TE ⠀)

Y.EH.OW.AH
WHICH IS PRONOUNCED
AS IT IS WRITTEN
I_EH_OU_AH

Its Story

Gérard Gertoux

> "The heavens declare the glory of God;..." *Psalm 19:1*

⠀⠀⠀⠀⠀merica,® Inc.
·k · Oxford

Copyright © 2002 by
University Press of America,® Inc.
4720 Boston Way
Lanham, Maryland 20706
UPA Acquisitions Department (301) 459-3366

12 Hid's Copse Rd.
Cumnor Hill, Oxford OX2 9JJ

British Library Cataloging in Publication Information Available

Library of Congress Cataloging-in-Publication Data

Gertoux, Gérard.
The name of God Y.eH.oW.aH which is pronounced as it is
written I_Eh_oU_Ah : its story / Gérard Gertoux.
p.   cm
Includes bibliographical references and index.
1. God—Name. 2. Tetragrammaton. 3. Names in the Bible. I. Title.

BT180.N2 G47 2002
231—dc21   2002018744 CIP

ISBN 0-7618-2204-6 (pbk. : alk. paper)

⊖™ The paper used in this publication meets the minimum
requirements of American National Standard for Information
Sciences—Permanence of Paper for Printed Library Materials,
ANSI Z39.48—1984

Table of contents

❖ **The Name** PART 1

❖ **Historical record**   PART 2

❖ Conclusion PART 3

❖ Appendix PART 4

❖ Index and notes PART 5

I would first like to thank the following people for their invaluable encouragement. It is with great pleasure that I quote their remarks while pointing out that they in no way constitute a guarantee on the conclusions of my research but show the reader the serious-mindedness of my work.

■ **E.J. Revell** (Professor emeritus at the University of Toronto): *«I was very interested to read the copy of your work which you sent me. Before reading your study, had no particular opinion on the pronunciation of the name of God. As a student in the 50's, I was told that scholars have determined that "Yahweh" was the ancient pronunciation. I did not find the argument well-grounded, but the view was held almost as an article of faith by my instructors, and I had no superior argument, so I ignored the problem. I have occasionally thought about it since, but I have not acquired any information that you have not noticed in your study. You have certainly collected more information on the question than any other study I know, and you are to be congratulated on the production of a valuable work. Many thanks for sending it to me.»*

■ **H. Cazelles** (Director of the Institut Catholique de Paris): *«Je vous remercie vivement de m'avoir envoyé votre "In Fame only?" d'une grande richesse de documentation. Je vais le déposer à la Bibliothèque Biblique pour le plus grand profit des chercheurs... Avec mes félicitations et remerciements.»*

■ **D.C. Hopkins** (Editor of the Near Eastern Archaeology): *«Thank you for submitting your rich and detailed study. Your topic is fascinating.»*

■ **G.W. Buchanan** (Editor of the Mellen Biblical Commentary) *«Let me thank you very much for sending me your excellent thesis. I trust that will soon have it published.»*

■ **S. Morag** (Professor at the Hebrew University of Jerusalem): *«The study is full of important evidence and gives a good survey of the research.»*

■ **E. Lipinski** (Professor, at the Katholieke Universiteit Leuven): «*Je tiens à vous remercier pour cet envoi et à vous féliciter pour le travail consciencieux dont cette recherche fait preuve. Je ne manquerai pas d'en faire usage si je reviens un jour à ce sujet.*»

■ **M. Harl** (Professor at the Université de Paris IV Sorbonne, translator and editor of the Bible d'Alexandrie): «*Votre envoi me remplit d'admiration... Encore une fois toutes mes félicitations.*»

■ **J. Bottéro** (Director at the E.P.H.E. assyrian department): «*Vous m'avez l'air à la fois très informé et très exigeant: vous vous en sortirez et nous ferez un beau travail, qui m'apprendra beaucoup de choses! (...) Vous avez un beau sujet de travail: j'aimerais bien voir paraître et lire votre thèse. C'est peut-être vous qui résoudrez les énigmes.*»

■ **E.A. Livingstone** (Doctor at the Oxford University): «*I sent your kind letter and the copy of your thesis to one of my colleagues who gave me much guidance over Old Testament material in the third edition of the Oxford Dictionary of the Christian Church (...), telling me that he found your thesis most interesting; he said your case was reasonable one, and well argued.*»

■ **D.N. Freedman** (Editor of the Anchor Bible): «*I was pleased to hear from you and to have your detailed treatment of this valuable and interesting subject, on which I have written from time to time. I have never been entirely satisfied with my own analysis and interpretation of the divine name in the Hebrew Bible, or with that of others, including my own teacher, W.F. Albright and his teacher (from whom Albright derived his position), Paul Haupt. At the same time, I haven't seen anything to persuade me of the superior value of another interpretation, but I will be glad to learn from your study and perhaps discover that you have finally solved this long-standing puzzle.*»

By the end of the present study, the reader will note that the conclusion may be summed up by one simple sentence: YHWH, the Tetragram, is the proper name of God, which is pronounced without difficulty because "it is read as it is written" according to the very words of the great Maimonides.

To succeed in understanding this simple, elementary truth, it was nevertheless necessary to closely examine the innumerable errors that have accumulated on this subject for at least twenty centuries. This led me into linguistic questions sometimes very technical that the non-specialist reader might find formidable. I have therefore annexed a lexicon explaining some notions which are essential to a good comprehension of the development followed.

✀ In addition, the more technical parts have been placed between two pairs of scissors to indicate them to the non-specialist reader, so that he may omit them (if he wishes) notably at the time of a first quick reading. [The first version of this work was *In Fame Only?*, referenced as thesis at the Institut Catholique de Paris (T594GER) 21, rue d'Assas F-75270] ✀

☞ To help the reader during the development of this historical record, some paragraphs include a pictograph index.

Part 1

The Name

The first gift that you received was your name. The last remembrance that will remain a long time after you, engraved on stone is your name. An unsigned check is worth nothing; your name is therefore really important, is it not? From an emotional viewpoint this is true; when one wants to know someone, the first question is: «What is your name?» Nevertheless, some refuse to apply the obvious to God.

God has a name. The Bible asserts it and all religions acknowledge it; then why do so few people know it? Usually, theologians retort that, either this name is too sacred to be used, or God wants to hide it, or that it is of no importance. However in the Bible, the only religious personage that systematically refused to use the Name is Satan. When Jesus debated with Satan, the discussion was enlightening as Jesus only used the Name, and Satan only the anonymous title 'God' (Mt 4:1-11)[#]. This antagonism is not new between those who avoid the name of God (Jr 23:27) and those who accept its use (Jr 10:25). Knowing the name of God is essential for salvation according to the Bible (Jl 2:32; Rm 10:13).

To begin, writing the name of God is not a problem: it is composed of four letters YHWH called the Tetragram. How is such a name pronounced? Dictionaries and encyclopedias indicate that Yahve (or Yahweh) is an uncertain vocalization, and that Jehovah is a barbarism originating from a wrong reading. As unbelievable as it may seem, this last affirmation is known to be false among scholars. This crude error has been denounced by Hebraists of all confessions, and with the support of the Vatican's Congregation of propaganda, but without result.

This name YHWH is read without difficulty because it is pronounced as it is written, or according to its letters as the Talmud says. In fact, up until 70 CE, on the day of Yom Kippur the high priests read the blessing in Numbers 6:24-27 pronouncing YHWH according to its letters, that is to say as it was written. Indeed, this name is the easiest one to read in the whole Bible because it is made up of four vowels as Flavius Josephus noted. The question of knowing which vowels accompanied the letters YHWH is absurd, for Masoretic vowels did not appear before the sixth century CE. Before this, Hebrew names were widely vocalized by the three letters Y, W, H, as the manuscripts of Qumrân widely confirm. The letter Y was read I (or E), the letter W: U (or O), and the letter H: A at the end of words. For example, YH was read IA, YHWDH was read IHUDA (Juda). If there was no vowel letter in a name the vowel *a* was often inserted; thus YSHQ was read: ISaHaQ (Isaac), etc. The name YHWH was therefore read IHUA (Ihoua). For the H, which was almost inaudible, to be better heard a mute *e* could be added, thus the name YHWDH read literally I-H-U-D-A then became I-eH-U-D-A, the exact equivalent of the Hebrew name Yehudah. This slight improvement gives the name YHWH the pronunciation I-eH-U-A (Iehoua), the equivalent of YeHoWaH in Masoretic punctuation. This coincidence is remarkable; even providential for those who believe that God watched over his Name (obviously without the copyists knowing!)

Did Jesus pronounce the Name? Having vigorously denounced human traditions that annulled divine commandments (Mt 15:3), it appears unlikely that he conformed to the non-biblical custom of not pronouncing the Name. When reading in the synagogue (Lk 4:16-20)[#] a part of the text of Isaiah (Is 61:1), he encountered the Tetragram. Even if the version in question was the Septuagint, this translation contained the Name (not Lord), as noted in all copies dated before 150 CE. According to the Masoretic text, at this time all theophoric names which had a part of the Tetragram integrated at their beginning were pronounced *without exception* YeHÔ-. Consequently, because the Tetragram is obviously the ultimate theophoric name, its reading had to be Yehô-aH to be consistent with all other theophoric names (YHWH can be read YHW-H). If the disputes are numerous, some appearing even legitimate, as a whole they constitute a body of proof that their objective is to eliminate the Name. But first, is a name *actually* important?

#In the translation of C Tresmontant (Catholic) one reads the name yhwh. In that of A. Chouraqui (Jewish) IhvH and in that of J.N. Darby (Protestant) *Lord, that is to say Jehovah according to the note on Matthew 1:20.

The power of the name

The need to name is fundamental: the name separates, distinguishes, makes irreplaceable. What mother would forget to give a name to her child? That which is unnamed is rejected; that which is unnamable is usually considered ignoble. Actually, the Latin etymology of ignominy is in fact the loss of the name.

In this domain, each society shows variable habits and needs, with some however remaining constant. Human beings and places that are significant for man are always and everywhere nameable; they are most often designated by a name. Nothing is more shameful for man than the loss of his name, and nothing is more despicable than the systems where men are deprived of their names. Institutions (prisons, concentration camps), where liberty is denied first deprive their members of any name, then assign them a number, modifiable, replaceable, personality destroying. But, not only human beings require names.

The places where men gather to live also have to be indicated by names. In addition, whenever a being, in the widest sense of the word, becomes important for someone, a name is required. In our culture, domesticated or tamed animals (in the circus, for example), ships, public establishments and some dwellings, are given names. This denominative method, when transferred, can fill new needs: some first names may serve to designate trucks, cyclones and even, horribly, lethal weapons. For example, the bomb that fell on Hiroshima was christened Little Boy. Elements of common language may also become names[1], such as the adjectives used by stockbreeders to designate their animals (Snowy, Blackie, etc.).

In modern societies, the State recognizes and imposes at the registry office, the family name. In the past, one was more often known by his nickname, imposed because of his origins or environment. This often happens still: at school, in a village or at the workplace for example. In contrast, the nickname can express the manner a character is perceived by public opinion (The Voice, Public Enemy n° 1, etc.) To impose their authority on populations, totalitarian systems have often forced people to change their name. We have examples in the history of Daniel and his companions. The debasement of a convict will be complete if he is designated by nothing more than a registration number[2].

A NAME IS MORE THAN A LABEL

The name represents the person. By my name or 'in the name of', I exercise authority. In knowing my name, others may have a power over me. Thus, my name does not mean only my physical person, my body, my words, my gestures and my actions. It applies to all extensions of my personality.

In times past, the titles (of nobility) of a lineage were symbolized by a coat of arms, placed on the gates of castles and on the doors of coaches. My initials suffice to mark my silverware, my linen or the luggage that belongs to me.

I put my signature on a piece of paper; my name legitimately represents me and is enough to bind me completely. A check is nothing; my name confers to it the value that I want to give it. If I buy a property my name will appear on the cadastre on that parcel, often a long time after my death. A letter addressed to my name is for me; nobody except me has the right to open it. If I give power of attorney to a proxy; I make him another me. If I adhere to a manifesto, commit myself to a loan, join an organization, in all these acts, "I give my name", and thus confer a bit of my authority. I have an author's copyright on all written documents signed by me and this right will be transmitted to my heirs. Obviously this list could go on (...) yet there is another side to it. As long as you do not know my name you cannot get any hold on me. Without civil status we have neither rights nor obligations. Recently, a man presented himself at a prison to serve his sentence. He was sent away because he had had his papers stolen along the way, and therefore no one had the right to admit him.

If you know me only by sight, you may say: «I do not know this person, I am unable to say what his name is.» You cannot call me. You cannot speak either well or ill of me. You cannot criticize me, slander me or denounce me. Yet it is quite different if you have managed to find the name 'to which I answer. I am obliged to answer, I may be called to account for my actions. Nobody likes to leave his name open to the curiosity of the indiscreet. This is no doubt one of the reasons why many telephone subscribers prefer unlisted numbers.

Furthermore, one of the principles of magic states that "the knowledge of a name confers a hold on the being that it designates". In their incantations, sorcerers pronounce the names of those they wish to put under an evil spell. The shouts of hatred uttered against political or other opponents during public demonstrations: «Death to so-and-so!» show remnants of this concept.

We cannot believe that the fate of a child is connected to its name. There is no name which in itself brings misfortune or luck. Nevertheless, the desire to give a newborn child in its cradle a favorable name is rather natural. Think about names given to houses or to boats. They generally express wishes of prosperity, happiness, happy travels. Many places in the city or country are given, in a similar way, the name of a patron saint. A name does not bind in an irrevocable way, but it expresses a wish, directs in a direction, places in a sphere of beliefs.

Heathen religions supply numerous examples of theophoric names created from the name of a god or a goddess. For the Assyrians, Assur's name can be found in Assurbanipal; for the Punics, there is Baal's name in Hannibal, etc. The Babylonians gave the name of their gods to the young Jews that they deported. These gods can be found in the names Belteshassar, Meshak, Shadrach, Abed-Nego, which were conferred on Daniel and his companions.

Jewish tradition since Abraham, is consistent. From the Torah of Moses until our days, believers of the most ancient monotheistic religion, in naming, recognize no names of heroes, saints or human patrons, but the sovereign power of God alone. There is no departure from this principle.

Jewish names are composed either from El (god) as in Daniel (God is my judge), Eliezer (God is my help), Eliya, etc., or from the Tetragram YHWH. From a biblical point of view, the name given to a child is an act of recognition towards God who gave the child. It can also be a prophecy; not a superstitious gesture to secure the future or to exorcise a curse, but, in faith, a testimony of confidence in divine direction to encourage the child and later the adult not to despair in difficult moments.

THE NAME IN THE BIBLE[3], A NAME IN ORDER TO EXIST

We read: «every family in heaven and on earth owes its name.» (Ep 3:14,15) God indeed formed the first human couple and endowed Adam and Eve with the power to beget children. So we may say that all the families of the earth owe him their name. He is also the Father of his heavenly family and because he calls the countless stars by their names (Ps 147:4), he undoubtedly gave names to the angels as well (Jg 13:18; Lk 1:19).

God granted the first man the privilege of naming the lower creatures (Gn 2:19). Adam apparently gave them descriptive names, as suggested by Hebrew name of some animals or even some plants: 'the one that crops' or 'that cuts' seems to apply to the caterpillar, 'fossorial animal' to the fox, 'the one that jumps' or 'that jumps up' to the antelope. The Hebrew name of the turtledove evidently imitates this bird's plaintive cry of 'tur-r-r tur-r-r.' The expression 'awakening one' designates the almond tree, apparently because of its being one of the earliest trees to bloom.

Sometimes men named places after themselves, their offspring, or their ancestors. Murderous Cain built a city and named it after his son Enoch. (Gn 4:17) Nobah began calling the conquered city of Kenath by his own name. (Nb 32:42) The Danites, after capturing Leshem, called that city Dan, this being the name of their forefather (Jos 19:47). As in the case of altars (Ex 17:14-16), wells (Gn 26:19-22), and springs (Jg 15:19), places were often named on the basis of events that occurred there. Examples of this are Babel (Gn 11:9), Beer-sheba (Gn 26:28-33), Bethel (Gn 28:10-19), Galeed (Gn 31:44-47), Succoth (Gn 33:17), Massah, Meribah (Ex 17:7), etc.

There were instances when physical features provided the basis for the names of places, mountains and rivers. The cities of Geba and Gibeah (both meaning 'Hill') doubtless got their names because they occupied hills. Lebanon (meaning 'White') may have received its name from the light color of its limestone cliffs and summits or from the circumstance that its upper slopes are covered with snow during a major part of the year. In view of their situation near wells, springs, and meadows, towns and cities were often given names prefixed by 'en' (fountain or spring), 'beer' (well), and 'abel' (meadow). Other names were derived from such characteristics as size, occupation, and produce. Examples are Bethlehem (House of Bread), Bethsaida (House of the Hunter (or, Fisherman)), Gath (Winepress), and Bezer (Fortress). Places were also called by the names of animals and plants, many of these names appearing in compound form. Among these were Aijalon (Place of the Hind; Place of the Stag), En-gedi (Fountain (Spring) of the Kid), En-eglaim (Fountain (Spring) of Two Calves), Akrabbim (Scorpions), Baal-tamar (Owner of the Palm Tree), and En-Tappuah (Fountain (Spring) of the Apple-Tree). Beth (house), baal (owner; master), and kiriath (town) frequently formed the initial part of compound names. So, for a Semite (this word comes from Shem, which means 'Name'), there is a principle:

> " *All that exists bears a name, and*
> *All that has a name bears a meaning*".

This notion appears in the very first pages of the Bible (Gn 1:5,8,10). If it is true for things and animals, how much more so for intelligent creatures.

In the earlier period of Biblical history, names were given to children at the time of birth. But later, Hebrew boys were named when they were circumcised on the eighth day. (Lk 1:59; 2:21) Usually either the father or the mother named the infant. (Gn 4:25; 5:29; 16:15; 19:37, 38; 29:32) One notable exception, however, was the son born to Boaz by Ruth. The neighbor ladies of Ruth's mother-in-law Naomi named the boy Obed (Servant; One Serving). (Rt 4:13-17) There were also times when parents received divine direction about the name to be given to their children. Among those receiving their names in this way were Ishmael (God Hears (Listens)) (Gn 16:11), Isaac (Laughter) (Gn 17:19), Solomon (from a root meaning 'peace') (1Ch 22:9), etc.

The name given to a child often reflected the circumstances associated with its birth or the feelings of its father or mother. (Gn 29:32–30:13,17-20,22-24; 35:18; 41:51, 52; Ex 2:22; 1S 1:20; 4:20-22) Eve named her firstborn Cain (Something Produced), for, as she said: «I have produced a man with the aid of Jehovah.» (Gn 4:1) Regarding him as a replacement for Abel, Eve gave the son born to her after Abel's murder the name Seth (Appointed; Put; Set). (Gn 4:25) Isaac named his younger twin son Jacob (One Seizing the Heel; Supplanter) because at birth this boy was holding on to the heel of Esau his brother. (Gn 25:26); (compare the case of Perez at Gn 38:28, 29.) Sometimes what an infant looked like at birth provided the basis for its name. The firstborn son of Isaac was called Esau (Hairy) on account of his unusual hairy appearance at birth. (Gn 25:25).

Names given to children were often combined with El (God) or an abbreviation of the divine name Jehovah. Such names could express the hope of parents, reflect their appreciation for having been blessed with offspring, or make acknowledgment to God. Examples are: Elnathan (God has given), Jeberechiah (may bless Yah), Jonathan (J[eh]o[vah] has given), Jehozabad (Jeho[vah] has endowed), Eldad (God has loved), Abdiel (Servant of God), Daniel (My Judge Is God) etc.

As indicated by the repetition of certain names in genealogical lists, it apparently became a common practice to name children after a relative (1Ch 6:9-36). It was for this reason that relatives and acquaintances objected to Elizabeth's wanting to name her newborn son John (Lk 1:61).

The designations for animals and plants were yet another source of names for people. Some of these names are Deborah (Bee), Dorcas or Tabitha (Gazelle), Jonah (Dove), Rachel (Ewe; Female Sheep), Shaphan (Rock Badger), and Tamar (Palm Tree).

Thus, more than today, where the name is chosen for its pleasing ring, in the past the choice depended on its pleasing meaning.

CHANGING NAMES

In the first century CE it was not uncommon for Jews, especially those living outside Israel or in cities having a mixed population of Jews and Gentiles, to have a Hebrew or an Aramaic name along with a Latin or Greek name. This may be why Dorcas was also called Tabitha and the apostle Paul was also named Saul. At times names came to be regarded as a reflection of an individual's personality or characteristic tendencies. Esau, with reference to his brother, remarked: «Is that not why his name is called Jacob [One Seizing the Heel; Supplanter], in that he should supplant me these two times? My birthright he has already taken, and here at this time he has taken my blessing!» (Gn 27:36) Abigail observed regarding her husband: «As his name is, so is he. Nabal [Senseless; Stupid] is his name, and senselessness is with him.» (1S 25:25) No longer considering her name to be appropriate in view of the calamities that had befallen her, Naomi said: «Do not call me Naomi [My Pleasantness]. Call me Mara [Bitter], for the Almighty has made it very bitter for me.» (Rt 1:20).

Sometimes for a particular purpose names were changed or a person might be given an additional name. While dying, Rachel called her newborn son Ben-oni (Son of My Mourning), but her bereaved husband Jacob chose to name him Benjamin (Son of the Right Hand) (Gn 35:16-19).

God changed the name of Abram to Abraham (Father of a Crowd (Multitude)) and that of Sarai to Sarah (Princess), both new names being prophetic. (Gn 17:5,6,15,16) Because of his perseverance in grappling with an angel, Jacob was told: «Your name will no longer be called Jacob but Israel [Contender (Perseverer) With God; or, God Contends], for you have contended with God and with men so that you at last prevailed.» (Gn 32:28) This change in name was a token of God's blessing and was later confirmed. (Gn 35:10) Evidently therefore, when the Scriptures prophetically speak of "a new name," the reference is to a name that would appropriately represent its bearer (Is 62:2; 65:15; Rv 3:12).

At times new names were given to persons elevated to high governmental positions or to those to whom special privileges were extended. Since such names were bestowed by superiors, the name change might also signify that the bearer of the new name was subject to its giver. Subsequent to his becoming Egypt's food administrator, Joseph was called Zaphenath-paneah. (Gn 41:44,45) Pharaoh Necho, when constituting Eliakim as vassal king of Judah, changed his name to Jehoiakim. (2K 23:34) Likewise, Nebuchadnezzar, in making Mattaniah his vassal, changed his name to Zedekiah. (2K 24:17) Daniel and his three Hebrew companions, Hananiah, Mishael, and Azariah, were given Babylonian names after being selected for special training in Babylon (Dn 1:3-7; 4:8).

To make a name for oneself, to have renown

In Scriptural usage, 'name' often denotes fame or reputation. (1Ch 14:17) Bringing a bad name upon someone meant making a false accusation against that person, marring his reputation. (Dt 22:19) To have one's name "cast out as wicked" would mean the loss of a good reputation. (Lk 6:22) It was to make "a celebrated name" for themselves in defiance of Jehovah that men began building a tower and a city after the Flood. (Gn 11:3,4) On the other hand, Jehovah promised to make Abram's name great if he would leave his country and relatives to go to another land. (Gn 12:1,2) Testifying to the fulfillment of that promise is the fact that to this day few names of ancient times have become as great as Abraham's, particularly as examples of outstanding faith. Millions still claim to be the heirs of the Abrahamic blessing because of fleshly descent. Similarly, Jehovah made David's name great by blessing him and granting him victories over the enemies of Israel (1S 18:30; 2S 7:9).

At birth a person has no reputation, and therefore his name is little more than a label. That is why Ecclesiastes 7:1 says: «A name is better than good oil, and the day of death than the day of one's being born.» Not at birth, but during the full course of a person's life does his 'name' take on real meaning in the sense of identifying him either as a person practicing righteousness or as one practicing wickedness. (Pr 22:1) By Jesus' faithfulness until death his name became the one name "given among men by which we must get saved," and he "inherited a name more excellent" than that of the angels. (Ac 4:12; Heb 1:3,4) But Solomon, for whom the hope was expressed that his name might become 'more splendid' than David's, went into death with the name of a backslider as to true worship. (1K 1:47; 11:6,9-11) «The very name of the wicked ones will rot,» or become an odious stench. (Pr 10:7) For this reason a good name «is to be chosen rather than abundant riches.» (Pr 22:1).

A NAME RECORDED OR ERASED?

A person dying without leaving behind male offspring had his name "taken away," as it were. (Nb 27:4; 2S 18:18) Therefore, the arrangement of brother-in-law marriage outlined by the Mosaic Law served to preserve the name of the dead man. (Dt 25:5, 6) On the other hand, the destruction of a nation, people, or family meant the wiping out of their name (Dt 7:24; 9:14; Jos 7:9; 1S 24: 21; Ps 9:5).

We thus understand that a nameless one symbolizes a senseless one (Jb 30:8) or, worse, an enemy to be cut off (Ps 41:5). In the same way, in his controversy with false gods, the true God announced that he would destroy and cut off the very names of their idols (Dt 12:3; Os 2:17; Za 13:2) to remove them (Is 2:18; Jos 23:7). On the other hand, God wished his name to be known, and it was principally for this that he opposed Pharaoh (Ex 9:16; Rm 9:17).

It appears that God, figuratively speaking, has been writing names in the book of life from "the founding of the world." (Rv 17:8) It seems that Abel's name was the first one to be registered in this symbolic roll. The names appearing on the scroll of life, however, are not names of persons who have been predestined to gain God's approval and life (Is 56:5). This is evident from the fact that the Scriptures speak of 'blotting out' names from "the book of life." So it appears that only when a person becomes a servant of God is his name written in "the book of life," and only if he continues faithful is his name retained in that book (Ex 32:32, 33; Rv 3:5; 17:8).

To Act 'In The Name Of'

To speak or to act 'in the name of' another denoted doing so as a representative of that one (Ex 5:23; Dt 10:8; 18:5, 7, 19-22; 1S 17:45; 1K 21:8; Is 3:12; 8:8, 10; 1Co 1:12, 13) and also assuming the consequences of this representation (Mt 24:9; Lk 9:48; Rv 2:3). Similarly, to receive a person in the name of someone would indicate recognition of that one. Therefore, to "receive a prophet in the name of a prophet" would signify receiving a prophet because of his being such (Mt 10:41). And to baptize in "the name of the Father and of the Son and of the holy spirit" would mean in recognition of the Father, the Son, and the holy spirit (Mt 28:19) that is in recognition of the authority linked to the name rather than the name itself, because it is not said 'the names' but 'the name'. Consequently, to act in the name of somebody implies having received the name (today we would say the signature or proxy), which confers the authority of the mandate giver (Lk 10:17), provided that it is legal (Mk 9:38,39; Ac 8:16; 19:13-16). In Old Semitic cultures an ambassador was view as the king himself[4].

Nevertheless, this delegation can make the authorship of the signature ambiguous. For example, it is easy to understand in the following passages: «Solomon built a house for him» (Ac 7:47), «Yarobam built Sichem» (1K 12:25), «he (Cain) engaged in building a city» (Gn 4:17), that the persons cited only (legally) gave their name to actions which they did not carry out personally. The confusion between the one who delegates authority to his representative can lead to a paradox as in the case of Jacob who having legally bought his first-born's right from Esau (Gn 25:33), could then say "legally" to his father: «I am Esau your first-born» (Gn 27:19). In the same way, John and James (Mk 10:35) can be confused with their agent, their mother (Mt 20:20). The delegating officer (Mt 8:5) can be confused with the elders he delegated (Lk 7:3); and more generally in the Bible, there is (a legal) confusion between the angel of God (Gn 16:7) and God himself (Gn 16:13).

Thus, we confuse the angel and Jehovah himself (Gn 16:7, 13), which is legitimate if the angel is the spokesman of God (Jn 1:14; Gn 18:2, 22, 33; 19:1). To avoid confusion between the legal representation and the identification with God, the spokesman angel refused to give his name (Gn 32:29; Jg 13:18), while other angels did give theirs (Dn 8:16; 10:13).

ANGEL'S NAMES, THE NAME OF GOD

The Bible contains the personal names of only two angels: Gabriel (brave one of God) and Michael (who [is] like God?) (Lk 1:26; Jude 9). Perhaps so as not to receive undue honor or veneration, angels at times did not reveal their names to persons to whom they appeared (Gn 32:29; Jg 13:17, 18). Like human names, the names of angels can be changed: thus the angel of the abyss (Rv 9:11) becomes Abaddon or Apollyon (destruction).

The one who gave man the power to name, reserved the right to take a name, the right to introduce himself. He even took the extraordinary risk of having his name deformed, scoffed at, blasphemed and even, incredibly, forgotten! We are encouraged to look for this Name of which it is said: «My people will know my name» (Is 52:6) and: «The name of Jehovah is a strong tower. Into it the righteous runs and is given protection» (Pr 18:10).

Is it actually possible to know this name, and what does this knowledge imply?

To know God's name

Knowing the Name implies much more than knowing the existence of its written form or its pronunciation (2Ch 6:33). In fact, it means knowing the very person of God: his intentions, his activities and his qualities, many things revealed in his Word (1K 8:41-43; 9:3,7; Ne 9:10). It is more than a simple intellectual knowledge, as we can see in the case of Moses, a man that God "knew by name", in other words whom he knew intimately (Ex 33:12). Moses had the privilege of seeing a demonstration of the glory of God and to hear him "proclaiming YHWH's name". It did not involve simply the repetition of this name, but the proclamation in his presence of God's attributes and actions (Ex 34:6,7). In the same way, the song of Moses, which contains these words: «I shall declare the name of Jehovah» tells about the links which God maintained with Israel and describes his personality (Dt 32:3-44).

On earth, Jesus Christ "made the name of God known" to his disciples (Jn 17:6,26). Although already knowing this name and being familiar with the works of God recorded in the Hebrew Scriptures, these disciples acquired a deeper knowledge of God thanks to the one "who is in the bosom position with the Father" (Jn 1:18).

In the same manner, when God announced to Moses that he had not made his name known to his ancestors in Exodus 6:3, Moses understood that God had not made known his fame (for the translation of 'name' by 'fame', see Gn 6:4; Nb 16:2; Rv 3:1; etc.) or his reputation to his ancestors (Ex 9:16; 2 7:23; Ne 9:10). It was not a question of the pronunciation of this name according to the context. Moreover, the Egyptians were also going to learn to know this name (Ex 7:5), not its pronunciation, which Pharaoh already knew (Ex 5:2).

It is therefore surprising to note that numerous commentators (although not all)[5], understand the passage of Exodus 6:3 in a literal way, that is, as concerning pronunciation.

Nevertheless, when a person uses the expression "he will find out what my name is" or "he will get to know me", we cannot naively believe that this person simply wishes to give lessons in diction. In fact, even today, people use the expression "to call things by their name" to mean, "to be very clear on things".

✄   A literal comprehension of the text would imply that the Name was not known before Moses, but this contradicts the Bible (Gn 4:26). This concept is at the root of the theory of sources, elohist for the texts where there is the name 'elohim', and jehovist for the texts where there is the name 'Jehovah' to designate God, the scribes having "skillfully" merged these two sources according to the authors of the theory of sources. ✄

TO KNOW BY NAME

Finally, not to know a name is to deny the position of the authority behind it (Ac 19:15). For example Nabal says: «Who is David?» (1S 25:10) and Pharaoh says: «Who is Jehovah?» (Ex 5:2). The question here does not relate to pronunciation! It is obvious that only those who obey God really know his name. (1Jn 4:8;5:2,3) Jehovah's assurance in Psalm 91:14 therefore applies to such persons: «I shall protect him because he has come to know my name.» The name itself is no magical charm, but the One designated by that name can provide protection for his devoted people.

Thus the name represents God himself. That is why the proverb says: «The name of Jehovah is a strong tower. Into it the righteous runs and is given protection.» (Pr 18:10) This is what persons who cast their burden on Jehovah do. (Ps 55:22) Likewise, to love (Ps 5:11), sing praises to (Ps 7:17), call upon (Gn 12:8), give thanks to (1Ch 16:35), swear by (Dt 6:13), remember (Ps 119:55), fear (Ps 61:5), search for (Ps 83:16), trust in (Ps 33:21), exalt (Ps 34:3), and hope in (Ps 52:9) the name is to do so with reference to God himself.

CALLING UPON THE NAME

A particular name might be 'called upon' a person, city, or building. Jacob, when adopting Joseph's sons as his own, stated: «Let my name be called upon them and the name of my fathers, Abraham and Isaac.» (Gn 48:16; Is 4:1; 44:5) Jehovah's name being called on the Israelites indicated that they were his people. (Dt 28:10; 2Ch 7:14; Is 43:7; 63:19; Dn 9:19) Jehovah also placed his name on Jerusalem and the temple, thereby accepting them as the rightful center of his worship. (2K 21:4,7) Joab chose not to complete the capture of Rabbah in order not to have his name called upon that city, that is, so as not to be credited with its capture (2S 12:28). Calling upon the Name therefore meant asking for protection or part of the glory (Rm 10:13; Ac 2:21; Jl 2:32).

WHEN THE NAME IS PLACED "ON" OR "IN"

In answer to an invocation, God placed his name upon his servants, to grant them protection and glory (as a husband does even today for his wife and for his children), (Nb 6:27; Is 43:7; Ac 15:14). God also placed his name upon Jerusalem and on its temple, showing that he recognized them as the center of his worship (2K 21:4,7). This principle is the same for other names that God places upon persons or buildings (Rv 3:12; 21:14). Consequently, the one receiving this name possesses some authority (as if he had a signature or proxy). Furthermore, for different missions, someone may receive several names (see "Changing names").

Finally, to indicate a representativeness or a permanent authority, the name (the signature giving authorization) is no longer placed upon the person (or the object), but in the person (Ex 23.21) or the object (1K 9:3). Jesus mentioned that he benefited from such an arrangement (Jn 17:11,12,22).

To BLASPHEME THE NAME

Because the Name represents God himself (Ps 75:1; 1Ch 17:24; Is 30:27), to speak abusively of God's name is to blaspheme God (Lv 24:11-16). Jehovah is jealous of his name, tolerating no rivalry or unfaithfulness in matters of worship (Ex 34:14; Ezk 5:13). Today some traces of such abuses can still be found among French expressions, that some use in a blasphemous sense, as "nom de Dieu" (in God's name) or "nom de nom" (in name of the name). The Israelites were commanded not even to mention the names of other gods (Ex 23:13; Jos 23:7). In view of the fact that the names of false gods appear in the Scriptures, evidently the prohibition concerned mentioning the names of false gods in a worshipful way.

Furthermore, because the Israelites bore the name of their God (Is 43:7,10), their bad actions reflected on the Name and profaned it (Ezk 36:23; Lv 18:21). We can better understand then the warning on the use of this name (Dt 5:11) or sometimes even the ban on using it (Am 6:10).

In Jesus' time, the charge of blasphemy against the Name could be wrongly applied to other cases (Mt 26:65; Lk 5:21; Jn 10:36), which was excessive; however, Christians had to watch not to blaspheme the Name by their behavior (Rm 2:24) and to be vigilant when using this name (2Tm 2:19).

To REMEMBER THE NAME

Thus far, we can see that God's name in the Bible is likened to God himself, his glory, his reputation, his authority; however, even though the pronunciation is secondary, God wished his name to be remembered (Ps 119:55). Today, no one would not want to forget the names of loved ones, because they take on a sentimental value. How much more serious it would be to forget God's name (Jr 23:27; Ps 44:20). On the other hand, those who serve him would preserve his name (Mi 4:5). Jesus entrusted his brothers with this mission (Heb 2:12), which would allow this name to spread among the nations (Ml 1:11), finally becoming, one day, the only name (Zc 14:9).

Finally, let us note Satan's reluctance[6] to use the divine name. The discussion with Jesus is a characteristic example, with Satan using the term God every time and Jesus, on the other hand, systematically using the divine name in his answers (Mt 4:1-10). Furthermore, to prove the resurrection Jesus referred to the Name and its meaning! (Lk 20:37). This aversion to the Name, also shared by the demons (Lk 4:34,41; 8:28), results from a refusal of intimacy with the One who is addressed, much like those who prefer to say 'Hello' rather than 'Hello so and so' (using his name) in order to keep their distance from an undesirable individual.

THE NAME OF GOD AMONG RELIGIONS

God's name is, in theory, the central element of the fabric of religion, because all religions speak of a Creator and call upon his name. However, for millions of Hindus, the creator God, Brahma does not receive any worship. For millions of members of Christendom, despite the daily recitation of the prayer called 'Our Father', which begins with «let your name be sanctified», the only name God has is the title Lord (or the Eternal One). Similarly, Muslims who recite the surahs of the Quran, which all begin with 'in the name of God' (except Surah IX), answer that God has 99 names, that is to say not one of his own; and finally the Jews, who recite the prayer called 'Shema Israel' in which they ask God's name to be blessed but refuse to pronounce it at the risk of committing a blasphemy.

Thus, despite the apparent respect people seem to have for it, God's name is only a title which does not play any practical part in daily life. Apparently, only exorcist priests and spiritualists attach importance to the invocation of God's name[7]. In France, the expression "nom de Dieu" (in God's name) is avoided in ordinary conversation, but few could explain why this expression is considered as a curse.

The Bible holds God's name sacred, therefore it should only be pronounced respectfully (Ex 20:7), otherwise one would incur the penalty of death for blasphemy (Lv 24:11,16).

However, to know and to call upon this name, that is to shout it with supplication (Ac 2:21; Rm 10:13; Jl 2:32), is one of the major conditions of staying alive during God's intervention and not experiencing the effects of his anger (Jr 10:25). Thus, to know this name means to survive. To be unaware of it means to condemn oneself to death.

There is therefore underway a fight to the death between those who would have this name known (Ex 9:16; Ml 3:16) and those who would have it forgotten (Jr 23:27; Ps 44:20). The Bible identifies the instigator of this disgraceful, diabolical plan; it is indeed easy to verify that God, in the Bible, does have a name of his own: YHWH, which cannot be translated by Lord (Adon), My Lord (Adoni), The Lord (Haadon), my Lords (Adonay), God (El), Eternal (Olam), Almighty (Shadday), Very-High (Elyon), Creator (Bore), Heavens (Shamaïm), etc.

The knowledge of the Name is thus at the heart of the controversy between Satan and Jesus.

Jesus, Satan, their controversy over the Name

Although the divine name appears at the beginning of the biblical account (Gn 2:4), translators of the Bible noticed that the Serpent, identified as the Devil by the Jews (Ws 2:24), Satan according to the Gospel (Rv 12:9), refused to use this name in his dialogue with Eve and preferred to use the anonymous title 'God' (Gn 3:1-5). This was not done at random but, throughout the Bible, without exception. On the other hand, Jesus systematically used the Name in speaking with the Devil (Mt 4:1-10); even Eve used it (Gn 4:1).

As we have seen, to recognize a name means to recognize the authority connected with this name. In deliberately refusing the authority of God, Satan also refuses to recognize his name, actively propagating his subversive attitude. The first religious controversy in the Bible concerned the use of the Name, as it appears in Genesis 4:26.

According to this verse, the translation of which is sometimes inadequate, the people began "to call upon the divine name". Some translators were bothered by this precision, because as the Name was already known, they thought it must be an error. However, the context of this verse indicates that mankind had become wicked (Gn 6:5); therefore when this name was invoked, 'shouted with pleading' according to the sense of the Hebrew term, it was with wrong intentions. The Targum of the Pentateuch confirms this explanation, stipulating about Genesis 4:26 that the people gave the divine name to their idols, as they also did repeatedly afterwards (Ex 32:4,5; Is 44:17). So, this verse, correctly rendered in the Hebrew text, implied that this invocation was made in an evil sense, and consequently with the aim of abusing the Name to discredit it. Afterward, a new large-scale attack against the Name would occur. Indeed, the profusion of names of deities resulting from polytheism would drown the one and only name under an avalanche of appellations. To protect themselves from this snare, the Israelites were to destroy the names of these idols (Ex 23:13; Dt 12:3), because the purpose of this proliferation of names was that the one and only Name be forgotten (Jr 23:27; Ps 44:20). Of course, the divine name had to be protected from such an eventuality (Dt 12:4).

To actively fight against this desecration, that is the elimination of the name, the Hebrews were encouraged to invoke or 'shout with pleading' this name (Dt 32:3). The main reason God opposed Pharaoh was to promote the proclamation of his Name in the whole earth (Ex 9:16), which is one of the themes of the Bible (Rm 9:17). In his foresight, from the beginning God anticipated the crushing of Satan's head by means of the Seed (Gn 3:15), whom Christians would later identify as Jesus (Ga 3:16). Thus, Jesus came mainly to destroy the works of the Devil (Heb 2:14) and especially to proclaim God's name (Heb 2:12) and make it better known (Jn 17:6,26). Indeed, to foil the satanic project, which unfortunately succeeded with the Jews (Jr 44:26), God had planned to delegate an angel (Is 63:9) with his Name in him (Ex 23:21). Jesus made it clear that he was indeed the holder of the Name (Jn 17:11). The identification of this angel would be essential in knowing the real name. Now, if the Name is the central element of the religious system around which everything revolves like the center of our galaxy which exercises its attraction on all the rest of the system, it is still invisible to the naked eye, implying the importance of identifying the angel, the guardian of the Name.

THE IDENTIFICATION OF JESUS AND SATAN

These two personages are among the most widely known today. Nevertheless, they came to light relatively recently in mankind's history. Few know exactly what makes them enemies. Who today really knows their history, their origin, the part they actually play, the implications their conflict has on the life of every human being, and especially why it is important to know what is at stake?

WHAT IS THE MEANING OF SATAN'S NAME?

Although very ancient, Moses knew it (Jb 1:6). Satan was not a very widespread name in literature before our era. Knowing the meaning of a name in Hebrew often gives an indication as to the function of a person. Indeed, Satan (שָׂטָן) means in Hebrew 'opponent, accuser'. This name is translated into Greek by Devil (Διάβολος) which in the Septuagint means 'slanderer, gossiper'. Satan received other names which are simply descriptions, for example Beelzebul (Mt 12:24), likely a deformation of Baalzebub (2K 1:2), the name of the god of Ekrôn. This name Baalzebub ('Master of the flies' in Hebrew) that can be found at Ugarit (14th century BCE), means 'the prince Baal' and was doubtless deformed as Baalzebul which means in Aramaic 'Master of the dung' (or 'Master of the lofty abode' in Hebrew!). We often find in rabbinical papers the term Belial (2Co 6:15), which means 'one without worth' in Hebrew or good-for-nothing (Pr 16:27), with other terms such as Tempter, Evil, Enemy, etc. The meaning of Satan's name is well established; moreover, in some verses, translators hesitate between keeping the name or translating it as in Psalm 109:6. On the other hand, his role as the god of the world in a fight against the God of the universe seems clearly defined only in Christian Greek writings (2Co 4:4).

It can be noted that in the Persian religion the conflict of the principle of bad (Ahriman) against the god of light (Ahura Mazda), was popularized about the seventh century before our era by Zarathustra. This vision of two conflicting entities, good and bad, became later, around the third century, Manicheism.

WHAT IS THEIR CURRENT ROLE ACCORDING TO RELIGIONS?

In the Christian religion, Jesus is considered above all as the Messiah, the Word and the Son of God, Satan being regarded as the Prince of the world or the principle of Evil. In the Muslim religion, Jesus (called 'Isa, the Arabic vocalization of the name Esau) is considered as the Messiah and God's Word (Quran 4:171); on the other hand, Shaytan the rebel is described as opposing God and man. In the Jewish religion, Jesus (Yehôshua'), that is to say Josue in Latin, is regarded as the servant of Moses, and Satan as God's adversary or as the principle of Evil.

If the name and role of Satan appear to be quite clear, on the other hand the name and the role of Jesus seem much more obscure. This has to do with the confusion over the Name, because to know the Messiah is to know the Name, and conversely, because the Messiah possesses the Name, according to what is written in Exodus 23:21: «My name is in him.»

Rather quickly, the Jews understood that this powerful angel would play a distinctive role. He was identified with the "angel of the face" (Is 63:9) and also with the great angelic prince, Michael, the defender of Israel (Dn 12:1). Because Michael is described as being more powerful than the other angels (Dn 10:20,21), it is evident that he was the leader of the angels, or archangel. This is confirmed in Jude 9 which tells of the dispute between the archangel Michael and Satan. Furthermore, the book of Revelation indicates that Michael and his angels waged war against the dragon and its angels (Rv 12:7). It is noteworthy that there is only one archangel in the Bible; even Satan, the leader of the evil angels, is not called an archangel. At the beginning of our era, the Jews gradually identified this powerful angel, who has the Name in him, with Metatron. Metatron is a pseudonym given that his true name, Yahoel, would have revealed God's name. Indeed, Yahoel means in Hebrew 'Yaho is God'. On the other hand, Christians identified the archangel Michael with Jesus (1Th 4:16; 2Th 1:7), but apparently they did not establish any link between the pronunciation of the divine name and the fact that Jesus possessed the Name in him (Jn 17:11,26).

After this rapid analysis, we can conclude that for Muslims, if 'Isa (Jesus) is the Messiah, this name did not play any part in finding the personal name of Allah (Allah is not really a name because it is simply a contraction of al-Ilah 'The

God'). Muslim tradition only maintains that God possesses 99 beautiful names, that is to say not one exclusively his own[8]. This tradition asserts however that the personal name of God (the hundredth one) will be known at the end of times. However, a well-known comment on the surah 27:40 of the Quran, called *Tafsir Al Jalalayn*, explains that «Asaph, son of Berekia, was a righteous man. He knew the greatest of the names, the name of God, by means of which, if it has been called, gives an answer». In addition, the Bible (The Holy Book according to surah 17:2) specifies that he used the name Jehovah (Asaph's psalm 83:18). Also, the name Berekia means, 'blessed by Yah'. For the Jews, it is Metatron, that is Yahoel, who possesses the Name. The name Yaho thus played a large role in Jewish mysticism. Finally, for Christians, it is Jesus who was recognized as the Messiah. However, if Jesus does possess the Name in him, how does this help us to find the divine name?

The name Jesus is simply the transcription of the Hebrew name Yeshua. If some dictionaries mention abnormalities concerning the meaning and pronunciation of this name, none stop to explain them. Nevertheless, it is worth analyzing further (in view of the historical record of the name of Jesus), because it enables us to establish that because of the assonance with the Tetragram, the Name is literally inside the name of Jesus.

Before examining the historical record of the Name, it is important to know on which basis specialists decide current vocalizations of Hebrew names, because the choice of method automatically affects the choice of vocalization.

[NB. Dates BCE given in this book reflect a consensus (not unanimous) among various specialists and are therefore only indicative of the chronology of the periods of history.]

The Name read distinctly

Thus far we have seen that modern critics have focused mainly on the pronunciation of the Name, "the Name read distinctly" according to the Talmud[9] (*Sifre Numbers 6:27*), and some linguists, such as the Knights of the Holy Grail, have tried to find this mythical pronunciation of the Tetragram. However, like sincere cabalists of the Middle Ages who wanted to find the secret of this pronunciation, modern linguists have come up with the same result: confusion. To avoid such disastrous results in this justifiable search it is necessary to establish clear guidelines. For example, the pronunciation of the name of Moses can be improved. In fact, taking Hebrew into account, one should pronounce this name Môshèh; however this is according to Masoretic Hebrew, and so this vocalization reflects the biblical language at the beginning of our era (or a little before). Going further back in time would result in the "more archaic" pronunciation Mushah, confirmed by the Arabic name Musa.

However, going back to a "more archaic" pronunciation introduces some confusion, as this archaic period (generally undated) is often open to any interpretation because of its obscurity. Thus, some attempt to make this "ancient" pronunciation clear by its probable Egyptian etymology 'mosis' (son), which could be found frequently at this time in Egyptian names like Thutmosis, Ahmosis, etc. However, partisans of exotic etymologies "forget" to indicate that the vocalization of Egyptian names is very hypothetical, some preferring to use the forms Thutmès, Ahmès, etc. Secondly, this Egyptian elucidation of Moses contradicts the biblical etymology in Exodus 2:10, which connects this name with the Hebrew verb 'to draw out' (Mashah in Hebrew).

Finally, ardent supporters of archaism who would like to find the pronunciation of Moses' name through its biblical etymology, will notice that this leads again to an impasse, because conjugation gives the form Mashûy, which means exactly in Hebrew '(being) drawn out'.

Name	according to:
Moses	English
Môshèh	Masoretic Hebrew
Môusè	Greek of the Septuagint
Musa	Arabic
Mashûy	Hebrew etymology
Mès	Egyptian etymology
Mosis	Egyptian etymology (via Greek)

☞   The previous example shows why trying to find an original pronunciation much before the beginning of our era is a quest that is more mystical than scientific. As convincing proof that this justifiable search can not go back much before the beginning of our era, the well known name Jesus illustrates all the problems encountered.

THE PRONUNCIATION OF JESUS' NAME

"At first", the name of Jesus, according to Masoretic Hebrew, was a transformation of the name Hôshéaʻ into Yehôshuaʻ (Nb 13:16), then abbreviated as Yéshuaʻ (1Ch 24:11). Afterwards Yéshuaʻ was pronounced Yéshuʻ in Aramaic, and Yéshu became Ièsous in the Greek Septuagint.

	HEBREW		ARAMAIC
הוֹשֵׁעַ	יְהוֹשׁוּעַ	יֵשׁוּעַ	יֵשׁוּעַ
Hôšéaʻ ›››	Yᵉhôšûaʻ ›››	Yéšûaʻ ›››	Yéšû'
Hoshéa	Yehôshua	Yéshua	Yéshu

ARAMAIC	GREEK	LATIN	ENGLISH
יֵשׁוּעַ	Ιησου[ς]	I[h]esu[s]	Jesus
Yéšû' ›››	Ièsou[s] ›››	Iesu[s] ›››	
Yéshu	Ièsou	Iesu	

Furthermore, to make the situation more complex, there are other transcriptions of this name. For example, Yehoshua became Josue in the Latin Vulgate and Yeshu gave the Greek form Jason!

HEBREW	LATIN	ENGLISH
יְהוֹשֻׁעַ	Josue	Joshua
Yᵉhôšûa ›››	Iosue	
Yehôshua	Iosue	

ARAMAIC		GREEK	ENGLISH
יֵשׁוּעַ	יְסוֹן	Ιασον	Jason
Yéšû' ›››	Yason ›››	Iason ›››	
Yéshu	Yason	Iason	

There exist currently therefore five possible pronunciations of the original name Yehôshua, that is to say: Jesus, Josue, Jason, Yéshua' and Yehôshua'. Which is the right one?

Most will acknowledge that to find the original version, the ideal would be to return to the Hebrew pronunciation. Nevertheless, even in this case, the Hebrew Bible gives two variants: Yehôshua' and Yéshua'. Which one is correct? If we confine ourselves to Jesus' time, the usual pronunciation was Yéshua, as confirmed by the excellent translation of Aquila (128-132), which translated this name Ièsoua (Ιησουα; Dt 1:38) into Greek. Furthermore, in setting up the beginning of our era as a reference period for proper names we have two sources of evidence of exceptional quality: the first one being the text of the Septuagint, which reflects Hebrew vocalization around 280 BCE; and the second the Masoretic text, which reflects Hebrew vocalization around 100 BCE (and even probably around 300 to 400 BCE)[10]. Paradoxically, the vocalization of the Masoretic text seems older than the one of the Septuagint, although its fixing is posterior. Besides, the Septuagint was revised on a Masoretic model as early as the first century CE.

Once this limit is established, the majority of biblical names can be improved according to their Masoretic vocalization, which makes them closer, not to the original, but to their pronunciation at the beginning of our era. Numerous modern translations follow this method, some (such as that of A.

Chouraqui) even for such venerable names as Moses, Jesus, Solomon, Noah, etc., which become again Moshè, Iéshoua', Shelomo, Noah, as in the first century. Can the pronunciation of the Tetragram be found, since at this time it was still pronounced, at least in the Temple? The answer is yes, in spite of the fact that this vocalization is not directly indicated either in the text of the Septuagint or in the Masoretic text.

METHODS TO RESTORE A PRONUNCIATION

This vocalization of the Name (in the first century) can be brought to light in several ways. For example, let us suppose that the Hebraic pronunciation of a name was lost; one could find it in at least four ways, each one being more or less reliable. The following are the four methods:

1- Etymologies method.
2- Sources method.
3- Onomastic method.
4- Letters method.

1- Etymology method. Assuming that the name reflects its etymology, where such exists.

2- Sources method. Assuming that the Greek names in the Septuagint used the correct vowels.

3- Onomastic method. Assuming that when a name was integrated into another it was not distorted.

4- Letters method. Assuming that when a name is written out in full, the vocalization according to its letters corresponds to its actual pronunciation. To read a name, one proceeds as follows: Y is read I, W is read Û and a final H is read A. A consonant is read alternately with a vowel, and when lacking a vowel one uses the sound *a*. A guttural consonant, even when accompanied by a vowel, is read with the sound *a*.

It is interesting to test the reliability of each of these four methods before applying them to the divine name. The following seven well-known names permit this verification.

■ Abraham

1- The etymology, in Genesis 17:5 indicates that this name means 'Father of a crowd', that is to say Abhamon in Hebrew like Baalhamon (Ct 8:11) which means 'Master of a crowd'.

2- The Septuagint uses the Greek form Abraam.

3- The name Abraham is connected with Abiram (1K 16:34), Abishûa (1Ch 8:4), for the beginning of the name (Ab). The final part 'raham' means nothing in Hebrew but it is connected with the name Raḥam (1Ch 2:44), meaning 'he had compassion'. The reconstructed form is Abraḥam (Note that the name Abra-ham, rather than Ab-raham, is similar to the expression 'I shall create them' or 'I shall beget them' [הֶם אֶבְרָא]).

4- This name 'brhm may be read A-ba-ra-ham according to its letters.

■ Jesus

1- The etymology of Jesus (Yéshûa) is found in Matthew 1:21 which gives the Hebrew form Yôshia', meaning, 'He will save'.

2- The Septuagint gives the Greek form Ièsous

3- The names connected to Jesus are Yesh'ayah (Ezr 8:7), Yish'i (1Ch 2:31), for the beginning, and Èlishûa' (2S 5:15) at the end. The reconstructed form is Yeshûa or Yishûa.

4- This name Yšw' is read I-šû-a' according to its letters, that is to say Ishûa'.

■ Noah

1- The etymology in Genesis 5:29 indicates that Noah (Noaḥ) 'will comfort'; therefore, if one assumes that this name means 'He comforted', one obtains Naḥam in Hebrew.

2- The Septuagint gives the Greek form Noé

3- The names connected with Noah are Yanôaḥ (2K 15:29) and Manôaḥ (Jg 13:2). The reconstructed form is Nôaḥ.

4- This name Nwḥ is read Nû-aḥ according to its letters.

■ Israel

1- The etymology in Genesis 32:28 indicates that Israel means 'He contended [with] God', as in Hoshea 12:3, or Seraél in Hebrew. Moreover Serayah (2S 8:17) means 'He contended [with] Yah'.

2- The Septuagint gives the Greek form Israèl

3- There are several names connected with Yisraél: for example, Yisraéli (2S 17:25) and Yisreélit (Lv 24:10 for the beginning of the name. At the end, the word él is well attested to, thus the most probable reconstructed form is Yisraél.

4- This name Yśr'l is read Iś-ra-'al according to its letters.

■ Juda

1- The etymology in Genesis 29:35 indicates that this name means 'He will laud', which gives the form Yôdèh or Yehôdèh (Ne 11:17) in Hebrew.

2- The Septuagint gives the form Iouda.

3- There are several names linked with Judah, for example Yehûdi (Jr 36:14, 21), Yehûdit (Gn 26:34), Yehûdim (Jr 43:9) for the beginning, and Hôdawyah (1Ch 9:7) for the end. The reconstructed form is therefore Yehûdah.

4- This name Yhwdh is read I-hû-da according to its letters.

■ Moses

1- The etymology in Exodus 2:10 indicates that this name means 'drawn out [of the water]', that is to say in Hebrew Mashûy ([being] drawn out). In Egyptian the sentence 'drawn out of the water' is pronounced *setja em mu* (st̠3 m mw) and the word 'son' is pronounced *mes* (ms) like in Ra-mes-es.

2- The Septuagint gives the form Môusès.

3- There is only one sure name linked with Moses, which is Nimeshi (2K 9:2). The reconstructed form is therefore Meshi.

4- This name Mwšh is read Mû-sha according to its letters.

■ Jerusalem

1- The etymology in Hebrews 7:2 indicates that the last part of this name Salem means 'peace'. The first part Yerû- literally means 'been founded' or 'foundation', that is to say 'city'. Therefore, the expression 'foundation of peace' gives Yerûshalôm in Hebrew.

2- The Septuagint gives the form Iérousalèm. Other works (Josephus and the books of Maccabees) give Iérousalüma.

3- There is only one name definitely connected to the final part of Jerusalem: it is Shalém (Ps 76:2). For the beginning, there is Yeruél (2Ch 20:16). The reconstructed form is therefore Yerushalém. Noticeably, the Masoretic text has several variants: Yerûshalayim (1Ch 3:5; 2Ch 25:1; Est 2:6; Jr 26:18), Yerûshalayem (2Ch 32:9; Ezk 8:3) and Yerûshelèm (Dn 6:11). Thus, despite the choice of the Masorets (Yerûshalaïm); the form Yerûshalém is currently privileged, because several concordant transcriptions of this name have been uncovered. For example, Urusalima (city of Salim) in the tablets of Ebla (-2300), Urusalim to Tell El-Amarna (-1300), and Urusalimmu in a text of Sennacherib (-700).

4- This name Yrwšlym is read I-ru-ša-lim (Irushalim) according to its letters.

■ Babel

1- The etymology, in Genesis 11:9 indicates that this name means 'confusion' or '[being] confused', which gives in Hebrew either Balûl (masculine), or Belûlâ (feminine). (Concerning the meaning 'gate of God' for the name Babel see the appendix B.)

2- The Septuagint has transcribed this name Babülôn.

3- There is only one definitely name connected to Babel: it is Zerûbabèl (Za 4:6). The reconstructed form is therefore: Babèl.

4- This name Bbl can be read Ba-bal according to its letters.

Assuming that the Masoretic text preserved the authentic pronunciation of these names in the first century (except perhaps for Jerusalem), we simply have to evaluate the gap between these names used as standards and the results of each method. To gauge objectively, 2 points may be given when a vowel (i, é, [e], è, a, o, û) is identical, and 1 point if it is close, for example an *a* put in the place of *è* or *o*. Additionally, as some consonants serve as vowels in Hebrew, one obtains Ya = ia, Yi = ï, Wa = ûa, Wu = û.

ACCORDING TO: REF.		ETYMOLOGIES		SOURCES	
Yéshûa	8	Yôshia	4	Ièsous	5
Abraham	6	Abhamon	5	Abraam	6
Noaḥ	4	Naḥam	3	Noé	2
Yisraél	6	Seraél	4	Israèl	5
Yehûdah	7	Yehôdèh	5	Iouda	6
Moshèh	4	Mashûy	1	Mousès	3
Babèl	4	Balûl	2	Babülon	2
Yerûshalém	9	Yerûshalom	7	Iérousalèm	8
100 %	48	65 %	31	77 %	37
Sarah	4	Sarah	4	Sarra	4
Shemûél	5	Shealtiél	3	Samouèl	3
Yôséph	6	Yôsiph	5	Iosèph	5
Kayin	4	Kanuy	2	Kain	4
Zebûlûn	5	Izebol	1	Zaboulon	3
Yaaqôb	8	Yaeqob	6	Iakôb	6
Ḥawuah	6	Ḥayiah	4	Éüa	4
100 %	86	65 %	56	77 %	66
Yhwh		Yihyèh		Iaô	

ACCORDING TO: REF.		ONOMASTIC		ITS LETTERS	
Yéshûa	8	Yéshûa	8	Ishûa	6
Abraham	6	Abraḥam	6	Abaraham	6
Noaḥ	4	Noaḥ	4	Nûaḥ	3

Yisraél	6	Yisraél	6	Israal	4
Yehûdah	7	Yehûdah	7	Ihûda	6
Moshèh	4	Meshi	0	Mûsha	2
Babèl	4	Babèl	4	Babal	3
Yerûshalém	9	Yerûshalém	9	Irûshalim	7
100 %	48	92 %	44	77 %	37
Sarah	4	-		Sara	4
Shemûél	5	-		Shamûal	2
Yôséph	6	-		Iûsaph	3
Kayin	4	-		Kin	2
Zebûlûn	5	-		Zabûlûn	4
Yaaqôb	8	-		Iaqûb	5
Ḥawuah	6	-		Aûa	6
100 %	86	92 %		73 %	63
Yhwh		**Yehowah**		**Ihûa**	

We see by means of the tables above that if one wished to find a name whose pronunciation was lost, the best method (92%) consists of finding this lost name inside other associated Hebrew names. This is the method based on an onomastic study of names. Second (77%), in order of reliability, there is the method of Greek transcriptions of names in the Septuagint. Third, but following closely (73%), one finds the method of reading a name by its letters. And finally, the inferior method (65%), is the one that consists of restoring a name by its etymology.

Paradoxically, it is this last method which is at present favored to find the pronunciation of the Tetragram. Very often this last method is combined with Greek occurrences of Iaô. It is possible to combine various methods and obtain a final pronunciation which is more reliable, but for that it is also necessary to know the origin of the differences resulting from each method to be able to evaluate them, case by case.

°ETYMOLOGIES METHOD

It is not the role of biblical etymology to be scientific. As proof, an examination of only a few examples shows that biblical explanations are more wordplays than linguistic definitions[11]. (For a further analysis see the Appendix B).

NAME	1- GRAMMATICAL ETYMOLOGY	2- BIBLICAL ETYMOLOGY	BEST AGREEMEMENT
Jesus	salvation	he will save	Joshua
Moses	drawing out	being drawn out	Nimshi
Israel	He will contend [.] God	He contended [.] God	Serayah
Yoséph	He will add	He will gather*	Asaph
Levi	[being] joined	he will be joined	-

Although there is an obvious link between the biblical definition and the etymology (in the grammatical sense), there is no absolute equivalence[12]. For example, the name Jesus is closer to the word *yeshûah* 'salvation' than to the word *yôshîa'* 'He will save'. In fact, biblical etymology is based more on wordplay, or on an assonance between words, than on a strict grammatical definition, because the primary goal of the Bible is to provide religious teaching. So, the etymology of a name actually constitutes a prophetic statement. For example, the name Moses, explained in Exodus 2:10 as 'being drawn out [of the water]', announced prophetically that a whole people would be also 'drawn out [of the water]' by means of the one who would become the man 'drawing out [of the water].' (Is 63:11,12.) Just as there can be several prophecies concerning a single person, there can also be several etymologies for a single name, which proves the imprecise character of these etymologies. For example, the name Yôséph means 'he will add', or Yôsiph in Hebrew (Gn 30:24), and as well as 'he will collect', or Yè'soph in Hebrew (Gn 30:23)*. Consequently, it sometimes happens that biblical etymologies are completely disconnected from the etymology in a technical sense[13].

NAME	1- GRAMMATICAL ETYMOLOGY	2- BIBLICAL ETYMOLOGY	BEST AGREEMENT
Samuel	being heard of God (see Appendix B)	asked to God	Shealtiel Saul
Noah	rest	he will comfort	Nahum Nehemia
Babel	gate [of] God	confusion	-
Reuben	see, a son	he has looked upon	
Cain	wrought ?	acquired	-
Abraham	Father had compassion ?	Father of a crowd	Baal-hamon
Zebulun	lofty abode	He will honour	Jezabèl

One can notice the "gulf" which separates these two sorts of etymologies. Rather than attempting to make them coincide, it is necessary to remember that the explanation of these gaps is always the same: the goal of biblical definitions is above all to communicate a religious message. Besides, what would be the purpose of explaining to the Hebrew people the meaning of a Hebrew name? It is obvious to a Hebrew that the name Noah *linguistically* means 'rest'; however the text of Genesis 5:29 makes it clear that this 'rest' would mean *biblically* 'he will comfort', because Noah was to play a comforting prophetic role. In addition, in the first century of our era, Barnabas, an Aramaic name which *linguistically* means 'son of prophecy' (Bar-nabuah) or perhaps 'son of Nabu' (Bar-nabau), would mean *biblically* 'son of comfort'. (Ac 4:36)

Thus, the Bible can notably modify the sense of a name in order to teach an important message for the future. For example, Babylonians probably called their city: Babel, as very old transcriptions of Bâb-ili literally meaning 'Gate of God' have been found (see the Appendix B). But the Bible would change this noble name to another, more fitting prophetic name: 'Confusion', because Babel would become the great symbol of religious confusion, according to Revelation 18:2,23. One would say today, to retain the biblical play on words, that this 'Gate of God' was rather 'Gap of God'. This way "of etymologizing"

names is known to be ancient since the Babylonians themselves
practiced it at the beginning of the second millennium before
our era. It is evident that most of these Babylonian etymologies
are considered outdated today, because they lean more on a
symbolic link and on the assonance between words than on their
linguistic link[14].

☞   Consequently, all these religious etymologies have no
linguistic value, because such was not their purpose. Besides,
those who would use Exodus 3:14 to find the Name should also
use Exodus 34:14, which says: «Jehovah whose name is jealous,
He is a Jealous God» as well as Isaiah 63:16, which says: «Ô
Jehovah, you are our Father. Our Repurcaser of long ago is your
name» and Hoshea 2:16, which says: «You will call me My
husband» and finally, why not, Zechariah 14:9, which says:
«My name is One.» It is clear that all these etymologies, should
naturally not be understood literally, unless God's name really is
One, Husband, Jealous God, Repurchaser, etc. Moreover, as
seen, Moses did not try to find out "which is God's name",
because he already knew it, but "what this name is", that is:
what would it mean for the Israelites?

°SOURCES METHOD

Some gaps resulting from Greek transcriptions of the
Septuagint can be explained by the following. First, in the Greek
language of this time, there was a phenomenon called iotacism,
which led mainly to the confusion of the sounds *i, é, è, ai*.
Secondly, the Septuagint was probably written in Alexandria in
an Aramaic environment; This sister language of Hebrew
vocalized words in a slightly different way, which doubtless
influenced some transcriptions. Thirdly, a Greek ear did not like
the guttural sounds of the Hebraic language, and, as Flavius
Josephus, for example, explains, numerous names were
hellenized to satisfy the Greek reader (Noah was transformed
into Noé, Yéshua' into Ièsous, etc.). These problems already
existed   in   other   languages: the   Akkadians   having

"akkadianized" Hebrew names, the Hebrews having "Hebraized" the Akkadian names, etc., each ones according to their auditory affinities.

The numerous occurrences of divine names[15] show a great variety in the transcription of names that were identical at first. The most critical case concerns the letters Y and W, which had a considerable evolution of pronunciation. For example, in Aramaic then in Hebrew, the letter W was successively pronounced[16] U > Ô / V > B̲ > B. Samaritans always confused[17] the sounds U and Ô. Given these conditions one can understand that to assess the value of a transcription, one needs to know when it appeared and who did it.

It is also necessary to check the exactitude of quotations. For example, a remark from the book of Theodoret (*Quaestiones in Exodum cap. XV*) is very often quoted to support the pronunciation Yahweh, because of the following sentence: «the name of God is pronounced Iabe (Ιαβε)». This remark is true, but Theodoret specified that he spoke about Samaritans and he added that the Jews pronounced this name Aïa. In another book (*Quaestiones in I Paral. cap. IX*)[18] he wrote that «the word Nethinim means in Hebrew 'gift of Iaô (Ιαω)', that is the God who is».

Theophoric names are very often quoted to determine the kind of worship which might have existed, but the context is of prime importance to get the right meaning of these names. For example, the name Baal means in Hebrew 'owner, master' as in Hosea 2:16, thus the Jewish name Bealyah (1Ch 12:5) must be translated by 'Master [is] Yah' rather than 'Baal [is] Yah', but the Edomite name Baalhanan (1Ch 1:49) must be translated by 'Baal has shown favor' rather than 'Owner has shown favor'. In the same way, the Jewish name Mikayah must be translated by 'Who is like Yah' but the Eblaïte name Mikaia has to be translated by 'Who is like mine [of god]' rather than 'Who is like Ia' because there was no worship of Yah at Ebla. Furthermore in Akkadian the word *ia* means 'mine' and *iau* means 'of mine' and not 'Yah He'.

In another example, a Phoenician prince was called either Iaubi'di or Ilubi'di in a Sargon's text around 720 BCE. From this data some concluded that Ilu (god) and Iau (mine?) are connected to the god of the Bible[19], but because this prince was Phoenician there is little chance that this god was linked with YHWH. Secondly, an identification from names is not very convincing if the context is partly known. Within the Bible itself this difficulty occurs, as in the case of King Abiyah (1Ch 3:10) who is also called Abiyahu (2Ch 13:20) and Abiyam (1K 14:31), probably because the words yahu (Yah himself) and yam (sea) were pronounced in the same way in certain languages, for example at Ugarit (14th century BCE) the god Yam (ym) was also spelt Yaw (yw)[20], in Persia the name Dari-*yaw*-ush (Darius) is also read Dari-*yam*-ush (6th century BCE). Because the name Miryam is spelt Maria or Mariam in the Greek Scriptures, some specialists believe that the ending *yam* may come from an old *yaw*[21] (In Akkadian the letter *w* was in time substituted by *m*).

°LETTERS METHOD

The process of reading according to its letters is, in principle, very rudimentary, because it contains only three sounds I (Y), U (W) and A, while the Hebraic language possesses seven (i, é, [e], è, a, o, u). In spite of this intrinsic handicap, this method of reading gives rather good results on the whole[22], because it respects the vocalic character of the Hebraic language which favors a vocalic reading of proper names instead of a consonantal reading (Aramaic). The group YW in a word will be read preferentially IO or IU in Hebrew, while Aramaic will prefer to read YaW or -YW-. One can see this peculiarity in some words written identically but pronounced differently.

NAME	ARAMAIC	REF.	HEBREW	REF.
Ywn	**Yaw**an	Gn 10:2	**Yo**nah	Jon 1:1
Drywš	Dar**yaw**èsh	Ezr 5:7	(Dar**yo**sh)	Ezr 10:16
Sywn	Si**yw**an	Est 8:9	**Si**yon	Is 1:8
Kywn	Ké**yw**an[23]	Am 5:26	Kiy**û**n	Am 5:26

Note that names not of Jewish origin such as Yavân, Darius, Sivân, Kaiwan (probably for anti-idolatrous reasons this name, spelt Raiphan [Ac 7:43], was modified to Kiyûn), have a consonantal pronunciation. On the other hand, in Jewish names the group YW is always vocalized IO or IU without exception. One notes the same phenomenon in the Peschitta, a Syriac translation of the Bible: for example, Io-séph (Lk 3:26) became Yaw-sèph, Io-nah (Lk 11:30) became Yaw-nan. The Aramaic influenced the Hebrew language greatly over a long period of time[24]; the opposite was less true.

To give an example showing the enormous influence of Aramaic on the Hebrew of the Bible, the expression 'brother [of] he' or 'his brother' in Hebrew, that is found very often in the Bible, is written 4 times in its Hebraic form 'aHIHU, and 113 times in its Aramaic form 'aHIW. All these variations have been the object of numerous studies[25]. By applying the results of this research, one can restore the pronunciation of the three divine names YH, YW or YHW, and YHWH, just before the beginning of our era.

GREEK		HEB	ARAM.	HEB	ARAM.	HEB	ARAM.
		YH		YW		YHWH	
(Iaû)	-400	îâ	Yah	îû	Yaw	îhûâ	Yahwah
Iaô	-100	îâ	Yah	îô	Yaw	îhôâ	Yahweh
Iaüe	+200	îâ	Yah	îô	Yav	îhôâ	Yahveh
Iabe	+300	îâ	Yah	îô	Yab	îhôâ	Yahbeh

As seen from this chart, Greek sources confirm without ambiguity the Aramaic vocalization. In fact, the problem remains down to today, because the Arabic language, which is related to the Aramaic language, vocalizes the word YHWD, not Ye-HUD (IHUD) as do the Jews, but Ya-HUD. This vocalization Ye- is proper to the Jews. One does not find it in other similar languages. For example, the word **Yehu**di in Hebrew is read **Yahu**diyun in Arabic, **Yau**dayyu in older Akkadian and **Yau**dayya in younger Akkadian[26] (Assyrian).

°ONOMASTIC METHOD

☞   This last method is the most reliable, because names are very stable with the passage of time, often much more so than common words of the language itself. Proper names are in a sense a memory of the sounds of the past or 'phonograms'. Furthermore, the Hebraic language was, despite some variations, very stable over a long period of time. For example, the Hebrew (Canaanite glosses transcribed) of El Amarna's letters dated the fourteenth century before our era can still be understood by a modern Israeli. So, one can reconstitute a name with great reliability if the name to be found is protected within several other names. Now, in this regard, the divine name has a significant advantage, because it was integrated into hundred of proper nouns. The only difficulty is to avoid confusing the great name YHWH (Jr 44:26), with the short name YH (Ps 68:5). These two names can moreover be used together, as in Isaiah 12:2 and 26:4, in Psalm 130:3, etc. Generally, the short name, Yah, more affectionate, was especially used in songs (Ex 15:2), as in David's psalms and in the frequent expression 'Praise Yah' (Alleluia). Because of this preeminence of the great name Yehowah with regard to the other name Yah, the Jews, as noted in the list hereafter, took scrupulously care to place it only at the head of proper names (Yehô-), and never at the end.

As the famous Jewish commentator Rashi of Troyes (1040-1105) noted in his commentary on Numbers 26:5 «The Holy One has linked his name YHWH (' ה) to theirs at the beginning and YH (י) at the end of their names in order to say according Psalm 122:4 "I shall witness that they are the sons of their fathers"».

M.T. (B.H.S.)	LXX (Rahlfs)	"LINGUISTIC" TRANSLATION (Brown,Driver,Briggs/ Gesenius)
'Abiyâ	Abia (1Ch 3:10)	my father (is) Yah
'Abiyahû	Abia (2Ch 13:20)	my father (is) Yah himself
'Adayâ	Adaia (1Ch 8:21)	[he] has decked, Yah
'Adayahû	Adaia (2Ch 23:1)	[he] has decked, Yah himself
'Adoniyâ	Adônia (1Ch 3:2)	my lord (is) Yah
'Adoniyahû	Adôniou (1K 1:8)	my lord (is) Yah himself
'Aḥazyâ	Okozias (2K 1:2)	(he) has grasped, Yah
'Aḥazyahû	Okoziou (2K 1:18)	(he) has grasped, Yah himself
'Aḥiyâ	Akia (1S 14:3)	my brother (is) Yah
'Aḥiyahû	Akia (2Ch 10:15)	my brother (is) Yah himself
'Aḥyô	(Aḥiw)* (2S 6:3)	brother of Yo/my brother (is) He
'Amaryâ	Amaria (Ezr 10:42)	(he) has said, Yah
'Amaryahû	Amarias (2Ch 19:11)	(he) has said, Yah himself
'Amasyâ	Amasias (2Ch 17:16)	(he) has carried the load, Yah
'Amasyâ	Amasias (Am. 7:10)	mighty (is) Yah
'Amasyahû	Améssiou (2K 14:18)	mighty (is) Yah himself
'Ananyâ	Anania (Ne 3:23)	(he) has covered, Yah
'Anayâ	Anaia (Ne 10:23)	(he) has answered, Yah
'Asayâ	Asaia (2Ch 34:20)	(he) has made, Yah
'Aṭalyâ	Atélia (Ezr 8:7)	exalted (is) Yah ?
'Aṭalyahû	Gotolia (2Ch 22:2)	exalted (is) Yah himself ?
'Aṭayâ	Ataia (Ne 11:4)	my time (is) Yah ?
'Aṣalyahû	Éséliou (2K 22:3)	(he) has reserved, Yah himself
'Azanyâ	Azania (Ne 10:10)	(he) has given ear, Yah
'Azaryâ	Azaria (1Ch 2:8)	(he) has helped, Yah
'Azaryahû	Azariou (2K 15:6)	(he) has helped, Yah himself
'Azazyahû	Ozazias (2Ch 31:13)	(he) has strengthened, Yah him.
Baaséyâ	Baasia (1Ch 6:25)	in the work of Yah ?
Baqbuqyâ	Bakbakias (Ne 12:9)	flask of Yah
Bealyâ	Baalia (1Ch 12:5)	Master (is) Yah
Bédyâ	Badaia (Ezr 10:35)	[ser]vant of Yah ?
Benayâ	Banaia (Ezr 10:25)	(he) has built up, Yah
Benayahû	Banaiou (Ezk 11:1)	(he) has built up, Yah himself
Bera'yâ	Baraia (1Ch 8:21)	(he) has created, Yah

Bèrèkyâ	Barakia (1Ch 3:20)	blessed by Yah
Bèrèkyahû	Barakiou (Za 1:7)	blessed by Yah himself
Besôdyâ	Basodia (Ne 3:6)	in the secret of Yah
Buqiyahû	Boukias (1Ch 25:4)	proved of Yah himself
Delayâ	Dalaia (Ne 7:62)	(he) has drawn up, Yah
Delayahû	Dalaias (Jr 36:12)	(he) has drawn up, Yah himself
Dôdawahû	Dôdia (2Ch 20:37)	beloved of (Yah) himself
'Éliyâ	Élia (Ezr 10:21)	my God (is) Yah
'Éliyahû	Éliou (1K 17:1)	my God (is) Yah himself
'Èlyehô'énay	Éliôènai (1Ch 26:3)	toward Yehô (are) my eyes
'Èlyô'énay	Éliôènai (1Ch 4:36)	toward Yô (are) my eyes
Gedalyâ	Gadalia (Ezr 10:18)	(is) great, Yah
Gedalyahû	Godolia (1Ch 25:3)	(is) great, Yah himself
Gemaryâ	Gamariou (Jr 29:3)	(he) has completed, Yah
Gemaryahû	Gamariou (Jr 36:10)	(he) has completed, Yah himself
Ḥaggiyâ	Aggia (1Ch 6:30)	feast of Yah
Ḥakalyâ	Akalia (Ne 1:1)	wait for Yah ?
Ḥananyâ	Anania (1Ch 8:24)	(he) has been gracious, Yah
Ḥananyahû	Ananiou (Jr 36:12)	(he) has been gracious Yah him.
Ḥasadyâ	Asadia (1Ch 3:20)	(is) kind, Yah
Ḥašabenyâ	Asbania (Ne 3:10)	(he) esteemed, Yah
Ḥašabyâ	Asabia (1Ch 25:19)	(he) has taken account, Yah
Ḥašabyahû	Asabia (2Ch 35:9)	(he) has taken account Yah him.
Ḥazayâ	Ozia (Ne 11:5)	(he) has seen, Yah
Ḥilqiyâ	Élkia (Ne 11:11)	my portion (share is) Yah
Ḥilqyahû	Kélkiou (Jr 1:1)	my portion (share is) Yah himself
Ḥizqiyâ	Ézékia (1Ch 3:23)	(he) has strengthened, Yah
Ḥizqiyahû	Ézékiou (2K 20:20)	(he) has strengthened, Yah him.
Ḥobayâ	Ébia (Ne 7:63)	(he) has hidden, Yah
Hôdawyâ	Odouia (1Ch 5:24)	give thanks to Yah
Hôdaywahû	Odouia (1Ch 3:24)	my splendor [is]wah himself ?
Hôdiyâ	Odouia (Ne 10:14)	splendour (is) Yah
Hôdwah	Oudouia (Ne 7:43)	praise []wah ?
Hôša'ayâ	Ôsaia (Ne 12:32)	(he) has saved, Yah
Kenanyâ	Kônénias (1Ch 15:27)	firm (is) Yah
Kenanyahû	Kônénia (1Ch.15:22)	firmly established (is) Yah him.

Kænanyahû	Kônéniou (2Ch 31:13)	firmly established (is) Yah him.
Kænyahû	Iékonias (Jr 22:24)	established by Yah himself
Mæ'adyâ	Maadias (Ne 12:5)	celebration [of] Yah ?
Ma'aséyâ	Maasaia (Ne 10:25)	work of Yah
Ma'aséyahû	Maassaiou (2Ch 26:11)	work of Yah himself
Ma'azyâ	Maazia (Ne 10:8)	stronghold (is) Yah
Ma'azyahû	Maassai (1Ch 24:18)	stronghold (is) Yah himself
Maḥséyâ	Maasaiou (Jr 51:59)	a refuge (is) Yah
Malkiyâ	Mélkia (Ne 10:3)	my king (is) Yah
Malkiyahû	Mélkiou (Jr 38:6)	my king (is) Yah himself
Matanyâ	Matania (Ezr 10:26)	gift of Yah
Matanyahû	Mattanias (2Ch 29:13)	gift of Yah himself
Matityâ	Matatia (Ezr 10:43)	gift of Yah
Matityahû	Mattathia (1Ch 15:18)	gift of Yah himself
Melatyâ	Maltias (Ne 3:7)	(he) has delivred, Yah
Mešèlèmyâ	Masalami (1Ch.9:21)	(he) repays, Yah
Mešèlèmyahû	Mosollamia (1Ch 26:1)	(he) repays, Yah himself
Mikayâ	Mikaia (Ne 12:35)	who (is) like Yah
Mikayahû	Mikaias (2Ch 17:7)	who (is) like Yah himself
Mikayehû	Mikaias (Jr 36:11)	who (is) like (Yah) himself
Miqenéyahû	Makénia (1Ch 15:18)	possession Yah himself
Môadyâ	Kairos (Ne 12:17)	celebration [of] Yah ?
Môriyâ	Amoria (2Ch 3:1)	provided by Yah ?
Ne'aryâ	Nôadia (1Ch 4:42)	youth of Yah
Nedabyâ	Nadabia (1Ch 3:18)	magnanimous (is) Yah
Neḥèmyâ	Néémia (Ne 7:7)	he comforts, Yah
Nériyâ	Nèriou (Jr 32:12)	my lamp (is) Yah
Nériyahû	Nèriou (Jr 36:14)	my lamp (is) Yah himself
Netanyâ	Natanias (1Ch 25:2)	(he) has given Yah
Netanyahû	Nataniou (Jr 36:14)	(he) has given Yah himself
Nô'adyâ	Nôadia (Ne 6:14)	meeting with, Yah
'Obadyâ	Abadia (Ezr 8:9)	servant of Yah
'Obadyahû	Abdiou (1K 18:3)	servant of Yah himself
Pedayâ	Padaia (Ne 3:25)	(he) has ransomed, Yah
Pedayahû	Padaia (1Ch 27:20)	(he) has ransomed, Yah himself
Pelalyâ	Palalia (Ne 11:12)	(he) arbitrated, Yah

Pelatyah	Paléttia (1Ch 4:42)	(he) has provided escape, Yah
Pelatyahû	Paltian (Ezr 11:1)	(he) has provided escape, Yah hi.
Pela'yâ	Péléîa (Ne 10:11)	(he) has been surpassing, Yah
Pelayâ	Palaia (1Ch 3:24)	(he) has distinguished, Yah
Peqahyâ	Pakéïas (2K 15:22)	(he) has opened (the eyes), Yah
Petahyâ	Pétaia (1Ch 24:16)	(he) has opened, Yah
Qôlayâ	Kôlia (Ne 11:7)	voice [of] Yah
Qûšayahû	Kisaiou (1Ch 15:17)	(he) has lured, Yah himself ?
Ra'amyâ	Daémia (Ne 7:7)	he) has thundered, Yah
Ramyâ	Ramia (Ezr 10:25)	exalted [is] Yah ?
Re'ayâ	Raia (1Ch 4:2)	(he) has seen, Yah
Re'élayâ	Réélias (Ezr 2:2)	(he) made to tremble, Yah
Rehabyâ	Raabia (1Ch 23:17)	(he) has widened, Yah
Rehabyahû	Raabias (1Ch 26:25)	(he) has widened, Yah himself
Remalyahû	Roméliou (2K 16:1)	(he) has adorned, Yah ?
Repayâ	Rapaia (1Ch 7:2)	(he) has healed, Yah
Semakyahû	Samakias (1Ch 26:7)	(he) has sustained, Yah himself
Sepanyâ	Sapania (1Ch.6:21)	(he) has treasured up, Yah
Sepanyahû	Soponian (2K.25:18)	(he) has treasured up, Yah him.
Serayâ	Saraia (Ne 11:11)	(he) has contended, Yah
Serayahû	Saraia (Jr 36:26)	(he) has contended, Yah himself
Šebanyâ	Sabania (Ne 10:11)	whose he built, Yah ?
Šebanyahû	Sobnia (1Ch 15:24)	whose he built Yah himself ?
Šeharyâ	Saaria (1Ch 8:26)	(he) has sought for, Yah ?
Šekanyâ	Sakania (Ezr 8:3)	residence of Yah
Šekanyahû	Sékonias (2Ch 31:15)	residence of Yah himself
Šèlèmyâ	Sélémia (Ezr 10:39)	[he] has rewarded, Yah
Šèlèmyahû	Sélémiou (Jr 36:14)	[he] has rewarded, Yah himself
Šemaryâ	Samaria (Ezr 10:32)	(he) has kept, Yah
Šemaryahû	Samaria (1Ch 12:5)	(he) has kept, Yah himself
Šema'yâ	Samaia (1Ch 3:22)	(he) has heard, Yah
Šema'yahû	Samaiou (Jr 26:20)	(he) has heard, Yah himself
Šepatyâ	Sapatia (1Ch 3:3)	(he) has judged, Yah
Šepatyahû	Sapatias (1Ch 27:16)	(he) has judged, Yah himself
Šérébyâ	Sarabia (Ne 12:8)	[has sent] parching heat, Yah

Ṣidqiyâ	Sédékias (1K 22:11)	my righteousness (is) Yah
Ṣidqiyahû	Sédékiou (1K 22:24)	my righteousness (is) Yah him.
Tebalyahû	Tablai (1Ch 26:11)	(he) has dipped, Yah himself
Tôbiyâ	Tôbia (Ne 7:62)	good (is) Yah
Tôbiyahû	Tôbias (2Ch 17:8)	good (is) Yah himself
'Ûriyâ	Ouria (Ezr 8:33)	my light (is) Yah
'Ûriyahû	Ourias (Jr 26:20)	my light (is) Yah himself
'Uziyâ	Ozia (Ezr 10:21)	my strength (is) Yah
'Uziyahû	Oziou (2Ch 26:22)	my strength (is) Yah himself
Ya'arèšyâ	Iarasia (1Ch 8:27)	(he) fattened up, Yah?
Ya'azanyâ	Iézonian (Jr 35:3)	(he) has given ear, Yah
Ya'azanyahû	Iézonias (Ezk 8:11)	(he) has given ear, Yah himself
Ya'aziyâ	Ozia (1Ch 24:26)	(he) has strengthened, Yah?
Yaḥzeyâ	Iazia (Ezr 10:15)	may behold, Yah
Yebèrèkyahû	Barakiou (Is 8:2)	(he) blessed, Yah himself
Yeda'eyâ	Iadia (Ne 11:10)	(he) has known, Yah
Yedayâ	Iédaia (Ne 3:10)	may he praises Yah?
Yedidyah	Idédi (2S 12:25)	beloved of Yah
Yèḥdeyahû	Iadia (1Ch 24:20)	may give joy, Yah himself
Yeḥiyâ	Iia (1Ch 15:24)	may live, Yah
Yeḥizqiyâ	Ézékia (Ezr 2:16)	may strengthen, Yah
Yeḥizqiyahû	Ézékiou (Jr 15:4)	may strengthen, Yah himself
Yehô'ada	Iôiada (1Ch 8:36)	Yeho has adorned
Yehô'adan	Iôadén (2Ch 25:1)	Yeho (is) pleasure
Yehô'adin	Iôadin (2K 14:2)	Yeho (is) pleasure
Yehô'aḥaz	Iôakaz (2Ch 36:1)	Yeho has grasped
Yehô'aš	Iôas (1K 14:8)	Yeho has bestowed?
Yehôḥanan	Iôanan (Ezr 10:28)	Yeho has been gracious
Yehônadab	Iônadab (2S 13:5)	Yeho (is) magnanimous
Yehônatan	Iônatan (1S 14:6)	Yeho has given
Yehôram	Iôram (2K 1:17)	Yeho (is) exalted
Yehôṣadaq	Iôsadak (1Ch 5:40)	Yeho did righteous
Yehôšab'at	Iôsabét (2Ch 22:11)	Yeho (is) an oath
Yehôšapat	Iôsapat (1Ch 18:15)	Yeho has judged
Yehôšèba'	Iôsabéé (2K 11:2)	Yeho (is) an oath
Yehôšûa'	Ièsou (2K 23:8)	[Yeho is] salvation

Yehôyada'	Iôadaé (1Ch 12:28)	Yeho may know
Yehôyak̲in	Iôak̲im (2K 24:12)	Yeho will firmly establish
Yehôyaqim	Iôakim (1Ch 3:15)	Yeho will raise up
Yehôyari̲b	Iari̲b (1Ch 24:7)	Yeho will plead
Yehôza̲bad	Iôzabad (1Ch 26:4)	Yeho will endow
Yéhû'	Ièou (1Ch 2:38)	Ye[hu is] himself
Yek̲ælyahû	K̲alia (2K 15:2)	(he) will able, Yah himself
Yek̲ænyâ	Iék̲onias (1Ch 3:16)	(he) will establish, Yah
Yek̲ænyahû	Iék̲onian (Jr 24:1)	(he) will establish, Yah himself
Yeqamyâ	Iékémia (1Ch 3:18)	(he) has raised up, Yah
Yeriyâ	Ioudias (1Ch 26:31)	(he) will see (provide?), Yah
Yeriyahû	Iédiou (1Ch 24:23)	(he) will see, Yah himself
Yeša'yâ	Iésia (Ezr 8:7)	(he) will save, Yah
Yeša'yahû	Esaias (Is 1:1)	(he) will save, Yah himself
Yéšûa'	Ièsou (1Ch 24:11)	[Yehua (is)] salvation
Yezanyâ	Iézonias (Jr 42:1)	(he) has given ear, Yah
Yezanyahû	Iézonias (Jr 40:8)	[(he) has given ear, Yah himself
Yi̲bneyâ	Ibanaa (1Ch 9:8)	(he) will build, Yah
Yi̲bniyâ	Banaia (1Ch 9:8)	(he) will build, Yah
Yigdalyahû	Godoliou (Jr 35:4)	(he shall make) great, Yah him.
Yip̲deyâ	Iép̲éria (1Ch 8:25)	(he) will ransom, Yah
Yir'îyâ	Sarouias (Jr 37:14)	(he) sees, Yah
Yirmeyâ	Iérmia (Ne 10:3)	(he) will exalt, Yah ?
Yirmeyahû	Iérémiou (2Ch 36:21)	(he) will exalt, Yah himself ?
Yišiyâ	Isia (1Ch 24:25)	(he) makes forget, Yah
Yišiyahû	Ièsouni (1Ch 12:7)	(he) makes forget, Yah himself
Yišma'yah	Samaias (1Ch 12:4)	may hear, Yah
Yišma'yahû	Samaias (1Ch 27:19)	may hear, Yah himself
Yismak̲yahû	Samak̲ia (2Ch 31:13)	(he) has supported, Yah himself
Yiziyâ	Iazia (Ezr 10:25)	(he) will gush forth, Yah
Yizraḥyâ	Iézria (1Ch 7:3)	(he) will shine forth, Yah
Yô'a̲b	Iôab (2S 8:16)	Yo (is) father
Yô'aḥ	Iôaa (1Ch 26:4)	Yo (is) brother
Yô'aḥaz	Iôak̲az (2Ch 34:8)	Yo has grasped
Yô'aš	Iôas (1K 22:26)	Yo has bestowed
Yô'éd	Iôad (Ne 11:7)	Yo (is) witness

Yô'él	Iôèl (1Ch 5:12)	Yo (is) God
Yô'èzèr	Iôazar (1Ch 12:7)	Yo (is) help
Yôḫa'	Iôḵa (1Ch 8:16)	Yo has been grac(ious) ?
Yôḫanan	Iôanan (Ne 12:22)	Yo has been gracious
Yôḵèbèd	Iôḵabéd (Ex 6:20)	Yo (is) glory
Yônadab	Iônadab (2S 13:3)	Yo (is) magnanimous
Yônatan	Iônatan (1S 14:1)	Yo has given
Yôqim	Iôakim (1Ch 4:22)	Yo has raised up
Yôram	Iôram (2K 8:21)	Yo (is) exalted
Yôṣadaq	Iôsédék (Ne 12:26)	Yo (does) righteous
Yôšapat	Iôsapat (1Ch 11:43)	Yo has judged
Yôšawyâ	Iôsia (1Ch 11:46)	(he) has assisted, Yah ?
Yôšibyâ	Isabia (1Ch 4:35)	(he) causes to dwell, Yah
Yo'šiyâ	Iôsiou (Za 6:10)	(he) will support, Yah?
Yo'šiyahû	Iôsia (Jr 1:2)	(he) will support, Yah himself?
Yôsipyâ	Iôsépia (Ezr 8:10)	(he) will add, Yah
Yôṭam	Iôaṭam (2K 15:36)	Yo (is) perfect
Yôyada	Iôada (Ne 12:22)	Yo may know
Yôyaḵin	Iôakim (Ezk 1:2)	Yo may firmly establish
Yôyaqim	Iôakim (Ne 12:10)	Yo may raise up
Yôyarib	Iôiarib (Ne 12:6)	Yo may plead
Yôzabad	Iôzabad (1Ch 12:4)	Yo has endowed
Yôzaḵar	Iéziḵar (2K 12:21)	Yo has remembered
Zebadyâ	Zabadia (1Ch 8:15)	(he) has endowed, Yah
Zebadyahû	Zabadias (1Ch 26:2)	(he) has endowed, Yah himself
Zeḵaryâ	Zaḵaria (Ezr 8:11)	(he) has remembered, Yah
Zeḵaryahû	Zaḵariou (2Ch 26:5)	(he) has remembered, Yah him.
Zeraḥyâ	Zaraia (Ezr 7:4)	(he) has shone, Yah ?

☞ One can see a noteworthy agreement between these two texts, despite the fact that they were handed down through some twenty centuries. Of course, there was some Aramaic influence in the Septuagint version and in the Hebrew text. But, the authentic vocalization seems to be close to the Hebrew Masoretic text. The first reason is that 60% of the texts found at Qumran[27] dated from 275 BCE to 70 CE agree with the Masoretic text[28], which consequently, also confirms its vocalization. A second reason is that the LXX itself was revised as early as the mid first century from a text close to the Masoretic text[29].

☞   Some remarks are necessary about the transcription of names in the Septuagint because one finds a curious phenomenon here. The sequence Yehô in Hebrew names became Iô in Greek simply because the letter *h* doesn't exist in Greek. Even in Hebrew this letter had become inaudible by the third century BCE. Furthermore, the letter *y* is pronounced *ü* in Greek, therefore Iô is the best transcription. The same is true for *yah* which became *ia*. However *yahû* is never transcribed iaou but rather at random by *ia* or *iou*. The names ending in *yahû* are systematically modified into *yah*, without exception. This change was made too often to be due to chance and is confirmed by the Qumrân texts. For example, in the oldest text (from 150 to 100 BCE) of Isaiah found at Qumrân[30], the ending of proper names in *yahû* were modified systematically to *yah*. This must have been a voluntary modification because the spelling is exact in some of the scribe's corrections, for example at Isaiah 1:1 and 38:21. On the other hand, in a more recent text of Isaiah[31] (from around 50 BCE) these modifications were not used. Finally, in the Septuagint itself the correct endings were restored. For example, in Aquila's translation near 130 CE, the name Iôs-ia reverted to Iôs-iaou (2K 23:16, 19, 23, 34), K̲élk-ias (also written K̲élk-iou) came back to Élk-iaou (2K 23:24), etc. The correct ending is *yaou*, confirmed by its presence on several seals dated around the seventh century before our Common Era.

From the preceding one can deduce that around the third century before our Common Era the Jews avoided the pronunciation yahû. Was this the pronunciation of the Name? The answer is no, because as we have seen, this name Yahû was the substitute used by the Jews in the letters (of Elephantine) dated of the fifth century before our Common Era. Two centuries later the veneration for the substitute equalled the reverence shown the Tetragram.

Is it still possible to find the pronunciation of the Name through the Septuagint? Yes, provided one keeps in mind this exception. The Tetragram was never put at the end of theophoric names but only at the beginning. In contrast the word El (God) can be found at the beginning of names such as Eleazar, Elqana, Eldad, etc., or at the end such as in Daniel, Gabriel, Bethel, etc. The same holds true for other words such as *adon* (lord) *'ab* (father) *'ah* (brother) and so forth.

Yehô'aḥaz	'Aḥazyah
Yehôḥanan	Ḥananyah
Yehônadab	Nedabyah
Yehônatan	Netanyah
Yehôṣadaq	Ṣidqiyah
Yehôšapaṭ	Šepaṭyah
Yehôšûa'	Yeša'yah
Yehôyada'	Yeda'eyah
Yehôzabad	Zebadyah

'Elḥanan	Ḥanan'él
'Elnatan	Netan'él
'Elîšapaṭ	
'Elîšûa'	
'Elyada'	Yedî'a'él
'Elzabad	Zabdî'él

☞ One can verify that, *without exception*, the theophoric names beginning in YHW- are vocalized YeHO- (IO- in the Septuagint), and those ending in -YHW are vocalized -YaHU (IA or IOU in the Septuagint). Additionally, the vowel *a* very often follows the sequence YeHO-, that is to say the "normal" sequence is YeHO-()a. A further study[32] has shown that this vocalic sequence is very frequent in biblical names (It is impossible to find, for example, YeHO-()i or YeHO-()é, etc.). The sequence YeHO-()a is so universal in theophoric names that some names have been 'theophorized' by assonance. There are some traces of this phenomenon, which happened before the editing of the Septuagint, in the following names: Iôa-tam (Jg 9:7, 57; 2K 15:5, 32; etc.), Iôa-kéim (1Ch 4:22), Iôa-s (1Ch 23:10, 11), Iôa-sar (1Ch 2:18), Iôa-kal (Jr 37:3), etc. In some cases the change is surprising for example when the name 'aḥaz-yahû is read Iôa-kas (2K 14:13). The oldest Greek occurence of this name Iôa- is found in a letter from Egypt dated 257 BCE where there is the name Iôa-nai[33].

A careful analysis of the names of the Septuagint allows us to conclude that towards the third century before our era the pronunciation Iaou had become too sacred to be written, and that the older pronunciation IÔA had a great influence, the beginning of certain names even becoming Iôa-. One can see that this powerful assonance is also at the origin of the transformation of Yehôshûa's name (Joshua) into Yéshûa (Jesus) instead of Yoshûa. In this case, the sequence YeHO-U-a- became Yé-U-a-. As a last point concerning pronunciation, the final H in the names ending in WH is always vocalized -A (endings in -èH result from a more ancient -aH[34]; for example the name Ninwéh is pronounced Ninua in a Cyrus's Assyrian text, dated the sixth century before our era).

M.T.	LXX	REFERENCE
'Alwah	Gôla	Gn 36:40
Ḥawah	Éuan	Gn 4:1
Išwah	Iésoua	Gn 46:17
'Iwah	Aua	2K 19:13
Ninwéh	Ninéuè	Gn 10:11
Puwah	Poua	Nb 26:23
Šawéh	Sauè	Gn 14:5
Tiqwah	Tékoué	2K 22:14

CONCLUSION ON THE PRONUNCIATION OF THE NAME

We have seen that, apart from the Masoretic vocalization, there are several methods to find the pronunciation of a name in the first century of our era. However, with the four methods of reconstruction, the one based on biblical etymology, which is in fact a religious teaching, by definition not scientific, cannot be used for this purpose. The three other methods give, on the other hand, concurrent results. In the case of the Tetragram, these three methods give successively the three pronunciations, Iaô, Yehowah and Ihûa. An examination of the historical context explains the conflict in Iaô. Indeed, at this time the Hebraic substitute YHW, or the Aramaic homologue YW, was still widely used among the Jews. Furthermore, the occurrences of Iaô evolved in time, simply reflecting the evolution of the pronunciation of the number 16 (which was forbidden), or YaW. Thus, there is a compatibility between the two pronunciations Yehowah and Ihûa, just as satisfactory as Yehûdah and Ihûda, Yésûa' and Isûa', etc. In view of this agreement, unanimity on the vocalization should have been easy to obtain!

Actually, several difficulties result from a faulty use of occurrences of the Name. Indeed, many authors "forget" to clarify time (which is crucial because of the use of substitutes for the Name), and place (which is crucial because of the language used [Hebrew or Aramaic], and so the vocalization). The historical record which follows will permit us to place the use of the divine names YHWH (Yehowah), YHW (Yahu), YW (Yaw) and YH (Yah) in their times and places respective.

Part 2

Historical record

From Adam to Moses

Regarding this period, the Bible is categorical: the Name is known. For example, Eve used it (Gn 4:1) and Abraham called upon it (Gn 12:8), that is, shouted with pleading according to the sense of the Hebrew term. How would an unpronounceable name be shouted? Furthermore, at this time and in all cultures[35] (Egyptian, Babylonian, etc.), a nameless god was a god who did not exist. Semitic culture is no exception; to be nameless is absurd (Jb 30:8).

MYSTICAL CONCEPT OF THE USE OF NAMES

A huge difference separates the Hebrews from other peoples concerning the perception of the name of a divinity: For the peoples of antiquity, the act of calling upon the name of a god forced this one to action, giving a magical power to the name; while to the Hebrew the fact of calling upon God's name was simply a plea and not an incantation (1K 8:33,34). This nuance is major. For example, in his dialogue with Jesus, Satan quoted Psalm 91:11,12 in the sense of God's being obligated to act; it was a mystical concept of prayer (similar to Aladdin's lamp). Jesus rectified this erroneous conception (Mt 4:6,7).

For the Egyptians, Babylonians[36], etc., a thing or being had a real existence only from the moment it received a name, and the fact of having this name created, for the one knowing it, a real power over the being or thing. This implies the importance of the exact pronunciation of the name[37], also its repetition to strengthen the power of the statement. Included in this power would be diagrammatic representations and the written word, which is language in visual form. These steps were taken in the belief of the possibility of exercising a constraint on the divinity if one used the correct words, consequently increasing the importance of ritual. This concept lead to paradoxical consequences. In order not to be compelled to act, the gods and Pharaohs would not divulge their true names but only pseudonyms. For example, the name Amon[38] means 'the hidden' because only initiates knew his real name and could so oblige him to act. To prevent someone from doing any harm, one literally destroyed his name (in fact his pseudonym). For example, the names of Pharaohs or gods fallen in disgrace were scratched out. In addition, in a lawsuit one never mentioned the name of the culprits, for fear of these names producing a bad influence later.

Thus, because of this mystical concept of the name[39], it was useless for ancient peoples to know and use the name of the god of the Hebrews, for at least two reasons. First, in a pragmatic way, these peoples could realize that the use of the Tetragram did not produce any advantage for them (Dt 7:6). Secondly, the conflicting relations of the Hebrews with their neighbors certainly brought the latter to consider the god of the Hebrews as an enemy, and as seen, to protect themselves from this influence, they thus avoided using his name. The only exception to this rule occurred when casting a spell on their enemies. They wrote the name of the enemy to be fought on a figurine representing this enemy then destroyed the figurine to seal the curse. Afterward, when the enemy was defeated, his gods were taken as booty and their names could be used "as by force" (Aladdin's lamp concept).

EXTRA-BIBLICAL TRACES OF THE DIVINE NAME

From the preceding, it seems that to find God's name is problematic (but possible under precise conditions). Even so, archaeologists propose several traces of the divine name during this period, but interpreting their findings is delicate. For example, in the tablets of Ebla written in cuneiform between 2400 and 1800 BCE appear several times names which could be theophoric, that is with the constituent 'ia' or 'ia-u' inside the name. Therefore, the name Mi-ka-ia could be translated by 'who [is] like ia', because the name Mi-ka-il means, 'who [is] like god'. However, the constituent 'ia' also means 'mine[40]', implying 'mine [of god]', which considerably weakens the identification of this name with that of the God of the Bible. Thus Mi-ka-ia can also be translated by 'who [is] like mine [of god]'. In addition, Ia-ra-mu can be translated by 'ia [is] exalted' or 'mine [of god is] exalted'; šu-mi-a-u can be translated by 'son of ia-u' or 'son of mine [of god]'; etc. In fact, these identifications are only based on homophony; (nothing permits us to say if this a coincidence or not.) Also, in the past, certain scholars connected the name Ju-piter (Jove-father) with the Tetragram, but without general agreement.

✂   The Babylonians names[41] Ya-u-um-ilu, Ya-u-ba-ni, etc., which one finds during the first dynasty (-1900-1600), present the same difficulty because one can translate Ya-u-um-ilu by 'Ya-u [is] a god' or 'mine [of god is] god', and Ya-u-ba-ni by 'Ya-u [is] creator' or 'mine [of god is] creator', etc. It is very improbable that these names are theophoric, because, as seen, the Babylonians did not direct worship to the God of the Bible. Secondly, if these names were of Hebraic origin, they would probably have been exchanged for Babylonians names, as in the case of Daniel and his companions (Dn 1:7).

Amorite names (around 1800 BCE) present the same problem. Certainly a name such as Ili-ya[42] can be translated by 'my god [is] ya[43]', but the religious context favors the translation 'my god [is] mine' (as in the biblical name Eliel which means 'my god [is] God'), because none of the Amorite writings which have been found confirm the existence of worship to the god Yah (or Yahu). Amorite names[44] present another peculiarity: some begin with the constituent Ya-wi-, which phonetically approximates the biblical divine name. For example, the Amorite name Ya-wi-AN corresponds exactly to the Akkadian name Ibašši-AN, which is read Ya-wi-i-la and which means 'he is god'[45] (more exactly 'he proves to be god') or, more probably 'He embraced, god'. This is shown by the name Yawi-dagan which means 'he is Dagan', or probably 'He embraced, Dagan' like the Yaḥawi dagan found at Ugarit[46] and not, of course 'Yawi [is] Dagan'. ✂

The expression 'He proves to be god' found among Amorite names is a theological definition identical to that of the

Bible (Ex 3:14), but it does not prove anything regarding the pronunciation of the Tetragram, except to accept these two things: first, that Amorite was a language identical to Hebrew, and secondly that the Tetragram became confused with its theological definition. However, this last assertion is doubtful, because, as seen, there are numerous exceptions in the Bible, notably concerning the most well known names for which the grammatical etymology is completely different from the biblical etymology. Moreover, at that time, this occurrence was frequent among Egyptian or Babylonian documents, where etymologies are more symbolic expressions than linguistic definitions (which were of little interest), that is more based on assonance or wordplay[47]. Therefore it is preferable to speak about religious etymologies. Furthermore, if the Tetragram was really equivalent to its biblical etymology 'He will [prove to] be', the Bible, or more exactly the Pentateuch, would have been illegible, because there would have been permanent confusions between thousands of Tetragrams (yhwh) and thousands of verbal forms 'He will [prove to] be' (yihyèh), which was never the case in Hebrew. On the other hand, in Aramaic, this confusion is possible with the verbal form 'He will [prove to] be' (YiHWèH)[48] and the name YeHoWaH.

Names found in Egyptian annals are more interesting, because during this period (-1750-1500), according to the Bible, the Hebrews lived in Egypt. In fact, Egyptian annals relate that during this period lived an Asiatic people called Hyksos, some of whose members even reigned over Egypt before being pushed out the country by Pharaoh Ahmosis. Around 280 BCE, the Egyptian priest Manethon specified, in his historic chronicles, that these myriads of renegades expelled from Egypt were the forefathers of the Jews who later occupied Judaea, founded Jerusalem and built the Temple (Some years previously, towards 300 BCE, the Greek writer Hecataeus of Abdera had already mentioned this event).

However, Egyptian annals relate that these Asiatics received Egyptian names[49], a practice confirmed by the Bible (Gn 41:45), making the use of these names extremely delicate, even impossible. For example, we find Egyptian persons of Asiatic origin named Touya and Youya, but the exact meaning of these names is unknown. The vizier of Amenophis III is called Aper-El or Aper-ia and his wife is called Uria[50]. We find also the divine name Horus-ia, or Horus-iau, during this period[51]. An Egyptian papyrus dated around 100 BCE mentions the name Horus-yah (or yahu) in an Aramaic hymn[52] translated into Demotic, very close to Psalm 20:2-7. But even here, these coincidences based on homophony are not really decisive, because these links are too accidental. Neither does a Greek goddess who was called Io prompt any link with the Tetragram.

The only notable point on Egyptian names concerns the fact that the Pharaohs registered their official names on scarabs, because in the Egyptian language there is a wordplay resulting from the homophony between the word 'scarab' (hepri) and the formula which means 'it comes to be'. It can be seen that this last expression is linked with the theological definition of the Tetragram in Exodus 3:14. The first name of the Pharaoh Thutmosis III is Mahahpiya meaning 'may the *being* [of Ra'] last'[53]. Pharaoh Wahkare Khety II (around -2100), to express that he was acting powerfully against the Bedouins, cried out to prove it: «as I live! *I am while I am*»[54], which proves that the theological concept of a God who "proves to be" had rival versions among the Egyptians and maybe among the Amorites.

PROBLEMS OF TRANSCRIPTION AND VOCALIZATION

✂   Notice that all these extra-biblical theophoric names which have just been listed favor the two radicals *ya* and *yahu*. Supposing that they reflect the divine names of the Bible, which we have seen is impossible to prove with current data, several problems remain to resolve, because the transcriptions of a name (king, city, etc.) into another language fluctuated, and numerous discrepancies are difficult to explain today. Furthermore, one cannot state with certainty anything concerning vowels in Semitic languages, because they are weak elements and thus variable. An example of one variation accepted in the transcription of names is the term 'Israelite', Yisréli in Hebrew (2S 17:25), considered to be the equivalent of the Akkadian name sir-'i-la-a-a (read Sir'ilaya) in Shalmaneser III's stele. Another example: the name Môab written in cuneiform Mu-'a-ba is also very often written Ma-'a-ba, because the sound *a* was esteemed and often preferred to the true vowel[55]!

A second problem, often left unsolved by the authors of commentaries, is that the cuneiform transcriptions in Akkadian are syllabic transcriptions which, regrettably, have only a single sign to represent the following sounds: ya, ye, yi, yu, wa, we, wi, wu. In fact, there is only a single specific sign to specify the sound ia, and none for the sound h. So, the name Yehudah can be transcribed, at best, only by Ia-u-da or Ia-ḫu-da; the name Yô'aš by Ia-aš or Ia-a-šu; etc. The logical consequence of this is that, if the Tetragram was pronounced Yehowah in Hebrew, the Akkadian transcription of this name could be, at best, that Ia-u-a or Ia-ḫu-a. We notice moreover that the name Yéhu' (Ièou in the Septuagint) was transcribed Ia-u-a (and Ia-u) in Shalmaneser III's texts[56], dated ninth century BCE. ✂

☞ The last problem: is the data resulting from theophoric names during this period biblically significant? Once again the answer is, unfortunately, negative. Actually, before Moses theophoric names are rare; there is only one mentioned explicitly in the Pentateuch. It is Yôkèbèd, which means 'Yô [is] glory'. In fact, the practice of theophoric names became widespread only in about the eleventh century BCE, dating from Solomon's administration.

✂ At present, the oldest theophoric name is likely Yôḥanan (ywḥnn), written[57] in paleo-Hebrew and dating from the eleventh century BCE. However, the influence of the name Yahu is so great that the name Yôḥanan is read instead Yawḥanan. Furthermore, there is a trend to vocalize all ancient names in Ya-, because of the belief that all Semitic names followed a general evolution Ya>Yi>Ye, according to a relatively well verified linguistic law (Barth-Ginsberg's law)[58]. However, this law is often applied back to front, that is Ye< Yi< Ya, which is evidently incorrect. For example, the name Yisra'él would have been spelt Ia-aš-ra-il at this time; but at Ebla, in documents dated from the end of the third millennium before our era, one finds the name Iš-ra-il, the exact equivalent of Yisraél. In fact, some studies prove that some verbal forms and names could have been vocalized Yi- rather than Ya- at Ebla[59]. For example, the name meaning 'He will set free, the upright [god]' or Yiptor-yašar in Hebrew (the name Jashar is found in Joshua 10:13), was spelt ip-dur-i-sar and not ia-ap-dur-ia-sar[60]. In addition, in Mari's texts[61], dating from the same period, specialists come to the same conclusion as to the vocalization Yi- rather than Ya- in numerous cases. For example, the Akkadian name I-krub (He blessed) is very often written Ia-krub[62]. Thus, among the oldest known texts, this law Ya >Yi >Ye shows numerous exceptions.

☞   Furthermore, if theophoric names were still pronounced Yaho- (in Hebrew) at the beginning of the third century BCE, translators of the Septuagint should have preserved these names in Iaô- because they generally kept the first vowel of proper nouns (Zakaria, Nathania, Qahath, instead of Zekaria, Nethania, Qehath, etc.). Among thousands of theophoric names in the Greek Bible, there are none which remained in Iaô- (or even in Ia- only), which should have been frequent if these names began in Yahow- (or Yaw-). For example, all the 'theophoric' names of the god Nabu (beginning in Nebu- in Hebrew) are written Nabou- in the Septuagint. So the beginning Iô- of theophoric names gives evidence of the vocalization Y(eh)o- and not Y(ah)o-.   ✄

So, to suppose that all the Hebrew theophoric names at present vocalized Yehô- would result from an "archaic" form Yahû- is indefensible if only on the basis of linguistic laws[63]. Not only does the vocalization of these names remain hypothetical, but even their sense or etymology reflects, in spite of philological justifications sometimes proposed, the convictions of modern authors rather than solidly turned out proofs[64].

From Moses to David

Moses played a large role in the spreading of the Name (Ex 3:14). However, to assert that the Tetragram was unknown before him, as we have seen, is to contradict the biblical text. Nevertheless, numerous biblists accept this assertion, or assert that the Tetragram is a verbal form which amounts to the same thing. In fact, to assimilate the divine name with a verbal form, is to tacitly admit it's equivalence to the definition of Exodus 3:14. Thus, either this name was not pronounceable before Moses, or the Hebrews of Moses' epoch did not understand Hebrew, implying the necessity of a grammatical explanation of the Name! This would be illogical and contradict the Bible itself. Furthermore, to use Exodus 6:3 to justify the fact that God's name was not known before Moses is to ignore that the word 'name' often has the sense of reputation in the Bible (Gn 6:4; Nb 16:2; etc.); It makes no sense to believe, as Maimonides indicated in his book *The Guide of the Perplexed*, that the knowledge of the proper pronunciation of the Name would have been able to induce the Israelites to action, because what reasonable motivation would be found in the knowledge of a correct pronunciation of the Tetragram?

The Israelites did not ask to know the pronunciation of the Name (because they already knew it), but rather the meaning of this name. Enslaved by the Egyptians for more than two centuries, it seemed that their God was powerless before Egyptian gods. Moreover, even Pharaoh later asked Moses a similar question: «Who is Yehowah so that I should obey his voice?» (Ex 5:2), in order to know what this name meant, and not the pronunciation which he obviously knew.

WHICH LANGUAGE DID MOSES SPEAK AND WRITE?

According to the Bible, Abraham is described as Hebrew (Gn 14:13) which implies that the Hebraic language was spoken at that time. It seems that Aramaic and Hebrew belonged to the same family even though there were some differences (Gn 31:47). These languages were called "the language of Canaan" (Is 19:18) which are classified today among North-West Semitic languages. The tablets of Tell el-Amarna (14th century BCE) call this language of Canaan as Kinahnu (a term used at Mari around 1800 BCE)[65]. This Hebrew very closely resembles the Hebrew of the Bible with two exceptions. First, it kept three archaic cases (nominative in u [ḫa-mu-du for *ḥamud* meaning precious], genitive in i [ḫa-ar-ri for *har* meaning mountain] and accusative in a [mu-ur-ra for *môr* meaning myrrh])[66]. Secondly it is written in Akkadian cuneiforms which may have modified its original vocalization. It seems likely that Hebrew must have been written in this way in the land of Canaan and that during their stay in Egypt the Hebrews tried to adapt their writing to Egyptian hieroglyphs. Numerous specialists suppose moreover that the alphabetical signs found near the Sinai and in Palestine (called proto-Sinaitic or proto-Canaanite) dated between 1700 and 1500 BCE are probably an adaptation of Egyptian hieroglyphs to write the Hebraic language[67]. These signs later evolved into proto-Hebrew or paleo-Hebrew, writing which one already finds on jars and mugs dated around the thirteenth century BCE.

According to the Bible, in the time of Josiah (7th century BCE), a copy of the Pentateuch written by Moses himself was found (2Ch 34:14,15), suggesting that he wrote in the paleo-Hebrew of Josiah's time. According to this account then, Moses would be the first who officialized the use of paleo-Hebrew, the first known alphabet in human history. Archaeology seems to agree with this version, as regards the chronology of the evolution of writing. It is interesting to note that the Greek historian Herodotus (-495-425) writes that the inventor of the alphabet was a certain Cadmos who lived towards 1500 BCE (*History II:145*) who came from Phoenicia and was the builder of Thebes according to Hesiod[68] (around 700 BCE). Cadmos gave these Phoenician characters to the Greeks who modified them in time (*History V:58*). The history of Cadmos resembles that of Moses who gave the Israelites 'The Book' (Ex 17:14). As a last interesting point, Cadmos does not mean anything in

Greek but comes very certainly from the Hebrew word Qèdèm which means 'East' or 'Oriental'. Indeed at the time of Job inhabitants of the Sinai were called 'sons of the East' (Job 1:3) or 'Orientals', that is to say Qadmonites (Gn 15:19), or Qadmoni 'eastern' (Ezk 47:18) in Hebrew.

Around 300 BCE, the Greek writer Hecataeus of Abdera wrote «When in ancient times a pestilence arose in Egypt, the common people ascribed their troubles to the workings of a divine agency; for indeed with many strangers of all sorts dwelling in their midst and practicing different rites of religion and sacrifice, their own traditional observances in honor of the gods had fallen into disuse. Hence the natives of the land surmised that unless they removed the foreigners, their troubles would never be resolved. At once, therefore, the aliens were driven from the country, and the most outstanding and active among them banded together and, as some say, were cast ashore in Greece and certain other regions; their leaders were notable men, chief among them being Danaos and Cadmos. But the greater number were driven into what is now called Judaea, which is not far distant from Egypt and was at that time utterly uninhabited. The colony was headed by a man called Moses, outstanding both for his wisdom and for his courage. On taking possession of the land he founded, besides other cities, one that is now the most renowned of all, called Jerusalem.»[69] Of course, this last sentence reflects a real embellishment, but the rest of the events seems to be correctly ascribed. Around 160 BCE, Jewish writer Eupolemus (1M 8:17) wrote that Moses was the inventor of the alphabet, which passed from him to the Phoenicians and from them to the Greeks[70]. Latin Historian, Diodorus (-90-21) noted that, in time, the story of Cadmos from Thebes in Egypt, was assimilated and modified by the Greeks, in order to agree with their own mythology (*History 1:23,4-8*).

Nothing in archaeology or history contradicts the biblical account. It is therefore reasonable to conclude that the 'eastern' (Cadmos) Moses did indeed write his account in paleo-Hebrew around 1500 BCE. This initial undertaking no doubt paved the way for the transmission of the alphabet as we know it today.

HOW TO UNDERSTAND EXODUS 3:13, 14

An inaccurate translation of Exodus 3:13 leads to a faulty understanding of this verse. In numerous Bibles one can read the question: «What is his name*?*» as in Judges 13:17, when Manoah wanted to know the name, that is the pronunciation of the name, of the angel who came to meet him; on the other hand the Israelites asked Moses: «How is his name?» that is «what does his name mean?» or «what does his fame mean?»

✂   One can verify that in Hebrew the interrogation 'what, how' is *mâ* (מָה) and 'who' is *mî* (מִי). Thus, there is a big difference between asking to know a name because one is in ignorance of it, as in Ezra 5:4, and asking the meaning of a name which one already knows, as in Genesis 32:27 where the angel asks Jacob to remind him of the meaning 'He will supplant' of his name, which meaning was already known to him (Gn 27:36), in order to give him a new one 'He will contend' (Gn 32:28). ✂

Thus, when Moses asked God: «How is his name?» God, in fact, gave the explanation «I shall be who/what I shall be» (*èhyèh ashèr èhyèh*). Even here, regrettably, numerous translators are influenced by Greek philosophy on the being as existing, developed by Plato in some of his works, including Parmenides. For example, the Septuagint was going translating this passage by 'I am the being' (*égô éimi o ôn* in Greek), that is: 'I am He who is'; while Aquila's translation, more faithful to Hebrew, translates this sentence by: 'I shall be: I shall be' (*ésomai ésomai* in Greek). As indicated by a study on the translation of this sentence, the difficulty results from translators who want to explain this translation by means of their personal beliefs very often influenced by Greek philosophy; otherwise there is no difficulty[71]. For example, one finds the word *èhyèh* just before (Ex 3:12) and just after (Ex 4:12,15) and here translators have no problem translating it by: «I shall be with you». Moreover the Talmud retains this explanation for the meaning of the Name (*Berakot 9b, Midrash Aggadah*).

It is true that the answer 'I shall be what(who) I shall be' requires an explanation of the context. Some translators indicate in notes that God, in fact, refused to answer, which is absurd with regard to the context, and constitutes a supplementary attack on the Name. The difficulty comes from the fact that the verb 'to be' in English has the meaning 'to exist', which it did not have in ancient Hebrew. In addition, dictionaries of biblical Hebrew indicate that this verb expresses both the idea 'to be' and 'to become'. To solve this problem and to avoid arbitrarily choosing to translate this verb by 'to be' or 'to become' depending on the context (which would show a lack of rigor), some translators have suggested replacing this double translation by only one which expresses this dynamic verb 'to be' with its two notions 'to be and to become'. The translation 'to prove to be' or 'to come to be' well expresses this double notion[72].

This sentence can be slightly improved in «I shall prove to be who I shall prove to be» or «I shall come to be who I shall come to be». The Egyptians could perfectly understand this expression because the Pharaohs used it for their own purposes to express power over their enemies. However, God showed he was going to end their pretensions by: «You will see who I am» that is to say: «I shall prove to be [the true God]».

This explanation is confirmed by a similar situation. God says in Exodus 33:19: «I will favor the one whom I will favor and I will show mercy to the one to whom I will show mercy» not to express an uncertainty or a refusal to intervene, but as a reminder that it depends on him alone, as confirmed in the Christian Greek Scriptures (Rm 9:15-18) which comment on this passage. Therefore, one could translate Exodus 33:19 by: «I will favor the one whom I want to favor and I will show mercy to the one to whom *I want* to show mercy.» In the same way, one could also translate «I shall prove to be who I shall prove to be» by «I shall prove to be who *I want* to prove to be». This type of expression is not unique to God as humans use it as well. For example, in John 19:22, «what I have written, I have written» can also be translated by «what *I want* to write, I have written». Also, «in the place where my lord the king will come to be (...) your servant will come to be» (2S 15:21), expresses the idea «in the place where my lord the king will come to be your servant *wants* to be»; or again, «by God's undeserved kindness I am what I am» (1Co 15:10) expresses the idea «by God's undeserved kindness I am what *I want* to be».

So, the expression 'I shall be' well translates the dominance of God's action, as he often reminded his servants: «I shall be with you» (Gn 26:3; 31:3; Dt 31:23; etc.), but sometimes also: «I shall not be with you» (Os 1:9). So, if God says in speaking about himself "I shall be who I shall be", in speaking about God one should say "He will be who He will be"; or, if one uses "I am who I am" one should say in speaking about God "He is who He is". Some biblists prefer the causal form "He causes to be who He causes to be" or "He causes to become who He causes to become". However, this choice is arbitrary, because, in the first place, the causative form of the verb 'to be' does not exist in Hebrew; secondly, the translator is influenced by the idea of a creative God who is making things, which constitutes an extrapolation of the text of Exodus 3:14, because God says "I shall be" and not "I cause to be" or "I cause to become". To respect the Hebrew text, the meaning of God's name is 'He will be' or more exactly 'He will prove to be', implying "He will prove to be [a Judge], [a Legislator], [a King], [a Rescuer], etc. (Is 33:22)".

RELIGIOUS ETYMOLOGY AND TECHNICAL ETYMOLOGY

Finally, to confuse the biblical definition 'He will be' (yhyh) with the vocalization of the Tetragram (yhwh), is to mix biblical etymologies with technical etymologies, which shows a serious misunderstanding of the role of these religious etymologies[73]. Indeed, why explain to a Hebrew the Hebraic meaning of a Hebrew name? For example, in Hebrew Noah means 'rest', but the Bible specifies that this name *will mean* 'comfort' (Gn 5:29). This meaning is obviously prophetic and not grammatical.

The pitfall of confusing religious and technical etymologies is very old. For example, the word 'comfort' was *modified* into 'rest' in the Septuagint. In the first century, a

Jewish writer, Philo, in order to explain technically the meaning of the name Abraham, proposed a Greek translation 'chosen father of noise', in his book on the changes of names (*De Mutatione Nominum §66*), while the Bible proposes 'father of a crowd of nations' (Gn 17:5) or 'father of numerous nations', according to the Septuagint. With good intentions, Philo *modified* the sentence 'father of a crowd' (Ab-hamôn) linking the word *raham*, which means nothing, to the word *ra'am* (רַעַם) which does mean 'noise' in Hebrew. Apollonius Molo, a Greek rhetor previously explained the name Abraham as 'friend of father'[74] (around 75 BCE). Today, translators do no better when they link the word *raham* to the word *raham* (רְחַם) meaning 'He comforted'. These translators forget that etymologies in the Bible are above all religious teachings. For example, the name Yehudah means 'He will laud', or Yôdèh in Hebrew, according to the expression 'I shall laud' of Genesis 29:35.

Hebrew name	Technical etymology	Religious etymology
Yehudah	Yudèh	Yôdèh
(Gn 29:35)	He will be lauded	He will laud
Yéshua'	Yeshua'h	Yôshia'
(Mt 1:21)	salvation	He will save
Yehouah	Yihwèh *in Aramaic*	Yihyèh
(Ex 3:14)	He will be (Qo 11:3)	He will be

✄   However, "technically" the name Yehudah (or Yudah) is phonetically closer to the hypothetical form Yudèh (houphal) which means, 'He will be lauded.' Many grammarians, not understanding the origin of these gaps, consider these to be popular etymologies. A study concerning the 60 etymologies of the Pentateuch concluded that about a quarter of them deviated strikingly from the technical sense, hence this study[75] preferred to refer to religious etymologies. From all this, it becomes evident that, with regard to the biblical explanation, the religious etymology seems "less rigorous". In fact, the two methods are based on inverse procedure. For example, the name Yehudah means *at the outset* 'He will laud', according to the biblical expression 'I shall laud'; then this form Yôdèh is modified by assonance[76] with Yehouah, God's name, to give the hybrid form Yehudah. On the other hand, "technically" this name is phonetically closer to the *hypothetical* 'He will be lauded'. ✄

AN EGYPTIAN TESTIMONY

To settle the question of the vocalization of the Tetragram, does archaeological testimony exist considering that, according to the Bible, only the Egyptians had a prolonged contact with the Hebrews? Reasonably, one can not hope to find a recording in hieroglyphs which tells of the exploits of the Hebrew god against the Egyptians. Furthermore, the Egyptian accounts that tell the history of their enemies are patently dishonest, notably regarding their defeats.

The Hyksos (from the Egyptian *ḥeqaw ḫa'st* which means 'leaders of foreign countries'), lived amicably with the Egyptians according to Egyptian annals, bringing a prosperity and a splendor under their management, several Hyksos having reigned as kings. Everything went well until the day the Hyksos King Apopi (around 1500 BCE) made Pharaoh Seqnenre Taa the following ridiculous demand «It will be necessary to remove hippopotamus from the canal at the east of the city, because they prevent me from sleeping, whether in the daytime or at night» which entailed a terrible war (not attested!). Kamose boasted of having chased out these "miserable" Asiatics who had brought chaos to the country because of King Apopi, the prince of Retenu (Syria-Palestine). The remark of the female Pharaoh Hatshepsut (around 1470 BCE) speaks volumes for the real origin of this war «I strengthened what was ruined. I raised what was in ruin since the time when the Asiatics were at Avaris in the Delta and when the vagabonds were among them, knocking down all which had been made; they steered without Ra' (...) I have made distant those whom the gods abominate»[77].

The Egyptian stories concerning the Hyksos, before and after King Apopi, are obviously contradictory[78], therefore the biblical version of facts concerning the Hebrews (Ex 12:37-40) is probably the correct one. The account of Pharaoh Seqnenre says that «King Apopi made him Seth as lord, and he would not serve any god who was in the land [except] Seth. And he built a temple of good and eternal work beside the House of King Apopi and he appeared [every] day to have sacrifice made daily to Seth». Most of this is true, except that the god Seth was the lord of evil, darkness, violence and disunion for the Egyptians (referring to the Hebrew god after the 10 plagues). Additionally, Pharaoh Kamose reproached some Egyptians with having abandoned Egypt, their mistress to go with Apopi a miserable Asiatic (who spent more than 40 years in Egypt). It is interesting to note that the name Apopi means 'pretty' in Hebrew (Jr 46:20). The Talmud of Jerusalem (*Nedarim 42c*) notes that a vow by Ipopi of Israel was valid.

If a recording in an Egyptian temple had mentioned the name Yehoua, after the departure of the Hebrews, it would inevitably have been chiseled out to remove it. However, a good specimen was found at Soleb[79], a short inscription dated about the time of Amenophis III (-1391 -1353). Additionally this short inscription is engraved in a shield used for subjugated peoples, according to the Egyptian way of describing.

This inscription is easy to decipher[80]. It can be transcribed: t3 š3-sw-w y-h-w3-w. This expression, vocalized in the conventional system by: ta' sha'suw yehua'w, can be translated by: «land of the Bedouins those of yehua'». It is interesting to note that the Shasus (Bedouins) would have meant to the Egyptians specific Bedouins staying with their bundles, in the region North of the Sinai. From the fifteenth to twelfth century BCE, the Hebrew settlers conquering Palestine were pejoratively called the Hapirus[81] by the Egyptians (The word 'Apiru/ Ḥabiru means 'wanderings' in Semitic languages[82].)

These hieroglyphic shields were short enough to escape possible erasure. Some specialists prefer to identify Yehua' with an unknown toponym. In any case, this distinction is impossible to prove, as in the cases of biblical toponyms like: 'land of Judah' (Dt 34:2); 'land of Rameses' (Gn 47:11); or with the Asiatic toponyms of this period (15th century BCE)[83] found in several Egyptian lists as '[land of] Jacob-El'; '[land of] Josep-El', '[land of] Lewi-El', etc., which obviously are also personal names.

✂   However, one notices a certain resistance to the vocalization of this name Yhw3, because the totality of dictionaries indicate either yhw', which is unreadable, or Yahweh which is not in agreement with the conventional vocalization, but never Yehua'. Some specialists quite correctly object that the vowels of Egyptian words are not well known[84]. However, for foreign words, which is the case here, Egyptian used a sort of standard alphabet with *matres lectionis*, that is of semi-consonants which served as vowels. In this system one finds the equivalences: 3 = a, w = u, ÿ = i, and that is exactly why reading by the conventional system gives acceptable results. For example in Merneptah's stele dated the thirteenth century BCE, the name Israel is transcribed in hieroglyphs Yÿsri31 and can be read Yisrial (conventional system), which is tolerable. However, some specialists who refuse the classic system, read this name Yasarial because of its antiquity. Nevertheless, almost a millennium before, at Ebla, one read this name Išrail, contradicting the reading Yasarial. So, in the current state of our knowledge, the conventional system of reading of hieroglyphs is the best alternative, and in this system the name (or toponym) Yhw3 is read 'technically' Yehua. (see the Appendix D) ✄

SHORT NAME AND GREAT NAME

☞ The reading Ya- results from a confusion between the two names of God: the great name YeHoWaH (Ps 83:18) and the short name YaH (Ps 68:4). The Jews treated these two names differently. They consented to pronounce the short name whereas the great name was replaced at about third century BCE by its substitute Adonay (Lord). So, one finds the short name Yah in the Christian Greek Scriptures in the expression Alleluia (Rv 19:1-6), which means 'Praise Yah'. Moreover, in the writings from Qumrân, the Tetragram was sometimes written in paleo-Hebrew inside a Hebrew text, which was not the case for the name Yah. One also notices that this name Yah was specially used in songs (Ex 15:2) and in psalms.

☞ In the same way, as there were theophoric names elaborated from the great name, that is, names beginning with Yehô- or its shortened form Y(eh)ô-, there were also theophoric names elaborated from Yah. However, a major observation must be noted in the Bible, either Greek or Hebraic: the Hebrews took care to make either their names begin with Yehô- or Yô-, or to end their names by -yah, but never the other way around, without exception. So, in the Bible, it is impossible to find, among hundred of existing theophoric names, a single name beginning with Yah-. So, those who vocalize YHWH by Yahweh are obliged to admit that the Tetragram, the ultimate theophoric name, does not belong to its family of theophoric

names, which is inconceivable. This absurdity appears upon
opening a dictionary, where one notices that the name Yahve is
completely isolated from other theophoric names like: Joshua,
Jonathan, Jesus, John, etc.

☞   In the same way that the initial part Yehô- was
abbreviated in Yô-, the final part -yah also had a diminutive -
yahu, the latter meaning in Hebrew 'Yah himself'. This term
appeared for two reasons. First, the Hebrew term *hu'* meaning
'himself' (implying God) began to play a large role in worship.
For example, to distance himself from other gods and to mark
his unchangeableness, God often expressed himself by using the
Hebraic expression *'ani hu'*, that is 'myself' or more exactly 'I,
himself' or 'It is I' (Dt 32:39; Is 52:6; etc.). Although human
beings did use this expression in speaking of themselves (1Ch
21:17), generally when one said 'He' or 'Himself' he was
referring to God (2K 2:14).

The Hebrews did not delay in integrating this divine
appellation into their names, as in the names Abihu' (my father
[is] He), or Elihu' (my god [is] He) or Yehu' (Ye[hou is] He).
Eventually, the final letter of these names being mute, was not
written any more. For example, the name Elihu' is very often
written Elihu. The names Abiyah (my father [is] Yah), and
Eliyah (my god [is] Yah) existing also, Yah and Hu' were linked
to obtain names like Abiyahu' (my father [is] Yah Himself), or
Eliyahu' (my god [is] Yah Himself).

☞   This association provoked the appearance of a new
divine name, which one does not find in the Bible, except at the
end of some theophoric names: the name Yah hu', abbreviated
in Yahu. The assonance of this expression with the Tetragram
doubtless favored the emergence of this abbreviation. Moreover,
one finds this name alone (YHW), written next to the Tetragram
(YHWH), in Kuntillet Ajrud's writings, dated the ninth century
BCE. To sum up, the name Yehu' results from a contraction of
YeHoWaH Hu' to YeHoW[aH]u' that is YeHoWu' or YeHU'.
On the other hand, YaHu results from the contraction of the two
names YaH-Hu' (The ending in *u*, as Eli-Hu' which became
Elihu, is not the exceptional residue of an archaic nominative[85]).

From David to Zedekiah

Numerous Hebrew writings with theophoric names in *yah* or *yahu* are found during this period and as well as several tetragrams. The oldest writing, the Moabite stone, dated from the mid ninth century, recounts a story of biblical events. This story is in agreement with the Bible (2K 3:4-27), and the Tetragram YHWH appears in the eighteenth line. Therefore, the Moabites knew the divine name and they could pronounce it!

✂   How did Moabites pronounce this name? As this language was very close to Hebrew, it is difficult to know. However, findings show that well-known Moabites names were written without *matres lectionis*. Thus Môab is written M'b on the Moabite Stone, while in the Bible it is written Mw'b, Kamûsh is written Kmš and Kmwš in the Bible. Names like Omri, Israel and Yhwh were considered to be foreign names and were probably written as they were pronounced, that is to say "according to their letters". Therefore 'mry was read Omri (and not Omray), Ysr'l was read Israel (and not Yasrael) and consequently Yhwh was read Ihua according to its letters, not Yahua or Yahue (see the Appendix E.)   ✂

Finding a vocalized occurrence of the divine name at this time, requires at least two conditions. First, that the Jews be overcome in a conflict, in order to have the conquerors' report mention the losers and their God. Secondly, that the language of the conquerors be vocalized, and at this time the only language which clearly vocalized the sounds ye, ya, yi, yu, we, wa, wi, wu, was Cypriot syllabary, called Linear B. Unfortunately, there are few writings in this language; furthermore, the Hebrews having had no conflict with Cyprus, no report of victory can be expected. The problem is the same with Greek, as this language really penetrated in Palestine only from the sixth century before our era. The Egyptian hieroglyphs of the time of Pharaoh Necho would be enlightening, if their vocalization was more reliable. Only the Assyrians and Babylonians are left fulfilling both conditions. However, as seen, the Akkadian language possesses only a single symbol to transcribe the sounds ye, ya, yi, yu, and has no specific sign for the sounds we, wa, wi, wu and h.

■ The Moabite Stone

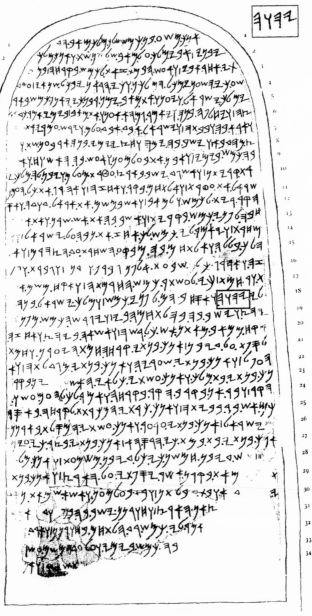

Although none of the theophoric names begin with Ya-
in the biblical text (M.T. or LXX), they are nevertheless all
vocalized by Ia- in Akkadian transcriptions.

English name:	Hebrew name (MT)	Greek name (LXX)	Akkadian name
Judah	Yehûdâ	Iouda	Iaḫudu
Jehu	Yéhû'	Ièou	Iaua
Jehoiachin	Yehôyakin	Iôakim	Iakukînu
Jehoahaz	Yehô'aḥaz	Iôakaz	Iauḥazu
Hezekiah	Ḥizqiyahû	Ézékiou	Ḥazaqiyau

✂   On the other hand the ending -yahû is correctly
transcribed in the name Hizqiyahû. Some specialists conclude
that these transcriptions are reliable and simply reflect the well-
known evolution Ya >Yi >Ye (Barth-Ginsberg's law). They
surmise as well that if the pronunciation had been Ye-, the
Akkadian would have instead used the symbol which represents
the vowel i-. Thus, the name Yehûdâ would have been
transliterated i-ḫu-da rather than ia-ḫu-da, but the name i-ḫu-da
is never found! However, Semitic languages favor consonants,
which are the stable elements of it; so, if the group Yi- can be
likened by default to the Akkadian symbol for i- (Yisraél being
transliterated Iš-ra-il), the group Ye- is closer to the symbol ia-
than to the symbol i-. It is interesting to note that the Amorite
name I-krub (He blessed) is very often spelt Ia-krub[86].
Furthermore, Akkadian transcriptions favor the sound *a* at the
beginning of words in spite of the actual vowel of origin.
Therefore, some specialists[87] estimate that the Akkadian symbol
ia- could also be read ie- or io-. ✂

INFLUENCE OF ARAMAIC ON HEBREW

By observing inscriptions where the divine name is
found, dating from the ninth and eighth centuries before our era,
one notices that the evolution of language effectively played a
role, notably with the influence of Aramaic on Hebrew.

At Kuntillet Ajrud, near the Sinai, writings dated around 800 BCE have been found[88]; they contain either the name YHW or the Tetragram YHWH. For example, the inscription below reads: «to Obadyaw son of Adnah may he be blessed by Yhw» (l'bdyw bn 'dnh brk h' lyhw)[89]

One can also read the following sentences:
«I bless YOU by Yhwh of Samaria and by [his] asherah» (brkt 'tkm lyhwh šmrn wl'šrth)
«I bless you by Yhwh of Teman and by [his] asherah» ('t brktk lyhwh tmn wl'šrth, asherah being a sacred pole, tree or totem, according to Deuteronomy 16:21,22)
«and let Yhw give unto him as to his heart» (wntn lh yhw klbbh)
«does good, Yhwh» (hytb yhwh)

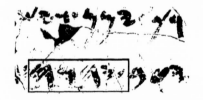

Dated at 775 BCE, a seal was found with the following inscription: «Miqneyaw servant of Yhwh / to Miqneyaw servant of Yhwh» (mqnyw 'bd yhwh / lmqnyw 'bd lyhwh)[90].

What is noticeable in these inscriptions is that these theophoric names end in -yaw and not in -yahu. How can this anomaly be explained? The reason is simple: the name *yaw* was pronounced in fact *yau*, which is a phonetic equivalent of *yahu*, because the *h* was hardly audible, especially in an Aramaic context. Indeed, one observes this anomaly only in inscriptions found outside Judaea, because in this territory theophoric names were always written with -yahu at the end not with -yaw. It is thought that Judaeans spoke a more correct Hebrew than the Hebrews of the North (Samaria and Galilee) whose language was more relaxed.

ARCHAEOLOGICAL EVIDENCES

At Khirbet el-Qom, about 30 km south-west of Jerusalem, an epitaph dated at 750 BCE was discovered, with the inscription: «Uriyahu the rich has written it, blessed be Uriyahu by Yhwh» ('ryhw h'šr ktbh brk 'ryhw lyhwh)[91]

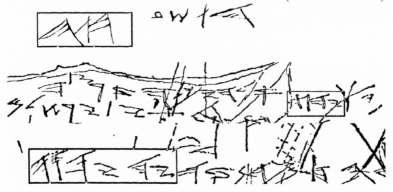

At Nahal Yishai near En-Guedi a cave was found with the following inscription dated at 700 BCE:

«blessed be Yhwh» (brk Yhwh)[92]

Hebrew inscriptions dated around -700 may be read on the walls of a burial cave at Khirbet Beit Lei (near Jerusalem).

The Tetragram appears in the following sentences:

«Save us [Y]hwh»
«Yhwh the god of the whole earth[93] (...) be merciful forgive Yh Yhwh».

    (A few letters are hard to read but the two words Yh Yhwh are clearly legible.)

■ Silver plaques[94]

Two silver plaques have been found at Ketef Hinnom near Jerusalem dated around 625 BCE. On plaque II there are three Tetragrams. It is interesting to note that the two plaques include the blessing from Numbers 6:24-25 thus this text is, at the present time, the oldest text of the Bible.

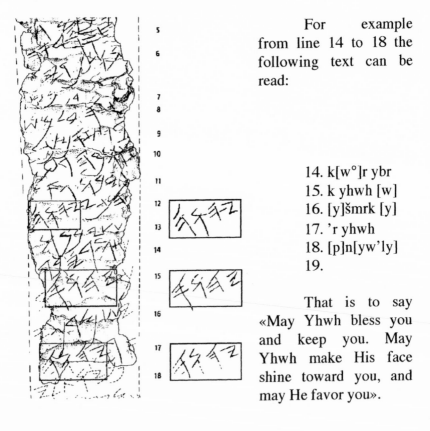

For example from line 14 to 18 the following text can be read:

14. k[w°]r ybr
15. k yhwh [w]
16. [y]šmrk [y]
17. 'r yhwh
18. [p]n[yw'ly]
19.

That is to say «May Yhwh bless you and keep you. May Yhwh make His face shine toward you, and may He favor you».

It is also interesting to note what is written in this verse: (Nb 6:27) «they must place my name upon the sons of Israel, that I myself may bless them», in other words the priests had to pronounce the divine Name with a loud voice upon the people to get the blessing. Actually, Jewish tradition tells us that the priests did this but only inside the temple, whereas elsewhere they used a substitute name. (*Sifre Numbers 39, 43*)[95]

■ Arad ostraca[96]

A few ostraca have been discovered at the site of Tell Arad. These texts date from 700 to 600 BCE. For example in ostracon N°18 we find the following text[97]:

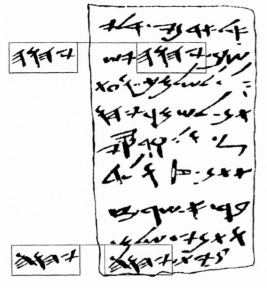

1. 'l 'dny.'ly
2. šb.yhwh yš
3. 'l lšlmk.w't
4. tn.lšmryhw
()
9. byt.yhwh

Which means: «To my lord Eliashib may Yhwh seek your welfare. And now give to Shemaryahu... (...) temple of Yhwh»

■ Lakish letters[98]

A few ostraca of the same period have been found at the site of Lakish dated around 600 BCE with the following inscription[99] on ostracon N°2: «To my lord Yoash. May Yhwh make my lord hear to a news of peace in this very day, in this very day. Who is your servant, a dog, in order for my lord to remember his servant? May Yhwh allow my lord (...)»

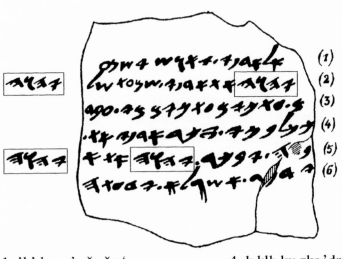

1- 'l 'dny.y'wš yšm'   4- k klb ky.zkr 'dny 't.
2- yhwh 't 'dny.šm't šl   5- [']bdh.ybkr.yhwh 't'
3- m.'t kym 't kym my.'bd   6- ()

This inscription agrees with the events which were described in Jeremiah 34:6,7.

☞   All of this evidence is useful in proving that the Tetragram was widely used in daily life until 600 BCE. From an archaeological point of view, the Tetragram disappeared, except in the Bible, just after this date, after the destruction of the first temple. In the period from 900 to 600 BCE about forty Tetragrams[100] can be found.

Thus, the Tetragram played a major role in worship[101], even though, as indicated in the Bible, the short name Yah was also used alone. The only difference is with regard to the divine name Yahû, which was never used on its own in the Bible but only at the end of theophoric names. Furthermore the spelling of this name is always *yahû* in the Bible (except, perhaps, for the name Aḥîô which stems from Aḥyaw). The main reason for this exception is that Yahû is a constructed form (Yah-hû') or more exactly a diminutive. Consequently, this name is used for less formal occasions as in theophoric names or in engravings on jars. For example, several jars[102] have been found dated around 750 BCE with names Yah (as in the Khirbet Beit Lei inscription) and Yahû (as in the Kuntillet Ajrud writings) stamped on them.

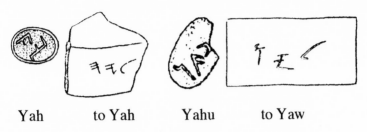

Yah   to Yah   Yahu   to Yaw

✀   Notice that these names are preceded by the Hebraic particle L which means 'to, for' (Is 44:5), implying that these objects were intended for the Temple, perhaps as tithes. In a few cases the name YHW, during the period of the second temple, is surmounted by a Hebrew symbol ℧ which means 'shekel', that is the collection for the sanctuary according to Exodus 30:13. During this period there are also some parallel inscriptions of LMLK which means 'to the king'.

One notices also that the letter H is sometimes written backwards and deformed, imitating its Aramaic equivalent. From this we can conclude that the Aramaic language had to begin influencing the Hebraic language very early, in its pronunciation as well as its writing. In the Aramaic language the dropping out of the H in words started quite early, around 800 BCE, with the endings -WHY often becoming WY[103]; and endings in -YHW (yahaw) becoming -YW[104] (-yaw or -yaû[105]). Additionally, the pronunciation of the letter heth Ḥ was also weak, because it was confused with the letter H in some words[106].

A little later, towards 400 BCE, the Hebraic language followed the same evolution with the pronunciation *aû* changing into *ô*[107]. In spite of these changes, theophoric names in Judaea[108] continued to be written with the ending -yahu. An engraving was even found at Tell Djedeideh, with the double spelling[109] yahu/ yaw: Shebanyahu Azaryahu (שבניהו עזריהו)

Shebanyaw Azaryaw (שבניו עזריו). ✀

From Zedekiah to Simon the Just

A major event would occur at the beginning of this period: the destruction of the first Temple and with it significant consequences for worship and later the pronunciation of the Name. As archaeology confirms, before this destruction the Name was widely used by the Hebrews, but, as Maimonides pointed out, it also confirms that the Name did not possess any mystical power. Knowing the proper pronunciation was for the Hebrews neither a material advantage, nor a protection against their enemies.

The biblical account of the events which occurred before and after the destruction of the First Temple helps us to understand the process of the progressive disappearance of the Name. Indeed, some years before 600 BCE, Pharaoh Necho defeated King Josiah then established Eliakim (God will raise up) as vassal and perhaps as provocation, changed his name to Jehoiakim (Yehô will raise up). This proves that Necho knew the great name of the God of the Hebrews (2K 23:34). Some years later, in a similar way and in the same context, the Babylonian king Nebuchadnezzar would establish as vassal King Mattaniah (gift of Yah) and change his name to Zedekiah (rightness of Yah). This proves that he also knew the divine name, but only the more familiar form Yah, and not the form of the great name (2K 24:17).

THE NAME NO LONGER USED BY NON-JEWS

It is easy to understand the chain of events after the destruction of the Temple. For the Hebrew people it was a terrible humiliation to be defeated by pagans. Likely at this time they took good care in the use of the holy name in order not to profane it (Ezk 36:20,21; Mal 1:6) and they surely remembered previous warnings on the subject (Is 52:5; Am 6:10). It is noteworthy that after the return from exile even the prophets avoided using the Name with non-Jews.

For example, Daniel used the Tetragram (Dn 1:2 9:2-20) but he used several substitutes with non-Jews: God in the heavens (Dn 2:28), Revealer of secrets (Dn 2:29), God of heaven (Dn 2:37,44), the Most High (Dn 4:17,24,32), the heavens (Dn 4:26). In the same way Ezra (-498?-398?) and Nehemiah used the Tetragram with the Jews (Ezr 3:10,11 8:28,29; Ne 4:14 8:9) but they used several substitutes with non-Jews: God (Ezr 5:17), the great God (Ezr 5:8), God of the heavens (Ezr 5:12; Ne 2:4,20), God of the heavens and the earth (Ezr 5:11). Furthermore, these non-Jews no longer used the Tetragram in their answers to the prophets. Cyrus was probably the last (just after 539 BCE) who used the name Jehovah (Ezr 1:2). In the book of Esther there is no Tetragram, but the last book (Malachi) written for the Jews, contains it.

CHANGE OF LANGUAGE AND WRITING.

Another very important consequence of the destruction of the first temple is the Jews' 70 years of captivity in Babylonia during which time the people learnt Aramaic. Thus, from this period some parts of the Bible were written in this language (Dn 2:4-7:28; Ezr 4:8-6:18 7:12-28). Therefore, when the Jews came back to Jerusalem a many of them had forgotten their mother tongue[110] (Ne 13:24). Hence, to make the Bible more readable, around 460 BCE, Ezra changed the old Hebrew characters into Aramaic characters or "modern Hebrew" (*Sanhedrin 21b*) and to help the people to understand, read the text and explained it (Ezr 7:6; Ne 8:8,9). On the other hand, the old Hebrew style was retained by the Samaritans in their writings (Ezr 4:7-10).

Although the Tetragram disappeared, the two other divine names Yah and Yahû remained in use until the beginning of the third century BCE. Thus several Aramaic papyri, written by Jews from 514 to 398 BCE, have been found in the towns of Elephantine and Padua[111] containing the names: Yhw (very often) Yhh (sometimes) and Yh (once)[112]. Furthermore, the name written Yhh has also been found in twelve ostraca[113].

YHW

✂   Some specialists read however the two names YHW and YHH in the same way. Based on the principle that these two names are identical in pronunciation, they deduce that only sound common to the two final *matres lectionis* is the sound Ô, because the letter W can be read in vowel either Û or Ô, and the H final can be read or Â or sometimes Ô. This astute conclusion is probably erroneous, for at least two reasons. In the first place, while in Hebrew does encounter the anomaly of a final H vocalized Ô, this peculiarity does not exist in Aramaic[114], the language in which these letters are written. Secondly, as the letter H had become almost inaudible, it was frequently doubled, as in the feminine suffix of the third person singular, written interchangeably H/ YH/ YH'/ YHH[115].   ✂

Thus, in Aramaic, the pronunciations of Yâ (YH), YaH (YHH) and Ya' (Y') are more or less the same; in fact, they are almost phonetic equivalents, as in the Aramaic name Yaw (YW) pronounced Yaû at this time, which is a phonetic equivalent of the Hebrew name Yahû (YHW). Moreover, in the Aramaic papyri of Egypt, one finds these same equivalents among theophoric names[116].

Name	at the beginning	at the end
Yâ	Yâ has given (YHNTN)	
		has judged, Yâ (Y'DNYH)
		has judged, Yâ (YDNYH)
		has acquired, Yâ (QNYH)
		my light [is] Yâ ('WRYH)
Yah	Yah [is] light (YHH'WR)	
		servant of Yah ('BDYHH)

Ya'		has acquired, Ya' (QNY') my light [is] Ya' (HWRY') has judged, Ya' (YDNY')
Yahû	Yahû has given (YHWNTN) Yahû [is] light (YHW'WR)	
		my father [is] Yahû ('BYHW) servant of Yahû ('BDYHW)
Yaw		brother of Yaw ('ḤYW) has covered, Yaw (ḤPYW)

✂   It is of note in this table that all the theophoric names are written with a rather free spelling (phonetic in fact), which contrasts enormously with the rigor of the Masoretic text. However, one does find the name YHH, instead of YH, in some codices[117]. It could be that, in an Aramaic context, the authors of these missives wanted to dissociate the divine name YH from the vocative particle YH meaning 'Oh!' as these two words are homonyms in Aramaic. What is more, it had the advantage of making the H more audible.

One finds these same fluctuations in the biblical text, which indicates by a point inside the letter (mappiq) if the final H must be pronounced or not. In the Bible all theophoric names ending in -yah are written without *mappiq* with the exception of Yedidyah (2S 12:25) and should thus be pronounced -yâ (יָה). On the other hand, the divine name Yah alone is always written with a *mappiq* except in Song of Solomon 8:6, and should be pronounced Yah (יָהּ) not Yâ.

These subtleties of pronunciation are without consequence in any case as to the meaning, or even the pronunciation of these words. It simply shows that the Masoretes wanted to keep all the nuances which had been passed on to them by tradition. Hence, they noted that word Yah could sometimes be pronounced Yiah (יִהּ) as in Psalms 94:7,12; 118:18, etc. In the same way, they noted that word 'divinity' pronounced Eloah in Hebrew is both noted with a *mappiq* (Jb 3:4; 6:4; 16:21), or Eloa, without a *mappiq* (Jb 4:9; 11:7; 15:8).

Finally, those that would pronounce the name YHH as YaHÔ, must remember that in the Bible there are no names ending in -HH which are vocalized -HÔ. The names ending by -HH are always vocalized -HÂ, as Bilhâ (Gn 29:29), Yogbehâ (Nb 32:35), etc. In addition, at Qumrân, words ending by -HH are always vocalized either -HÂ, or - ÂH. ✄

To the problems of pronunciation, which obscure the existence of these two names Yah and Yahu, are added the problems of writing. The Jews of the time of Ezra had abandoned their former writing, paleo-Hebrew, to square Hebrew characters, but they would continue, out of nostalgia, to use the former script for prestigious inscriptions such as coins, seals, and of course to write the divine names. However, the influence of Aramaic, which affected the pronunciation of Hebrew, also affected its writing. For example, about 60 jars with the name YH, and 40 with the name YHW[118], stamped on them, dated between 500 and 300 BCE, have been found.

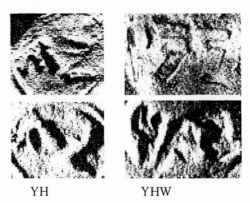

YH   YHW

At first, these stamps were read Yah and Yahû (YH and YHW), but under the influence of Israeli specialists, all these stamps are now read Yehud (YHD). However, these specialists candidly recognize that this reading poses problems[119]. Indeed, one would have to suppose that there was an evolution of the writing of this name read Yehûdâ (YHWDH) in full writing, as on Arad ostracon[120] n°40, dated around 750 BCE, into the name Yehud (YHD)[121] written defectively, which goes against normal evolution and would constitute a unique event of reverse evolution. Then, it would be necessary to suppose that the Jews preferred in this case to use a foreign script, paleo-Aramaic, rather than their own paleo-Hebrew[122]. This would be contrary to the fact that, out of nationalism, the Jews always favored their former type of writing, paleo-Hebrew, on their coins, at least until Bar-Kochba's revolt in 135 of our era. The confusion in reading between Yahû and Yehud began when coins that actually were marked Yehud (YHD) were found.

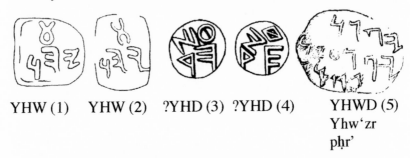

YHW (1)   YHW (2)   ?YHD (3)   ?YHD (4)   YHWD (5)
                                                  Yhw'zr
                                                  pḥr'

All the stamps above are at present read Yehud[123]. Even without being an expert, one can note an aberration in reading. Stamps n°3 and 4 are read YeHuD (YHD) because they are written in paleo-Hebrew. Stamp n°5 is read YeHUD (YHWD) because it is written in paleo-Aramaic. By observing closely, one sees that the shape of the letter H is different, yet this shape is typical because at this time there is no confusion of letters in paleo-Aramaic[124]. Therefore, in stamps n°1 and 2, the H can not be paleo-Aramaic but only paleo-Hebrew. So, if one letter is written in paleo-Hebrew the rest of the word would be too, because it would be illogical to suppose that a writer wrote the letters of one using two different scripts. This assertion can be verified by the inscriptions on these coins of Judaea[125].

YHD (1)   YH? (2)   YHDH (3)

Yehud (YHD) is mentioned on coin n°1, and Yehudâ (YHDH) on coin n°3. Only coin n°2 poses problem because logically it should be read Yahû (YHW)[126] in paleo-Hebrew, but the H may also be read in paleo-Aramaic style. Because of the Aramaic influence, variations in writing this letter are frequent in paleo-Hebrew[127]. One can moreover observe below, in this study of inscriptions on stamps and seals, a wide variety of shapes in paleo-Hebrew[128].

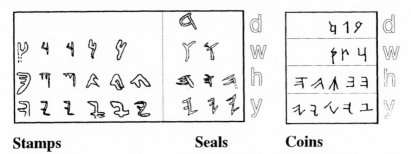

| **Stamps** | **Seals** | **Coins** |

This variety is less evident on the seals than on the stamps. No doubt, this conservatism in seals exists because they were made by professional 'printers'. As to the coins, which are from a later period (from the 3rd to 1st century BCE), one notices an even greater degeneracy of paleo-Hebrew[129].

JUDAEA: A NAME MADE SACRED.

Additionally, the reading of some stamps as Yehud poses problems of chronology. In fact, according to the Bible, the jurisdictional district of Yehud (Judaea) appeared after 600 BCE (Esz 5:8). Paradoxically some stamps are dated[130] more than one century before the existence of this district. Certain specialists admit that the epigraphic analysis must agree with historic data[131], and therefore these stamps should be read Yah (YH) and Yahû (YHW), not Yehud (YHD). Because the names Yah and Yahû existed before the seventh century BCE and also after the second century CE, if all the stamps are read Yehud, these two names would have mysteriously disappeared during this period. Finally, if the stamp marked YH is considered as an abbreviation of the name Yehud (YHD), it is necessary to conclude that the Jews of this time allowed confusion to arise between the divine name Yah (YH) and this abbreviation. This supposition seems absurd because when the Jews changed their system of numbering[132], about the second century BCE, they scrupulously avoided the confusion of the new numbers with the two divine names. So, the number 15 was never written YH but rather TW; also the number 16 was never written YW but TZ; moreover, this modification remains to our day.

To harmonize the paleographical, archaeological, historical, and biblical data, one may assume that the following progression of events took place. Before 600 BCE, the Jews of the land of Judah spoke and wrote Hebrew, in fact paleo-Hebrew. They used the Tetragram widely and sometimes the names Yah and Yahu. After the fall of Babylon, when they returned to Jerusalem, many Jews learnt to speak and write in Aramaic, and many could no longer speak their mother tongue, Hebrew. Therefore, Ezra, according to the Talmud (*Sanhedrin 21b*), around 460 BCE, would rewrite the Bible in these new Aramaic characters, that is to say modern Hebrew.

Regarding the Name, we note that the Jews, after their return from exile, would no longer use the Tetragram with non-Jews, but only the two substitutes Yah and Yahu, as at Elephantine and Padua. Furthermore the number of theophoric names using *yahu* declines sharply[133] from this period on. The Talmud (*Yoma 39b*) indicates that at about the third century BCE, at the time of high priest Simon the Just, the use of the Tetragram was reserved for the Temple only, and it specifies that in time even the divine names stamped on jars would be removed to protect their holiness (*Šabbat 61b, 'Arakin 6a*).

On the other hand, the use of the name Judaea would grow. So, after the fall of Babylon (539 BCE) the jurisdictional district of Judah (Ezr 5:8) with its governors appears (Hg 1:1). One can note that the Hebrew name Yehudah (Ezr 4:6) is pronounced Yehud in Aramaic (Ezr 7:14). During the period of the 70 years of captivity there were only inspectors or superintendents in Judaea. Moreover, an Aramaic seal[134], dated around 550 BCE, was found with the (below) inscription «Inspector of Judaea [Yehud]» (LPQD YHD), which shows the precision of biblical terms to indicate these rulers, as the Bible makes a distinction between the inspector's title (*paqid* in Hebrew) which Gedaliah received (2K 25:19-23) and the governor's title (*pèhah* in Hebrew) that was first received by Zerubabel (Hg 1:14) then by all his successors (Ne 5:15).

 This inscription does not pose any problem to read, because the two letters D and W can not be confused. Although Babylonians may have preferred to use the expression Yehud (YHD) for the name Yehudah (YHWDH), the Jews of Egypt, on the other hand, from the fifth to third century BCE, preferred to write this name in plene writing as YHWDH or YHWD, but never YHD[135].

The resemblance between the Aramaic name Yehud (YHD) and the Hebrew name Yahû (YHW) certainly favored the emergence of the Hebrew name Yehud on stamps and coins, because, as seen, this defective spelling in Hebrew is abnormal. Furthermore, when in observing the chronological frequency of these two names, one notices that, at about the third century BCE, there is a reversal of the trend, with inscriptions of Yehud (YHD) replacing inscriptions of Yahû (YHW). Actually, this reversal shows the slow change from Juda (Yehudah) as a religious realm into Judaea (Yehud) as a political district. It also shows the emergence of a nationalistic concept of power as opposed to the power of religion. This competition between Yahû and Yehud would eventually result, in the first century, in the choice between God and Caesar (Jn 19:15).

SOME VOCALIZED OCCURRENCES OF THE NAME

The Greek language began to spread widely[136] from the sixth century BCE, and a Greek listener would have been able to identify this name during a reading of the Bible. Moreover, according to Eusebius, there were translations of the Bible into Greek during this period[137], but the letter of Aristeas (*Letter of Aristeas XII, 312-316*)[138] specifies that the quotations of these translations failed. Theopompus (-378-323) and then Theodektes (-375-334) tried, but they received «divine punishment, temporary madness for the former and momentary cataracts for the latter». Around 300 BCE, Hecataeus of Abdera[139] mentioned the existence of the law of Moses, but without clarifying if it was a Greek text. However, Greek prevailed very early in the synagogues, as proven by one of the earliest (dated 246-221 BCE) of the dedicatory inscriptions[140] from Schedia (near Alexandria). The place of prayer was an elementary synagogue according to the text of Acts 16:13,16.

«On behalf of king Ptolemy and queen Berenice his sister and wife and their children, the Jews (dedicate) the place of prayer»

Since, according to the Talmud, the Jews used the Name outside the Temple until Simon the Just, are there some vocalized occurrences of the Tetragram (see the Appendix B) during this period from 600 to 300 BCE? Actually, the only biblical testimony of the Name written in Greek is very late, in a manuscript of the Septuagint (4QLXXLevb) dated first century BCE, where one can read Iaô (Ιαω) in place of the Tetragram. But, in view of the context, one can only conclude that it is probably the Hebraic substitute Yahû. It is interesting to note that according to Ecclesiastes 11:3 the Aramaic word meaning yhwh 'He will be' was vocalized Yehû' (and probably Yehû'a before 900 BCE) in Hebrew.

§ 2.5 [-300-0]

From Simon the Just to Jesus

At the beginning of the third century most people spoke Aramaic, and most tradesmen also spoke Greek. The Jewish aristocracy spoke Greek[141] and Hebrew but this latter language was probably a little different from the Biblical Hebrew, just as common Greek, or Koïne is a little different from literary Greek[142]. Thus, in order to improve the people's comprehension, the Hebrew text of the Bible was paraphrased in Aramaic. This vernacular translation was called the Targum. Mainly to help the Greek speaking Jews of the Diaspora, a Greek translation[143] of the Pentateuch, the Septuagint was made around 280 BCE.

■ Papyrus Fouad 266

☞ It is interesting to see how the translators solved the problem of rendering the Tetragram into Greek, because at this time the Jews avoided its use, regarding the Name as sacred. Even so, there was no prohibition against it. The solution was very simple. As one can see in this papyrus[144] (dated between 100 and 50 BCE) the Name was written in Hebrew characters, like the ones chosen by Ezra, inside a Greek text.

YAHU: A DECLINING SUBSTITUTE OF THE NAME

This substitution[145] of the Name was used until 135, no Greek text of the Bible before 150 CE having been found using Kurios instead of the Tetragram. This procedure chosen by Jewish copyists, involved two unfortunate consequences. Firstly, as the name Yahû was still used by Jewish people at this time, 'to protect' this substitute for the Tetragram, all theophoric names ending with *yahû* were modified to *ia* or *iou*, according to the preference of the translator induced by Greek declensions. Thus, in the Septuagint, in spite of thousands of theophoric names, there are none ending in -iaou.

☞   The second and worse consequence to justify their choice these Jewish translators modified verses in the Bible. Thus, Leviticus 24:15,16 became in the LXX «(...) a man who will curse God will bring the offence, but in order to have named the name of the Lord, he would have to die absolutely, the entire assembly of Israel should stone him with stones; the alien resident as the native, in order to have named the name of the Lord, he would have to die absolutely»[146]. Paradoxically, as noted by Philo, a Jewish philosopher of the first century (-20 to 50), to name God was worse than to curse him! (*De Vita Mosis II, 203-206*).

As might be expected in return, this innovation influenced Jewish worship. Indeed, the Septuagint forbade Greek speaking Jews to pronounce the Name, while Hebrew speaking Jews could continue to use it, making a paradoxical situation for bilingual Jews. The Talmud of Babylon (*Yoma 39b*) indicates that in practice, the use of a substitute for the Tetragram became widespread in Israel at this time, except inside the Temple of Jerusalem. This speed in the chain of events is easily explained by a rapidly expanding Hellenism in Israel, which already had entailed a decline in worship, as confirmed by certain Jewish historic books (1M 1:11-15,41-57; 2M 4:14; 6:6). The prohibition on the Name written in Greek affected the majority of the Jewish population which then adopted this custom[147].

According to the historic testimonies of the Talmud of Babylon, the Letter of Aristeas and the Jewish Antiquities[148] of Flavius Josephus, the translation of the Septuagint (-280) and the disappearance of the Name in Israel were contemporary events[149], since all these accounts indicate that Ptolemy Philadelphus and Simon the Just lived at the same moment[150]. However, to try to harmonize certain incompatible historic data, many specialists prefer at present to move these dates forward to around 200 BCE. Finally, according to the Palestinian Talmud (*Yoma 3,6-7*), the complete disappearance of the Name took place after the destruction of the second Temple in the year 70.

☞   During the intervening period which preceded the destruction of the Temple, the Talmud (*Sotah 7,6 Tamid 33b*) makes it clear that substitutes of the Name were used in Palestinian liturgy. These substitutes were numerous, as one can notice in the literature of this time (2M 1:24 , 25; 15:3; Si 23:4; 50:14-19). However, singing, with its technical constraints, would favor two of these substitutes: 'my Lord' (Adonay in Hebrew), which is a plural of intensity meaning 'my lords' as in Genesis 19:2; and 'God' (Elohim in Hebrew) which is he also a plural of intensity meaning 'gods'. This second substitute is mainly used in the place of YHWH in the expression 'my Lord YHWH', which was read 'my Lord God' to avoid the repetition 'my Lord my Lord'. One can note that these two Hebrew substitutes, Adonay and Elohim, also have their Aramaic equivalents, used notably in the Targums: Mariya' (The Lord) and Elaha' (The God).

Singing certainly favored these substitutes. Even though we do not know the exact cantillation of the biblical texts[151], we know, for example, that the Psalms were sung to ancient melodies known at this time, which are moreover indicated the superscriptions (Psalms 9; 22; 45; 46; 59; 60; 69; 75; 80; 81; 84; 120-134). We also know that these songs inaugurated under David's administration, were sung at least until 70 of our era (Mt 26:30; Jc 5:13). After the disappearance of the Temple, then the Hebraic language, these melodies were probably lost. Logically if the Name was replaced by a substitute from about third century BCE, and if the Psalms were sung from the tenth century BCE until the first century CE, we can conclude that in order not to modify the melody, they chose a substitute of the same syllabic structure as the Name. The two substitutes used ('a-do-nay and 'è-lo-him) do have an identical syllabic structure of two and a half syllables (1/2,1,1), exactly the same as that of the divine name Ye-ho-wah.

✄   A second detail derived from the constraints of song, is that assonance[152] played a large role in ancient poetry. To help singers to remember Psalms, which were sometimes rather long, the text contained acrostics, parallelisms, word plays and assonance. For example, in Psalm 3:8 one can read: «layehowah hayešû'ah 'al'ammeka birkatèka»; in Psalm 118:25,26 one can read the sentence: «'ana' yehowah hôšî'ah na' 'ana' yehowah haslîhah na'». This last Psalm was well known shown by its use in Matthew 21:9 and 23:39. The Talmud (*Sukka 3:9*) also points out that the Name was used in this blessing, but it quotes it in Aramaic «ana Shema hosanna». In the Targums found at Qumrân[153], dated the first century BCE, the common substitute was Èlaha (אֱלָהָא) meaning, 'The God' (see Dn 2:20; 3:26), an adaptation of the Hebrew word Èlôah (אֱלוֹהַ) meaning, 'God [Himself]'. Specialists consider that assonance also played a role in the forming of names such as Yehudah[154]. The Talmud itself noted this resemblance of Yehudah's name with the Tetragram (*Sotah 10b 36b*).   ✄

ADONAY VERSUS JEHOVAH

Using the substitute Adonay in place of the Name entailed other consequences. When the scribes made copies of the Bible under dictation they sometimes confused the word Adonay with the tetragrams pronounced Adonay. This way of copying was inadvisable, because it engendered errors, but as it saved time it was regrettably used. The Sopherims, who were the precursors of the Masoretes, fortunately found these 134 places, as seen by reading the Masoretical note of Genesis 18:3, where a Tetragram was replaced by Adonay. For example, in the oldest text of Isaiah (from 150 to 100 BCE) found at Qumrân (1Q^a), sixteen times 'Adonay' took place of the Tetragram.

Furthermore, the process which consisted of writing the Name in Hebrew inside a Greek text impressed the Jewish copyists, who, wishing also to show their reverence for the Name, sometimes wrote the Name in paleo-Hebrew inside the Hebrew text.

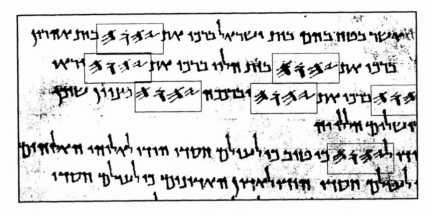

As one can see in this copy of the book of Psalms[155], dated 30-50 CE, tetragrams were written in good paleo-Hebrew. This procedure influenced in return the copyists of the Septuagint who also tried to imitate these strange tetragrams.

☞ As seen in the copy[156] reproduced here, dated around the beginning of our era, the writing of this paleo-Hebrew was of much inferior quality. Furthermore, this procedure favored a mystic attitude toward divine names. In addition, the Talmud points out that they had started to remove these names that had been stamped on jars in order to protect their holiness. (*'Arakin 6a; Šabbat 61b*)

Also, out of respect, the Name was to be avoid the conversation, as proven by these remarks, from Jewish books written in the second century BCE: «Do not accustom into the habit of naming the Holy One» and «someone who is

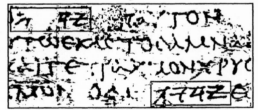

continually swearing and uttering the Name will not be exempt from sin.» (Si 23:9,10). It was held that the privilege of pronouncing the Name was strictly reserved for use inside the Temple (Si 50:20), and that it should not be communicated to foreigners (Ws 14:21). Outside Palestine, the copies of the Septuagint which have been found, show a rapid deterioration in writing of the letters of the Name, as in this copy from Egypt dated from the beginning of our era[157].

When the Jews changed their system of numbering[158], between the third and the first century BCE, they modified the numbers 15 and 16. Instead of using YH (10+5) and YW (10+6) to represent these numbers, they used in their place TW (9+6 !) and TZ (9+7 !). On the other hand, some centuries earlier (about the fourth century BCE) the number YW had been used for a measure of liquid[159] (see the Appendix H).

	Old system (Bible)	New system	
14	ארבעה עשר	יד	YD
15	חמשה עשר	טו instead of יה	TW (YH)
16	ששה עשר	טז instead of יו	TZ (YW)
17	שבעה עשר	יז	YZ

This modification can be explained easily in an Aramaic context. Indeed, in this language the names YHW and YW were pronounced identically before 200 BCE (Yahû and Yaw, since the letter H was inaudible). This fact can be verified in that all theophoric names which ended in -yahû in Judaea, where Hebrew was spoken, were written -yaw in territories outside Judaea (Samaria) where Aramaic was spoken.

Furthermore, slight variations that arose in the pronunciation of the Aramaic language explain the differences found in works of ancient authors. Actually, it is thought that there were two periods for Aramaic: from 700 to 200 BCE there was an official Aramaic, which became from 200 BCE to 200 CE middle Aramaic. Hebrew encountered approximately the same periods when the Hebrew of the second temple became rabbinical Hebrew. The main changes concerned precisely the pronunciation of the letters *y* and *w* (ay $\Rightarrow$ é, aw $\Rightarrow$ ô, hû $\Rightarrow$ ô/ w, éhû $\Rightarrow$ aw, etc.)[160] The end result was that the pronunciation of the letter waw in Aramaic varied successively in time[161]: *w* $\Rightarrow$ *v* $\Rightarrow$ *b*, rendered in Greek by: *u* $\Rightarrow$ *ô* / *ü* $\Rightarrow$ *b* (*b* is pronounced as bv). For example, the word Aramaic Yaw progressively became in Greek: (Iaou) $\Rightarrow$ Iaô $\Rightarrow$ Iaüe $\Rightarrow$ Iabe, as seen below.

AUTHOR	ERA	TONGUE	NAMÉ
Terentius Varro[162]	-116 -27	Latin	Iao
LXX papyrus[163]	-100-1	Greek	Iaô
Diodorus Siculus[164].	-90-21?	Greek	Iaô
Irenaeus of Lyon[165]	130-202	Greek	Iaô
Gnostic writer[166]	150-180	Coptic	Yaüe
Clement of Alexandria[167]	150-215?	Greek	Iaoué
Tertullian[168]	155-222	Latin	Iao
Gnostic writer[169]	200?	Ethiopian	Yâwê
Origen[170]	185-253	Greek	Iaô
Eusebius[171]	265-340	Greek	Iaô
Epiphanius[172]	315-403	Greek	Iabé
Jerome[173]	347-419	Latin	Iaho
Theodoret[174]	393-458	Greek	Iabé

☞   When giving the pronunciation of the divine name, these authors never specify whether it is the Aramaic substitute YW (or YHW), or the great name YHWH reserved for the Temple (see the general chronology in the Appendix A). Even though in a papyrus of the Septuagint, dated the first century BCE, one finds Iaô in the place of the Tetragram, again, it is probably the substitute, because at Qumrân it was forbidden to vocalize the Name at the risk of exclusion from the community. Additionally the historian Titus-Livius (-59 17) wrote[175] «in the Temple of Jerusalem, the god is not named.» The other subtle factor which would dissuade a Jew knowing the complete Name from revealing it to a foreigner, was the improper confusion with the Latin name Ioua meaning 'girl of Iouis [Jupiter]' or 'Jupiteret', according to Varro![176]

Confusion between Jehovah and Jupiter

When Varro wrote, that the god of the Jews is called Iao by the Chaldeans, his testimony seems to be reliable because, as one can see, the name Iaô is indeed written in the LXX below (1st century BCE) in place of the Tetragram. However, when Varro quoted this name Iaô, he did not know that it was only a substitute.

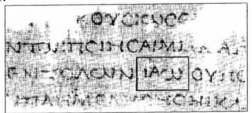
IAÔ

Strangely, the famous scholar Augustine of Hippo (354-430) wrote around 400 that «Varro was rightly writing that the Jews worship the god Jupiter![177] (*deum Iudaeorum Iouem putauit*)». Therefore, Augustine confused the name of Jupiter (Ioue) with the name of God (Iaô or perhaps Ioua). Valerius Maximus, a Latin historian who was also a contemporary of Philo wrote (around 30 CE) in his book, quoted by Ianuarius

Nepotianus at the end of the fifth century, that (in 139 BCE) «the praetor Cornelius Hispalus expelled at home the Jews who tried corrupting Roman manners by their worship of Sabazi Iouis». However, as the Romans already worshipped the god Jupiter (Iouei) which was never the case for the Jews, this strange name Sabazi Iouis must be an approximation for the Hebrew name Sabaoth Ioua (or Iaô), which is a more plausible conclusion[178].

This confusion permits an explanation of odd events quoted by two reliable historians. For example, the author of the book of Maccabees (2M 6:2) explained that (in 167 BCE) King Epiphanes «tried to desecrate the Temple of Jerusalem by dedicating it to Olympian Zeus (Διος Ολυμπιου) and this one of Garizim to Hospitable Zeus (Διος Ξενιου) *according to what the inhabitants of the place asked.*» As we know the Samaritans and the Jews worshipped the same God and they would never have asked permission to worship Jupiter from a pagan king. A plausible explanation is that they asked, perhaps, to dedicate the Temple to Hospitable Iaô (or Ioua), a slight modification of the divine name (Hospitable meaning more precisely 'Protector of strangers'). The historian Flavius Josephus gave some more details on this event. In his book (*Jewish Antiquities XII, 261*) he explained that the Samaritans worship the Most Great God of the Jews and after they erected a temple without a name, asked that it be dedicated to Hellenic Zeus (Διος Ελληνιου). As the name of the Hebrew God has never been Zeus (the Latin Iouei) a more plausible explanation is that the Samaritans asked to dedicate their temple to a *Greek Iaô* rather than to Iaô (or Ioua) alone. Last remark, the deity on the coin with Yahu may be identified with the Latin god Jupiter (Ioui).

YHW
(Yahu)

IOVI VICTORI
(Jupiter victorious)

(ZEUS)

The shape of the Hebrew coin with Yahu (dated 5th-4th century BCE) may have been influenced by numerous Greek coins, dated from this time, with the god Zeus holding an eagle on his right hand[179].

Another factor that may favored the confusion between YHWH and Jupiter is their nearness of function (both of them are considered as head master of heavens as explained in the *Letter of Aristeas §16*) and their nearness of pronunciation. For example, the Jews of Elephantine (5th century BCE) used the Aramaic word *yhwh* (vocalized *yihweh* which means 'he will prove to be'), very frequently in their letters, but the name of Jupiter was Ioue at this time which is very close to the Aramaic word *yihweh* that is an equivalent of *iioue* in Latin.

Additionally, Pausanias a Greek writer (2nd century CE) reports in his book (*Description of Greece X 12:10*) that the prophetesses at the prestigious oracle at Dodona were the first to sing (beginning of the third century before our common era): «Zeus was, Zeus is, Zeus shall be. O mighty Zeus!» a formula close to the sentence found in the book of Revelation: «Jehovah God, the One who is and who was and who is coming, the Almighty» (Rv 1:8).

It is interesting to note that the first writer who gave a description of the Almighty as a king seated on his throne with wheels, was the prophet Daniel in 536 before our common era when he wrote: «the Ancient of Days sat down. His clothing was white just like snow, and the hair of his head was like clean wool. His throne was flames of fire, its wheels were a burning fire» (Dn 7:9).

From Jesus to Justin

At the beginning of our Common Era reverence for the name of God was great, the expression «let your name be sanctified» (Mt 6:9) is quite representative of this period, but in daily life this reverence was over exaggerated. For example, the Tetragram was pronounced exactly as it was written but only inside the temple and elsewhere a substitute was used. However, even inside the temple when reading of the blessing of Numbers 6:23-27 the utterance of the divine name was drowned out by the singing of the priests (*Yoma 3:6/ 40d/ 66a*).

Usually, Adonay was used as the main substitute in the Palestinian liturgy (*Sotah 40b 7,6*) and sometimes Elohim (*Damascus Document XV,1*)[180]. In daily life many substitutes were used as seen in the Talmud or in the New Testament (the Heavens, Father, the Almighty, the Blessed One, Power, the Name, etc.) The only exception seems to have been in greetings, since the Talmud (*Berakot 63a 9,9*) noted that the divine name was to be used in this case. However this was likely the name Yah (*Berakot 9,1*) because this name was still sung in Psalms like in the expression Hallelu-Yah which means 'Praise Yah'. This expression is found in the book of Revelation (Rv 19:1,3) written by the apostle John around 96 of our era.

As one can see in portion of the book of Psalms found at Qumran[181], the name Yah was written normally while on the other hand, the Tetragram was written in paleo-Hebrew. Furthermore several times 'Adonay' takes the place of the Tetragram. Many peculiarities[182] from these scrolls may be explained today without difficulty. The use of paleo-Hebrew[183], which was sometimes also used to write the Hebrew word El (God) simply shows the extreme reverence with which the scribes treated divine names. To erase a divine Name was forbidden (*Šebu'ot 35a*), but in case of a mistake the copyist was able to 'virtually' delete a letter by writing points above it or underneath it[184]. It was also possible to rectify an omission by writing above. For example, in the sequence Yhwh Adonay (Is

3:15 28:16 30:15 65:13) probably pronounced [Adonay] Adonay, the copyist only wrote Adonay once[185]. Then, after checking, he added the missing occurrences of Adonay over the tetragrams, not to indicate the pronunciation of the Name, but because he had forgotten them.

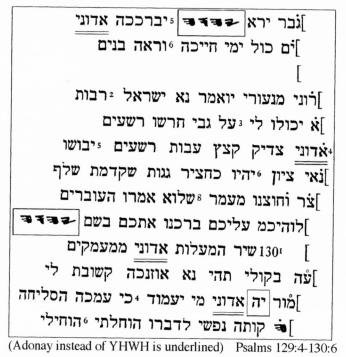

(Adonay instead of YHWH is underlined)   Psalms 129:4-130:6

THE USE OF THE NAME IN THE TEMPLE

☞   Of course, the pronunciation 'Adonay' was well known. However, the name that was read in a loud voice inside the temple (*Qiddušin 71a, Yoma 40d, Tamid 30b*) was not Adonay but the name according to its letters, therefore it was possible for a priest to know the exact pronunciation. The main difficulty lies in the valuation of the Aramaic influence of the popular substitute Iaô, because this reading seems to agree with the theophoric names. However, the exact pronunciation was in Hebrew not in Aramaic; thus, the data drawn from theophoric names in Aramaic is misleading.

NAME	CONSONANT	ARAMAIC	PHONETIC
Yehôshaphat	Yhwšpt	Yahawšapat	Iâôshafat
Ahiô	'hyw	'Aḥyaw	Ahiaô
Ahiyah	'hyhw	'Aḥyahaw	Ahîâô

NAME	CONSONANT	HEBREW	PHONETIC
Yehoshaphat	Yhwšpt	Yehôšapat	Ieôshafat
Ahiô	'hyw	'Aḥyô	Ahiô
Ahiyah	'hyhw	'Aḥiyahû	Ahîaû

One can note that the Aramaic pronunciations seem to be more consistent because in each case the divine name found in these theophoric names is read phonetically Iaô while in Hebrew we find Ieô, Iô and Iaû. Furthermore, at Qumran, very often the words written *wh* were vocalized *ôh* in the Masoretic text[186]. Thus, impressed by this body of evidence pointing to Iaô, many scholars have concluded that the pronunciation of YHWH could have been YaHWoH[187].

However, reconstituted vocalization contradicts all the witnesses who had access to the pronunciation of the Name in the Temple during the first century. For example Flavius Josephus (37-100), who knew the priesthood of this time very well, made it clear when the Romans attacked the Temple, the Jews called upon the fear-inspiring name of God[188]. He wrote he had no right to reveal this name to his reader[189], however he did give information of primary importance on the pronunciation he wanted to conceal.

☞   One can read the following remark in the work *The Jewish War V:235* «The high priest had his head dressed with a tiara of fine linen embroidered with a purple border, and surrounded by another crown in gold which had in relief the sacred letters; these ones are four vowels» This description is excellent; moreover, it completes the one found in Exodus 28:36-39. However, as we know, there are no vowels in Hebrew but only consonants. Regrettably, instead of explaining this visible abnormality, certain commentators (influenced by the form Yahweh) mislead the readers of Josephus by indicating in a note that this reading was IAUE. Now, it is obvious that the 'sacred letters' indicated the Tetragram written in paleo-Hebrew, not Greek. Furthermore, in Hebrew these consonants Y, W, H, do serve as vowels; they are in fact called 'mothers of reading' (matres lectionis). The writings of Qumrân show that in the first century Y used as vowel served only to indicate the sounds I and É, W served only for the sounds Ô and U, and a final H served for the sound A. These equivalences may be verified in thousands of words. Additionally, the H was used as a vowel only at the end of words, never within them[190]. So, to read the name YHWH as four vowels would be IHUA that is IEUA, because between two vowels the H is heard as a slight E.

☞   A second testimony on pronunciation, is the Talmud itself where the Tetragram is called the *shem hamephorash* meaning "the name distinctly read" or "the name read according to its letters". Some cabalists affirm that the word *mephorash* means 'hidden', but it is easy to verify the correct meaning of this word in the Bible itself (Ne 8:8; Ezr 4:18). The Talmud (*Sanhedrin 101a 10:1*) forbade the use of the divine Name for magical purposes, and Rabbi Abba Shaûl (130-160?) also prohibited the use biblical quotations containing the Tetragram for exorcising purposes and the *pronunciation of the Tetragram according to its letters*, warning that those transgressing this command would forfeit their portion in the world to come.

The phrase "to pronounce the Name according to its letters" means pronouncing the Name as it is written, or according to the sound of its letters, which is different than spelling a name according to its letters. Actually, it was authorized to spell the name YHWH according to its letters (because the Talmud itself did it), that is in Hebrew Yod, He, Waw, He (or Y, H, W, H in English); on the other hand, it was forbidden to pronounce it according to these same letters.

In Hebrew, the majority of proper names in plene writing can be read according to their letters. In the first century, these equivalents existed Y = I, W = U, and H = A at the end of words. Additionally, consonants mostly always alternate with a vowel in the reading of these names, except in the case of a guttural or an H at the end, which are vocalized *a*. When a vowel is not indicated in a name, consonants are vocalized with an *a*. This style of reading is usual in Hebrew, for example with some famous names or a few names with an orthography close to the Tetragram.

NAME READ ACCORDING	TO ITS CONSONANTS	TO ITS LETTERS	TO THE SEPTUAGINT	TO THE MASORETES
1 Ch 3:5	Yrwšlym	Irušalim	Iérousalèm	Yerušalayim
Gn 29:35	Yhwdh	Ihuda	Iouda	Yehudah
Gn 25:19	'brhm	'Abaraham	Abraam	'Abraham
Gn 25:19	Yṣḥq	Iṣaḥaq	Isaak	Yiṣḥaq
Lv 26:42	Yʻqwb	Iʻaqub	Iakôb	Yaʻaqôb
2 Ch 27:1	Yrwšh	Iruša	Iérousa	Yerušah
Gn 46:17	Yšwh	Išua	Iésoua	Yišwah
1 Ch 2:38	Yhw'	Ihu'	Ièou	Yéhu'
Gn 3:14	Yhwh	Ihua	(Kurios)	(Adonay)

In the chart above we see a remarkable agreement with the reading of these names according to the Septuagint and their reading according to their letters (in the Hebrew language).

A third testimony, still from this epoch, coming from persons who had access to the priesthood, is that of the translators of the Septuagint. This text had fixed the vocalization of proper names just before the custom to no longer use the Name outside the Temple was adopted. Note that all theophoric names beginning in YHW-() in the Hebrew Bible were vocalized Iô-(a) in the Septuagint and never Ia-. So, the divine name, constituting the theophoric name par excellence (that is to say YHW-H), to be in agreement with all the other theophoric names should have been vocalized IÔ-A in Greek, or, if one restores the mute H which did not exist in Greek, IHÔA.

This vocalization IHÔA, or IeHÔA taking into account the theophoric names of the Masoretic text, permits us to explain an anomaly in the texts of Qumrân. It was forbidden to pronounce the divine name during a reading of a biblical text, punishable by excommunication from the community[191].

Therefore, to apply this rule, it was necessary to know the pronunciation of this name. To respect prohibition, often in certain texts the Tetragram was replaced by the substitute 'Himself'[192], pronounced *Hu'* in Hebrew, also used in the Targums[193]. However, this last word was written *Hu'a* with a harmonic *a*[194]. The main reason for this change seems to be assonance with the divine name. The forbidden name Yehua could actually be replaced by the similar expression Yah Hu'a, which was allowed. One can note that the Arabic language has kept this ancient expression Ya Huwa (I [is] he)[195] up until today in Surah 27:9 of the Quran: «Ô Moses! *Him it is I* Allah the Almighty, the Wise one.»[196]

Was there really a prohibition on pronouncing the Tetragram in the first century? The answer is no, as, according to the Talmud this prohibition appeared from the middle of the second century. Actually the Bible itself never mentioned such a prohibition, forbidding only blasphemy (Lv 24:11,16) and later, this notion was enlarged to include apostasy (Mt 9:3 26:65).

THE USE OF THE NAME BY EARLY CHRISTIANS

Did Jesus pronounce the Name? In the first place, as he strongly denounced human traditions which annulled divine dictates (Mt 15:3), it seems unlikely that he complied with this unbiblical custom of not pronouncing the Name. Secondly, the Gospel makes clear that Jesus read (Lk 4:16-20) a part of Isaiah's text (Is 61:1) in a synagogue, and these verses contain the Tetragram. Even if it was the text of the Septuagint, at this time this translation contained the Name in Hebrew, as noted in all copies of this text dated before 150 CE.

Did the fact that Jesus pronounced the Name surprise his listeners? As they were Galilean, they must have spoken Aramaic and must also known the substitute Yaw, archaeology supplying numerous Greek sources of evidence using Iaô. Furthermore, the name Yaho played a large role in Jewish mysticism[197]. For example, we find it in a work written around 80 CE (*Apocalypse of Abraham 10:3-11:5*), where we read the following remark concerning Iaôel, a visible agent of God: «Iaôel (Iaô [is] God) of the same name, through the mediation of my ineffable name»[198]; In order to hide his name, this angel Yahoel was later called Metatron. As seen, even at Qumrân and in spite of the prohibition, the names Yah and Hu'a were authorized, and consequently also the expression Yah Hu'a, that is 'Yah Himself'. One can easily understand that the Hebraic pronunciation of the Name, although it was slightly different from its Aramaic substitutes, must have been be identified by Galilean audience. Moreover, today this same situation exists: when a person reads the Bible, he can choose between the Hebrew name Jehovah and the Aramaic name Yahweh; the audience will understand without a problem.

However, Jesus (and also his disciples) used this name cautiously, and to avoid being judged as a blasphemer during his trial he respected the judicial prohibition (*Sanhedrin 56a 7,5*) not to pronounce the Name before the final judgement. For this reason, during this trial many substitutes were used such as; «the living God, power (Mt 26:63,64), the Blessed One (Mk 14:61)», hence, from his trial up until his death, Jesus did not use the divine Name. This problem affected the early Christians of Jewish origin because they were regarded by the Jews as apostates (Dt 13:10) and therefore as blasphemers deserving of death (Ac 26:10). This penalty was executed if they pronounced the Name before the final verdict as Stephen did[199]. In fact, Stephen was first accused of blasphemous sayings (Ac 6:11,12). Then, during his judgement before the Sanhedrin he quoted the famous episode of the explanation of the Name (Ac 7:30-33) and he pronounced the Name three times (Ac 7:31,33,49) that was considered a profanation of the Name (*Sanhedrin 7:5*) for which he was stoned (Ac 7:58). One can understand that Christians used the name cautiously because they ran the risk of losing their life (see the Appendix G).

Outside Israel, the situation was not any easier because of a law on superstitions (Lex superstitio illicita) which involved the death penalty for introducing a new unauthorized deity. [Nobody will have different or new gods, neither will they worship unknown private gods, unless they have a public authorization]. For example, Socrates (-470-399) was put to death because of this law. Of course, the apostle Paul knew this law (Ac 16:21 17:18 18:13) and therefore, he avoided using the Tetragram in his speeches, preferring substitutes such as "deities, God, Lord of heaven and earth, the Divine Being" (Ac 17:21-32). To sum up, in each instance the wiser choice for early Christians was to use the divine Name very cautiously[200]. On the other hand knowledge of the name of Jesus was an important new teaching (Mt 12:21; Jn 16:24 20:31; Ac 4:17-18 9:15; Ro 1:5; 1Jn 5:13) and even exorcists discovered it was a powerful name (Mk 9:38; Mt 7:22).

How did early Christians write the Tetragram when they copied the Bible? As they were of Jewish origin (Judeo-Christian), they had accepted the Greek Septuagint (which was a Jewish translation) and they continued to propagate it[201]. At first, they probably followed the Jewish custom of writing the Name in Hebrew within a Greek text[202], at least until the death of the last apostle (of Jewish extraction) around 100 of our era (2Th 2:7). It is interesting to note that Rabbi Tarphon *(Šabbat 116a)*, between 90 and 130 CE relates the problem of the destruction of heretical (Christian) texts containing the Tetragram.

INVENTION OF 'SACRED NAMES' BY EARLY CHRISTIANS

☞   After the destruction of the Temple in the year 70, and the official malediction[203] of Christians (Judeo-Christians) by the Jews around 90-100, profound changes would occur. First of all, Hebrew would practically cease to be spoken after the second century[204]. Furthermore, with the internationalization of Christianity, the strange Jewish custom of writing an "old Hebrew word" that one pronounces 'Lord' (Kurios in Greek) would be abandoned by mostly the pagano-Christian copyists[205], probably between 70 et 135 CE, and they would simply to write the word 'Lord' in place of the strange Hebrew Tetragram. However, the sequence Kurios YHWH posed a problem of translation. Note the wide selection of solutions offered to translate this expression, which became in Greek 'Kurios Kurios', 'Kurios Theos', 'Kurios Adonay' or 'Kurios' (verified in the Concordance of Hatch and Redpath). It also engendered a lot of variants in the Gospel[206].

☞ The Jews, reacting against Christians, would in time reject their translation of the Septuagint and produce new versions[207], such as that of Aquila (129) of Symmachus (165) and Theodotion (175?). At the beginning of Christianity (until 135), most copies of the New Testament were probably made by Judeo-Christians in a same manner[208], by writing the Name in paleo-Hebrew within the Greek text. This kind of writing was used (with more and more roughness) until the end of the third century CE. For example in this Samaritan inscription[209] found at Syracuse and dated second century CE, one can read the following verse «Do arise, Jehovah, and let your enemies be scattered» (Nb 10:35).

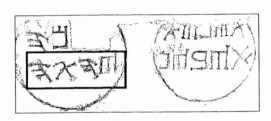

[QW]MH YHWH WYPṢW 'YBYK

Thus, the use of paleo-Hebrew was the standard of writing for the Jews to write the Tetragram from around 50 BCE to 250 CE. The Jews who became Christians, probably followed this way of proceeding (until 135 CE), but from 70, pagans who became Christians (the majority after 100 CE) were not able to understand the paleo-Hebrew writing and they ceased to use it.

Origen confirmed (around 250 CE), in his comment on Psalms[210], this Jewish custom of writing the Tetragram in old Hebrew embedded in the Greek text as one can see hereafter in this copy of Aquila's translation[211] dated fifth century CE.

But are there any traces of this ancient practice? Yes, in two cases at least. The first case concerns the oldest Christian papyrus (P52), the only one belonging to this period, since it is dated 125 CE. This papyrus contains an anomaly which one does not find again in any of the later Christian manuscripts. In actual fact, this manuscript is an exception among all the texts of the Gospels because there is no *nomina sacra* process[212], that is to say names considered as sacred were not replaced by abbreviations. Thus one can conclude that the Tetragram was written in full (see the Appendix C).

The second case, concerns the inexplicable number of errors leading to confusion between the terms 'Lord' and 'God' in the Gospel. As we have seen, the expression Kurios YHWH posed a difficult problem for the translators of the Septuagint. This expression is much rarer in the Gospels; on the other hand, the title 'Lord' (Kurios) is frequently applied to Jesus, which could lead to confusion with the other 'Lord', the translation of YHWH. So, some copyists, to avoid this confusion, preferred to translate YHWH by 'God' (Theos) or simply to omit this name, as noted in the following passages: Lk 1:68; Ac 2:17; 6:7; 7:37; 10:33; 12:24; 13:5,44,48; 15:40; 19:20; 20:28; Rm 14:4; Col 3:13,16; 2 Tm 2:14; Jm 3:9; Jude 5; Rv 18:8. The list of variants is considerable for these few verses[213]. Why did translators stumbled over the reading or understanding of such simple and well known words as 'God' and 'Lord'? Some specialists admit that several times 'Lord' or 'God' took the place of YHWH[214].

These replacements were done early, since after the second century of our era no more traces of the writing and pronunciation of the Name[215] are found, except among a few Christian scholars. Paradoxically, a Christian reader might even believe that the God of the Bible was called Sabaôth, because this name is found in the expression Lord Sabaôth (Κυριος Σαβαωθ) in Romans 9:29 and in James 5:4.

The fact that God's name played an important role during two first centuries among Christians, can be verified it in the works of several writers of this time, whose remarks show that they held the Name in veneration[216].

Author	Era	Works
Clement of Rome	? -96	*Epistle to Corinthians* (43:2, 6; 45:7 58:1; 59:2, 3; 60:4; 64)
?	70-100	*The Didache* (10:2, 3; 14:3)
Ignatius of Antioch	? -117	*Letter to Ephesians* (1:2; 3:1; 7:1) *Letter to Magnesians* (1:2) *Letter to Philadelphians* (10:1, 2)
Hermas	? -140	*The Shepherd* (9:9; 10:1; 11:5 12:3 23:4)
Polycarp	70-160	*Letter to Philippians* (10:3) *The Martyrdom* (14:1)

☞   However, these writers use the substitute Lord (Kurios) instead of the divine Name, even when quoting the Holy Scriptures. Nevertheless, they cautiously avoided causing a confusion between YHWH (indicated by 'Lord' and 'The God') and Jesus (indicated by 'The Lord' and 'God'). Thus the presence or the absence of the article permitted the reader to know whom they were speaking about Jesus or YHWH[217]. Unfortunately, this subtlety disappeared very soon after the second century of our common era.

Was this term 'Lord' understood as a proper name at this time? The answer is no, in spite of apparent evidence. For example, Polycarp said he couldn't say «Caesar is Lord» (*The Martyrdom of Polycarp 8:2*), Josephus related that Jews refused to recognize Caesar as a Lord or to pronounce this word (*The Jewish war 7:418*), and finally the apostle Paul said: «there are (...) many lords, there is actually to us (...) one Lord» (1Co 8:5,6). But it is easy to dispel the misunderstanding of these quotations.

First, in the Gospel itself this term is only a title and was used in connection with human beings (Jn 12:21 20:15; Ac 16:30.) Also, Philo Judaeus (-20? to 50 CE?), a Jewish philosopher used this word with regard to a mere man 'Lord Gaius' (*Legatio ad Gaium 44-46.*) This title is found as well in correspondence from the Bar-Kokhba period (135 CE) written in Hebrew or in Greek[218]. Additionally, this title encountered no opposition at this time from political authorities.

In fact the explanation is very simple in that the title 'Lord' may have both a political and a religious meaning. However, for early Christians there was a difference between political titles which must be respected (Rm 13:7) and religious titles which must be rejected (Mt 23:8-10). Caesar held a plurality of offices as a religious pontiff and also as a political leader. Tertullian explained that therein the real lay problem (*Apologetic 34:1*), because for a Christian to say 'Lord' in a political sense acceptable but in a religious sense only God was worthy to receive such a title. Thus, when Polycarp was asked to say «Caesar is Lord» the context shows that he was asked to follow a regular procedure (*The Martyrdom of Polycarp 9:2*) which would imply recognizing Caesar as a pontiff, and that was impossible.

As the title Lord was used for God only, the importance of the Name itself for Christians quickly faded[219]. Many factors played a role in bringing about the disappearance of the Name: A wrong translation of Leviticus 24:15,16, a mystical reverence toward the Tetragram, the influence of legislation on superstitions, the increase of persecution, the important role played by the new name of Jesus and the influence of Greek philosophy which proposed the impossibility of men to name God.

PHILOSOPHERS AND RELIGIOUS TEACHERS OPPOSE THE
NAME

Surprisingly, philosophers and religious teachers have
been the most damaging opponents of the Name[220]. They were
strongly influenced by several works of Plato (-427-347)
wherein he explained that no name could perfectly designate
God, furthermore: «to have a name implies an older person who
gave you this name, therefore God has no name» (*Timaios 28b,c
Kratylos 400d Parmenides 142a*). Incredibly, in time these
arguments influenced Bible teaching about the divine Name.

For example, Philo (-20? 50?) a Jewish philosopher of
the first century had a good biblical knowledge and knew that
the Tetragram was the divine name pronounced inside the
temple since he related: «there was a gold plaque shaped in a
ring and bearing four engraved characters of a name which had
the right to hear and to pronounce in the holy place those ones
whose ears and tongue have been purified by wisdom, and
nobody else and absolutely nowhere else» (*De Vita Mosis
II:114-132*)[221] However in the same work, paradoxically, he
explains, commenting on Exodus 3:14 from the LXX translation
that God has no name of his own! (*De Vita Mosis I:75*).

To reconcile these two wholly opposite statements he
proceeded by steps. First, he justified the custom of not
pronouncing God's name with the analogy that children, out of
reverence for their parents use substitutes like father or mother
(or dad and mom) rather than their name (*De Vita Mosis II,207*).
Then he stated that the name of God is itself a substitute because
God refused to reveal his name to man. To prove this he
quoted[222] Exodus 6:3 and Genesis 32:29. Thus, he spent a lot of
time trying to prove that God's name was not a real name![223]

However, his Hebrew knowledge was incomplete,
because in spite of his knowing the two substitutes for the divine
name 'Lord' (Adonay in Hebrew or Kurios in Greek) and 'God'
(Elohim in Hebrew or Theos in Greek) most of his quotations
were from the Greek LXX. For example, when he explained the
changing of the name Oséé (salvation) into Ièsous in Numbers

13:16, he translated Ièsous: "Salvation of the Lord"[224]. Furthermore, he misunderstood the meaning of the old Hebrew characters of the Tetragram because he thought that these were symbols of numbers (*De Vita Mosis II:115*)!

Justin (100-165) a Christian philosopher, is another example of this insidious opposition to the Name. Like Philo, Justin often commented in his works that it was impossible for man to name God[225], and once more his main argument came from *Timaios*, a work of Plato (*Apologies II:6,1*). However, an interesting anomaly is found in his quotations (like the passage of Mika 4:1-7 quoted in his *Dialogue with Tryphon §109*) which permits us to conclude that he knew the writing of God's name. His quotations of the Bible did not correspond exactly with the LXX or with the Masoretic text but only with these texts found at Qumran.

In spite of the Tetragram clearly appearing in paleo-Hebrew in this Greek text[226], Justin did not understand it as a proper name. Perhaps he thought that it was an archaic procedure for writing the word 'Lord'. At this time, even Irenaeus of Lyons (130-202) believed that the word IAÔ (Ιαω in Greek, [Iah] in Latin) meant 'Lord' in primitive Hebrew

(*Against Heresies II, 24:2*). Very fast, the understanding of the paleo-Hebrew became chaotic. For example, in this Aramaic inscription[227], written by a Jew before 70 CE, the two names Jerusalem and Judah are written with degenerated letters.

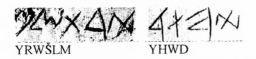

YRWŠLM   YHWD

Irenaeus esteemed that the use of this Hebrew word IAÔ to denote the Name of the unknown Father, was intended to impress gullible minds in worship of mysteries (*Against Heresies I, 21:3*).

☞   Thus, this philosophical activity in time produced many gnostic sects[228] with however two distinct trends. The main group maintained that God is unnamable because whoever has a name is the creation of another. One finds this reasoning in a text (*Eugnostos the Blessed III:3,72*)[229] dated as early as 50-100 CE. Another work (*Ascension of Isaiah 7:37; 8:7; 9:6*) written around 100 of our era states that God cannot be named and that the name of Jesus had not been revealed. This first trend was in reaction to the idolatrous practice of naming many gods connected with polytheism.

A second less widespread trend stressed the importance of calling upon the name of God in worship (which had to be kept secret as explained Lucius Apuleius (125-180) in his book entitled *Apologia* chapter LXIV, written around 150 CE). This process generated a lot of new mystical names such as: Yaoth, which means in Hebrew 'Yah [is] sign/ letter/ miracle', Yaldabaoth 'She gave birth in the sign', Yao 'Yah, himself', and so forth. In his book Irenaeus denounced such a profusion of names (*Against Heresies I, 11:4*), which was, in fact, a return to polytheism. He explained that in Hebrew all these names were only mere designations of the same God, because Adonaï means 'Unnamable and glorious', Eloe 'The true God', Sabaoth 'The first heaven', Iaoth 'He who makes ills away', and so on (*Against Heresies II, 35:3*).

He also made clear in his book that among the list of heretics, Marcion (85-160) was the first (around 140 CE) who had the audacity to mutilate the Scriptures (*Against heresies I, 27:2-4*). Concerning this apostate, Tertullian reported that one of his modifications was in the *Our Father* prayer in which «Let your <u>Name</u> be sanctified» became «Let your <u>spirit</u> be sanctified» in copies of Marcion.

Recent studies show that early Christians (before 70 CE) were mainly Judeo-Christians; that is to say Jews who became Christians and above all looked to Jesus as the Messiah (Christos in Greek). Afterward, between 70 and 135 CE, this small group of Christians would be quickly submerged in the mass of the pagano-Christians, that is heathens who became Christians and who instead saw in Jesus a new Lord (Kurios in Greek). Paradoxically, Judeo-Christians would be considered heretics by Jews and by "Christians" alike (the Jews labeled them as the sect of the Nazarenes in Acts 24:5, and the "Christians" treated them as partisans of the circumcision in Acts 15:1-5). This entailed their rejection, which would be complete after 135 CE, by the two groups[230].

Aristo of Pella, a Judeo-Christian, tried in vain to answer some Jewish objections, in his book entitled *A Disputation of Jason and Papiscus*[231] (written around 135 CE). For example, against the charge that Christianity was an apostasy from the Jewish religion, he explained that it was held that the Mosaic law, as far as it relates to outward rites and ceremonies, was only a temporary institution for the Jewish nation, foreshadowing the substance of Christianity based on a new covenant (Jr 31:31). In addition, Abraham was declared just before he was circumcised. To the objection that the divinity of Jesus contradicts the unity of God and is a blasphemy, he replied that Christians believe likewise in only one God. The Old Testament itself makes a distinction with the appearance of the three men at Mamre (Gn 18:22,33) one of whom was confessedly God, yet distinct from the Creator.

§ 2.7 [150-400]

From Justin to Jerome

Very soon a clever new interpretation would rise, which would reconcile the two trends of Gnosticism concerning the name of God. It is written: «everyone who calls on the name of YHWH will be saved» (Ac 2:21; Rm 9:17 10:13) but YHWH was read 'Lord' at this time. Furthermore, Jesus was also called 'The Lord' and since he came to save, according to his name, an identification between the name YHWH and the person of Jesus qualified as Lord was soon made with time in Christendom, the next step would be the complete identification of the 'Lord' (YHWH) with 'the Lord' (Jesus). This teaching is clearly explained in a work dated around 140-180 CE, called *The Gospel of Truth*[232], which says «The name of the Father is the Son (...) He gave him his name which belonged to him (...) For indeed the Father's name is not spoken, but it is apparent through a Son» This innovation soon became official. Justin asserted, for example, in his *Dialogue with Tryphon*, written around 150 CE, that in the book of Exodus Moses revealed this mystery «The name of God is Jesus.»[233] To justify this revelation, Justin wrote, in chapters 58 and 75 of his book, of having received it from God himself! In his *Against Heresies*[234] written around 180-200 CE, Irenaeus of Lyons adhered to this teaching as well.

GENERALIZATION OF ABBREVIATIONS

It is easy to understand that, in such a context, the generalization of the *nomina sacra*, that is the names regarded as sacred, must have been complete. Indeed, although some strange Hebrew names in the biblical text were left, they were in any case pronounced *Lord* (Kurios in Greek). So (after 70 CE), the Christian copyists invented the procedure of the *nomina sacra*. This procedure[235] which consisted of writing sacred names shortened and overlined became widespread. For example, the Greek word KYRIOC was written K̄C̄, KYRIE was written K̄Ē, IESOYC was written ĪC̄, etc. This method of replacing a sacred name by an abbreviation was doubtless inspired by the Jewish custom[236] of replacing the sacred name YhwH by YH.

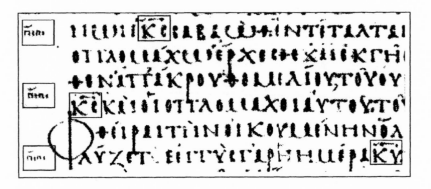

As seen in this codex[237] of the sixth century, the word $\overline{KC}$ took the place of the divine name. However, each time, the copyist indicated the presence of the Tetragram (written Π I Π I) in the margin, furthermore, as a marginal note in Ezekiel 1:2 and 11:1 the name Iaô (Iαω) appeared. Several hexaplar manuscripts (Q, 86, 88, 234mg, 264) were written in this way[238]. The procedure of the *nomina sacra* was systematically used in all Christian manuscripts after 135 CE, as verified in the following papyri: P90 and Egerton 2 (written around 150)[239], P46 and P66 (around 200), in the Sinaïticus (3rd century), etc. In time, when Greek was replaced by Latin, the sacred names were replaced by their Latin equivalents so these abbreviations were replaced by the term Dominus (Lord in Latin). As we have seen, the Greek copyists had sometimes hesitated between 'Lord' and 'God' (Kurios and Theos in Greek) to translate the Tetragram. The Latin copyists would perpetuate this confusion between the terms Dominus and Deus in Latin.

This confusion did not take place in the Jewish world, because the writing of the Tetragram was maintained in the Bible. This was, however, a notable exception as in other religious writings such as the Targums, the Mishna, the Talmud, etc., the Tetragram was replaced by substitutes. In fact, a particular substitute in time played a dominating role and eventually came to the fore: the abbreviation YY (").

Its history is rather ancient, because early on the letter *yod* Y had become an abbreviation of the name YHWH. For example the name Abdy (2 Ch 29:12) means 'servant of Y[ah]', and Yéhu (1 Ch 2:38) means 'Yé[hu it is] He', etc. Certain errors in the Septuagint can be explained by the presence of this abbreviation[240] of a single Y for the Tetragram. As already seen, at about second century before our era, when the Jews changed their system of numbering, they avoided using the symbols YH and YW for the numbers 15 and 16, because in the Aramaic language, one could vocalize these words in YaH and YaW, the two substitutes for the Name. Although the secular use of the first one (YH) was tolerated, this was not case for the second (YW). One can notice in the writings from Qumrân, that the Hebraic letters Y (י) and W (ו) may be easily confused, which naturally engendered some errors of reading. So, by confusing the name YW (יו) with YY (יי), one was freed from the ban on its use, because while there was little difference in writing, to use the latter name offended no one. In time, YY was also written YYY[241] and even occasionally YYYY! For example, YY written in paleo-Hebrew (𐤆𐤆) was found in a papyrus[242] of the Bible dating from the third century CE.

Regarding pronunciation, the Jews mainly used the permanent *qere* Adonay in their liturgy, but in daily life they used the usual *qere* Hashem (הַשֵּׁם) which means 'The Name' and which is found in Leviticus 24:11, or more often, its Aramaic equivalent Shema (שְׁמָא). It is interesting that the Samaritans continue to use this old *qere*[243] to read the Tetragram in the Bible. The name YaW or YaHaW (that is Iaô in Greek) was considered, as we have seen, as an equivalent of the Name in an Aramaic environment.

In a Hebraic environment one finds its equivalent Yahû (YHW), which played an important role in Jewish mysticism. For example, it is called the great name next to YHWH in the *Sepher Yetsirah I §13* (Book of Forming)[244], written around the third century CE. As one can see among these samples (above), numerous amulets of this time, written in Greek, contain the name Iaô, occasionally written backwards[245]. Sometimes other names like: Ia, Sabaot/ Sabao, Adonai, Iaot, etc., are found, but the most frequently found in these Greek amulets is Iaô[246].

So, a good correspondence exists between the Greek name Iaô and its Hebrew counterpart Yhw (Yahu), also between the names Ia and Yh (Yah), Sabaôt and Ṣb'wt (Ṣebaot), Adonai and 'dwny. To confirm this equivalence, one can compare Greek amulets with Jewish amulets[247] of this epoch (150-400).

YH   YHW   YHW   YH

Even though the name IEOA (Ιεωα) is rare, it is found in a few papyri from this time[248]. For example in *The Gospel of the Egyptians*[249] the following sentence is written: «O glorious name, really truly, o existing aeon, ιἐἑΟUÔA (more exactly ιιιεεεεηηηηοοοουυυυωωωωααααα), his unrevealable name is inscribed on the tablet (...) the Father of the light of everything, he who came forth from the silence (...) he whose name is an invisible symbol. A hidden, invisible mystery came forth ιἐΟUἐAΟ (each vowel is repeated 22 times).» These vocalizations are interesting, because they are previous to the punctuation of the Hebrew text, and they prove that the vocalization Iaô was not completely universal. Moreover, Eusebius (265-340), a Greek writer, well versed in the Bible, wrote in his *Praeparatio Evangelica XI:6,36-37*: «The name (of God) which a person is not allowed to pronounce, has four letters in Hebrew and seven vowels (Iéêouôa?) in Greek.»[250]

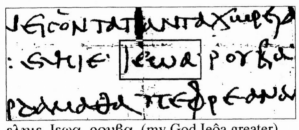

ελημε Ιεωα ρουβα (my God Ieôa greater)

Unfortunately, this knowledge which was conserved for a time in a few esoteric circles, soon became incomprehensible because of being mixed with ever increasing extra-biblical influences. Additionally, rabbinical Hebrew replaced biblical Hebrew among religious leaders while most of the people started to speak Aramaic and in time, Arabic. The Jewish aristocracy preferred for its part the use of Greek[251].

Around the fourth century, Greek itself was supplanted by Latin. Thus Jerome began (382) his new Latin translation of the Bible, *The Vulgate* which officially replaced the Old Latin (Vetus Latina), a Latin translation of the second century. This famous translator gave some worthwhile information in his commentary on Psalm 8:2: «The name of the Lord in Hebrew has four letters, Yod He Waw He, which is the proper name of God which some people through ignorance, write Π I Π I (instead of הוהי) in Greek and which can be pronounced Yaho[252].»

These remarks of Jerome confirm that at this time the complete disappearance of God's name was "well underway". Moreover, Jerome wrote in his prologue of the books of Samuel and Kings (*Prologus Galeatus*): «And we find the name of God, the Tetragram, in certain Greek volumes even to this day expressed in ancient letters.»

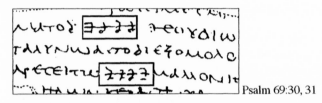
Psalm 69:30, 31

With regard to Tetragrams written in paleo-Hebrew, the disappearance was faster than those written in standard Hebrew. The whimsical style of this copy dated around 300 CE, which is a part of a LXX revised by Symmachus[253] confirms that the copyists of that time had a total incomprehension of the reading of the divine name. The Samaritans still used the paleo-Hebrew, but their writing moved away from its original shape as one can see in this inscription (below)[254] dated third century CE.

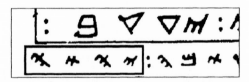

But, contrary to Christian translators, Jewish copyists carried on the use of writing the Name in paleo-Hebrew until 250 CE (then in modern Hebrew within the Greek text.) A little later, Eusebius and then Jerome would point out that the Jews used again modern Hebrew to write the Name, and that regrettably these letters (הוהי) were confused with Greek characters of similar shape (Π I Π I), as one can observe in many hexaplar (six columns) copies[255].

James of Edesse, in about the seventh century, still observed this curious phenomenon of writing the Name Π I Π I (for יהוה). One can see the use of 'modern' Hebrew to write the Name in this Ambrosian manuscript[256] of the ninth century CE.

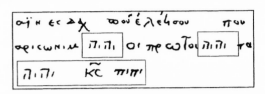

As one can imagine, these rapid changes would also have an impact on the LXX of Jewish origin in which God's name in Hebrew occured. The Christian copyists, in copying out these manuscripts, would first transform these names (very often יהוה became Π I Π I), then replace them by the Greek abbreviation KC. There was also a case where the copyist actually read the word Π I Π I in Greek, or Pypy. For example, Bishop Paul of Tella, in his Syriac translation of the Septuagint, around 616, used this strange name Pypy refer to God[257]. In another comment believed to be by Evagrius Ponticus (345-399), we find the following remark: «The Tetragram, which is ineffable, was written in Hebrew: Ioth, e, ouau, e, that is to say, πιπι the God![258]» Strangely enough, he said that the name of the Lord is: ioth, e, ouab, eth, with the Hebrew letter "s" (called shin) in the middle. What did he mean exactly, since the Name of Jesus in Hebrew is different (יהושע instead of יהשוה)? Maybe, he meant that the name 'Jesus' is pronounced Jehoshuah (or Jehoshua') in Hebrew[259]. In the LXX of Aquila the name Jesus is written Iesoua (Iησουα in Dt 1:38), so according to Evagrius' reasoning the Tetragram would have been pronounced Ieoua.

WAS THE TETRAGRAM PRONOUNCED YAHO?

Regarding pronunciation, it is interesting to note that Eusebius quoted a writer of great antiquity (before 1200 BCE?) called Sanchuniathon who spoke about the Jews in chapter four of his work entitled *Phoenician History*. Philo of Byblos translated this work into Greek, at the beginning of our era, and Porphyry (234-305) was familiar with it. Sanchuniathon maintened that he got his information from Ieroubal the priest of IÉÜÔ (Ιευω)[260], that is Jerubbaal (-1300?-1199) found in Juges 7:1. This last vocalization could indeed be a vestige of the pronunciation of the Tetragram, since many Hebrew names lost the final 'a' in Greek transcriptions (e.g. Noa̲h̲ which became Noé, Yéshua' which became Ièsous, etc.) In addition, the Hebrew name Yehouah could have become IÉÜÔ in Greek. This testimony, considered by Eusebius as valid (although he made no link with the divine name, because the accepted pronunciation in his time was Iaô as proven by his remarks in his book *Evangelical Demonstration*), is interesting in view of its antiquity.

☞   Numerous linguists postulate that, even though this name was pronounced Yehouah in the first century, this pronunciation in fact would result from an "archaic" Yahowah or Yahwoh with a classic fall (because of the stressed accent) of the initial vowel, so the first syllable Ya- became Ye-. Now, although change is witnessed in numerous names (although the influence of the Aramaic language on the Hebrew could also explain this modification), there is no trace of this phenomenon for the divine name. For example, the "modern" names Zekaryah, Nethanyah, Sedôm, etc., in "ancient times" would have been pronounced Zakaryah, Nathanyah, Saduma, etc., because the Septuagint kept the old forms with their initial vowel (Zakaria, Nathania, Sodoma, etc.), thus retaining numerous traces of this process which took place during third century before our era[261].

✄   If, according to the hypothesis of the previously mentioned linguists, theophoric names were still pronounced Yaho- (in Hebrew) at the beginning of third century BCE, the translators of the LXX should have kept these names as Iaô-. Now, among the thousands of theophoric names in the Greek (or Hebraic) Bible, none remained as Iaô- or even simply as Ia-. Furthermore, the only exception proposed is the name Jason of Aramaic origin (Ia-sôn; Ac 17:7), the likely equivalent of the Hebrew name Jesus (Yé-shua). So, linguistic laws cannot be used to explain why the Septuagint did not retain any trace of this term Iaô-, which should nevertheless have been very common if the Name had been Yahwoh. Additionally, if the Name had been Yahwoh, the "archaic" pronunciation of the usual name Yôtam (which is found 25 times in the Hebrew Bible) might logically have been Yawtam (Yahwoh being likely to be abbreviated into Yaw-). Unfortunately, its Greek transcription is never Iaôtam (like Nékaô instead of Nekô) or Iautam (like Nabau instead of Nabû), but always Iôatam. In a same manner the transcription of the name Yôqîm is Iôakim (1Ch 4:22), the name Yôah is transcribed Iôaa (1Ch 26:4), the name Yûkal is transcribed Iôakal (Jr 38:1), etc. Thus, according to the Septuagint the "archaic" pronunciation of the name Yô was Iôa, not Iaô or Iau. Furthermore, the name John is written YHWHNN in Hebrew, making the first part of the name, YHWH, very similar to the Tetragram YHWH. If the name Yehowah is rendered as Iaô it would be logical to render the name Yehoha-nan similarly as Iaô-nan, but that is not the case.

A second explanation proposed was that: there was a transformation of the name Iaô for theological reasons (the protection of God's name). This second assertion, which is based on accepted fact, is also refutable. Actually, if the Tetragram was pronounced Yahwoh (the form Yahowah is absurd, because it means in Hebrew 'Yah [is] howah', that is to say 'disaster'), the complete name (which would be surprising) would have been integrated at the beginning of theophoric names, and so these names with Yaho- would have become Iô- (the form noted in the LXX with only rare exceptions such as Ié-zikar, Ié-zébouth [2 K 12:21]; Iè-soué [1Ch 7:27]; -iarib [1Ch 24:7]). This transformation would be illogical, since when endings of -yahû were modified, both -ia and -iou are used; Now the transformation Iaô- into Iô- should have been unanimous (which is difficult to believe since even when the Christian copyists exchanged the divine name for the title 'Lord' some preferred the title 'God') and in disagreement with the previous choice of -ia for the ending of theophoric names (the theological choice of

ia- was the most logical because it kept the short form (Yah) of
the divine name).   ✂

The most reasonable explanation is to assume that the
Greek term Iô- simply results from the Hebrew Y(eh)o-.

From Jerome to the Masoretes

The process that led to not pronouncing the Tetragram would lead to new ideas. In the Christian world, as "demonstrated" by the writer Dionysus the Pseudo-Areopagite in his book entitled *The Divine Names*, written around 540, «it is impossible for man to name God». In the Jewish world, its pronunciation had become so uncertain that many began to believe that it would once again be revealed in the messianic time of the world to come. On the other hand, other Jews imagined that since it had be lost, only those who knew it could benefit from a specific protective power still linked with the exact pronunciation of this Name (*Pessikta Rabbati ch. 22 fol. 114b*). This kind of belief in time generated a powerful trend towards biblical esotericism and cabalistic speculations about the Name.

In consulting any works of this time (5th-6th century) one notices that, nevertheless, there were still some pockets of resistance. For example, the name Iaô (Iαω) is still mentioned in some copies of the Septuagint[262] in reference to theophoric names, and in some Apocryphal Christian writings[263] which apply it to Jesus (*Book of the Resurrection of Bartholomew 6:1*).

Some authors, such as Severi of Antioch (465-538), used the form IÔA

Ω΄σαινεὶ δ᾿ ιπλασια ζόμϑνος, ὁ Θεὸς ὁ Θεός, Ι᾿ωά
ᾧ κ᾿ Ε᾿λά, παρ Ε᾿βραίοις ὁ Θεὸς ὀνομά ζεῖ, ἴν.
ἐκ τὐτυ μάθης, Α᾿γιον ἁγίων ἐῇ τὸ ἔτος, κᾳ-ϑὸ

(Iωα) in a series of comments[264] on chapter eight of John's gospel (Jn 8:58), pointing out that it was God's name in Hebrew. Another book (*Eulogy of John the Baptist 129:30*) alluded to the name IÔA written in Greek *iota, omega, alpha*. In the codex[265] Coislinianus dated sixth century, several theophoric names are explained owing to the Greek word *aoratos* (αορατος) meaning 'invisible' and read IÔA. The word *aoratos* (found in the LXX in Genesis 1:2), or *arretos* (αρρητος) meaning 'unspeakable', is equivalent to the Latin word 'ineffable'.

| IOA | "invisible" | (Codex Coislinianus, 6th century CE) |

In commenting on a work of Severi of Antioch, the famous scholar James of Edesse (633-708) made clear around 675 in a technical comment, that the copyists of the Septuagint (of his time) were divided over whether to write the divine name Adonay, to keep it within the Greek text in the form Π Ι Π Ι (corresponding in fact to the Hebrew name YHYH as he mentioned), or to translate it as Kurios and write it in the margin of the manuscript[266]. The erudite Photius (815?-897) explained around 870, in his letter N°162 to Amphiloc[267], that the Tetragram was written with four evanescent letters called in Hebrew iôth, alph, ouauth, èth, and that this name was pronounced Aïa by the Jews but Iabe (Ιαβε) by the Samaritans.

These quotations are however exceptional, because the greater majority tended towards the ineffability of God's name. Isidore of Sevilla for example (560-636), knew God's ten names (El, Eloim, Eloe, Sabaoth, Elion, Eie, Adonai, Ia, Tetragram, Saddai)[268] owing to Jerome's letter number 25, but he thought that the unspeakable Tetragram resulted from the double name Iala. Similarly, Albinus Flaccus Alcuini (735-804), a famous translator of the Bible into Latin, specified that although God's name was written Jod He Vau Heth, it was read Domini (Lord in Latin), because this name was ineffable[269].

All of these remarks are from scholars who had some notions of Hebrew, but they do not reflect the general knowledge of the readers of the Bible, who did not know, for the immense majority, that God had a name. If the Name had disappeared from the Bible, with the exception of the Hebraic text, one might suspect its presence due to Hebraic theophoric names, but the very pronunciation of Hebrew itself had become varied in the Jewish world and therefore incoherent.

☞   In order to fix the pronunciation of vowels around 400 CE, Nestorian Syriac[270] began to punctuate their texts. Probably owing to this influence, a group of Jews called the Masoretes, around 500 CE, decided to punctuate the Hebrew text in order to keep the authentic pronunciation and cantillation[271]. In the beginning, only questionable words received a specific pointing, that is they indicated by a group of points which vowel was to be pronounced; but in time, towards the ninth century, the entire text was handled this way[272]. It is interesting to note that this complex system grew in stages, with first the Palestinian system then the Babylonian and finally the Tiberian, which prevailed overall[273]. The main purpose of the Masoretes was to protect the original writing and spelling of the Hebrew text of the Bible. They tried to rediscover a reliable archetype by referring only to trustworthy manuscripts and also by relying on their memory, which was phenomenal[274]. The final result of these works commands admiration today, because in spite of an impressive sum of knowledge accumulated since, no one has done better. The only improvement has been to clarify some of their 'errors'.

It is probable that the Masoretes did not know the causes of the variations they observed in the Bible, however they noted them scrupulously. For example it is interesting that 90% of their remarks are about the 'mothers of reading' (matres lectionis)[275]. This fact proves that they misunderstood the exact role of these letters, which may be explained by several factors. Firstly, their mother tongue was Aramaic, shown by the Masorah (marginal notes) written in this tongue. Secondly they were strongly influenced by Arabic rules of grammar of their time, Arabic being a sister tongue. Thirdly they ignored the fact that the biblical text had been partly vocalized long before, owing to the *matres lectionis* (otherwise reading would have been impossible). Consequently, the Masoretes vocalized the biblical text a second time. It is interesting to note that the old Babylonian system of punctuation (around 700 CE) used six vowel signs and some of these represent Hebrew letters. For example, the vowel *æ* is a small aïn, the vowel *u* a simplified waw, the vowel *i* a simplified yod and the vowel *a* is considered a part of the letter aleph[276]. (Mandaic also developed a full system of vowel-writing but in a more rudimentary way).

THE MASORETES VOCALIZE THE TETRAGRAM

As seen in the Appendix A, the Hebraic Bible possesses two systems of vocalization. A system of *matres lectionis*, the oldest, and the system of vowel-points invented by the Masoretes. Very often these two systems overlap. In spite of the rigor of the Masoretic system, the mixed system remains ambiguous, because it is difficult to know if these particular consonants are used as vowels (matres lectionis) or remain true consonants.

✂ For example, the word ‘WN (עָוֹן; Ps 51:7), could be read ‘aON, but it should be read ‘aWoN (עָווֹן; Ps 59:5). In the same manner, the well known name YŚR’L (יִשְׂרָאֵל) should be read YiSRa’éL in the mixed system and not ISRa’éL. Certainly, these variations are slight, and it is not really important to know the exact reading, for example, of the name: PuWWaH (Gn 46:13), PuWaH (Nb 26:23), PU’aH (Jg 10:1), or to choose between PIHU and PIW (Ex 4:15), etc. However, these ambiguities of reading often concern theophoric names, and the choice of reading either Yi-, I- or Ye- is not always evident[277]. ✂

Because of the way this system worked, the remark of the Talmud forbidding the pronunciation of the Tetragram according to its letters, could no longer be understood. Furthermore, the Masoretes read the Name by its usual substitute: Adonay. However, they encountered an unexpected difficulty when it became necessary to point this word. In the beginning, as this *qere* was well known, only the Tetragram in the expression Adonay YHWH was pointed with the vowels of the word Èlohim, to avoid the repetition Adonay Adonay. So, the expression ’aDoNaY YéHoWiH was read ’aDoNaY ’èLoHiM, and not, of course, Adonay Yèhowih. However, to prevent the belief that these vowels were the real vowels of the Name, the Masoretes finally pointed all the tetragrams. Because the vowels of ’aDoNaY (אֲדֹנָי) are *a*, *o*, *a*, the Name should have been pointed YaHoWaH (יֲהֹוָה); but one never encounters this form, except in few ancient Babylonian codices (manuscript $B15_1$ of Cambridge University and manuscript T-S A 39.11 dated 953)[278]. Note that the Babylonian vocalization is slightly different from the Palestinian vocalization, but it might have influenced some copyists of the Arabic Bible made around 960 CE by the famous Karaite commentator Yefet ben Eli (920-1010), since the name Yahwah (or Yahuwah) is found a few times in this Bible[279].

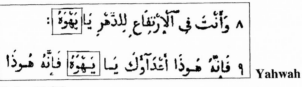

Psalm 92:8,9 — **Yahwah**

Yâh Huwa

(manuscript dated 10th century CE) [280]

Some serious works put forward a grammatical reason to justify the change of the first vowel *a* into *e*. This explanation is illogical for three reasons[281]. First, in the case of the word YèHoWiH (יֱהֹוִה), read Èlohim, one can verify in many codices that the vowel *è* of this word was not modified into *e* to give the form YeHoWiH (יְהֹוִה). Secondly, when the Masoretes indicate that a word to be read (*qere*) is different from the written word (*kethib*), it is to show that this word is indeed different, and that there is no link between the two words. Thirdly, before the twelfth century, the Tetragram was not pointed *e, o, a*, but only *e, a*[282], and sometimes with even only one final *a*, which would exclude grammatical reasons, because it becomes impossible to explain the disappearance of the vowel *o* in this way.

THE ORIGIN OF THE DIVINE QERE

The reason for this "anomaly" is nevertheless very simple. If the Tetragram had really been pointed with the vowels of the word Adonay, that is YaHoWaH, this form would have presented a crippling inconvenience for reading. Indeed, if a reader inadvertently read the vowels of this word with its consonants, which was entirely possible, this reader would commit blasphemy, because the word HoWaH in the Bible (Is 47:11; Ezk 7:26) means 'disaster', and so the expression YaHoWaH read literally means 'YaH [is] disas-'. So, to avoid this kind of error, the Masoretes wisely chose another *qere*. Since they designated this name by its Aramaic expression *SHeMa'* (שְׁמָא), meaning simply 'The Name'[283] (an expression which the Samaritans use even today to read the Name[284]), they simply pointed the Tetragram with the vowels *e, a* of the word *SheMa'*, obtaining the form YeHWaH, to indicate that the Name should be read Adonay, and not Èlohim.

✄   It is interesting to note that a homonym of the word disaster (HoWaH הֹוָה), meaning 'coming to be', was also modified to avoid a blasphemous misinterpretation. So, the expression YeHoWaH HoWaH in Exodus 9:3, meaning 'Yehowah coming to be', was modified into YeHoWaH HOYaH (יְהֹוָה הֹוָיָה). ✄

In the Targum of Ruth[285] seen below the Tetragram is pointed YeHWaH in the Hebrew text, and YeYa in the Aramaic text. However this form of pointing was never stable as one can verify in many codices from this epoch.

(YeHWaH   YeYa)

Later, a change becomes noticeable in the *qeres* of the divine name. A mutual influence of the two *qeres* YeHWaH and YèHoWiH is evident , because after the twelfth century, the two other forms YeHoWaH and YeHWiH also appear. Thus, there would be a gradual standardization, from the twelfth century to the fifteenth century of the two forms YeHoWaH and YèHoWiH in Jewish Bibles, forms kept by Rudolf Kittel (BHK) in his early Biblia Hebraica. On the other hand, later scholarly editions (BHS) would return to the older forms YeHWaH and YeHWiH.

☞   Thus, the current form YeHoWaH, which one finds in Jewish Bibles, is the product of a long history. What is more, this complex process took place without the knowledge of the protagonists. One can suppose that if God really attaches importance to his name, all these coincidences were not necessarily accidental. In the greatest of paradoxes, the system of the *qere/ kethib* which was supposed to protect God's name really did protect it, except for this 'amusing' detail; the Name was coded by its own vowels, which has to be the epitome of coding. Consequently, in the debate with those that laugh at the 'naive' reading Yehowah, perhaps the naives are not the ones we might think.

This practice of the *qere/ kethib*, which consists of pronouncing one word in place of another, was used at first as a protection against idolatry. For example, when God asked in Hoshea 2:16 to stop using the word Baal ('owner') as a title for him, it was doubtless to help the Israelites to distance themselves from Baal worship. However, they even applied this command to proper names. For example, Eshbaal (1Ch 8:33) became Ishbosheth (2S 2:8), and Jerubbaal (Jg 6:32) became Jerubbesheth (2S 11:21). So, the word Baal (owner) was replaced by the word Boshet ('shame'). This system had the serious drawback of modifying the biblical text, so the system of the *qere/ kethib* was invented to note the places where the word written Baal would in fact be pronounced Boshet.

The Masoretes kept this old tradition by indicating next to the written word the vowels of the word to be read. For example, the god Molok (Ac 7:43) was written MLK in the Hebraic Bible, so the Masoretes punctuated this word with the vowels *o, è* of the word BoŠèT to indicate that MLK should be read Boshèt, or 'shame'. Thus, one obtains, in the text, the hybrid form MoLèK (1K 11:7) which the Septuagint vocalized Molok. Many modern Bibles, however produced by translators who did not know of this complex system, transcribe it simply Molèk, actually mixing the vowels *o, è* of the word to be read Boshèt with the consonants MLK of the written word. Thus, to be unaware that this system had been conceived at first to protect the exclusivity of the Name, really is 'a shame'.

From the Masoretes to Maimonides

This period seems particularly rich for the revival of the Bible in the East, since numerous codices were published. The point of departure for this publishing seems to be the fortuitous discovery of very old scrolls, near Jericho[286], about the year 800. After this date several high quality codices appear[287]. As for the divine name in the Hebraic Bible, copyists vacillated for a long time before standardizing the various *qeres*.

		QERE	
DATE	CODEX	ADONAY	ÈLOHIM
1008	Leningrad B19a[288]	יְהוָֹה (e, ,a)	יֱהוִֹה (e, ,i)
930	Aleppo[289]	יְהוָה (e, ,a)	יֱהוִֹה (e,o,i)
	Palatini[290]	יְהוָה (, ,a)	יֱהוִֹה (è,o,i)
900 <	(Geniza)[291] **	יְהוָה (e, ,a)	יֱהוִֹה (e, ,i)
1105	Reuchlianus[292]	יְהוָה (e, ,a)	יֱהוִֹה (è, ,i)
916	Petrograd[293] **	יהוה (, ,)	יֱהוִֹה (è,o,i)
	Urbinati 2[294]	יְהוָה (, ,a)	יְהוִֹה (, ,i)
950	Or.4445	יְהוָה (e, ,a)	יֱהוִֹה (e, ,i)
1286	Paris Hébreu 1	יְהוָה (e, ,a)	יֱהוִֹה (è,o,i)
900?	Berlin[295]	יְהוָה (, ,a)	יהוֹה (, ,)

** (partial Babylonian vocalization)

At same time, with the works of Saadia Gaon (892-942) a parsing of the text appeared which would be continued by numerous grammarians[296]. During this same period in the West, the distribution of the Bible saw a considerable acceleration, at the instigation of Charlemagne who asked to promote the distribution of the Bible text in all his realm. By a surprising coincidence, this also took place around the year 800, and to fulfill his request, the Vulgate revised by Alcuin was preferred to the Old Latin (Vetus Latina).

This complex system of multiple *qeres* produced numerous errors within the same codex. For example, in the codex B19a, which is considered by specialists to be one of the best copies, there are seven different pointings of the Tetragram. The most frequent error is the transformation of the vowels *e, a* of the *qere* into *e, o, a*[297], or the vowels *e, i* into *e, o, i*[298].

QERE	ADONAY	ÈLOHIM	
usual	יְהוָה (e, ,a)	יְהוִה (e, ,i)	
Gn 3:14	יְהֹוָה (e,o,a)	יֱהוִה (è, ,i)	Gn 15:2, 8
Ps 144:15	יַהוָה (a, ,a)	יְהֹוִה (e,o,i)	1K 2:26
		יֱהֹוִה (è,o,i)	Jg 16:28

The situation is identical for other codices. The most frequent error is the transformation *e, a* into *e, o, a*, thus the changing of the form YeHWaH into YeHoWaH, which one finds in the Aleppo codex (Ezk 3:13; etc.) and in the Or4445 codex (Ex 16:7; 40:29; etc.) These errors are very old and can be observed on reproductions of biblical fragments[299] dated between 700 and 900. Something that doubtless facilitated this kind of error, in spite of the scrupulous attention of the copyists, was the presence of a sign of cantillation, the *rebia*, which was very difficult to differentiate from the point representing the vowel *o*. So, from the twelfth to the fifteenth century CE the *qere* *e, a* (kept by the present BHS) changed into *e, o, a* (kept by the former BHK) which would become the standard *qere* in Jewish Bibles.

IN THE MUSLIM WORLD

At the beginning of the tenth century the Hebrew Bible was translated (and transliterated) into Arabic by some Karaites[300], mostly living in Basora (Irak), who used the Arabic *matres lectionis* (alif = a, ya' = i, waw = u) to vocalize the entire biblical text[301]. However, because of the lack of *shewa* (e) the name Yehwah was punctuated Yahwah, which is found in some modern Arabic Bibles. It is interesting to note that in certain Babylonian manuscripts of this time, the divine name was also punctuated Yahowah, which became Yahuwah (read as Yâ Huwa 'O He' in Arabic). This later vocalization may have influenced several imams, such as Abu-l-Qâsim-al-Junayd (?-910) or Faḫr ad-Din Râzî (1149-1209), who, knowing the 99 beautiful names of God, explained that the supreme Name (*ism-al-a'ẓam*) of God was Yâ Huwa not Allâh[302]. (Yahwah and Yahuwah are found in modern Arabic Bibles)[303].

In the Christian World

This sudden revival of the work of edition and distribution of the Bible would be at the origin of a chain reaction which would finally end in the revival of the Name. Indeed, in order to understand the Bible better, the nobility and clergy would value more and more annotations (or glosses) on Jewish history and Hebraic philology. Anselm of Laon (1050-1117) systemized the use of these biblical glosses. In time, this plentiful accumulation of notes was compiled (in 1170) by Petrus Comestor (1100?-1179) in his famous work entitled *Historia Scholastica*. During this period, dictionaries and concordances to make the study of the Bible easy also appeared. In spite of its quality, this intellectual search did not reach the people. However, a rich trader of Lyons, Peter Waldo (1140-1205?) who had been touched by the evangelic message decided, from 1170 on, to preach this message to the people. To do this, he asked two priests to translate the Latin Bible into the common language, and immediately began preaching with these rudimentary copies. Pope Alexander III (1105?-1181) had approved his initiative in 1179, but not long after (1184) his disciples were excommunicated. This movement apparently enjoyed a rapid expansion, so the clergy organized mendicant orders, like the Dominicans and Franciscans, with the aim of suppressing this heresy. This counter-attack required however a plentiful production of Bibles with a text that was unanimously approved so the services of the academics were called upon.

To improve the study of the text, an English academic, Stephen Langton (1150-1228), during his time at the University of Paris, standardized the use of chapters[304] (in 1203). This Bible became a reference. It is interesting to note that at the end of the book of Revelation, a glossary of Hebrew words (Aaz apprehendens) and an interpretation of Hebrew names are found. However, the translation of certain theophoric names began to create a predicament. For example, the name Ioel is translated 'The Lord (Dominus in Latin) is God', Adonia 'The Lord is Lord', Elia 'The God is Lord', etc. On the other hand, the word Alleluia is sometimes translated by 'Praise Ia'. This dilemma of translation between 'The Lord' and 'Ia' was in fact only the "tip of the iceberg" of problems in understanding the Hebrew text.

In order to better understand the Hebrew language, Christian scholars began an exchange with Hebrew scholars although not without disagreement[305]. Additionally, a small number of Jews had converted to Catholicism and they greatly improved the knowledge of Hebrew and above all of divine Names. For example, Petrus Alfunsus (1062-1110?), called Moses Sephardi before his baptism (1106), was probably the first one to connect the 'ineffable' trinity with the 'ineffable' Tetragram. Thus, he clarified the meaning of several names like:

Eloha (god), Elohai (my gods/ my God), Elohi (my god), Elohim (gods/ God), Adon (lord), Adoni (my lord), Adonai (my lords/ my Lord), but he said that the Tetragram was secret, written with only three letters (י, ה, ו) and four figures (יהוה, יה, הו, וה) or three geometrical figures in one[306]. Petrus Blesensis (1135-

1204), a Christian writer, completed these remarks. He said, in his short treatise against the Jews[307], and to prove the trinity, that the name of God was made up of four figures: 'Io, he, vaf, he' God's name, 'Io, he', another name of God (Iah) and two altered names of God: 'he, vaf' (Hu) and 'vaf, he' (?). The Name thus began to reappear in the Christian world.

IN THE JEWISH WORLD

Within the Jewish world drastic changes occurred as well. From the eleventh to the twelfth century the expansion of Christendom with its crusades and the spreading of Islam generated pressure from outside, but the greatest destabilization came from Jewish circles themselves. Philosophy, Gnosticism and mystical even astrological beliefs became increasingly influential mainly due to the third century work, entitled *Sepher Yetsirah* (Book of Forming) which speculated on the letters of the divine names. In order to contend with such influences Maimonides (1138-1204, Rabbi Moses ben Maïmon) a Jewish scholar and famous talmudist, put forward a whole new definition of Judaism. His reasoning centered on the Name of God, the Tetragram, which was explained in his book entitled *The Guide of the Perplexed*[308], written in 1190. There he exposed the following powerful reasoning: the God of the philosophers did not require worship only polite acknowledgement of his existence, since it would be impossible to establish relations with a nameless God (Elohim). Then he proved that the Tetragram YHWH is the personal name of God, that is to say the name distinctly read (Shem hamephorash), which is different from all the other names such as: Adonay, Shadday, Elohim (which are only divine titles having an etymology), because the Tetragram has no etymology.

☞   However, Maimonides knew well the problem of the pronunciation, since Jewish tradition stated that it had been lost. On the other hand, he also knew that some Jews believed in the almost magical influence of the letters or the precise pronunciation of divine names, but he warned his readers against such practices as being pure invention or foolishness. The remarkable aspect of his argumentation lies in the fact that he managed to avoid controversy on such a sensitive subject. He asserted that in fact it was only true worship which had been lost, and not the authentic pronunciation of the Tetragram, since this was still possible according to its letters. To support this basic idea (true worship is more important than correct pronunciation), he quoted *Sotah 38a* to prove that the name is the essence of God and that is the reason it should not be misused, then he quoted Zechariah 14:9 to prove the oneness of this name, also *Sifre Numbers 6:23-27* to show that the priests were obliged to bless by this name only.

Then, to prove that the pronunciation of the Name did not pose any problem in the past, and that it had no magical aspect, he quoted *Qiddušin 71a*, which said that this name was passed on by certain rabbis to their sons. Also, according to *Yoma 39b*, this pronunciation was widely used before the priesthood of Simon the Just, which proved the insignificance of a magical concept, because at this time the Name was used for its spiritual not supernatural aspect. Maimonides insisted on the fact that what was necessary to find was the spirituality connected to this Name, and not the exact pronunciation. In order to demonstrate this important idea of understanding the sense and not the sound conveyed by this name, he quoted a relevant example. Exodus 6:3 indicates that before Moses the Name was not known. Naturally this refers to the exact meaning of the Name, and not its pronunciation, because it would be unreasonable to believe that a correct pronunciation would have suddenly been able to incite the Israelites to action, unless the pronunciation had magical power, a supposition disproved by subsequent events. To conclude his demonstration, Maimonides quoted Exodus 3:14 to show that the expression *èhyèh ashèr èhyèh*, which can be translated as 'I shall be who I shall be', was above all a spiritual teaching. Because the Tetragram had no "linguistic etymology", this link with the verb 'to be (haya)' expressed above all a "religious etymology", that is a teaching about God, who can be defined as «the Being who is the being» or «the necessary being». It is interesting to observe that Judah Halevi (1075-1141), another Jewish scholar, put forward almost the same arguments in his book *The Kuzari*[309] published some years before, in 1140. He wrote that the main difference between the God of Abraham and the God of Aristotle was the Tetragram (*Kuzari IV:16*). He proved also that this name was the personal name of God (idem IV:1) and that it meant "He will be with you". To show once again that it was the meaning of this name which was important and not the pronunciation, he quoted Exodus 5:2 where Pharaoh asked to know the Name: not the pronunciation which he used, but the authority of this Name (idem IV:15). He pointed out that the letters of the Tetragram have the remarkable property of being *matres lectionis*, that is the vowels associated with other consonants, much as the spirit is associated with the body and makes it live (idem IV:3).

These two scholars gave convergent information which marked a turning point in the history of the Name. However, the expression "pronounced according to its letters" which Maimonides used is strictly exact only in Hebrew (vowel letters as pointed out by Judah Halevi). Joachim of Flora (Gioacchino da Fiore) gave a Greek transliteration of the Tetragram (I-E-U-E, or IEUE) in his work entitled *Expositio in Apocalypsim*[310], that he finished in 1195. He also used the expression «Adonay IEUE tetragramaton nomen» in another book entitled *Liber Figurarum*[311]. As seen in this illustration, Joachim of Flora (1130-1202) also gave the three other names: IE, EV, VE, which he associated with the Father, the Son and the Holy Spirit!

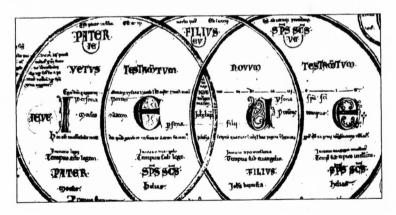

The vocalization of the Tetragram (IEUE) associated with the name of Jesus (EU) would soon be improved by Pope Innocent III (1160-1216) in one of his sermons[312] written around 1200. Indeed, he noticed that the Hebraic letters of the Tetragram Ioth, Eth, Vau (that is Y, H, W) were used as vowels, and that the name IESUS had exactly the same vowels I, E and U as the divine name. Like Joachim of Flora, he broke up the divine name IEUE into IE-EU-UE, which led him to suppose that the name IE-SUS contained God's name IE. He also drew a parallel between the name written IEVE, pronounced Adonai, and the name written IHS but pronounced IESUS. The link between these two names would afterwards play a determining role in the process of vocalization of the Tetragram.

In the years that followed, knowledge of the Hebraic language would progress considerably, involving notably the role of *matres lectionis*. For example, the famous scholar Roger Bacon (1214-1294) wrote in his Hebraic grammar[313] that in Hebrew there are six vowels "aleph, he, vav, heth, iod, ain" close to the usual Masoretic vowel-points. (The French erudite Fabre d'Olivet also explained in his Hebraic grammar the following equivalence: aleph = â, he = è, heth = é, waw = ô/ u, yod = î, aïn = wo.)[314] Moreover, Judah Halevi had already specified in his work that the yod (Y) served as vowel I, the waw (W) served as O, and that the he (H) and the aleph (') served as A. [It is interesting to note that the old Babylonian system of punctuation (around 700 CE) used six vowel signs and some of these represent Hebrew letters]. According to these rudimentary indications, one could already read the name YHWH "according to its letters", approximately as I-H-O-A [since the letter H is never used as a vowel within words; in that exceptional case the use of the letter aleph is preferred, as Ramoth (Jos 21:38) written Ra'moth (Dt 4:43), but most of the time this pointing was not necessary because the sound *a* was usual.] The name YH is pronounced according to its letters IA in Hebrew, IH in Latin and IE in Greek. Also, the name YHWDH is pronounced according to its letters IHUDA (Yehudah) in Hebrew, IHUDE (Jude) in Latin and IEUDE in Greek.

The book entitled *Ysagoge in Theologiam* (Introduction into Theologies) written around 1150, specified that in Hebrew the Tetragram is pointed with the vowels *e, a* (יְהוָה), but the place where the Name had been vocalized has regrettably disappeared in subsequent copies![315]

From Maimonides to Tyndale

During this period there were well qualified Hebrew scholars, and one of the most remarkable of the thirteenth century was no doubt Wilhelmi de la Mara[316] (?-1290). This writer lived in Paris where he wrote his main work *Biblical Glossary of the Hebrew and Greek Vocabulary*[317], between approximately 1260 and 1270, in which he explained grammar and pronunciation of the Hebraic language. One of his key innovations, which contributed to the improvement of the study of this language, was the establishment of an equivalence between the Latin alphabet and the Hebrew alphabet. For example, the Hebrew name Jehu is spelled in Hebrew Iod, he, vau, aleph, which is written in Latin I.h.v.a. He made numerous remarks concerning the pronunciation of Hebrew names. For example, he pointed out that the name Iesus of the Septuagint was the equivalent of the name Iosue of the Vulgate, but that this name was pronounced Iehossua' in Hebrew. He clarified that the letter vau could, as in Latin, serves either as a consonant (V), or as a vowel (U). Finally, concerning the tetragramaton (sic), he indicated that it was written in Hebrew Iod, he, vau, he, but was pronounced Adonay. Also, this unspeakable name was Semamphoras in Hebrew. At the same time, another scholar called Gerardus de Hoyo wrote in his work entitled *Book of the Three Comments*[318] that the ineffable Tetragram is written in Hebrew iod, he, vaf, he, and pronounced Adonai, but Ia in the word Allelu-ia.

Parallel to this knowledge of the language, Maimonides' work soon became an authority, among Christian scholars as well as Jewish scholars. Christian academics often referred to it in their controversies with Jewish theologians of the Law. The case of Raymond Martini (1220-1284) is a good example. This Spanish monk used the spelling Yohoua, for God's name, in his work *Pugio Fidei* (Dagger of Faith) published in 1278, as seen in the copy hereafter[319]. It is clear that this scholar who knew the Hebrew form (YeHoWaH) did not transcribe it Yehouah in

Latin as might be expected, but Yohoua. In his work, Raymond
Martini explained at length the reasons for his choice. He quoted
talmudic references given by R. Moseh Ben Maymon in his
Guide of the Perplexed, especially those of chapters 60-64 of
part I, which concern the Name. Thus, the Tetragram, the only
name of God according to Zekariah 14:9, was written in Hebrew
Iod He Vau He, and pronounced Adonai. This name was
indicated by the expression Shemhamephoras, which means "the
Name distinctly read" or "the Name read according to its
letters". However, a rabbi of second century, Abba Saul, had
forbidden the pronunciation of this name according to its letters.
This remark led Raymond Martin to deduce that the Name was
pronounced Y-H-U-A that is Yhoua or Yohoua. (At this time,
the unusual transcription Y rather than I is frequent [Elohym for
Elohim, Helye for Eli, etc.]. The letter H was also variable [Jesu,
Hiesu, Jhesu and Iehsu][320].)

Raymond Martini did not claim that this was the exact
pronunciation, but insisted on the necessity of using it[321],
quoting Isaiah 52:6, which said: «For that reason my people will
know my name.» (It is interesting to note that during this period

a standardization of the *qere* of the divine name occurred. The *qere* "e, a" (which are in fact the vowels of the Aramaic word Shema 'The Name' inserted for Adonay) became "e, o, a." On the other hand, the *qere* Elohim has either "e, i" or "è, o, i".)

Most of the academics who followed would not be interested themselves on the question of the pronunciation. For example, Arnaldus of Villanueva (1240-1311), a former student of Raymond Martini, would indeed be most interested in God's name, shown by his work entitled *Allocutio super Tetragramaton*[322] published in 1292, but his considerations on the pronunciation of the Name are more of cabalistic nature. Although at the beginning of his book Arnaldus of Villanueva explained, as did Raymond Martini, that the Tetragram should be used (he too quoted Isaiah 52:6), he added, quoting Isaiah 29:11, that the current impossibility for Jews to pronounce this name was prophesied since it was written in this passage: «Read this out loud, please, "and he has to say" : I am unable, for it is sealed up.» In the remainder of his account, he mixed the vocalism and symbolism of the letters, in order to make links between the name 'Jesus' and the Tetragram. Although he mentioned the equivalences of the consonants Y and V with their respective vowels I and U, he did not come to any conclusion on the pronunciation of the Tetragram but instead he linked its resemblance written IHVH, with the name of Jesus, written either IHS, or IHESVS. He then speculated on the place of these letters I, H, V within these names and on their respective symbolism in proving the Trinity. Interestingly, even though his demonstration was somewhat convoluted, it would assure (after Evagrius Ponticus and Pope Innocent III) the link between the two names IHVH and IHSV.

Soon after, another scholar, Porchetus de Salvaticis (?-1315), completed a book entitled *Porchetus' Victory Against the Ungodly Hebrews*[323], published in 1303. Like Raymond Martini, he used the spelling Yohouah (Ihouah in the edition of 1520), a vocalization which was in agreement with the theophoric names of his work (example: Yohoyaqim for Joaqim). He never used the spelling Yehouah.

ce·dedi te cloim: pharoni. Et
fic ifit'·sieur dictu eft·ps·lex
x)·g. Ego dixi telohym uos·Et
eft uocano regem mefflam no
mune fuo. Et qo eft nomen ei?
yohouab. ur yoo/he/uau·be·
nomen ei? sieur dictu eft ·exo:
xv·a·dominus uu pugne·yod
he/uau/he· nomen ipf. Idiou
oum eft ualde· qo fup̄·i tradui
one· inpereq beleq· habetur q·
one uur pugne· ero·xv·a·eft
deus fk̄ et benedictus·equitaf
fup equu rubeu. Et in tradicie
p̄muffa·in glofa·pfalmoṛ qua;

neduis tebalisṭa uu̇·uocant·
haberur̄·q̄ð ueap eft uecane mef
fuam neite·fuo/qo eft yohouab
ur̄yoð·he·uau·be· Et q̄ comin
uur pugne eft mefflas· Cuẏ·9·
nomen efi·yoð/he·uau/be·a·
ip̄ certifi·num eft mefflam et
dicun·Nemo eim pacpat eu;
uo·ifte gloriaffimo noie ap
apuato foli·fibi ut iapofteil
eft·€ Cum itaq; pfatus eques
fit deus fk̄ ebenedictus ut p̄n
cui efi· Et one yb̄e x̄p̄ fucnet
fias·uur fimul·deue·ut p̄ios
atharum eft·roote corpus fuu.

Like Raymond Martini, he quoted Rabi Mosse ben Maimon abundantly to justify his assertions on the Name. He repeated that the Tetragram, written Yod He Uau He, was the only name of God. He quoted verses of Jeremiah's book (Jr 23:5,6; 33:15,16) to point out that the Messiah had received God's name in his name, because, according to these verses, the name of the Messiah must mean 'YHWH is our righteousness'. He insisted on the fact that one had to mention God's name to be blessed (Ps 20:1,7; 79:6,9; Mi 5:4), and that this name could not have disappeared, because, according to the Bible «only the very name of the wicked ones will rot» (Pr 10:7). Finally, concerning pronunciation, he showed the absurdity of agreeing on one hand to pronounce the shortened name Iah in the expression Hallelujah and of refusing on the other hand to pronounce YHWH, since YH and YHWH are considered, each separately, to be God's name (Ps 68:4; 83:18); Thus why allow the pronunciation of one and not the other?

These relevant remarks were reserved for the small circle of the Christian and Jewish scholars in their debates. However, most of the population was in deep ignorance on this subject, and, to make matters worse, some erudite theologians taught their flocks that it was absurd to name God. For example, the famous theologian Thomas Gallus (?-1246), abbot of Verceil, asserted in many of his works on God's name, such as *De*

Divinis Nominibus published in 1242, that it was impossible for man to name God. The only hope was that in time the powerful arguments of the Hebrew scholars would eventually succeed, but this did not take into account two powerful factors, one Jewish and the other Christian, which would prevent the dissemination of this information about the Name.

The most subtle opposition came from Jews themselves. At this time, the divine name had become the object of extreme veneration for some. For example, Abraham ibn Ezra (1092-1167) wrote a book entitled the *Book of the Name*, published in 1155, favoring an almost mystic attitude to the Tetragram. This attitude, as well as other forms of esotericism, was at the origin of the work of Maimonides, who tried to introduce more rational behavior into the worship of God.

Contrary to what one might have think, the maimonidian argumentation, instead of diminishing mystic concepts, would stir them up by reaction to it. Indeed, scandalized that, according to Maimonides, the invocation of the Name could have only a spiritual and not a real effect, the Cabal movement, appeared in the South of France (Provence) which would try to demonstrate the power of invocation of the letters of the Name.

By a strange twist of irony, it was in fact R. Abraham Abulafia (1240-1291), one of the first commentators of the *Guide of the Perplexed*, who became an influential catalyst of the cabalistic point of view, introducing new esoterical elements which was exactly what Maimonides had contended[324].

THE CABAL

How did Abulafia achieve this incredible tour de force? First, he recognized that he was indebted to Maimonides for his powerful elucidations, then he declared his acceptance of the whole of Maimonides' views, except one: the knowledge of the Name. For example, he said «Effectively, I inform you that the true knowledge of the Name cannot be learnt, neither the *Sepher Yetsirah* (Book of Forming) alone, even if you know all the commentaries about it, nor the *Guide of the Perplexed*, even if you know all the commentaries about it. But only when these two kinds of knowledge, from these two books, are linked together.»[325] He declared afterward: «In the Name, my reason has found a ladder which allows it to ascend to steps of visions. And the whole set of the word is achieved in it by examination and experimentation. Unknown to philosophers, his name is the key to understanding.»[326] Continuing his mystical quest, Abulafia received a "disclosure from God" around 1280 which said to him: «*He is I and I am He*, it is forbidden to disclose this statement in a clearer way. But the secret of the corporal name is the Messiah of God.»[327]

So, cabalists developed a contradictory attitude toward the Name. They seemed to value the Tetragram, since they even called its vocalization "ardent desire" (Ḥéšèq in Hebrew), an acronym which served to code the three vowels "e, o, a" of the Tetragram (these vowels are called in Hebrew: Ḥolam [o], Šewa [e], Qamats [a], constituting the word ḤéŠèQ)[328]. However, it is interesting to note what Abulafia thought of this obvious pronunciation YeHoWaH. He wrote: «To the fools [the mass of uneducated people] it has been forbidden to pronounce this name, that is why they don't pronounce it according to its true name [but only in a roundabout way]. The persons in the know received the permission to pronounce it and great was their joy to know the way (procedures) to pronounce it correctly.» He concluded that it was for this purpose that God wanted his name to remain hidden to the public and be disclosed only to the initiated. Abraham Abulafia said (around 1280) that the genuine divine name is in fact AHUI (aleph, he, waw, yod) and that YHWH is the hidden name made of consonants of concealment![329] Around 1270, another cabalist, Jacob ben Jacob Cohen, developed a different idea, which ended up in more or less the same result. In fact, he asserted that God actually had 72 authentic names.

In time cabalists discovered endless new names, each one more authentic and more hidden than the other. They arrived at the surprising conclusion that the Name is Torah itself (The Christians had concluded that the Name is Jesus himself).

These searches led to the following conclusion: God had indeed a proper name which had many facets, reflecting all the other holy names, but none of them were his alone.

This outcome was exactly what Maimonides and also Judah Halevi had fought against. The effective result of all this complex learning was to discredit obvious pronunciations of the Name, such as Ihua (read according to its letters) or even better Yehowah, in the eyes of Hebraists.

THE INQUISITION

The second factor which worked against the spreading of the name came from Christian circles. The clergy, in order to neutralize the preaching of the Waldenses, asked for them to be banned. Pope Innocent III forbade the laity to preach (1199); then he forbade the translation of the Bible into the common language without his permission, and he demanded that all unauthorized Bibles be burnt. That was the beginning of the Inquisition, and it rapidly became dangerous even to own a single Bible[330].

In this animated context, the Name would naturally fall again in the domain of a few scholars. For example, a skillful talmudist, Abner de Burgos (1270-1340), called Alfonso of Valladolid after his conversion to Catholicism around 1330, wrote a book entitled *Display of Justice* (Mostrador de Justicia)[331], in which he often used, at least in the beginning, the name *yehabe* (sometimes also spelt *yahabe*, *yahaba* or *yaba*). This Tetragram vocalized *yehabe* (in Spanish *b* is pronounced as *v*) is more an attempt at translation of the name ('he will make to be' or 'he will constitute', *piel* form of the verb 'to be' in Hebrew), than a reading according to its letters.

☞   Subsequently, because of violent religious conflicts, exchanges among Christian and Jewish scholars disappeared. So, Nicholas of Lyra (1270-1349) was certainly one of the last important Hebrew Christians of this time. In his comments on the Bible (*Postillæ super Totam Bibliam*, between 1330 and 1340), those on Exodus 3:14 and Jeremiah 23:6 are interesting, because he made reference to Rashi and to Maimonides. He even made clear that the Latin expression 'I am who I am' (ego sum qui sum) should be corrected to read 'I shall be who I shall be' (ero qui ero) taking into account the Hebrew. Concerning the pronunciation of the Name, he contented himself with recalling the information given by Maimonides.

On the other hand, a famous talmudist, Pablo de Sancta Maria of Burgos (Paulus Burgensis, 1353-1435), converted to Catholicism in 1390, copied the Bible of Nicholas of Lyra adding his own comments to those already existing, including one concerning the pronunciation of the Name. After comments on Exodus 3:14, he indicated that the Tetragram was spelt Y.h.b.h (or maybe Y.h.v.h), and that this name was very close to the name of Ihesus, because these two names both had four letters, the first letter and the third one being the same (written p and v in the oldest manuscript[332], probably for y and v). He pointed out that the consonants y and v could serve as vowels (i and u), and that the Hebraic gutturals, that is the h final and the ayn, were unknown in the Latin language, which increased the resemblance between these two names. However, he did not vocalize either of these names in the Hebraic language. These specialists' remarks apparently confused certain copyists in the Latin language who did not know Hebrew. There are numerous variants in copies, because certain copyists wrote the name of Ihesus in the form of four Latin letters Iesu, to move closer to the name Ihvh; but, in that case, the previous remarks must left the reader perplexed as to the identification of the third letter! (What Pablo of Burgos meant, was simply that the Tetragram Y.h.b.h [יהוה] in Hebrew, is close to the name Ihesus [ישוע], because these two names "read according to their letters" are rather similar in their writing and their pronunciation, e.g. I.h.u.a and I.š.u.a', with the equivalence: Y = I, V = U, H final = ' = A.)

An erudite theologian, Cardinal Nicholas of Cusa (1401-1464), was fascinated by this subject on which he commented repeatedly in his sermons. In his personal library he possessed the work of Arnaldus of Villanueva entitled *Allocutio super Tetragramaton*, and dedicated his first sermon (on John 1:1) to explaining the links between God's name and the name of Jesus. For example, in this sermon entitled *In Principio Erat Verbum* (In the beginning was the Word), written around 1428, he explained, based on rabbi Moyses's works, the various names of God (Adonai, Jah, Sabaoth, Schaddai, etc.) and the meaning of the Tetragram, which he vocalized Iehoua[333]. In this sermon, he began to develop the idea that Jesus was the 'speakable' element (the Word) of the 'unspeakable (ineffable)' God. He explained in another sermon[334], written around 1440, that the name of Jesus means 'savior' is pronounced Ihesua in Hebrew, and this name 'Savior' is also the Word of God. He indicated that the unspeakable name is Ihehoua in Hebrew. In two other sermons[335], written in 1441, he pursued the connection between the unspeakable Greek Tetragram, spelt Iot, He, Vau, He, and the 'speakable' name of Ihesus which he often wrote Ihûs.

Then in a sermon[336] written in 1445, he explained in detail the grammatical reasons permitting a link between these two names. God's name is the Greek Tetragram which is spelt in Hebrew Ioth, He, Vau, He; these four letters serve as vowels, corresponding to I, E, O, A in Greek, because in this language there is no specific vowel for the sound OU (the letter U in Greek is pronounced as the French Ü). So, in Greek, the transcription IEOUA would be more exact and would better reflect the OU sound of the Hebrew name Ieoua, becoming in Latin Iehova or Ihehova, because the letter H is inaudible and the vowel U also serves as a consonant (V). He noted finally that the Hebraic form IESUA of the name 'Jesus' is distinguished from the divine name only by a holy letter "s" (*shin* in Hebrew) which is interpreted as the 'elocution' or the Word of God, also the salvation of God. He would continue this parallel, between God's name (Ieoua) and the name of Jesus (Iesoua) in yet another sermon[337].

However towards the end of his life he wrote several important works (*De Possest* in 1460, *Non Aliud* in 1462, etc.), to explain the purely symbolic character of God's name which had all names and so none in particular. Contrary to his books, his sermons were not widely diffused.

HUMANISM

Cultivated readers nevertheless began to take advantage of this important information. For example, Denys the Carthusian (Denys van Leeuwen, monk of Rickel, 1402-1471), who was friend of Nicholas of Cusa, was also a fervent reader of 'Rabbi Paulus'. Denys wrote, between 1452 and 1457 (the first edition of this book no doubt being lost), a commentary on the book of Exodus entitled *Enarrationes in Exodum*, where he explained that from Pablo of Burgos he knew God's name, vocalized Iehoua in following versions[338]. These authors simply used the link of pronunciation between the name of Jesus and the Tetragram. The Hebraic pronunciation of the name of Jesus being known (Iesoua in Latin), it became easy, by exchanging the letter s of this name for the letter h, to find the pronunciation Iehoua. Moreover, even those who were not Hebrew scholars could find this pronunciation with access to Aquila's translation. However, as the spelling of the name of Jesus varied (Iesu, Ihesu, Hiesu), these fluctuations also influenced the vocalization of the Tetragram. For example, Marsilio Ficino (1433-1499) indicated in his work entitled *Book of the Christian Religion*[339], published around 1474, that God's name was Hiehouahi and that this name expressed all the tenses of the verb 'to be'.

cet folus recte pnūciare fciebat nome illud dei propriū: qd
eft apud uos præ cæteris uenerādū.& quia quatuor folū litteris cóftat: & illis quidem uocalibus difficillime omnium
pronunciatur. fonat autem ferme in hunc modum.
¶ Hiehouahi.i. fuit:eft erit. Atq hæc maior hebreorū pars
opināt. Si ita é:cū nihil apud uos hoc noie fanctius habeat

☞   Thus towards the end of the fifteenth century, due to the works of several Christian humanists, there was a renewal of interest for the Hebrew language as well as God's name, found indirectly by means of the name of Jesus. However, once again, the influence of the Cabal[340] would slow down this progress. For example, Paulus de Heredia a Christian cabalist published a book entitled *Epistle of Secrets*[341] (1488) in which he explained that God's name is Yehauue because it means 'He will generate' in Hebrew (*piel* form of the verb 'to be').

> ſunt uerba diuerſa quæ unū oſtēdunt. Poſtꝗ
> aūt hoc tibi aperui animaduerte nomē ꝗtuor
> lꝛaꝫ put ſcriptio ē. & ſic ſcribiſ i hebraico
>   id eſt ⌐ychauuc¬ ipſū deū generātē ſignificaſ

Johannes Reuchlin (1455-1522), one of the founders of Hebraic and Greek studies in Europe, was also fascinated by the Cabal. In 1494, he published a book entitled *De Verbo Mirifico* (*The Wonderful Word*)[342], where he explained both the rules of pronunciation of the name of Jesus and the Tetragram, but also the symbolic links between these two names due to their letters. He explained in his book that the name Ihesu (a spelling certainly favored because of its Greek homologue IHΣOY) was in fact a deformation of the name Ihosue, and that therefore this name could be improved, because the final part had disappeared in Greek then Latin transcriptions. He remarked that this final part had sometimes been protected in the Vulgate, because the name Iesu was also spelt Iesue in Ezr 3:2 and in 1S 6:14 (this shape is also found in the Septuagint in 1Ch 7:27). Then he emphasized that this Greek transcription IESUE had the advantage of reintroducing the four vowels of the divine name (which implied that God's name must be read IEUE), but, the Latin transcription of the Tetragram being IHVH, to harmonize these two transcriptions he specified that the Greek letter E was the equivalent of the Latin H; so the Greek form IESUE would give the Latin form IHSVH, which made its link with the Latin form of the Tetragram IHVH more convincing. In following editions, this resemblance was perfected by clarifying the Hebraic forms of these names IHSVH (יהשוה) and IHVH (יהוה), which produced a result contrary to the expected effect. Indeed, serious hebraists could verify that this Hebraic form of the name of Jesus had never existed in the Hebrew Bible. Furthermore, in Hebrew, Jesus was not pronounced Iesue but, as seen, Iesoua (even the name ISVH (ישוה) in Genesis 46:17 is pronounced Iesoua not Isue in the Septuagint).

One can note some embarrassment in the biblical commentary of the Hebraist Jacques Lefèvre d'Étaples (1435-1536) in his translation of the book of Psalms in French, entitled *Quincuplex Psalterium* (Quintuple Psalms)[343] which appeared in 1509. Due to the remarks of Johannes Reuchlin, Jacques Lefèvre d'Étaples noted that it was easy to pronounce the Tetragram IHVH as it is written, that is I-he-u-he which gives the Latin form Ihevhe. He observed however that according to Reuchlin the Hebraic form of the name of Jesus was Ihesuha (I-he-su-ha), while it should have been Ihesuhe (I-he-su-he). Some years later, in 1514, when he published[344] sermons of the cardinal of Cusa, he used the form Iehova without comment.

Wanting to solve this tangle, one of the most brilliant scholars of this time, the Italian humanist Giovanni Pico della Mirandola (1463-1494), friend and former student of Marsilio Ficino, attacked this problem in his book entitled *Disputianum Adversus Astrologos* (Dispute against the Astrologers), which was published in 1496. Due to his vast knowledge he made brilliant links, which however proved to be rather daring. To prove the superiority of the Bible he tried to demonstrate that heathen religions were in fact plagiarisms of biblical religion. He asserted for example that the Roman god Jupiter was in fact an idolatrous imitation of the God of the Hebrews, and that even the etymology of this name Jupiter 'Ioue-pater' (Jove-father) was a fraudulent copy of it[345].

This link, daring because it was not defensible, simply resulted from a phonetic analogy made by Giovanni Pico della Mirandola. As Chateillon explained in his commentary[346] on Matthew 1:21, this pronunciation could easily be corrected as Ioua, much like the name Iosue could be improved to Iosua, and this new equivalence Iosua for the name of Jesus and Ioua for the divine name permitted the harmonization of all the data. The name Ioua was found within the name Iosua, the name 'Ioua-

'pater' could be deformed as Ju-piter, and finally Ioua, which contains four vowels, corresponded to the pronunciation "according to its letters" of the Hebrew name Y-H-W-H (that is I-H-U-A, with a mute H). This new pronunciation Ioua (or Jova, as in Latin the pronunciation is the same) began to spread[347].

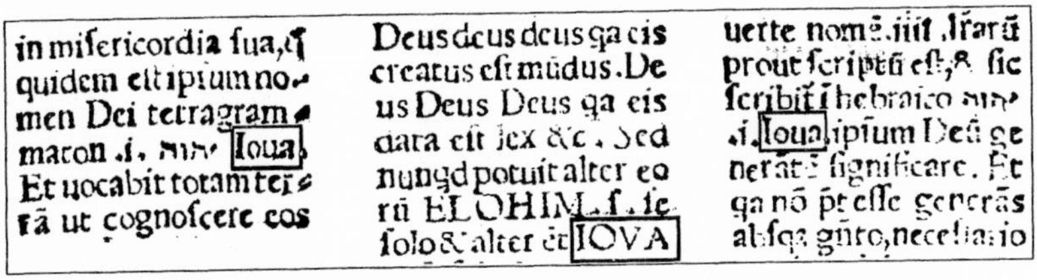

in mifericordia fua, q̃ quidem eſt ipſum no- men Dei tetragram maton .i. �ʜ Ioua Et uocabit totam teſ- rã ut cognoſcere eos	Deus deus deus q̃a cis creatus eſt mũdus. De us Deus Deus q̃a eis aata eſt iex &c. Sed nunq̃d potuit alter eo rũ ELOHIM .f. le folo & alter et IOVA	uerte nomẽ .iiii .lrarũ prout ſcriptũ eſt, & fic ſcribiti hebraico ᴀɪᴘ .i. Ioua ipſum Deũ ge nerat̃ fignificare. Et q̃a nõ pt eſſe generãs alſq̃: gñto, neceſiaio

It is found in the verses of certain Bibles. For example, a friend of Pico della Mirandola, Agostino Justiniani (1470-1536), used it in his comments on the Psalms[348] published in 1516. He believed that the name Ioua was an alteration of the name Jupiter. Sebastien Chateillon explained in his book[349] entitled *Dialogorum Sacrorum* (Holy Dialogues) published in 1549 that this name IOVA, even though it might have a link with the name Iupiter, should be used in the Bible, which he did in his Latin translation of 1551 and later in his French translation[350] of 1555 (see below.)

f. Ioua uerra.	Ieditmoutõ, e en hivn brulage au lieu de fon fis: e nõma celle place Ioua réc: ey dit-on auiourdui, en la montagne Ioua fera veu. E lãge du Seigñr criɑ A

(Genesis 22:14)

From Tyndale to the American Standard Version

☞   In order to clear up the variants of pronunciation of the Tetragram, Pietro Galatino (1460-1540) dedicated a good part of his work entitled *De Arcanis Catholice Ueritatis* (Concerning Secrets of the universal truth)[351], published in 1518, to explaining the (Hebraic) reasons for this pronunciation. First, he quoted profusely from the book of Maimonides *The Guide of the Perplexed*, especially chapters 60-64 of the first part, as a reminder that the Tetragram is the proper name of God and that it can be pronounced according to its letters. However, he demonstrated that the pronunciation Ioua, accepted in his time, was inaccurate and he gave the reasons why. He explained for example that the proper name Iuda, written יודה (YWDH), was an abbreviation of the name Iehuda written יהודה (YHWDH). All Hebrew proper names beginning in YHW- [יהו] are moreover always vocalized Ieh-. Consequently, if the Tetragram was really pronounced Ioua it would have been written in Hebrew יְוַה (YWH), which was never the case. So, because the Tetragram is written יהוה (YHWH), one should hear the letter H inside the Name. He concluded that, because this name is pronounced according to its letters, the best transcription was the form I-eh-ou-a (Iehoua), rather than the form I-ou-a used for example by Agostino Justiniani, a friend of Pico della Mirandola, in his polyglot translation of Psalms published in 1516.

If Galatino had transcribed the Masoretic form directly, he would have obtained Yehouah and not Iehoua. Also, French translator Pierre Robert Olivétan (1506?-1538) recognized in his *Apology of the Translator*[352] written in 1535, that God's name in Hebrew was Iehouah rather than Ioua, because the latter form did not express the aspiration of the letter H.

The form Iehoua is obviously very close to the Masoretic form, but nevertheless not completely identical. Contrary to the assertion of all current dictionaries, this vocalized form does not stem from an erroneous reading of the Tetragram in the Hebraic Bible. Actually, this vocalization of the divine name resulting in Iehoua is extremely surprising, as its resemblance to the Masoretic form is a strange coincidence (?).

Galatino's demonstration was progressively accepted by several Hebraists. So, when new editions of ancient works, were published (after 1520) the various vocalizations Yohoua, Ihouah (found in the book of Porchetus, published in 1521; see the copy here), Iôa, Hiehouahi, etc., were gradually replaced by Iehoua, considered to be the most reliable, then rapidly, by Iehouah. Martin Luther (1483-1546) was aware of this name from Nicholas of Cusa's sermons, rather than the writings of his 'spiritual father' Johannes Wessel Gansfort (1419-1489) who preferred[353] the form Iohauah (see below).

For example, in a sermon (1526) on Jeremiah 23:1-8 he wrote «This name Iehouah, Lord, belongs exclusively to the true God.»[354] (the same year, Sebastian Münster (1489-1552), the best German scholar in Hebrew of this time, used the name Iehova in his Chaldean grammar[355].)

Luther wrote in 1543, with characteristic frankness: «That they [the Jews] now allege the name Iehouah to be unpronounceable, they do not know what they are talking about (...) if it can be written with pen and ink, why should it not be spoken, which is much better than being written with pen and ink? Why do they not also call it unwriteable, unreadable or unthinkable? All things considered, there is something foul.»[356] From this remark we deduce that the pronunciation Iehouah of the Tetragram was no longer disputed.

William Tyndale, with his burning desire to make the Bible known to the people made a new translation. The Name first appeared in an English Bible in 1530, when he published a translation of the first five books of the Bible. He included the name of God, usually spelled Iehouah, in several verses (Gn 15:2; Ex 6:3 15:3 17:16 23:17 33:19 34:23; Dt 3:24), and he wrote in a note in this edition: «Iehovah is God's name (...) Morever as oft as thou seist LORD in great letters (except there be any error in the printing) it is in Hebrew Iehovah». It is interesting to note that most English translations of this time mentioned the name of God, very often in Exodus 6:3, except for the Coverdale translation (1535). Matthew's Bible (1537) explained about Exodus 6:3: «Iehouah is the name of God, and none creature has been named like it, it means: this one who is himself and who depends of no thing». This name appeared for the first time in a dictionary[357] in 1557.

☞   This apparent general agreement on the pronunciation was of short duration, as several factors would again join to greatly impede its spreading. The first one was conformism. For example, when Martin Luther published in 1534 his complete translation of the Bible based on the original languages, he did not use God's name, that he knew well, as we have seen, but preferred to use the substitute HERR (Lord). (but, the same year 1534, Sebastian Münster used the name Iehova in Exodus 6:3 when he published his own translation, despite that he thought this name came from Iouis, that is Jupiter.)[358]

Another example of this vacillating attitude is John Calvin (1509-1564). In most of his books and sermons, he regularly encouraged his readers not to use God's name! For example in 1555 in his comment on Deuteronomy 5:11 he condemned the use of God's name[359]. However, a few years before (1535) he prefaced Olivetan's Bible which used the name Iehouah and a few years later (1563) when he published his comments on the five books of Moses[360], he systematically used the form Iehoua including in the biblical text and denounced in his comment on Exodus 6:3 the Jewish superstition which lead to replacing Iehouæ with Adonaï.

The second reason for the end of the general agreement on pronunciation was the appearance of a rival form, representing an "attempt at translation" of the Tetragram rather than an approximate transcription. William Tyndale had introduced the name Iehouah into some verses of his translation (1530); Sebastian Châteillon did it also but using the name Ioua (1551). On the other hand, in his second version 1537) Pierre Olivetan, hesitating to use the name Iehouah (because of the form Ioua which he mentioned), replaced it by the attempt at translation: 'Eternal', except in some verses (Gn 22:14; Ex 6:3; etc.)[361] where he left Iehouah. Some hebraists such as François Vatable (1485-1547) and Paul Fagius (1504-1549) used Iehouah, that encouraged Robert Estienne (1503-1559) to use it systematically (also written Iehouæ or Iehoua)[362] when he published his Bible (Psalms) in Latin in 1556. Martin Bucer did yet the same, a few years before, in 1547.

RETURN TO THE QUESTION OF ETYMOLOGIES

The origin of this discord, and thus of this rival form, came this time paradoxically from increased knowledge of the rules of Hebrew grammar. For example, Santes Pagnino (1470-1541), doubtless the best hebraist of his time (he was the first scholar, after Jerome, to translate the Bible directly from Hebrew into Latin, and he was also the first to systematically number chapters and verses in a printed Bible[363]), effectively improved the usual Latin names of Josue to Iehosvah, Jesus to Iesua, etc. Some would see in his translation of such names a guarantee of the pronunciation Iehovah. He explained in his Thesaurus[364], which appeared a little later in 1529, that the word *yhwh*, which he vocalized *yèhèwèh* (יְהֶוֶה), came from a verb 'to be' (*hawah*; הוה) and that this word *yhwh* meant in Aramaic 'He will be'. Johannes Mercerus (?-1570) also contributed to this Thesaurus and explained in his comments on the book of Genesis that according to Exodus 3:14 the Tetragram would mean 'He will be' (*erit* in Latin).

In an incredible combination of circumstances, this information, still considered as valid today, with the exception of a few details, was nevertheless at the origin of a great confusion over the Name. Before this date, not much credit was given to Greek transcriptions of Iaô (Ιαω); at the most some associated them to the Hebraic form Yahu (יהו) of the divine name. After this date, the form Iaô would gradually be associated with the Tetragram to support the "archaic" form Yahwèh (יַהְוֶה)[365]. In a curious shift, the near totality of theologians investigated this new track on the vocalization of the Name, that is YHWH = 'He will be', confusing the linguistic etymology and the biblical explanation, which is above all a religious teaching (For example, Mercerus despite his remark about the meaning 'He will be', did not think that the name Iehoua could come from a grammatical form of the Hebrew verb 'to be')[366]. However, Michael Servetus (1511-1553) still preferred (in 1531) the name Iehouah as being closer to the word Iesuah 'salvation' in Hebrew than its supposed grammatical form (imperfect *piel* at the time!)[367]. For example, this form *yehauue* 'He will generate', is found in the book of Paulus de Heredia (1488), a Christian cabalist.

Strongly influenced by the remarks of Johannes Reuchlin and Giovanni Pico della Mirandola, the grammarians of this time believed that Iehoua was an improvement on the name Jupiter, a deformation of Ioua-pater meaning 'Father Ioua'. Angelo Canini[368] clarified however, in his grammar written in 1554, that he preferred Iehoua to Ioua, because Iehoua more closely resembled names Ieshoua and Iehouda.

Suspicion towards the vocalization Iehoua was progressive. The hebraist theologian Gilbert Genebrard (1537-1597) wrote in 1568, in his book on the Trinity[369], that the name Iehoua resulted from a change of the heathen name Ioue (Jupiter) into Ioua then Iehoua; he specified that in Hebrew the form yhwh should be read Iehue. Translator Benito Arias Montano (1527-1598) explained in one of his books (1572), that the divine name was never read Iehovih or Iehovah by the Masoretes and he agreed with Genebrard that the old pronunciation was probably Iehveh. Being afraid to favor a name of heathen origin, since he too thought Iehoua resulted from a transformation of Iouis into Ioua, he replaced this name in his Latin translation of Psalms[370] (1574) with IA (the surer and shorter form). Cardinal Robert Bellarmin[371] asserted moreover (in 1578) that the form Iehoua was erroneous, because it had the vowels *e, o, a*, of the *qere* Adonay (*a, o, a* becoming *e, o, a* for grammatical reasons!)

However, that Jewish erudite Immanuel Tremellius (1510-1580) was not affected by all these statements is shown by his choice to systematically use the name Jehova in his Latin translation of the Hebrew Bible[372] (1579). In addition, scholar Jerome Prado[373] (1547-1595) distinguished (in 1594) between the Hebrew name Iehoua and its Hebrew meaning Iihieu 'He will be'. Another scholar, Louis Alcazar[374] (1554-1613) also distinguished the pronunciation Iehoua from its Hebrew etymology, but he preferred the meaning *ihie hoia ve haia* that is 'He will be, He is and He was'.

If all the Bible scholars recognize that biblical etymologies are sometimes puzzling (which is not surprising since they are often in fact a play on words), rare are those who accept this reality for the Tetragram. To support this major point, it is important to realize that a study of biblical etymologies concerning proper nouns showed that in half the cases, these etymologies had an "elastic" link with the "linguistic" etymology, and that in a quarter of cases there was no link at all, apart from the assonance of words[375]. We can illustrate this problem by examining a few of the many cases where the etymological connection is 'stretched'.

✁   The biblical etymology of the name Judah (Yehudah) for example, is given at Genesis 29:35, where it reads «I shall laud Jehovah. She therefore called his name Judah.» Because the sentence 'I shall laud [Jehovah]' referred to Judah, in speaking about him one would say 'he will laud [Jehovah]', which constitutes the biblical etymology of this name. 'I shall laud' is said in Hebrew *'ôdèh* (אוֹדֶה imperfect of hiphil, 1st person of singular), from which obtained 'he will laud', in Hebrew *yôdèh* (יוֹדֶה imperfect of hiphil, 3rd person of singular) or *yehôdèh* (יְהוֹדֶה, Ne 11:17). Yet, this etymology is linguistically incorrect, because the form *yôdèh* or *yehôdèh* differs from the Masoretical vocalization Yehûdah. In view of this slight disagreement, some linguists rectify this etymology. They assume that at first the form had to be *yûdèh* (יוּדֶה imperfect of huphal, 3rd person singular) meaning 'he will be lauded'. This correction has two inconveniences: In the first place, the supposed verbal form of the verb 'to laud' (huphal) does not exist in Hebrew and, the biblical message which was 'he will laud' is modified to 'he will be lauded', which is a mild but undeniable deviation from the truth. The biblical explanation is much subtler. In the previous explanation, an important word of the definition 'he will laud [Jehovah]', the Tetragram itself is ignored. A rigorous translation of this expression into Hebrew would be 'yehôdèh [Yehowah]'. The biblical writer would have then integrated the Tetragram, by assonance, into the word *yehôdèh*; so, 'yehôdèh [Yehowah]' became 'Yehûdah.' ✁

In another example, the biblical etymology of the name of Jesus (Yéshua‘), given in Matthew 1:21, is: «You must call his name Jesus, because he will save his people from their sins.» The identification is simple; the name Jesus means biblically 'he will save', or in Hebrew *yôshia‘* (יוֹשִׁיעַ imperfect of *hiphil*, 3rd person singular) or sometimes *yehôshia‘* (יְהוֹשִׁיעַ; 1S 17:47; Ps 116:6). Once again, this etymology is "linguistically" incorrect because the form *yôshia‘* (or *yehôshia‘*) differs from the Masoretical vocalization Yéshua‘.

Paradoxically, biblical dictionaries gloss over this anomaly and translate the name Jesus as 'Jehovah is salvation'. By giving this definition, they change 'he will save' (*yôshia‘*) to 'salvation' (*yeshua‘h*), thereby tacitly admitting, by the translation 'Jehovah is salvation' and not simply 'salvation' (*yeshua‘h* in Hebrew), that this word has a strong assonance with the Tetragram. In the biblical etymology 'He will save', God is in effect, implied in the 'He'. Therefore, Jesus actually means '[Jehovah] will save', or in Hebrew *[Yehowah] yôshia‘*; the Bible writer then integrated the Tetragram, by assonance, into the word *yôshia‘* of the expression *[Yehowah] yôshia‘*, which becomes simply *Yéshua‘*.

NAME	BIBLICAL ETYMOLOGY	MASORETIC POINTING	PHILOLOGICAL CHOICE
Judah	Yôdèh (יוֹדֶה)	Yehûdah (יְהוּדָה)	Yehûdâ (Ihuda)
Jesus	Yôshia‘ (יוֹשִׁיעַ)	Yéshûa‘ (יֵשׁוּעַ)	Yeshûa‘ (Išu‘)
Jehovah (Hebrew)	Yihyèh (יִהְיֶה)	Yehowah (יְהוָֹה) Yehwah* (יְהוָה)	Yehûâ (Ihua)
He will be (Aramaic)	Yihwèh (יִהְוֶה)	Yehû' (יְהוּא)	Yahwah (Yhwh)

*before 1100

In this table, the reading of names in the Hebrew text is closer to their reading according to their letters (philological choice) than their "linguistically" reconstructed form from biblical etymology. The reason for this agreement is simple. The Bible determines the meaning of names, not according to their vowels which can change with time, but according to a divine declaration which can be translated without ambiguity in all languages. God's name is no exception to this rule; from the beginning it could be read according to its letters, but the 'religious' not 'linguistic' meaning was later given to Moses. Therefore, it is not necessary to mix 'linguistically' the philological pronunciation Iehouah of the Tetragram, according to its letters, with the biblical etymology of Exodus 3:14, otherwise this mixture would create confusion (BaBèL according to the BiBLe).

Moreover, even today, this natural reading of the Tetragram does not pose a problem. Indeed, even though the Jews refuse at present to pronounce the name YHWH, they pronounce two similar words without problem, such as the name YHWH-NN which is read Yehôha-nan, and N-YHWH (soothing) which is read N-ihôah in any dictionary. So, the "natural" pronunciation of the Name is Yehôah or Yehouah.

✄   On the other hand, the meaning of the Tetragram is given in Exodus 3:14. When God says, in speaking about himself, 'I shall be', in Hebrew *'èhyèh* (אֶהְיֶה imperfect of *qal* 1st person singular), somebody speaking about God should say 'He will be', in Hebrew *yihyèh* (יִהְיֶה, imperfect of qal 3rd person singular). The translation 'He is' rather than 'He will be' is doubly ambiguous. In biblical Hebrew all occurrences of the verb HYH in the imperfect conjugation, with a few possible exceptions, refer to the future. So it would be strange to have a present reference in this case; secondly, the translation 'He is' can be understood in the sense that 'He exists', which would be absurd for a Semite since the existence of God could not be disputed (Ps 14:1). Furthermore, the expression 'He is' in the sense of 'He exists' is different in ancient Hebrew, being *yèsh* (יֵשׁ) not *yihyèh* or *yihwèh*. Some scholars rectify the biblical form 'He will be' by another verbal form of their own 'He causes to be', which has two serious drawbacks. First of all, this verbal form (hiphil) of the verb 'to be' does not exist in Hebrew; next, the biblical meaning of the expression 'I shall be' must be technically rectified to become 'I cause to be' or 'I cause to become'. Some scholars recognize that the hypothetical Yahweh is a choice that is more theological than philological[376].   ✂

THE FORM JEHOVAH

In spite of the controversy between Iehouah versus Iahue, until 1900 most of Hebraists considered the form Iahue as dubious. For example, Baruch Spinoza used the name Jehova in his treatise entitled *Tractatus Theologico-politicus* published in 1670, also in his grammar of Hebrew *Compendium Grammatices Linguæ Hebrææ*[377]. In the latter he wrote that the pointing "e, o, a" of the Tetragram represented the three tenses, the past, the present and the future of the verb 'to be'. (In 1765 the famous Voltaire explained in his *Philosophical Dictionary* that God's name was Jéova in French, since it came from an ancient name with four vowels as Ieuo or Ioua.)

A French erudite, Antoine Fabre d'Olivet (1767-1825), said in his work entitled *The Hebrew Language Restored* published in 1823, that the best pronunciation of the divine Name according to its letters was Ihôah/ Iôhah/ Jhôah[378]. Moreover, when he began to translate the Bible (Genesis, chapters I to X), he systematically used the name Ihôah in his translation. Antoine Fabre d'Olivet, renowned polyglot, knew numerous oriental languages, which made him favor the philological rather than theological choice, in that he refused to mix the sound with the sense of the word.

Paul Drach, a rabbi converted to Catholicism, explained in his work *Harmony Between the Church and the Synagogue* published in 1842, why it was logical that the pronunciation Yehova, which was in agreement with the beginning of all theophoric names, was the authentic pronunciation, contrary to the form Yahvé of Samaritan origin[379]. He disproved the foolish criticisms against the form Yehova, like the charge of erroneous reading attributed to Galatino, quoting Raymond Martini and Porchetus de Salvaticis to reject this assertion. Then he demonstrated the unreasonableness of the transmutation of the vowels *a, o, a* of the word Adonay into *e, o, a*, since this hypothetical grammatical rule (one contrary to the nature of the *qere / kethib*) was already demolished in the word Èlohim which keeps its three vowels *è, o, i* without the need to change them to *e, o, i*. Yet, in spite of the support of Vatican at this time, these refutations had no great effect.

Although having numerous detractors, the pronunciation Jehovah still had, in the beginning of our century, numerous defenders. For example, Jewish professor J.H. Levy explained why he preferred the form Y'howah, instead of Yahweh, in his article published in 1903 in *The Jewish Quarterly Review*[380]. Also, in 1923, the famous Catholic grammarian Paul Joüon preferred the older form Jéhovah rather than the hypothetical Yahweh[381]. In the Encyclopedic Dictionary of the Bible published in 1935, Protestant Professor Alexander Westphal also preferred the name Jéhovah to the form Yahvé, because, according to him, grammatical explanations were of lesser value than biblical explanations[382].

NAME OF VERSION:	PUBLISHED IN:	DIVINE NAME RENDERED (SOMETIMES)
ENGLISH		
Tyndale	1530	Lorde (Iehouah)
Rheims-Douay	1582-1610	Lord
King James Version	1611	LORD (Jehovah)
Young	1862-98	Jehovah
English Revised	1881-95	LORD (Jehovah)
Emphasised Bible	1878-1902	Yahweh
American Standard	1901	Jehovah
An American Translation	1923-39	LORD (Yahweh)
Revised Standard	1946-52	LORD
New English Bible	1961-70	LORD (Jehovah)
Today's English Version	1966-76	LORD
Revised Authorised Version	1979-82	LORD
New World Translation	1984	Jehovah
New Jerusalem Bible	1985	Yahweh
Third Millenium Bible	1998	LORD (Jehovah)

SPANISH		
Reina	1569	Iehoua
Valera	1602	Jehovà
Moderna	1893	Jehovà
Nàcar-Colunga	1944	Yavé
Evaristo Martin Nieto	1964	Yavé
Serafin de Ausejo	1965	Yahvéh, Señor
Biblia de Jerusalén	1967	Yahveh
Cantera-Iglesias	1975	Yahveh
Nueva Biblia Español	1975	Señor
PORTUGUESE		
Almeida	1681,1750	Jehovah
Figueiredo	1778-90	Senhor
Matos Soares	1927-30	Senhor
Pontificio Instituto Biblico	1967	Javé
Jerusalém	1976, 1981	Iahweh
GERMAN		
Luther	1522, 1534	HErr
Zwingli (Zürcher)	1531	HERR, HERREN
Elberfelder	1855, 1871	Jehovah
Menge	1926	HErr
Bibel in heutigem Deutsch	1967	Herr
Einheitsübersetzung	1972, 1974	Herr, Jahwe
Revidierte Elberfelder	1975, 1985	HERR, Jahwe
FRENCH		
Olivétan	1535, 1537	Éternel (Iehouah)
Castellion	1555	Ioua
Darby	1859, 1885	Éternel (Jéhovah)
Crampon	1894-1904	Jéhovah
Jérusalem	1948-54	Yahvé
T.O.B.	1971-75	Seigneur
Osty	1973	Yahvé
Segond révisée	1978	Éternel
Français courant	1982	Seigneur
Chouraqui	1986	IhvH

DUTCH		
Statenvertaling	1637	HEERE
Leidse Vertaling	1899-1912	Jahwe
Petrus-Canisiusvertaling	1929-39	Jahweh
NBG-Vertaling	1939-51	HERE
Willibrordvertaling	1961-75	Jahwe
Groot Nieuws Bijbel	1972-83	Heer
ITALIAN		
Brucioli	1541	Signore (Ieova)
Diodati	1607, 1641	Signore
Riveduta	1921-30	Eterno
Nardoni	1960	Signore, Jahweh
Pontificio Instituto Biblico	1923-58	Signore, Jahve
Garofalo	1960	Jahve, Signore
Concordata	1968	Signore, Iavè
Parola del Signore	1976-85	Signore
LATIN		
S. Münster	1534	Dominus (Iehova)
F. Vatable	1545	Dominus (Iehoua)
M. Bucer (Psalms)	1547	Iehouah/ Iehouæ
S. Castellion	1551	Ioua
F. Vatable (R. Estienne)	1557	Iehouah
I. Tremellius	1579	Jehova

☞   In the New Testament, the introduction of the divine name was slower, but the process began, paradoxically, with controversies among Jews and Christians. During their exchanges, these protagonists used Matthew's gospel written in Hebrew (which seems to be a copy of a Hebraic original rather than a translation from Greek). These Hebraic copies of Matthew's book are very old, as they are found in works such as: *Sepher Nestor Hakomer* (The Book of Nestor the Idolatrous Priest)[383], which is dated from the sixth to the ninth century. The priest Nestorius lived from 380 to 451 CE, but the Book of Nestor was completed later.

> ישו היה בורח מן השטן והיה מתפלל וצם
> ארבעים יום בהר. והנה בא השטן ואמר לו, אם אתה
> בן אלהים תאמר לאבן הזאת שתעשה לחם ותאכל
> ממנו. ויאמר ישו, כתיב כי לא על הלחם לבדו
> יחיה האדם, ולקחו השטן ויעלהו במרום ההיכל בעיר
> הקדש, וא"ל אם אתה בן אלוה השלך עצמך מלמעלה
> למטה ולא ימצאך נזק כלום. ויאמר ישו אל השטן
> הלא כתיב לא תנסו את ‏ה' ‏ אלהיכם. ועוד אמר
> השטן לישו, ראה העולם כולו ומלכותו ושלטנותו
> וכל הטוב אשר בו לי הוא ואם תכרע ותשתחוה לי
> השתחויה אחת אתנהו לך. ויען ישו הלא תרע כי
> כתוב בתורה את ‏ה' ‏ אלהיך תירא ואותו בעבור. ומזה

Matthew 4:1-10 in the *Book of Nestor* dated from the 6th to the 9th century [ישי = Jesus, ' ה = Hashem 'The Name']

- The Milhamot HaShem by Jacob ben Reuben (1170)
- Sepher Joseph Hamekane by Rabbi Joseph ben Nathan Official (13th century)
- Le Nizzahon Vetus (latter part of the thirteenth century)
- Even Bohan by Shem-Tob ben Isaac Ibn Shaprut (1385).

The appearance of the divine name as 'The Name' (HaShem) instead of the classical 'The Lord' in Christian texts quoted by Jews is interesting, to say the least[384]. The next step was the replacement of this divine name H' with the Tetragram.

In the middle of the sixteenth century, there were several scholarly translations of the New Testament with the Tetragram:
Anton Margaritha -Gospels (heb.) Leipzig 1533.
Sebastian Münster -Matthew (heb. lat.) Basel 1537.
J. Quinquarboreus -Matthew (heb.) Paris 1551.
J. Mercier -Matthew (heb. lat.) Paris 1555 Ed. J. du Tillet (ייי).
F. Petri -Gospels (heb.) Wittemberg 1573.

For example the Tetragram is found in the following translations: the first one (1599), where Ephesians 5:17 is translated[385] into Hebrew.

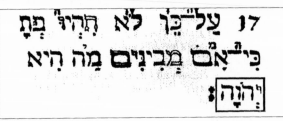

9 Kah modtaanukeg negonſháchtg, kah
aſukauon heg wuttauatonkquiſuog,kah nu-
waog, Hoſaun̄a wunnaumonuh David, ona-
numau noh paont ut ꝏweſuongauid Jebovah,
Hoſanna quanunkquiſit.
10 Kah *d* paont Jeruſalem, wame otan

Matthew 21:9 translated[386] into the Massachusett language (1661)

As for Hebrew Scriptures, a few translators of Greek Scriptures preferred to use the form Ioua rather than the usual Iehoua. For example, Dominikus von Brentano used the name Iehovah in Mark 12:29 (1796) but some years later (1805) another German translator used the name Ihouah in Luke 4:18.

At the beginning of the twentieth century there was a remarkable agreement among first scholarly translations directly made from Hebrew, because in spite of the fact they were of different origin, the name Jehovah (or Iehovah) was systematically used (except the Bible of Ledrain who was an Agnostic and preferred to use the more technical name Iahvé because it meant 'He causes to be', according to him[387]).

Bible (from Hebrew)	Language	Published	Religion
Samuel Cahen	French	1832-1856	Jew
Michael Glucharev	Russian	1860-1867	Orthodox
Eugène Ledrain	French	1879-1899	Agnostic
American Std Version	English	-1901	Protestant
Augustin Crampon	French	1894-1904	Catholic

An analysis of the table by observing on previous pages shows that after 1904 (the year which marked a consensus of choice) all translators changed their opinion: the Jews went back to the term Eternal (no Jewish translation used the name Yahweh), the Catholics, Protestants and the Orthodox went back again to God, Lord, Yahweh, etc. In spite of this sudden and spectacular reversal of opinions among translators, the impetus given at the beginning of the century had been too powerful to be completely reversed, thus the form Yehowah or an equivalent can be found in Bibles of the following languages:

TONGUE	DIVINE NAME	TONGUE	DIVINE NAME
Afrikaans	Jehovah	Maori	Ihowa
Albanian	Jehovait	Marshall	Jeova
Bicol	Jehova	Moore	Zeova
Bislama	Jeova	Ndonga	Jehova
Cantonese	Yehwowah	Niue	Iehova
Cebuano	Jehova	Norwegian	Jehova
Chichewa	Yehova	Paluan	Jehovah
Croatian	Jehovini	Pangasinan	Jehova
Czech	Jehovovi	Papiamento	Jehova
Danish	Jehova	Pidgin Melan.	Jehova
Dutch	Jehovah	Pidgin Salom.	Jehovah
Efik	Jehovah	Polish	Jehowy
English	Jehovah	Ponape	Siohwa
Estonian	Jehoova	Portuguese	Jeova
Ewe	Yehowa	Rarotonga	Iehova
Fijian	Jiova	Romanian	Iehova
Finnish	Jehova	Samar-leyte	Jehova
French	Jéhovah	Samoan	Ieova
Futuna	Ihova	Sango	Jéhovah
Ga	Yehowa	Sepedi	Jehofa
German	Jehova	Sesotho	Jehova
Goun	Jehovah	Shona	Jehovha
Greek	Iékhoba	Sinhalese	Jehova
Greenlander	Jehovap	Slovenian	Jehovove
Haoussa	Jehovah	Spanish	Jehova
Hiligaynon	Jehova	Sranan tongo	Jehovah
Hiri motu	Iehova	Swahili	Yehova
Hungarian	Jehova	Swedish	Jehova
Icelandic	Jehova	Tagalog	Jehovah
Igbo	Jehova	Tahitian	Iehova
Iloko	Jehova	Tongan	Sihova
Indonesian	Yehuwa	Truk	Jiowa
Italian	Geova	Tshiluba	Yehowa

Japanese	Ehoba	Tsonga	Yehova
Kikamba	Yehova	Tswana	Jehofa
Kiluba	Yehova	Turkish	Yehova
Kinyarwanda	Yehova	Tuvalu	Ieova
Kirundi	Yehova	Twi	Yehowa
Kisi	Jehowaa	Venda	Yehova
Kwanyama	Jehova	Vietnamese	Giêhôva
Lingala	Jéhovah	Xhosa	uYehova
Luganda	Yakuwa	Yap	Jehovah
Malagasy	Jehovah	Yoruba	Jehofa
Maltese	Jehovah	Zulu	uJehova

As seen, this chart does show some variations[388], but they are for the most part negligible. The Jews at present use the term Eternal in their translations of the Bible; on the other hand, some museums in Israel use the name Yahve (or Yahweh), and religious authorities favor the name Ye.ho.va[389]. Additionally non-superstitious Jewish translators always favored the name Jehovah in their translations of the Bible.

NAME OF VERSION: (JEWISH)	TONGUE	PUBLISHED IN:	DIVINE NAME RENDERED
Immanuel Tremellius	Latin	1579	Jehova
Baruch Spinoza	Latin	1670	Jehova*
Samuel Cahen	French	1836	Iehovah
Alexander Harkavy	English	1936	Jehovah**

*(Bible partly translated) Ex 6:2;3; Ex 15:11; 18:11 Is 58:14; Jr 9:24; 22:16; Ezk 20:26
**Gn 22:14 Ex 6:3; 17:15; Jg 6:24; Ps 83:18; Is 12:2

The name of Jesus and its connections to the Name

As seen in the previous chapter, God's name Iehouah and later Jehovah, found its place in an overwhelming majority of Bibles from 1500 till 1900. The name of Jesus played a very surprising and poorly known role in finding this vocalization. The name Jesus (in fact Joshua) is ancient, since Moses knew it in its Hebraic form Yehôshua (Nb 13:16). At first glance, the meaning of this name seems well established since the majority of dictionaries agree on the translation[390] 'Jehovah [is] salvation'. A close examination however reveals that, the history of the writing and pronunciation of this name is more complex than would seem, but also rich in teachings. Thus, from the beginning, this name has been connected to the turbulent history of the Tetragram. Numbers 13:16, gives the following explanation «Moses continued to call Hoshéaʻ the son of Nun: Yehoshuaʻ.»

☞ The name Jesus is already unique among theophoric names because it possesses three different spellings (in the Masoretic text). Next to the classic spelling, there is the full vocalization Yehôshûaʻ (יהושע; Dt 3:21; Jg 2:7) and the frequently encountered abbreviation Yéshûaʻ (ישוע). Secondly, the construction of this name is abnormal. All theophoric names (i.e. including a part of the divine name within) are built on the same model. For example, Nathan means in Hebrew 'He has given', 'He' being God. This name becomes theophoric by adding to its end the short name Yah (Nathan-yah, means 'He has given, Yah'), or the diminutive Yahû (Yah-himself, to obtain Nathan-yahû, which means, 'He has given, Yah-himself'). One can also obtain a theophoric name by adding Yehô- to the beginning, giving Yehô-nathan which means 'Yehô has given', or the shortened form Yô-nathan, Yô- being the abbreviated form of Y(eh)ô-. There are therefore only a maximum of four possibilities for any given theophoric name.

Nathan	He has given	2S 7:2
Nathan-Yah	He has given -Yah	1Ch 25:2
Nathan-Yahû	He has given -Yah himself	Jr 36:14
Yehô-Nathan	Yehô - has given	1S 14:6
Yô-Nathan	Yô - has given	1S 14:1

All theophoric names follow this rule of construction, with only two exceptions: Yéhu' and Yéshua'. The explanation for these abnormalities is instructive, because it highlights the powerful influence of the Tetragram on these names.

For Yéhu' the construction should normally have been Yehô-hu' meaning 'Yehô [is] Himself', much like Èlihu' means 'my God [is] Himself'. However, Yehôhu' is spelt in Hebrew YHWH-W' with a complete Tetragram inside, which would be disrespectful to the Name. The logical abbreviation would be YWH-W' (Yôhu') with the usual drop of the almost inaudible letter H, whereas it is abbreviated Yéhu'. This abnormal vocalization is confirmed in the Septuagint where Ièou (Ιηου) can be read in the Greek text.

To explain this abnormality very few satisfactory solutions are proposed. Some surmise that Yéhu' is not a theophoric name, but results from a contraction of the ancient name Yehi-hu' (He will prove to be Himself) to Yehé-hu' then to Yé-hu'; but nothing confirms this assumption. So, most consider that this name is indeed theophoric. But how can this oddity, found also in the name of Jesus, be explained?

Note, that the vocalization of several Hebrew names which would normally be *o-u* becomes either *é-u*, or *i-u*, with a dissimulation of the first vowel. The reason for this modification is not clear[391]. Yet, it can nevertheless be explained in that many names have an assonance with the divine name Iehoua. There seems to be a general leaning towards the vocalic serie i-o-a (or é-o-a). For example, the name Yehôdèh (he will laud) is in fact vocalized Yehudah; Urushalim (city of Shalém) becomes Yerushalém; etc. Yéhu is therefore a theophoric name due to its assonance, since Yéhu is closer to Yehua than Yôhu.

The case of the name Jesus is even more extraordinary. The Septuagint transcribed all Hebrew names beginning with Yehô- as Ihô-, or Iô- since the Greek language has no letter *h*. However, Numbers 13:16 reads: «Moses gave Nave the son of Ause his name Iesou.» The contraction of Yehô- to Iè- is abnormal because all these names, with this single exception, were read Iô- in the Septuagint. Moreover, in the Latin Vulgate, this name was corrected to Josue. How can this difference be explained? First of all, in an Aramaic context, the majority of -*a* endings in Hebrew names disappeared, so it should have read Josu. But what about the abnormal transformation of *o* into *é*? In fact, only a knowledge of the history of the Name answers this question in a satisfactory way.

WHICH IS THE MEANING OF THE NAME JESUS?

Hoshéa' means 'to cause salvation' or simply 'salvation', which is close to Hoshia' (He caused salvation). The construction of this theophoric name should have been Yehô-hoshéa' (Yehô [is] salvation) or Yehô-hoshia' (Yehô caused salvation), but the writing would have included the Tetragram, because Yehôhoshéa is spelt YHWH-WS'; so it was abbreviated to Yehôshua' (YH-WS'). This last version, as well as its vocalization resulting from the Masoretic text, seems very reliable, because the identical form is found on several seals dated from the eighth to the sixth century before our era[392]. However, the form Yehô-shua' is not theophoric in a classic way. The word *shua'* means 'noble, generous' and not 'salvation'. Moreover this name is found in the following forms: Shua' (Gn 38:2), Abishua' (1Ch 8:4), Élishua' (1Ch 14:5), Malkishua' (1Ch 10:2). Furthermore, the abbreviation Yéshua, which appears very early (1Ch 24:11) is surprising, because the form Yôshua would have been much more logical Y(eh)ô- becoming Yô- with the classic drop of the H.

Some Hebraists, to explain this oddity, suppose that this name was not theophoric at first, but that rather it was the name 'He will prove to be magnanimous', that is Yehi-shua' (יְהִי־שׁוּעַ),

which changed to Yehé-shua' (יְהִי־שׁוּעַ) then Yé-shua' (יֵשׁוּעַ), but this theory remains nevertheless hypothetical[393].

Furthermore, it contradicts all Jewish and Christian authors from the beginning of our era, who always explained that this name meant 'salvation'. For example, in the Greek version of Ben Sirach written towards the end of second century before our common era, is found the following remark: «Josue son of Nûn (...) he who, well deserving his name, proved himself great to save the elect (Si 46:1).» Philo (-20 to 50), a Jewish philosopher, explained in one of his books that Ôsèé means 'so-and-so is saved', and Ièsou 'Lord's salvation' (*De Mutatione Nominum, 121*). In the Talmud of Babylon, this explanation of the name Yehôshua' is found 'Yah, He will cause your salvation' (יהושע יה יושיע יושיעך; *Sotah 34b*). Christian authors of the first century also always connected this name to salvation without specifying whether if it was theophoric. For example, in Matthew 1:21 the author says that this name means 'He will save'. Justin also pointed out that this name means 'Savior' (*Apologies I,33:7*) but regretted that the Jews had forgotten the meaning of it (*Dialogue with Tryphon 113:2*).

It would seem therefore that in the first century only the divine meaning of this name posed a problem; but the explanation of *shua'* meaning 'noble' was never retained. Because this word has another meaning which is 'to call for help' being close to 'to cause salvation', commentators apparently agreed to merge these two meanings. For example, Eusebius, around 310 CE, in his book *The Evangelical Demonstration IV,17:23*, indicated that name Ièsu in Greek, becomes Iôsoué in Latin, but that in Hebrew it is read Isoua and means 'Iaô is salvation', since Iaô is God's name in Hebrew (idem X,8:28). At first, this explanation seems satisfactory because it confirms the others. Furthermore, all Greek and Latin witnesses of the first century BCE (Terentius Varro, Diodorus Siculus, LXX-4QLXXLevb) use the form Iaô for the divine name. We have also seen that the name Iaô played an important role in Jewish mysticism[394]; moreover, it is found inscribed on numerous amulets of this time.

In a book written around 80 CE (*Apocalypse of Abraham 10:3-11:5*), it is said that the mediatory angel Metatron is also called Yahoel, because his name is like God's name (Yahoel meaning in Hebrew: Yaho [is] God). The *Sepher Yetsirah I:13* (Book of Forming) specifies that next to the name YHWH there is also the great name YHW. Jewish commentators therefore identified the angel who has God's name in him, according to Exodus 23:21, with Metatron and with the archangel Michael.

Jerome specified, in a commentary on Psalm 8:2, that the Tetragram which is spelt Yod, He, Uau, He, may be pronounced Yaho. The numbers 15 and 16, which should have been written in Hebrew YH and YW, would replaced by TW and TZ, because in Aramaic pronouncing them YaH and YaW, the two divine names would sire, Ia and Iaô in Greek.

As for the pronunciation Isoua, it also appears to be correct, as verified by consulting Jewish translator Aquila, whose translation, made towards 130 CE, is considered to be very reliable and very literal. For example, he transcribed the name Yehôshua' which is found in Deuteronomy 1:28 as Ièsoua, thus confirming the choice of the Septuagint 'Ièsou' (in an Aramaic context the *a* final dropped). Paradoxically, if Iaô is God's name, it becomes impossible to explain how it was contracted to Ié in the name Ièsoua, unless Iaô is not the pronunciation of the Tetragram which was in current use at the Temple of Jerusalem until 70 CE. In fact, Flavius Josephus (a Jewish writer who was Pharisee and thus was familiar with the priesthood) indicates in one of his books that some Jews knew the great Name, and that this name (Tetragram) was constituted of four vowels (*The Jewish War V:235,438*). In the context of the first century (epoch of Qumrân), this information is easy to understand because it is a reading of the letters Y, W, H which also serve as vowels (matres lectionis) or I, U, A . Moreover, Abba Shaül, by the middle of the second century, would forbid the pronunciation of the Name according to its letters (*Sanhedrin 101a*). The destruction of the Temple in 70 CE would accelerate the process of the disappearance of the Name, because by the end of the second century Hebrew was rarely spoken and had been replaced by Aramaic. Therefore these remarks were no longer understood.

Consonants of the Hebrew name	Name pronounced according to: its letters	the Septuagint
YH	IA	Ia
YHWDH	IHUDA	Iouda
YŠW'	ISU'a	Ièsou
Y'QWB	I'aQUB	Iakôb
YSḤQ	ISaḤaQ	Isaak
YRWŠLYM	IRUŠaLIM	Iérousalèm
YHWH	IHUA	Kurios

The reading of these Hebrew names according to their letters corresponds well enough to their Greek vocalizations in the Septuagint, and even the name Jesus, read Isoua, is fairly close to the reading of Eusebius. However, the reading Ihoua of the Tetragram seems to be uncorrected to Iaô. In fact, this Greek name corresponds to the Hebrew substitute Yahu (YHW) which the Jews already used regularly at Elephantine during the fifth century before our era. It is also found at Kuntillet Ajrud (around 800 BCE) next to YHWH.

Eusebius, a highly qualified Hebraist, recognized in his commentaries on Psalms that the name Jesus was in fact phonetically very close to the word 'salvation' (Isoua) in Hebrew, but that it 'meant' Ia[395], Ia being the name of the 'Lord' God usually pronounced Adonai and sometimes written in Hebrew within the Greek text.

So, like Yehu's name which became theophoric by assonance, the logical abbreviation Yôshua' became Yéshua' to more closely resemble the vocalic series e-u-a of Yehowah, which one finds in all other theophoric names (Yehônatan, Yehônadab, Yehôram, Yehôyaqim, etc.)

Even though, in papyri of the third and fourth century, God's name is found written under the forms: Iéôa, Iéêôoua, etc., the majority of amulets bear the name Iaô, which obscures the assonance of theophoric names with the divine name. Only

Evagrius Ponticus, from about the fourth century, brought the Tetragram and the name of the Lord together which he supposed was written YHSWH[396].

WHAT IS THE HISTORY OF THE NAME JESUS?

As seen, the writing YHWŠ' (יהושע) from the Masoretic text seems very reliable (thus confirming the vocalization Yehôshua'), because it is found in identical form on seals dated from the eighth to the sixth century before our era. Furthermore, the Jews always considered the name Yéshua' as a theophoric name evoking salvation, for at least two reasons.

First: the cause of salvation would come indisputably from God. It was therefore understood Yehôshua' could be translated as '[YHWH] will cause salvation' and Yéshua' as 'salvation [of YHWH]'. The second reason is more decisive. The Jews considered it a great privilege to receive a letter of God's name in their name in order to get closer to it and to benefit from its holiness. For example, the Talmud indicates that Joseph received an H (in Psalm 81:6) because of his holiness, since Yôseph is written here YeHôseph, and that Juda (Yehûdah), received all the letters of the divine name (YHWdH) because of his very great holiness (*Sotah 10b; 36b*). Concerning Yéshua, it is written (*Sotah 34b*) that this name means 'YH will cause your salvation', because it received a Y, Hoshéa' (HWŠ') becoming YeHôshua' (Y-HWŠ'), according to Numbers 13:16. In fact, variations in pronunciation may have been favored by proximity to other names which had a similar meaning such as Isaiah (Yesha'yah, 'He saved, Yah'), or the word *yeshu'ah* ('being saved' or 'liberation'). So, the name Yehôshua' (יהושע), whose meaning was close to Yehôshia' (יהושיע) meaning 'He will cause salvation', could be abbreviated to Yéshua' (ישוע) similar to the word *yeshu'ah* (ישועה) which means 'salvation', for a good reason. Indeed, all theophoric names in the Masoretic text follow the phonetic pattern 'Yehô-a'. Series such as Yehô-i, Yehô-é, etc., are never found, only notable exception being Yehôshua' introducing the series Yehô-u-a.

☞   The scribes thus 'theophorized' this name by slightly modifying its writing and pronunciation. So, the name Yehôshua' (YHWŠ') became Yéhshua' (YHŠW'). Qumrân's biblical texts show that this name, written YHWŠ' (יהושע) in the Masoretic text, is written in paleo-Hebrew dated from the third and second century before our era in the form YHŠW' (יהשוע)[397], that is without the first W but always with the second. This is perplexing, because generally Qumrân's spelling is rather generous with matres lectionis. One also finds this abnormality in several biblical texts, dated the first century before our era, written in classical Hebrew[398]. On the other hand, some books, such as the book of Joshua, contain a variety in spelling of this name, going from YHŠ' (יהשע) to YHŠW' (יהשוע) and YHWŠW' (יהושע). (at this time the Tetragram YHWH was probably heard as four vowels I.E.U.A)[399]

Name	YHŠW'	YHWDH	YHW'	YHWH
equivalence	I.E.S.U.'a	I.E.U.D.A	I.E.U.'	I.E.U.A
Hebrew	Yeshûa'	Yehûdah	Yéhû'	Yehowah

✂   This anomaly of writing could explain the anomalies of pronunciation of this name. According to the use of *matres lectionis* at Qumrân, the name YHŠW' should be read IHŠUa', that is Yeshua', because the H had become inaudible. However, the consonant-vowel alternation permitted the reading of this name as IHaŠUa', that is Yashua', especially since it means, 'being saved'. In the bilingual mail of Bar-Kochba, written towards 125 CE, this name, always written YŠW' in Hebrew (ישוע), is transcribed in many different ways in Greek such as Ièsou, Iassou and even Èsou[400]. It is likely that this confusion is at the origin of the Greek name Jason.   ✂

Because of the assonance with the divine name IHÔA, some other names were 'theophorized'. For example, in the Septuagint, numerous names had their beginning improved with IÔA-: Iôatam (Jg 9:7,57); Iôakéim (1Ch 4:22); Iôas (1Ch 23:10,11); Iôasar (1Ch 2:18); Iôakal (Jr 37:3); Iôakas (2K 14:13); etc. Even in Bar-Kochba's letters (around 125 CE) the name Joseph, spelt YWSP (יוסף) in the Masoretic text, is always written either Yehôsèph (יהוסף), or Yôhasèph (יוהסף) and transcribed Iôsèpos in Greek.

The fate of these two names would continue to be closely connected. The Christians pronounced the Tetragram 'Lord' (Kurios in Greek), the equivalent of the Hebrew 'My Lord' (Adonay). Furthermore, between 100 and 135 CE, Christian copyists, not understanding Hebrew would quickly replace the Tetragram written in Hebrew within a Greek text (as verified in all versions of the Septuagint written before the second century) with Lord (or sometimes with God). Several authors of the two first centuries (Clement of Rome, Ignatius of Antioch, Polycarp, Hermas, etc.) recognized that God's name played an important role. However, some authors of this same time indicated that for them, God's name was Jesus! This identification is clearly expressed in the work entitled *The Gospel of Truth*. It is confirmed by Justin (*Dialogue with Tryphon 75*) and by Irenaeus of Lyons (*Against Heresies IV, 17,6*).

The Jews, in an excess of reverence, wrote YH to indicate YHWH; Christians did the same with the Greek term KURIOS (Lord), which applied to God but also to Jesus. They wrote it in the abbreviated form KS surmounted by a line, or KE for KURIE, etc. Jesus, in this context, deserved the same treatment. According to this process of *nomina sacra*, his name should also be regarded as sacred, thus IHSOUS became IS (or IHS); IHSOU became IU, etc. Note that the oldest Christian papyrus (P52), dated around 125 CE, does not contain this form of sacred names, which permits us to suppose that this process became systematic only after 135 CE.

On the other hand, Jewish polemicists, to distinguish this name from the biblical name Yeshu' (Joshua), preferred to write it YSW (ישו) in their controversies, in agreement with its Aramaic pronunciation Yeshu. It is written this way in the Talmud of Babylon (*Sanhedrin 43a*), and in Nestor's book (written between the sixth and ninth century of our era) etc. The explanation of this spelling is variable. Irenaeus of Lyons (177), in his book *Against Heresies II:24,2*, explained that this name

Jesus, written ISW in Hebrew, means in that language «Iaho Samaïm Wa'arets», that is 'Lord of the Heaven and of the Earth'. On the other hand, in *Toledoth Yeshû* (written after the sixth century of our era?) the following explanation is found on the meaning of YŠW in Hebrew «Ymah Shemo Uzikrino», that is "that one erases his name and his recollection."

The method of writing Jesus in abbreviation would last until the fourth century, because when the Bible was translated from Greek into Latin the term KS was replaced by Dominus (Lord in Latin) and IS by IESUS, however sometimes the abbreviation IHS (IES in Greek) was retained. Irenaeus explained in his book (*Against Heresies I:3,2*) that some Gnostics thought of deriving mystic information from these Greek abbreviations, because IH (iota, eta) represented the Greek number 18. For example, the author of a work written between 115 and 135 (*Epistle of Barnabe 9:8*)[401] made a link between the number 318 of Genesis 14:14, written TIH in Greek, and the 'standard' (T) of Jesus (IH)!

From the fourth to the sixth century the confusion would become complete. At this time, versions of the Septuagint with the name Iaô in some comments on theophoric names were still found. On the other hand, Severi of Antioch, commenting on John chapter 8, in a chain of verses, used Iôa for the Name. Isidore of Sevilla having apparently read letter XXV of Jerome to Marsala, thought that the Tetragram came from the name IAIA; finally Pseudo-Denys (in his work *The Divine Names*) had concluded that it was impossible to name God. The Jews thought that the right pronunciation belonged to the messianic world to come, and that the arrival of the Messiah would reveal the authentic pronunciation.

From the sixth to the tenth century, the Masoretes punctuated the biblical text. Their choice concerning the Tetragram is interesting. Indeed, this divine name, which was pronounced Adonay, was not punctuated by *a, o, a*, the vowels of the word 'aDoNaY; this would have given the form YaHoWaH, a risky word. Indeed, an absent-minded reader might have read these vowels with their consonants, which would have given 'Yah (is) calam-', because Howah means calamity in Hebrew (see Isaiah 47:11 and Ezekiel 7:26). The Masoretes thus wisely and fortunately chose to punctuate the Tetragram by its secular *qere* "e, a", that is the vowels of the Aramaic word ŠeMa' (שְׁמָא) meaning simply 'The Name', a word which the Jews pronounce once again today in Hebrew HaŠéM (הַשֵּׁם), as in Leviticus 24:11. So, YHWH became during this period YeHWaH.

In the twelfth century, several events would start the process which would end up in finding again the meaning and the pronunciation of the divine Name and of the name of Jesus. Under the influence of the *qeres* Adonay and Èlohim, the vowel o was added to the secular *qere* Shema, (YeHWaH becoming YeHoWaH). In parallel, Juda Halevi specified in his book (*The Kuzari IV:1-16*) that the Tetragram is God's unique name, and that these letters Y, W, H serve as vowels, that is to say I, O, A, for all other consonants. Maimonides, a renowned Talmudist, confirmed in his book (*The Guide of the Perplexed I:61-64*) that YHWH is the only name without an etymology, contrary to other divine names. He also made it clear that true worship alone had been lost, because the pronunciation of the divine name could always be found according to its letters. These remarks of Maimonides would inspire numerous Christian commentators. Joachim of Flora transcribed the Tetragram according to its Greek letters obtaining IEUE. He then decomposed this name into three, IE for the Father, EU for the Son and UE for the Holy Spirit. Pope Innocent III would pursue this link between the divine name IEUE, which he also wrote IE-EU-UE, and the name Jesus written IE-SUS.

In the thirteenth century, Hebraist Raymond Martini favored the Hebraic form Yohoua. Porchetus de Salvaticis used the name Yohouah several times in his book *Porchetus' Victory Against the Ungodly Hebrews*, and pointed out that God had given this name to the Messiah according to Jeremiah 23:5, 6. At this time, the position of the letter H varied. For example, the name Iesu was improved to Ihesus, sometimes to Hiesu and sometimes even to Iehsu. Arnaldus of Villanueva, student of

Raymond Martini, would connect these two names due to their respective Latin transcriptions, that is IHVH and IHSV, in his work dedicated to the Tetragram. Christian Cabal would connect these two names, through the pronunciation of vowel letters and their symbolism.

In the fourteenth century, Pablo de Santa Maria, a former rabbi, clarified that the Tetragram and Jesus both had four letters in Hebrew, and that the first and the third were identical vowels.

In the fifteenth century, Cardinal Nicholas of Cusa, in his sermons, would again link these two names by indicating that IESUA, the Hebraic form of the name Jesus, is close to the Greek Tetragram IEOUA, as this name in Hebrew is spelt with four vowels (I-E-O-A). Johannes Reuchlin, in his work *De Verbo Mirifico*, would pursue this link. Noticing that the name Iesu was sometimes transcribed in the Vulgate as IESUE, he supposed that this name which came from the Greek Septuagint could be transcribed into Latin by IHSUH (because the Latin letter H corresponds to the Greek E.)

In the sixteenth century, Jacques Lefèvre d'Étaple noticed that though the Tetragram must be read I-HE-U-HE according to its letters, the name Jesus in Hebrew was not I-he-sû-he but rather I-he-sû-ha. Christian Hebraists of this time even believed that the Jews had voluntarily removed the final *a* of the name Jesus to remove a part of its divinity. To improve this name, the great Hebraist Santes Pagnino thus transcribed the names Iosue and Iesus into Iehosvah and Iesua in his Latin translation of the Bible in 1528.

However, subsequent translations would all return to the names Joshua and Jesus, with the exception of Jewish translations which would retain Ieshoua and Iehoshoua, as did Samuel Cahen (from 1836 till 1852). However, after 1856, the name Iehovah would be replaced by Eternal in the later editions. Nevertheless, the Name would remain, though veiled, in the names Yéshua and Yehudah by its assonance, because these names would "normally" have been pronounced Yôshua and Yehôdèh.

While the name Yehowah should have been predominant, it has been widely attacked since the beginning of the century. It is interesting to note that the Bible itself associates the end of this controversy with the end of times to come (Ezk 38:16, 23).

Part 3

Conclusion

The controversy comes to an end

Jewish and Muslim traditions predict a supernatural revelation of the divine name at the end of time. But, since miracles have more to do with faith than reason, we prefer the «reasonable» route by consulting the Bible text which plainly states that God would make his name known in all the earth (Ex 9:16; Rm 9:17). This being the case, it would seem reasonable to conclude that, in order for the nations to hope in his name (Mt 12:21) and to be saved (Rm 10:13), the name must be accessible to all, hence translated with the rest of the Bible.

The first translators of the Bible, those of the Septuagint, sidestepped the issue by keeping the divine name in Hebrew characters within the Greek text. Later, Christian copyists of pagan origin, unacquainted with Hebrew, replaced this incomprehensible "sign" by the word 'Lord' or by its abbreviation, in order to retain a certain sacredness of the divine name. Later translations were often based on the Septuagint text and so the Name seemed destined to oblivion.

At the end of the fourth century, however, a new situation emerged. Jerome, a Hebrew scholar, made a revision of the Latin version of the Bible using the Hebrew text itself. Regrettably, at the time knowledge of Hebrew was declining and, still more seriously, the divine Name, having been replaced by substitutes, got its pronunciation from them. Jerome simply noted the problem, commenting that the Hebrew Tetragram was written «yod he waw he» and could be pronounced Iaho. For the next 800 years this scanty explanation was all that was available to the well-read concerning the Name. The first hope for scholars would wait for an improved understanding of Hebrew.

REVIVAL OF THE HEBREW LANGUAGE PLAYS A ROLE

☞ Even though he recognized that knowledge of Hebrew had seriously declined, Maimonides' work *The Guide of the Perplexed* gave a powerful stimulus to Christian Hebrew scholars in their search for the correct pronunciation of the Tetragram. The initial assumption was that the Name was pronounced as it is written. However, the understanding of Biblical Hebrew was still weak, and so the first attempts at establishing the correct pronunciation were flawed.

Author	Name used (Bible)*	/reprint	Date	/
Judah Halevi	(IHOA?)		1140	
Joachim of Flora	IEUE		1195	
Pope Innocent III	IEUE		1200	
Raymond Martini	YOHOUA	JEHOVA	1278	1651
Arnaldus of Villanueva	IHVH		1292	
Porchetus de Salvaticis	YOHOUAH	IHOUAH	1303	1520
Alfonso of Valladolid	YEHABE		1330	
Pablo of Burgos	YHVH		1390	
Nicholas of Cusa	IEHOUA	IEHOVA	1428	1514
Nicholas of Cusa	IHEHOUA	IEHOVA	1440	1514
Nicholas of Cusa	IEOA		1445	
Denys the Carthusian	?	IEHOUA	1455?	1534
Marsilio Ficino	HIEHOUAHI	IEHOUAH	1474	1559
Johann Wessel Gansfort	?	IOHAUAH	1480?	1521
Paulus de Heredia	YEHAUUE		1488	
Johannes Reuchlin	(IEUE?)		1494	
John Pic della Mirandola	(IOUÆ?)		1496?	
Jacques Lefèvre d'Étaples	IHEVHE		1509	
Jacques Lefèvre d'Étaples	IEHOVA		1514	
Agostino Justiniani	IOUA		1516	
Pietro Galatino	IEHOUA		1518	
Martin Luther	IEHOUAH		1526	
Sebastian Münster	IEHOVA		1526	
Wylliam Tyndale	**IEHOUAH***		1530	
Michael Servetus	IEHOUAH		1531	
Giacoma de vio Cajetan	IEHOUAH		1531	
Sebastian Münster	**IEHOVA***		1534	
Pierre Robert Olivétan	**IEHOUAH***		1535	
Antonio Brucioli	**IEOVA***		1541	
François Vatable	**IEHOUAH***		1545	
Martin Bucer	**IEHOUAH***		1547	
Sébastien Chateillon	IOVA/**IOUA***		1549/	1551

This table summarizes the various attempts at pronouncing the Name and reveals two important details: firstly, that these Hebrew scholars did not believe that the Tetragram was unpronounceable; secondly, that the well-known Masoretic punctuation YeHoWaH, which at face value is pronounced Yehouah or Iehouah, played no role in establishing their various suggested forms as evidenced by the fact that none of them refer to it, even though Maimonides' work is often quoted.

WHY SUCH A DISPARITY?

At first glance the bewildering array of spelling attempts seems to obscure the search for a precise rendering of the Name. But this is not really the case because each conclusion is the result of a justifiable compromise. For example, the first choice IEUE corresponds to the succinct equivalence Y=I, H=E and W=U; furthermore, this rendition has the advantage of being close to the name IESU, as noted by Pope Innocent III.

These arguments were then adopted by Johannes Reuchlin, and later (1509) by Jacques Lefèvre d'Etaples who used a Latin variant in this version: Y=I, H=HE and W=U. However, Lefèvre d'Etaples mentions a weakness that he found annoying: the name of Jesus in Hebrew was not IESUE, even though this form sometimes appears in the Vulgate, but IESUA. According to this reasoning, if the divine name was close to the theophoric name Jesus in the past, the precise form of the Name should have been IEUA (and not IEUE).

IHESV intelligatur:nichil abſonū.Nã deiſero authore Paulo eſt nomē quod eſt ſuper omne nomē. & de quo ad Romanos:IHESVS Chriſtus hert & hodie ipſe & in ſecula.qđ & toti verſui quadrat. & de quo Petrus in Aĉtis.nõ eſt in aliquo alio ſalus.nec eni aliud eſt nomē ſub celo datū hominis bus:in quo oporteat nos ſaluos fieri.quod & ſequēti verſui haud inaccomodabile videtur,vbi dicit. & benedicentur in ipſo oēs tribus terre:omnes gentes magnificabunt eū.Cuſa in ſermonibus:ſens ſit hoc admirabile & benediĉtū nomē:totū in ſe claudere cum media ſinid eſt f littera magnum del ineffabile nomen tetragrāmaton quatuor litteris ioth he/vau/he conflatū.quod his litteris noſtris quoquo paĉto repreſentare poſſumus I HE V HE.iunĉtim ſic IHEVHE.iunge igitur ſin id eſt f in medio:fiet IHESVHE nomē benediĉtū regis noſtri & ſaluatoris omniū.& deo icarnato/ineffa bile factum eſt effabile.Illud idē ſcripſit Mirandula.& de eodē librū edidit elegantiſſimus & ſine cõ trouerſia inter Sueuos doĉtiſſimus Ioannes Capnion/cuius paulo ante meminimus.quē quidē li=

dia littera hincinde triadē conectente.tuc eni veſtigiū ſue veritati ſuoɋ exeplari inſertū id eſt qđ ad imaginē & ſimilitudinē dei fuerat in principio creatū a diuino verbo aſſūptū: & tūc ineffabile eſfabile factū eſt.vt in annotationibꝰ pſalmi 7 i dictū eſt, ꝑpriū ſic repſentat IHSVH.cõmune ſic IHSVA & interdū metatheſi litterarū IHVSA.℄ Sĉdo verſu. poccupem꜀ facié eius in cõfeſſiõe:

The presence of the letter H does not fundamentally improve the pronunciation of the Name. The cardinal of Cusa explained in his sermons that this Latin letter simply allowed a better pronunciation of the Hebrew letter 'He'. To express the Tetragram in the Greek language, he preferred the form I-E-O-A rather than I-E-Ü-A, because he thought that the sound O was closer to W in Greek, while recognizing that the ideal would be to use a vowel (non-existent in Greek) to express the sound U. It would give I-E-OU-A, or I-EH-OU-A in Latin, written Iehova, as seen in his first sermon shown below (circa 1428).

The name Iesu was frequently written Ihesu in Latin, the name Iehova was also written Ihehova in his sermons, but cardinal Nicholas of Cusa preferred the form Iehoua (or Iehova, U and V being the same sound in Latin).

THE FIRST PROBLEM: IEHOUA OR IOUA?

The translators who favored the writings of Maimonides (based on the Talmud) chose the form Ioua, because the Name was pronounced as it was spelled. (Uses of the letter Y are scholarly transcriptions, but the letter I is more commonly used in Latin; furthermore, the introduction of the letter H in the name Ioua was simply a spelling enhancement.) The only point that bothered the translators with this pronunciation was the resemblance to the Latin word Ioua, meaning 'girl of Jupiter' or 'Jupiterette,' a point already noticed by the Latin writer Varro (116 to 27 BCE). This homonym led several scholars (including John Pico della Mirandol) to believe that the name Jupiter was derived from an adaptation of the expression Ioua-pater (Ioua father) into Ioue-piter (Jupiter). The translator Sébastien Chateillon used this to argue that if the heathen had used the divine name by chance, albeit deformed, all the more reason that Christians should use it.

O S dialogos , fratres charifsimi , compofui-mus,vt pueri haberent, vnde eadem opera , & mores Chriftianos,& orationem latinam difcerent . Itaque eorum ruditati in primo libro feruiui-mus,fermone facilimo,coque mi-nùs eleganti,& tamen latino vten tes:& pueris quafi præmanfum ci bum in os inferentes . In cæteris iam elegantiùs loqui cœpimus. Quod autē Dei nomen I O V A Hebræū vfurpauimus,quod nul, lum Dei proprium nomen latine extat(nifi forte Iupiter , fed id,vt pollutum,omittamus)id etfi prin cipiò videbitur fortaffe durius,ta-men vfu mòllefcet:& quod

E V S hæc omnia Ifraëlitis ad hunc modum effatus eft: Ego fum Ioua Deus tuus, qui te eduxi ex domicilio fer uitutis Aegyptiæ.
1 Deos alios nullos,præter me,habeto.
2 Simulachrum vllius rei,quæ extet aut fuprà in cœlo , aut infrà in terra, aut in aquis fub terra, ne facito, néve ea vene-rator, néve colito. Nam ego Ioua Deus tuus , Deus impatiens focij , parentum culpam etiam in liberos perfequor , etiam ad pronepotes vfque , & abnepotes ofo-rum mei : clementiaq; vtor ad millefimam vfque ftirpem erga mei amantes , meáque præcepta conferuantes.
3 Ioue Dei tui nomen inaniter ne adhi-beto:neq;enim finet impunitum Ioua, qui

Following the example of early translators, Pierre Robert Olivétan, preferred to use the form Iehouah in his Bible translation (of 1535), while recognizing that the Tetragram could also be pronounced Ioua. At this time (1535), Hebrew scholar Agostino Steuco[402] (1496-1548) wrote that the name Iehouah could come from an alteration of the Latin name Ioue. However, German translator Sebastian Münster used the name Iehova (1534) in Exodus 6:3 despite thinking that this name came from the name Iouis, that is Jupiter.

> en la fin Noe pour Noah. Toutessoys ce est esteinbze
> et perbze letymosogie/et signification des motz.
> Prenos exemple de יהוה Jeßouaß/resi se Seignr ou
> Eternes. Si maintenant on beust oster ses aspirations
> ה ß ce sera Joua: et plus ne sera ce quis repzesentoit.
>
> son origine (au plus pzes quis ma este possible) par ce
> mot / Eternes. Car יהוה Jeßouaß bient de יהוה/qui
> bauft a dtre que(Est).   Dz nya is que suy qui bzapz

The Talmud's linguistic argument being both simple and
strong, some translators argued in favor of this pronunciation as
we can see in the following: the German Bible[403] of Johann
Babor (of 1805), which uses the form Ihoua in Luke 4:18, or in
the French Bible (a partial translation) of Antoine Fabre d'Olivet
of 1823 which systematically uses IHÔAH (Gn 8:20,21 below.)

ten Jsaias, und als er es aufrollte, **18** fiel er auf folgende Stelle: ich werde vom Geiste des Jhova an- getrieben, der mich erfohren hat),	sey. Jesus aber sprach zu ihnen, **23** ihr könnt mir freylich das Sprich- wort vorhalten: Arzt! hilf dir selbst! verrichte auch in deinem Ba-

וַיִּבֶן נֹחַ מִזְבֵּחַ לַיהוָה וַיִּקַּח מִכֹּל הַבְּהֵמָה הַטְּהֹרָה וּמִכֹּל הָעוֹף הַטָּהוֹר וַיַּעַל עֹלֹת בַּמִּזְבֵּחַ:	20. Et-il-édifia, *Noah*, un-lieu de-sacrifice à IHÔAH; et-il-prit de- tout-quadrupède de-la-pureté, et- de-tout-volatile de-la-pureté; et- il-éleva une-élévation (il fit exhaler une exhalaison) de-ce-lieu-de-sa- crifice.
וַיָּרַח יְהוָה אֶת־רֵיחַ הַנִּיחֹחַ וַיֹּאמֶר יְהוָה אֶל־לִבּוֹ לֹא־אֹסִף לְקַלֵּל עוֹד אֶת־	21. Et-il-respira, IHÔAH, cet- esprit-odorant de-douceur; et-il- dit, IHÔAH, devers-le-cœur-sien,

The linguist Fabre d'Olivet preferred the pronunciation
Ihôah to the classic Iehovah because it followed the natural
reading of the Hebrew letters. Augustin Crampon (1826-1894)
systematically used the name Jova in his Latin translation[404]
(1856) rather than Jehovah.

Effatum Jovæ ad Dominum meum :
« Sede ad dexteram meam,
usque dum posuero hostes tuos scabellum pedibus tuis. »

2. Baculum potentiæ tuæ emittet (protendet) Jova ex Sione :
impera in medio hostium tuorum.

3. Populus tuus spontaneæ oblationes die militiæ tuæ
in ornatu sancto, ex utero auroræ tibi ros juventutis tuæ.

4. Juravit Jova, nec pœnitebit eum :
« Tu es sacerdos in perpetuum,
secundum rationem Melchisedeci. »

5. O Jova, Dominus (Messias) ad dexteram tuam *adest,*
inde confringit in die iræ suæ reges (hostiles).

Psalm 110:1-5

However, he came back to the name Jéhovah in his latter French translation (1894). As seen, the Hebrew pronunciation of theophoric names, particularly the name of Jesus, strongly influenced translators. And since the Masoretic text proved to be particularly reliable, it was gradually accepted.

THE ROLE OF THEOPHORIC NAMES

From the first attempts at determining the pronunciation of the Name (during the twelfth century), Hebrew scholars understood the connection with other Bible names (hence Ieve and Iesv are compared). Porchetus de Salvaticis pronounced theophoric names as Yoho- (For example he used Yohoyaquim instead of Jehoakim.), and so the original Youa became Yohouah in order to harmonize with the other theophoric names in his book. The name that most influenced the pronunciation of the Name was that of Jesus, which is pronounced Ieshoua in Hebrew. The Cardinal of Cusa established a parallel in some of his sermons (already noted by Evagrius Ponticus in the fourth century CE) between the two names 'Iehoua' and 'Iesoua.'

Furthermore, as Michael Servetus remarked in his treatise against the Trinity in 1531, the name Iehouah is very close to the Hebrew word 'salvation' (Iesuah), which is the biblical meaning of the name of Jesus (Iesua).

> lus *er* salutare. Chriftus *er* Euangelium; hoc *faluia* re Chriftum effe interpretatur Lu+. *er* 3.*er* Acto. xlt 1. Eadem ratione angelus, nomen Iefu , faluatorē interpretatus eft. De eodem, iuxta dictū Habacuc tē xit Maria, Exultabit fpiritus meus in Deo *falutari* meo, Habacuc enim dixerat, In Elohim *faluari meo.* Et licet Iehouah dicatur faluare, quia per Chriftum faluat, tamen nunq̃ coniunguntur, nunquàm legitur יהוה ישׁוע Sed quod eft etiā notabile poft no men Iehouah, addi folet de ישׁוע יהוה id eft, de
>
> hic eft Elohim, Chriftus faluator. Similiter patre dc monftrato, ifte eft Iehouah, *er* letabimur in Iefuato, id eft, in Iefu eius, m falutari eius Chrifto : eft enim nomen eius ישׁוע Iefuah, quod etiam ponitur Pfal. 9.12.13.19.20.105. *er* alijs q̃pluribus locis. poteft יהוה , id eft, effentie fons, effentiarum ge nitor, effe facies effentians, effendi caufa. Cabaliftis fua fecretarelinquo: *er* plane dico, q̃ (ut Iod fcheua tum nobis indicat) eft futurum piel, quod eft fignifi cationis actiuæ, à radice הוה feu potius היה mu

This link seemed more convincing to him than the grammatical form presented by some Cabalists of the same period: a imperfect *piel* (at present vocalized YeHaWèH and meaning 'he will make to be' or 'he will constitute'). This Hebrew form was also used by Abner of Burgos, a converted Spanish Jew, in his work *Display of Justice* (1330) and by Paulus de Heredia in his book called *Epistle of Secrets* (1488).

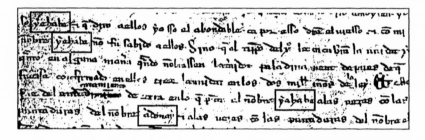

This grammatical form never managed to convince the translators for the following reasons: it is rarely used (not found in the Bible); its pronunciation is unclear (Abner of Burgos could not decide between 'yehabe', 'yahabe', 'yahaba', etc.); it is difficult to define; and finally, this form (*piel* of the verb 'to be') is not mentioned in Biblical or Talmudic comments about the Name.

By the end of the fifteenth century, largely because of the works of Johannes Reuchlin and Giovanni Pico della Mirandola concerning the link between the name of God and the name of Jesus, a debate arose to determine the exact Hebrew pronunciation of the name of God, given the two possibilities.

Name:	YHSW' (Jesus)	YHWH
in Greek	I E S U E	I E U E
in Latin	I O S U E	I O U E
in Hebrew (1)	I O S U A	I O U A
in Hebrew (2)	IEHOSUA	IEHOUA

The determining factor in overcoming the translators' reluctance to chose between the forms Iehoua and Ioua was Pietro Galatino's work. By quoting Maimonides' *The Guide of the Perplexed* he showed that, since the Name is pronounced as it is spelled, it should be Ioua (he noted that the similarity with the name Jouis or Jovis, the former name of Jupiter, was simply coincidental). This form Ioua was different from the substitute Adonaï that the Jews pronounced when they read the Tetragram.

> meum eft unicum mihi.Hæc oia prędiďa Rabbi Mofes ben Maimon.
> **CAPNIO** . Dic obfecro : hoc nomen quatuor literarum , ut fcriptū
> eft,ſiue ut literę ipſę fonant : quomodo proferatur. GALATINVS.
> Quidam ex noftris aiunt : hoc nomen in noftris literis fonare ⌐Ioua⌐. A
> quo dicunt forte apud antiquos nomen Iouis irępfiffe . Sed maxime
> pfeďo errāt:huiufmói gētilitatis blasfemiā tā fanďo nomini inferētes.
> Non.n.hę quatuor literę יהוה fi ut punďatę funt,legantʹ ⌐Ioua⌐reddunt:
> fed(ut ipe optime nofti) ⌐Iehoua⌐efficiūt.quis Iudęi illud pronūciare ut
> fcriptū ē,nō audeāt:fed loco ei̇, אדני Adonai qd̓ idē ē qd̓ Dñs:pferāt.
> Qui autēm illud in noftris literis.⌐Ioua⌐fonare cōtendunt :

He still felt, however, that the form Ioua remained inaccurate when compared to the Masoretic pronunciation of other Hebrew names. For example, when a name began with the full form YHW- in Hebrew, it was always pronounced Ieho- although it could be abbreviated as YW- or Io- such as when Iehosua becomes Iosua, etc. This explanation marked an important step in establishing the divine name as Iehoua, and thus convinced some translators to use it in their translations of the Bible, at least in certain verses.

literam fimul per fyncopam auferri. Nam exêpli gratia, יהודה Iehuda, nô nunq יודה Iuda & fcribit & ,pnûciat:& יהושע Iehofua יושע Iofua, & יהויכין Iehoiachin יכין Ioiachin & תהלים tehilim תלים tillim . Et reliqua multa id genus . Quod fimiliter quoq̃ in hoc nomine Dei magno fieri uolunt . Qua ex re illud Ioua apud nos fonare inferunt: cum in eo fceua litera he literam gucturis præcedat . Quod fi uerum eflet:ipfum nomen non יהוה fed יוה fine fceua & he litera fcriberetur. cipue apud Talmudiftas.Ipfum igit nomê Dei tetragrammaton cum fceua & he litera quæ lenem habet afpiratiorê, & fcribi & pronunciari, neceffe eft . Quare caueant , qui illud apud nos Ioua fonare affirmant. Non enim Ioua nec Ieoua, fed Iehoua cum leni afpiratione, ficut fcri-

The English translator William Tyndale used this name in his Bible (1530), as did the French translator Pierre Robert Olivétan (1535), and others. Later, some other translators went further by using it throughout the entire Bible text, for example the German translator Martin Bucer (1547), the French translator Robert Estienne (1556), the Spanish translator Casiodoro de Reina (1569), and others. However, if the name Iehoua had a friendly rival in Ioua, this soon changed with the arrival of a new form, which appeared at the beginning of the seventeenth century: the name Iahue.

SECOND DILEMMA: IEHOUA OR IAHUE?

The debate over the use of Iehoua or Ioua had been a quarrel restricted to Hebrew scholars. However, when the conclusions of their debate began reaching the general public it became much more theological and controversial. The first antagonist was Archbishop Gilbert Genebrard, who, in his book written in 1568 to defend the Trinity, dedicated several pages to the name in an effort to refute S. Casteillon, P. Galatin, S. Pagnin, and others.

First of all, he rejected Chateillon's Ioua using Saint Augustine's explanation, via Varro, that the Jews had worshiped Ioue (Jupiter!), and therefore the use of Ioua was a return to paganism. In the foreword to his commentary on Psalms he went so far as to state that the name Ioua was barbarian, fictitious and irreligious. Concerning the writings of Clement of Alexandria ('Iaou'), Jerome ('Iaho') and Theodoret ('Iabe'), he considered these as mere variations of Ioue, and that these testimonies appeared unreliable because, at the time they were written, the Jews had not pronounced the Name for several centuries. Lastly, he claimed that P. Galatin (as well as S. Pagnin), who had used the form 'Iehoua,' had not accounted for the theological meaning 'He is' when searching for the right pronunciation. Indeed, since the translation of the Septuagint it was known that the definition of the divine Name was essentially 'He is'. Genebrard tried to confirm this definition due to his knowledge of the Hebrew language. So, since in Exodus 3:14 God calls himself 'I am', (in Hebrew *Ehie*), one should say, when speaking about God, 'He is', that is in Hebrew *Iihie*. Grammatically, the form *Iihie* was likely derived from a more archaic form *Iehue*, suggested in 1550 by Luigi Lippomano[405] (1496-1559). Genebrard then pointed out that Abbot Joachim of Flora used this more exact form ('Ieue') in his book on the Apocalypse.

Genebrard's explanation, although unable to convince, impressed many because of its intellectual approach, and, during the century that followed Bible commentators often noted this form Iehue (or Iiheue) when using the more accepted Iehoua. However, in spite of the masterly presentation, it remained theoretic because of lack of early proof (later, to mitigate this discrepancy, Protestant theologians re-examined the historical evidence of the first centuries). Genebrard's major contribution was to introduce the theological meaning of the Name into the search for its pronunciation, a process that provoked a profusion of new pronunciations due to the ever increasing knowledge of the Hebrew language and its history.

✂ For example, in 1603, Jan Drusius (1550-1616) published a long article dedicated to the pronunciation of the Name[406]. His main arguments were that the Masoretic punctuation of the Tetragram could not be used as a basis for pronouncing the Name because it was a *qere*; so the form

Iehovih (resulting from the *qere* elohim) would be nonsense. He thus concluded that Iehovah was also a barbarism. He repeated the same arguments as Genebrard against Ioua, and then reminded his audience that according to the best grammarians of his time the expression 'He is' should be pronounced Ieheve. This form is found in Johannes Merceri's Thesaurus (?-1570) and that of Santes Pagnino (1470-1541) under the Hebrew form YèHèWèH (West Aramaic Peal imperfect) meaning 'He will be' which is now pronounced YiHWèH. He then theorized, using a few examples that the form Ieheve (or Iihveh) resulted from an archaic Iahave (or Iahveh), and in conclusion noted that this form Iahave was identical to the Samaritan pronunciation Iave given by Theodoret.

In 1616, Cornelius a-Lapide (1567-1637) published a commentary on the Pentateuch. While considering Exodus 6:3 he explained that according to the work of St Augustine (*liber 1 cap. 22 Consensu Evangelist*) the name Iehova developed from paganism, that is to say: Iehova ← Ioua ← Ioue (Jupiter). He explained that the name Jeheva would be better because it meant 'He is' in the archaic version of the past tense, and when modernized becomes: iive (יְהְיֶה)← Jeheve (יֶהֱוֶה)← Jeheva (יְהֶוָה).

Louis Cappel (1585-1658) dedicated almost one hundred pages to the pronunciation of the Name in one of his articles[407] published in 1650. As well as resuming many of Drusius' arguments, he explained a few new ideas. He maintained that the first syllable was certainly Iah-, because many names had lost their initial vowel, for example Nabô which had become Nebô, but he noted that the most ancient witnesses (hence the most reliable) usually used Iaô. He preferred Iahuoh to Iahave or Iahue. However the form Iahue eventually took over for two important reasons; first of all, it retained the first syllable Ia- as determined by the most ancient sources (it was also similar to the versions provided by Epiphanius, Theodoret and Clement of Alexandria), and, above all, it was close to a grammatical form beginning with Ya-, meaning 'He will cause to be' or 'He will make exist' (first suggested by Johannes Leclerc (1657-1736) around 1700.) This form would be a *hypothetical imperfect hiphil*, vocalized YaHaYèH resulting from an archaic [?] YaHaWèH. The cabalistic approach was in fact more "scientific" (!), because it was based on the *probable imperfect piel* form YeHaWèH meaning 'He will make to be' or 'He will cause to become'). ✄

This very complicated explanation intended to justify the form Yahweh disconcerted some translators who had used the "simplistic" Iehoua (after all, the name Iehoua had been used in most Bibles for four centuries). Towards the end of the nineteenth century, a few began using this "new" form in their translation. At the beginning of the twentieth century Yahweh proved dominant. Unfortunately for this rendition, the knowledge of the Hebrew language was still progressing, and so some linguists noticed that the final '-èH' could not be archaic because it was derived from an older sound '-aH.' The debate revived once again with some proposing Yahw-ah in order to conform to this new discovery and others proposing Yahwo-h, arguing that the letter W served as a vowel, as in the names Jericho-h or Nebo-h. Naturally, this linguists' quarrel concerning the pronunciation of the Name created confusion among most translators (to avoid taking sides in this debate, most current scientific works simply avoid vocalizing the Tetragram and have reverted to the 'silent' form YHWH.)

The Jerusalem Bible recognizes[408] that «at present the causative form 'He causes to be' is an old explanation, but it is more probably a qal form, that is 'He is.'» because in Exodus 3:14 the Hebrew Bible uses a *qal* form and not a *hiphil* form 'I cause to become what I cause to become.' Professor Freedman wrote: «I have never been entirely satisfied with my own analysis and interpretation of the divine name in the Hebrew Bible, or with that of others, including my own teacher, W.F. Albright and his teacher (from whom Albright derived his position), Paul Haupt.» He stated «However, the name could be a unique or singular use of the causative stem.» This cannot be taken seriously because there is not evidence. The causative form of the verb 'to become, to be' does not exist in Hebrew and it has never existed. As "Faith is the evident demonstration, with the power of reason", can we believe in it? Furthermore, Professor Freedman chose this analysis not for grammatical reasons but for theological reasons (See his own comment in the *Anchor Bible Dictionary*.)[409] For example, to prove the causative form Professor Albright in his book *From the Stone Age to Christianity*[410] supposed that the true name could be rediscovered through names coming from false religions (Babylonian and Egyptian). He then supposed that the formula of Exodus 3:14 was modified to fit his first hypothesis. By saying that, Professor Albright modified the biblical formula. Even in 1906, the Brown, Driver and Briggs dictionary stated: «Many recent scholars explain יַהְוֶה as Hiph. of הוה (...) But most take it as Qal of הוה.» At present, competent scholars know such as L. Pirot, A. Clamer[411], that the causative form can not be taken into account for two main reasons. Firstly, the causative form of the verb 'to be' is not known in Hebrew, furthermore to express a causative sense, the Piel form was used. Secondly, this philosophical notion did not come from Hebrew (but from Greek philosophy) and the more natural meaning is: 'I shall be with you' according to Exodus 3:12.

LAST DILEMMA: IEHOUA OR YHWH?

The explanations used by translators to justify their use of YHWH (unpronounceable) instead of a pronounceable form, are, firstly the uncertainty of the pronunciation and secondly ecumenical respect (!) for Jewish tradition (now 2000 years old) which prohibits the pronunciation of the Name. But if these arguments were valid, why not also apply them to the name Jesus, which would become YŠW' or simply JS or JHS as used by early Christians (before 400 CE.) This would even have the advantage of being more coherent theologically with the written form YHWH!

However, as we can see, the name YŠW' is easily read IeŠUa' *as it is spelled* (in Hebrew), YHWDH is read IeHUDA and YHWH is read IeHUA, and indisputably so!

Conclusion concerning the Name

God's name seems to resemble the sword wedged in the anvil of Merlin's legend of the Enchanter. Although all of the Realm's powerful men tried to remove it, only the simple young man was able to draw it from the anvil specifically because his simpleness made him unaware of the problem. In the past children could easily read the Name because it was pronounced as it is written! Things took a funny twist when the Masoretes decided to revise the pronunciation of the Hebrew text and chose, by a long and complex process, to use the vowels *e, o, a* with the name. In the fairy tale the sword was magic and Merlin took care to avoid its being taken by an imposter. In a similar way, the One who had the Bible written promised also to care for its preservation (Ps 12:6,7). Considering the importance He placed on His name, we can conclude that it also was protected.

As noted by Maimonides in his work *The Guide of the Perplexed*, it is impossible to have a deep relationship with a nameless God (Elohim). Juda Halevi expressed the same idea in his book *The Kuzari*, explaining that knowing the God of the philosophers cannot be considered worship, but is simply a polite recognition of His existence. These two authors agree in that what differentiated the God of Abraham from the God of Aristotle was his name, a unique name, not a simple title or honorary designation as God, Lord or Almighty, but a proper noun, the Tetragram YHWH. Moreover, when a person wishes to meet someone, do they not usually start by first asking their name? "What is your name?" has been the start of many a happy relationship.

So, what should we call God? YHWH, or its Latin transcription IHVH, is unpronounceable in our modern languages. The Greek transcription IEUE has the advantage of being pronounceable, but in the first century, when the high priest read the blessing of Numbers 6:24-27 in the Temple, or when Jesus read Isaiah 61:1 in the synagogue of Nazareth, they pronounced the Name in Hebrew. Maimonides knew Hebrew, and due to his extensive knowledge of the Talmud he also knew that the pronunciation of the Name became forbidden only at the time of Abba Shaül in the second century, and that before the priesthood of Simon the Just (3rd century before our era) the name was used even outside of the Temple. How was it pronounced? Maimonides does not dwell on the question because he felt, quite rightly, that the worship of God was more important than the pronunciation of the Name, which, at the time was not considered to be a problem since it was pronounced the way it was written. Juda Halevi noted that the vowels needed to be able to pronounce Hebrew words were exactly the letters of the Tetragram, I for the Y, O for the W and A for the H. So the only Hebrew name for which we know all the vowels is the Tetragram, and, as noted by Flavius Josephus, the Name is unique because it is constituted, not of four consonants, but of four vowels (that is IHOA, because the H is a vowel only at the end of a word. However, between two vowels the letter H is always pronounced like an E, that is to say IEOA, which is better than the form IEOE proposed by J. du Verdier (1843) in his Hebrew grammar[412] based on the natural reading according to certain vowel letters (ע י ו ה א).

In the Bible, refusal to pronounce the name of a god is a refusal to worship the god in question. That is why the Israelites were never to mention the name of other gods (Ex 23:13; Jos 23:7), thus indicating their refusal to worship them. Since the refusal to pronounce the Name meant a refusal to worship, Satan, by means of the seers of Baal, urged the Israelites to abandon the pronunciation of the Tetragram (Jr 23:27). History shows that unfortunately he succeeded (Jr 44:26). Jeremiah had nevertheless warned that refusing to pronounce the Name would be fatal, even to non-Israelites, when God intervened to pour out his fury (Jr 10:25). Yes, in that day, it will be imperative to call on the Name in order to be saved (Jl 2:32, Rm 10:13).

Today, the situation is similar; the "prophets of Baal" are still present. They claim to serve the true God while citing various reasons to refuse to name him. For example, some object by reasoning that naming God is a very great responsibility. But, a letter to Timothy stipulates that in order to do so we must renounce unrighteousness (2Tm 2:19). Definitely a worthy goal! Others assert that they would use it if they knew the exact pronunciation. But what do they mean by 'exact'? They reply: "The pronunciation at the time of Moses (or even before!) is the true pronunciation." But if you place the bar high enough, even a world champion will miss (it is interesting however to note that the Tetragram written in hieroglyphics, found at Soleb and dated fourteenth century before our era, is normally read Yehua!). By insisting on going back so far in time they imply that the pronunciation used by the high priests in the Temple (of the first century), and by Jesus in his reading aloud of Isaiah's text, was wrong. They are thus trying to be 'more catholic than the Pope'. Indeed, to think that the high priest of Israel, the highest authority for the Jews, and that Jesus, the founder of the Christianity and the highest authority for all Christians, did not pronounce the name correctly could be considered the height of presumption!

Some stress the impossibility of knowing the exact first-century pronunciation of the Name. This last objection is refutable, because, as we have discussed, according to the Masoretic text, theophoric names, which have a part of the Tetragram integrated at the beginning of the name, were, at that time, all pronounced YeHÔ-, *without exception*. Consequently, because the Tetragram is the theophoric name par excellence (arguing otherwise would be absurd), and since it is spelled YHW-H, its reading must be YeHÔ-aH in order to conform to all other theophoric names.

Some will object that Greek sources of the first century all use Iaô. But this does prove that they were still 'trying' to pronounce God's name at that time. However, those reliable sources change with time, eventually supporting the pronunciation of the Hebrew substitute Yahu (or its Aramaic equivalent YaW) and not that of the Tetragram, which was mainly reserved for Temple use. Indeed, before -200, the Septuagint avoids the name Iaou; from -200 to 150, one finds support for Iaô; then from 150 to 300 Iaüé appears; and finally after the year 300 it becomes Iabé. In fact, it seems similar to the Aramaic pronunciation of the number 16 (YW), a pronunciation abandoned by the Jews up to now.

To support this observation, note that writers of that time period and who had access to the priesthood agree; furthermore, these are people who knew the Temple pronunciation and also knew of the substitute used elsewhere. The first witness is the Talmud, which specifies that in the Temple, before its destruction, the name was pronounced as it was spelled (or according to its letters). The second witness is Flavius Josephus, who explains that the name, as pronounced in the Temple, was written with four vowels. These statements, of course, only apply to the Hebrew language. In the first century, Hebrew words were pronounced as follows: Y was used for the sound I / É, W for the sound Û/ O, and H at the end of a word became A. For example, the divine name YH is read IA, the name YHWDH = IHUDA, the name YŠW' = IŠUa', etc. It is possible to improve these pronunciations slightly in order to bring out some of the consonants: Hence, the name I-H-U-D-A becomes I-eH-U-D-A, the name I-Š-U-a' becomes I-eŠ-U-a', and the pronunciation I-H-U-A of the Tetragram becomes I-eH-U-A (pronounced as the four vowels IEUA)[413].

Because of these writings, which were understood by Hebrew scholars only towards the end of the twelfth century, Christian scholars determined the pronunciation of the Name, and not because of an erroneous reading of the Tetragram of the Hebrew Bible, as many specialists still believe (that would have resulted in Yehouah rather than Iehoua). Certainly, it is strange that the Masoretes chose the vowels "*e, o, a,*" since they pronounced this name Adonay. "Chance" would have it that they first choose the vowels "*e, a*" of the Aramaic word Shema' (The Name). Eventually (after 1100), influenced by the vowel "*o*" common to both Adonay and Elohim, they transformed the group "*e, a*" into "*e, o, a.*"

Modern scholars argue that we should not accord too much importance to the Bible text and that, in any case, there are too many uncertainties, thus ironically making their own doubt a certainty. According to this notion, some claim that the Biblical text evolved from primitive sources (of unknown identity and time period!) and that the Name itself must have also evolved from some archaic source (again identity and time period unknown!), and could possibly be Yah. In reality, the theory of Evolution is omnipresent in every step of their reasoning. As we know, according to this "gospel of evolution", the first woman is no longer Eve, but Lucy. As Psalm 100:3 shows, the Bible warns against this way of thinking because he who believes in Evolution ceases to bless His Name (Ps 100:4).

In 1753 a French doctor penned the above mentioned theory of ancient, unknown sources[414] (imagined first by H.B. Witter in 1711), and the touchstone of his explanation was the divine Name. Since God was called either Iehouah, or Elohim, in the Bible, he concluded that there had been two gods (Iehouah and Elohim) and so at least two ancient sources!

Using the Bible itself, the "evolutionists" reason that the patriarch Abraham could not have blessed and called upon His Name, because five centuries later Moses asked God "What is your name?" (Ex 3:13) which according to them proves that the Name was previously unknown. The passage at Exodus 6:3 seems to support their conclusion because God states that he did not make His Name known to Abraham. However, by their explanation, the "evolutionists" take a leaf from the theologian's book by interpreting the biblical answer. Now, Moses exact question (!) was rather: «If they say to me, 'What about his name?' What shall I say to them?» His question is concerning the meaning ('How, what' [Hebrew pronoun mâ]) and not the pronunciation ('who' [Hebrew pronoun mî]), as in Judges 13:17 where Manoah asked the question because he did not know the name of the angel speaking to him (Jg 13:6). As Juda Halevi points out, Pharaoh himself knew the Name because he asked: «Who is Yehuah?» (Ex 5:2) However, he apparently did not understand its meaning. So, as shown by Maimonides, the meaning of the word 'name' in Exodus 6:3 must pertain to reputation as in Genesis 6:4, Numbers 16:2, etc., otherwise we would be led to conclude that simply revealing the pronunciation would have motivated the Israelites to action, which seems implausible.

In fact the Bible differentiates between the pronunciation of a name and its corresponding reputation. Pharaoh's above-mentioned question helps us to understand two aspects of the name: the actual name and its subsequent reputation. We read in Exodus 9:16: «For this cause I have kept you in existence, for the sake of showing you my power [hence my reputation] and in order to have my name declared in all the earth.» So, even though these two aspects are related, we must distinguish between them, not mistaking the pronunciation 'Yehouah' for its reputation, that is its religious meaning (He will be). This definition comes from God's own declaration, speaking of himself as 'I shall be' (Ex 3:14). We could hence conclude that when speaking about God we could say: 'He will be' (in Hebrew *yihyèh* or *yahwèh*?), an understandable disparity because we are not discussing the same thing. We note that the well-known name Yehudah (pronunciation) seems to be similar to the meaning of *Yôdèh* (He will laud); and the name Yéshua' (pronunciation) resembles the meaning of *Yôshia'* (He will save), etc.

This confusion between the pronunciation and the reputation creates a tendency to mistake God for Jesus. It is true that the following statement is Biblical: "God exalted him (Jesus) to a superior position and kindly gave him the name that is above every other name." (Ph 2:9). Some Bible references state that Jesus is given God's name at this point. This is another example of confusing name and reputation, and this for at least three reasons. Firstly, Jesus had already received God's name well before this account, as he states at John 17:11,12: «Holy Father, watch over them on account of your name which you have given me.» However, since even his disciples never addressed Jesus as the Tetragram, we must understand that, as he stated himself, he is simply speaking of: «The glory that you have given me» (Jn 17:22). This practice of equating God's name with God's glory is an ancient custom (Ex 33:18,19; Is 42:8). Secondly, the name of Jesus has always been different from God's name, as can be seen in the last book of the Christian Bible (Rv 3:12; 14:1). Thirdly, even the Bible itself asserts that 'God's name' is not all-powerful, because 'God's word' is placed higher than his name (Ps 138:2). Then, why did Jesus specify that God had given him his name? What exactly does this expression mean when found in the Bible?

The explanation is very simple! When somebody gives his name to another, he is simply authorizing that person to sign or speak in his name. That is the over-all meaning of the Bible expression (1K 21:8; Est 3:12; 8:8,10; Lk 10:17). The principle of delegating a name to another authorizes someone to speak or to sign in that person's name, thus granting authority to his agent and hence a part of the glory of the delegator. For example, God placed his name on his people (Nb 6:27; Ac 15:14), that is, he authorized them to speak and to act in his name (Ex 5:23; Dt 10:8; 18:5,7; 1S 17:45). At times, when this legal covenant or "Power of Attorney" to make decisions in his name becomes permanent, the name is considered not *on* but *in* the empowered agent (Ex 23:21; 1K 9:3; 2K 21:4,7). However, the legal sharing of authority between the delegator and his agent can sometimes become blurred.

Obviously, if the agent oversteps his mandate, the authority of the delegator becomes invalid (Dt 18:19-22; Ac 19:13-16). But, in Jesus' case, the agent's action remains valid, even though it may seem strange to some (Mk 9:38,39). When we read that «Solomon built a house for him» (Ac 7:47), or «Jeroboam proceeded to build Sichem» (1K 12:25), «He (Cain) engaged in building a city» (Gn 4:17), it is obvious that these persons simply (legally) attributed their name to actions which they did not personally carry out. In some cases, however, this ambiguity can become paradoxical. For example, Jacob, having legally bought the right of Esau the first-born (Gn 25:33), can then state "legally" to his father: «I am Esau your first-born.» (Gn 27:19). Similarly, it is easy to confuse the two delegators John and James (Mk 10:35) with their agent, their mother (Mt 20:20). One can mistake the delegating officer of Matthew 8:5 with the elders whom he delegated (Lk 7:3); and, often in the

Bible, there is (legal) confusion between the angel of God (Gn 16:7) and God himself (Gn 16:13).

Of course the angels spoke in the name of God; moreover in Hebrew the word 'angel' signifies 'messenger'. However, the Bible distinguishes between these occasional spokesmen and the personal spokesman of God (Is 63:9). This spokesman possesses permanent authority because God's name is *in* him (Ex 23:21). This angel could be "legally" called by Jehovah's name (Gn 18:2,22,23; 19:1); but, in order to avoid confusion when questioned, he refused to give this own name (Gn 32:29; Jg 13:18) thus avoiding the mistaking of the 'legal' person for the 'authentic' person of God. This is not the only case in the Bible. For example, Moses, although he was 'legally' established as 'God' (Ex 4:16; 7:1) never claimed to be God; but the Law of Moses is still considered God's law. Also, certain men were 'legally' established as gods (Ps 82:6; Jn 10:34,35), but never claimed to be gods, even though, while acting as judges, they 'legally' represented God (Ex 21:6; Dt 1:16,17).

This legal aspect of the name is necessary in order to avoid misunderstanding. So, the Bible does not contradict itself at all when it says that one «Cannot see the (authentic) person of God and live» (Ex 33:20,23; Jn 1:18), while on the other hand saying that some people could see the (legal) person of God and live (Ex 33:11; Gn 32:24,28-30; Jg 13:22; Jn 14:9). In this last case, we understand that those who saw God (legally) in actual fact saw one of his representatives (physically). Hence, the contradictions are resolved when we understand that when God gives his name to angels or to human beings he simply authorizes them to speak in his name as spokesman. This mandate can be momentary or permanent, restricted or expanded, God obviously being the one who fixes the limits of the delegated powers resulting from the use of his name. Receiving the name (Ex 23:21) denotes receiving authority (Mt 28:18).

Christians identified Jesus as the one who received the authority of the Name. For Jews of our day only the Messiah will be able to reveal the exact pronunciation of the Tetragram.

But, Jesus asserted in Hebrew 2:12: «I will announce your name to my brothers.» However, since this promise concerning God's name was not fulfilled in the first century it must be considered a prophecy for a future time. The prophet Micah also predicted that during the final period of days each would walk in the name of his god, but that his people would walk in the name of Yehouah (Mi 4.1,5).

The Jews thought too that the expression "to have the name in one's self" could be understood in a symbolic sense (as a person in authority), but that it must also have a literal significance, as do most Bible prophecies. Thus, according to the Talmud (*Baba Batra 75b*), the name of the King Messiah is «Yehouah our Righteousness» (Jr 23:5,6). However, Jewish tradition (*Ḥagigah 15a; Sanhedrin 38b*) gradually identified this powerful personage with the angel Metatron, his true name being Yahôel, from which some came to the conclusion that God's name must be Yahôh. If the Jews had recognized Jesus as the Messiah and used the same reasoning (Rm 3:21-26), they would have deduced that the name which is phonetically in Yéshua' is Yehua. The name Yahô had the problem of not corresponding well with the name Yehudah, since the Talmud (*Sotah 10b, 36b*) states that God's name was contained in that name. The Gospels confirm that Juda received great authority with time (Mt 2:6; Heb 7:14). Furthermore, we can see that the name, which exists phonetically in Yehuda, is also in Yehoua. Interestingly Israeli researchers indicate that «the angel of the face» (Is 63:9) was called Yôshoua by the Judeo-Christians, and not Metatron or Yahoel, and that is why Jews always use this name 'Jesus' (Yôshoua) in their ritual[415] new year invocation.

The idea that the controversy over the Name would be resolved during the final period of days is indicated many times by the prophet Ezekiel in his expression: «Then they will have to know that I am Yehouah.» The Gospels clearly indicate that Jesus came to destroy the works of the Devil (1Jn 3:8) and eventually to destroy the Devil himself at the end of time (Heb 2:14). However, is the conflict between these two persons an ancient issue? If so, do the Hebrew Scriptures mention it?

Actually, in his foresight, God established from the outset the way this controversy would end. Even more remarkably, without fear of defeat he revealed it in writing, declaring from ancient times that his powerful Behemoth[416] (Rv 5:5) would, in a grande finale, bruise the seventh and last head of the Leviathan with its sword.

To love the truth, the Name and incense

To love God means to love truth (2Th 2:10) be it oral (Jn 14:6) or in its written form, the Bible (Jn 17:17). In any case, these two forms converge (Jn 1:14; 8:42,47). How can we recognize truth? According to the Bible, truth has a specific odor (2Co 2:14-16), which attracts some and repulses others. Indeed, according to this letter addressed to the Corinthians, conquerors provided incense to be burned during their triumphant procession, thus highlighting their victory. This incense "smelled" thus of glory and honor. On the other hand, for the losers this incense became a smell of death because it reminded them of their imminent execution.

The Bible often stresses the importance of incense, which symbolizes the intimacy of spiritual relations with God. That is why they always had to use incense in Temple worship, a specific and unique recipe that was protected from secular use by the death penalty (Ex 30:7,37,38). To prepare a prayer meant to prepare incense (Ps 141:2) and to say a prayer meant to burn incense (Rv 5:8). However, the odor of this spiritual incense was pleasant only if the name of the person who prayed had a good odor itself (Qo 7:1). The name of a wise person was comparable to perfumed oil because of his wisdom (Qo 10:1; Ph 4:18); the name of a wicked person stank because of its decay (Gn 34:30, Pr 10:7). Consequently, the name of the supreme Wise One could be only a pleasant scent for the wise.

This basic idea is seen in the Song of Salomon. Indeed, Jews as well as Christians understand in this song concerning the indestructible love of the shepherdess for her bridegroom a representation of the indestructible affection of the chosen people for their God. This magnificent song begins with the expression: «Like a perfumed oil that is poured out is your name» (Sg 1:3). There is Hebrew play-on-words between the word 'your name' (Šemèka) and 'your perfumed oil'

(Šemanèka), because God's name is comparable to incense. In old Hebrew this word 'incense' is Qeturah, like the name of the wife who comforted Abraham (Gn 25:1), and it is understandable that, for Abraham, his wife Qeturah really had a name of incense, a name he loved. Today, a popular Judeo-Arab proverb ironically says[417] «I have for you so much love that I have forgotten your name», but it goes without saying that for Abraham, God's name could not be forgotten because it was Incense, the ultimate Name, the Name par excellence.

Part 4

Appendix

Glossary, Chronology

■ List of abbreviations:

A.S.O.R.	American Schools of Oriental Research; Newhaven
A.L.H.	Academia Litterarum Heidelbergensis, Hamburg
B.A.S.O.R.	Bulletin of the American Schools of Oriental Research; Newhaven
B.H.S.	Biblia Hebraica Stuttgartensia
B.I.O.S.C.S	Bulletin of the International Organization for the Septuagint and Cognate Studies; USA
B.O.S.E.B.	Bibliothèque Œcuménique des Sciences et Études Bibliques; Paris
C.A.T.A.B.	Centre d'Analyse et de Traitement Automatique de la Bible; Lyon
C.R.A.I.L.	Comptes Rendus de l'Académie des Inscriptions & Belles-Lettres; Paris
E.B.O.R.C.	Études Bibliques et Orientales de Religions Comparées; Leiden
H.U.C.A.	Hebrew Union College Annual; Cincinnati
I.E.J.	Israel Exploration Journal; Jerusalem
J.B.L.	Journal of Biblical Literature; Philadelphia
J.J.S.	Journal of Jewish Studies; London
J.S.O.T.	Journal of the Study of the Old Testament; Sheffield
LAPO	Littératures Anciennes du Proches-Orient
LXX	Septuagint (Ralhfs)
M.T.	Masoretic Text (BHS)
O.T.S.	OudTestamentische Studien; Leiden
P.L.	Patrologiæ Latina; Paris
R.B.	Revue Biblique; Paris
V.T.	Vetus Testamentum; Leyde
Z.A.W.	Zeitschrift für die Alttestamentliche Wissenschaft; Berlin
Z.D.M.G	Zeitschrift des Deutschen Morgendländiscen Gesellschaft, Leipzig

The abbreviations of the biblical books are the same as those of the Jerusalem Bible. The biblical quotations are taken from the New World Translation or the Jerusalem Bible.

References to the Talmud in this book are standardized according to the two usual editions. For example: *Sotah 40b; 7,6* refers to:

Sotah 40b - The Babylonian Talmud -I. Epstein. London 1948
Sotah 7,6 - Le Talmud de Jérusalem -M. Schwab. Paris 1933
(see also - Textes rabbiniques -J. Bonsirven. Roma 1955)

Abbreviations in Alphabetical order according to the Jerusalem Bible (1968)

Ac	Acts	Lk	Luke
Am	Amos	Lm	Lamentations
Ba	Baruch	Lv	Leviticus
1Ch	1 Chronicles	1M	1 Maccabees
2Ch	2 Chronicles	2M	2 Maccabees
1Co	1 Corinthians	Mi	Micah
2Co	2 Corinthians	Mk	Mark
Col	Colossians	Ml	Malachi
Dn	Daniel	Mt	Matthew
Dt	Deuteronomy	Na	Nahum
Ep	Ephesians	Nb	Numbers
Est	Esther	Ne	Nehemiah
Ex	Exodus	Ob	Obadiah
Ezk	Ezekiel	1P	1 Peter
Ezr	Ezra	2P	2 Peter
Ga	Galatians	Ph	Philippians
Gn	Genesis	Phm	Philemon
Hab	Habakkuk	Pr	Proverbs
Heb	Hebrews	Ps	Psalms
Hg	Haggai	Qo	Ecclesiastes
Ho	Hosea	Rm	Romans
Is	Isaiah	Rt	Ruth
Jb	Job	Rv	Revelation
Jdt	Judith	1S	1 Samuel
Jg	Judges	2S	2 Samuel
Jl	Joel	Sg	Song of Songs
Jm	James	Si	Ecclesiasticus
Jn	John	Tb	Tobit
1Jn	1 John	1Th	1 Thessalonians
2Jn	2 John	2Th	2 Thessalonians
3Jn	3 John	1Tm	1 Timothy
Jon	Jonah	2Tm	2 Timothy
Jos	Joshua	Tt	Titus
Jr	Jeremiah	Ws	Wisdom
Jude	Jude	Zc	Zechariah
1K	1 Kings	Zp	Zephaniah
2K	2 Kings	*	notes

■ Alphabet

Hebrew Old	New	Letter name	Transcr.	Greek letter	value
	א	Alèph	'		'
	ב	Béth	b	(β)	b
			b̲	B β	bv
	כ		b̲	(β,υ)	v
	ג	Gîmèl	g	Γ γ	g
	ג		g	(γ)	g/r
	ד	Dalèth	d	(δ,τ)	d/t
			d	Δ δ	d
	ד		d̲	(δ,θ)	d/z
	ה	Hé	h		h
	ה		h		h
	ו	Waw	w	(υ,ου)	w
	ו		ww	(υ,ου)	ouw
	ז	Zayin	z	Z ζ	z
	ח	Héth	ḥ		h/kh
	ט	Téth	t	T τ	t
	י	Yôd	y	(ι)	y
			yy	(ι)	iy
	כ	Kaph	k	K κ	k
	כ		k̲	X χ	kh
	ל	Lamèd	l	Λ λ	l
	מ	Mém	m	M μ	m
	נ	Noun	n	N ν	n
	ע	Ayin	'		'/g
	ס	Samèkh	s	Σ σ	s
	פ	Pé	p	Π π	p
	פ		p̲	Φ φ	ph
	צ	Tsadé	s̲		ts
	ק	Qôph	q	(κ)	q
	ר	Résh	r	P ρ	r
	ש	Sîn	s	Σ σ	s
	ש	Shîn	š		sh
	ת	Taw	t	T τ	t
	ת	Thaw	t̲	Θ θ	th
			x	Ξ ξ	x
				Ψ ψ	ps

■ Vowels:

i	é	è	a	æ	o	ô	u	ü
								(e)

Masoretic vowel-points

Matres lectionis (with their vowel-points)

Greek vowels

I	E	H	A	AY	O	Ω	OY	Y
ι	ε	η	α	αυ	ο	ω	ου	υ
							(ε,η)	

■ Lexicon:

Kethib

Aramaic word which means '[what is] written'. This expression indicates the consonants of the written word, because before the sixth century of our era the biblical text was written in Hebrew without its vowel-points. For example, the *kethib* of the word Molok (Ac 7:43) is MLK. The Masoretes would have had to punctuate this *kethib* M*o*L*o*K (with the vowels *o, o*).

Qere

Aramaic word which means '[what is] read'. This expression indicates the (Masoretic) vowels of the word to be read. For example, the *qere* of the word Molok (1K 11:7) is *o, è*, which are the (Masoretic) vowels of the word B*o*SH*è*T which means 'shame' in Hebrew. Translators who by ignorance mix this *qere o, è*, (shame) with its *kethib* (MLK) obtain the mixed form M*o*L*è*K (on the other hand, the name Molok is read in the Septuagint as in Acts 7:43).

Matres lectionis

This Latin expression which means 'mothers of reading' mainly indicates the three consonants Y, W and H, being used as vowels in the pre-Masoretic text. Y is used to vocalize the sound I (or E), W for the sound U (or O) and H at the end of words for the sound A. A word is in *plene writing* if its vowels are indicated with their *matres lectionis*, otherwise a word is in *defective writing*. For example the word DWD in *plene writing* is read DOD (which means 'beloved'), but DaWaD in *defective writing* can also be read. The name David (DaWiD) is often written with its *mater lectionis* (that is DWYD instead of DWD) which allows the unambiguous pronunciation DaWID (one supposes a regular sequence consonant-vowel). In *plene writing* DLYLH is read (reading according to its letters) DaLILA, HGR is read HaGaR, YṢḤQ is read IṢaḤaQ, Y'QWB is read I'aQÔB, 'BRHM is read 'aBaRaHaM, 'DM is read 'aDaM, YHWDH is read IHUDA, etc.

Theophoric name

A proper noun which contains either the divine name Yah, or a part of the complete divine name Yehowah. For example, Yehô-natan and Eli-yah are theophoric names. Theophoric names are found in the Muslim Quran (Surah VI:85), in the Catholic Vulgate or in the Orthodox Septuagint, but only the Jewish Torah has kept the correct pronunciation and the exact meaning.

N.W.T.	Zechariah	John	Jesus	Elijah
Quran	Zakarîyâ	Yaḥyâ	'Isa	Ilyâs
Vulgate	Zaccharia	Iohanan	Iosue	Helia
LXX	Zakaria	Iôanan	Ièsou	Élia
Torah	Zekaryah	Yehoḥanân	Yéšûa'	'Éliyahû
Meaning of names	He has remembered Yah	Yeho[uah] has been gracious	[Yehouah is] salvation	My God is Yah himself

Religious etymology

This expression indicates the etymology given by the biblical text, and which can be different from the grammatical or technical etymology. For example, the name Noah means in Hebrew 'rest' (Nuah), but the Bible connects this name to the idea of 'comfort' (Gn 5:29). To avoid confusion between these two etymologies, it could be said that 'rest' is the technical etymology, while 'comfort' is the religious etymology.

Grammatical form

The Hebraic 'conjugation' of a verb is characterized by two aspects (perfect and imperfect) which one returns in English by three tenses (past, present, future), three stems (simple, intensive, causative) and three conditions (active, passive, reflexive). For example, for the Hebrew verb "to kill" in the perfect state, the third masculine person of the singular gives the following seven (possible) combinations:

Form (perfect)	Simple	Resultative/ Factitive	Causative
Active	qatal (**qal**) he killed	qittél (**piél**) he brought into a dead state	hiqtil (**hiphil**) he caused to kill
Passive	niqtal (**niphal**) he was killed	quttal (**pual**) he was brought into a dead state	hoqtal (**hophal**) he was caused to kill
Reflexive		hitqattél (**hitpaél**) he killed himself	

The form *qal* of the verb "to kill" in Hebrew for the third masculine person of the singular in the perfect aspect is the word *qatal* (see table above). Most of the time this word can be translated by 'he killed'. In the imperfect aspect, the form *qal* of the verb 'to kill' in Hebrew for the third masculine person of the singular is the word *yiqtol* which can be translated by a future tense 'he will kill' or a present tense 'he kills'.

■ Chronology of main events

To help the reader a rough chronology has been made. The names between brackets are based on witnesses but there is no archeological proof. The grey colored zones point to a period of important activity.

BIBLICAL WITNESSES BEFORE OUR COMMON ERA

Date	Old Hebrew	Hebrew	Greek	Comments
-1500	𐤉𐤄𐤅𐤄?			Pentateuch written by Moses according to Exodus 17:14
-1400				
-1300				
-1200				
-1100				
-1000				
-900				
-800				
-700	𐤉𐤄𐤅𐤄			Silver plates of Ketef Hinnom Hilkiah found the book of
-600	(𐤉𐤄𐤅𐤄)			Moses (2Ch 34:14)
-500	(𐤉𐤄𐤅𐤄)	(יהוה)		Ezra catalogued the Bible in Hebrew.
-400	(𐤉𐤄𐤅𐤄)	(יהוה)		
-300	𐤉𐤄𐤅𐤄	(יהוה)	(יהוה)	Qumran manuscripts
-200	𐤉𐤄𐤅𐤄	יהוה	יהוה	Papyrus Fouad 266
-100	𐤉𐤄𐤅𐤄	𐤉𐤄𐤅𐤄	𐤉𐤄𐤅𐤄	One papyrus of the LXX with I A Ω
000				

BIBLICAL WITNESSES IN OUR COMMON ERA

Date	Hebrew	Greek (then others) LXX	NT	Comments
000	𐤉𐤄𐤅𐤄	𐤉𐤄𐤅𐤄	(𐤉𐤄𐤅𐤄)	The oldest papyrus of the NT is dated 125 (P52)
100	(𐤉𐤄𐤅𐤄)	𐤉𐤄𐤅𐤄	K̄C̄	*Nomina sacra* process started between 70 and 135
200	(𐤉𐤄𐤅𐤄)	𐤉𐤄𐤅𐤄	K̄C̄	Hebrew is no longer used in daily life.
300	('יהו(ה	ΠΙΠΙ.	K̄C̄	The Jews used Hebrew again to write the Name
400	('יהו(ה	ΠΙΠΙ הוהי	Lord	Vulgate used *Dominus* (Lord)
500	יהוה	ΠΙΠΙ	Lord	Masoretes began to point the Hebrew text.
600	יְהוָה	ΠΙΠΙ	Lord 'ה	A few manuscripts of the NT in Hebrew (book of Nestor) have
700	יְהוָה	Lord	Lord	the expression H' which means "the Name"
800	יְהוָה	Lord ΠΙΠΙ	Lord	Last copies of the Septuagint with the name pypy.
900	יְהוָה	Lord	Lord	
1000	יְהוָה	Lord	Lord	
1100	יְהֹוָה	Lord	Lord 'ה	The pointing Yehwah became Yehowah in the Hebrew Bible
1200	יְהֹוָה	Lord	Lord 'ה	
1300	יְהֹוָה	Lord	Lord 'ה	Shem Tob manuscript of Matthew in Hebrew
1400	יְהֹוָה	Lord	Lord	
1500	יְהֹוָה	Iehouah	Lord	Printing of manuscripts. Tyndale used the name Iehouah
1600	יְהֹוָה	Jehovah	Lord	The form Iehouah and Ioua are both attacked.
1700	יְהֹוָה	Jehovah	Lord	The grammatical form Iahue is proposed by Drusius
1800	יְהֹוָה	Jehovah	Lord	Numerous biblical Societies.
1900	יְהֹוָה	Yahweh	YHWH	The name Yhwh is found in a few NT.
2000				

EXTRA-BIBLICAL WITNESSES BEFORE OUR COMMON ERA

Date	YHWH	YHW	YH	Comments
-2000				Patriarchal period
-1900				
-1800				
-1700				Hyksos period (-1750 -1500)
-1600				
-1500				Hyksos are expelled from Egypt and arrive in Palestine
-1400	ꓑꓭꓺ (Yehua')			Egyptian shields from Soleb
-1300				
-1200	(ヨ Y ヨ Z) (Ieüô)			Sanchuniathon testimony
-1100				
-1000				First Temple building
-900	𐤉𐤄𐤅𐤄			Mesha stele
-800	𐤉𐤄𐤅𐤄	𐤉𐤄𐤅		Kuntillet Ajrud inscriptions
-700	𐤉𐤄𐤅𐤄	(𐤉𐤄𐤅)	𐤉𐤄	Lakish, Arad, Khirbet el Qom inscriptions
-600		𐤉𐤄𐤅	𐤉𐤄	First Temple destroyed. Jar stamps with Yh / Yhw. Yehud inscriptions
-500	יהו	יהה	Second Temple. Modern Hebrew is adopted. Elephantine letters.
-400	𐡉𐡄𐡅	𐡉𐡄	Old Hebrew is used again. Many variants of writings.
-300	𐡉𐡄𐡅	𐡉𐡄	LXX translation (-280)
-200				Jar stamps are taken away. The use of the Name is avoided.
-100		I A Ω		Latin Varro ang Greek Diodorus of Sicily witnesses
000				

EXTRA-BIBLICAL WITNESSES IN OUR COMMON ERA

Date	YHWH	YHW	YH	Comments
000				Beginning of Christianity. Second Temple destroyed (70)
100	𐤉𐤄𐤅𐤄	I A Ω יהו	I A יה	Philon of Byblos spoke of IEÜÔ. Greek and Jewish amulets.
200	𐤉𐤄𐤅𐤄	I A Ω יהו	I A יה	A few magical papyri with IEÔA or IEEÔOUA.
300		I A B E יהו	I A יה	Samaritan inscriptions of Yhwh with a pronunciation of Iabe.
400				Vulgate finished
500	I Ω A	I A Ω		Some comments in the LXX mention the name IAÔ. Severi of Antioch IÔA
600				IÔA found in the Codex Coislinianus
700				
800				Charlemagne asked to spread the Bible (in Europe).
900				
1000				
1100	IEUE			Maimonides Joachim de Flore Pope Innocent III
1200	Yohoua			Raymond Martin Porchetus de Salvaticis
1300	Yehabe			Abner de Burgos
1400	Iehoua			Cardinal Nicolaus of Cusa
1500	Jehovah			Beginning of Humanism. The Hebrew tongue became well-known in Europe
1600	Jehovah			
1700	Jehovah			
1800	Jehovah			
1900	Yahweh			
2000				

Interpretation of the Hebrew names

GRAMMATICAL DIFFICULTIES (EX. ABDIEL)

The vast majority of Hebrew names are interpreted simply from their grammatical meaning. For example, the name Daniel means 'my judge [is] God' or Obadyah which means 'servant [of] Yah'. On the other hand there are some problems for a few names (less than one quarter of the total) notably the divine names; there are some problems. So, the names Abdiel, Gabriel, etc., can not be directly be translated by 'my servant [is] God', 'my brave one [is] God', etc., without obtaining a nonsensical meaning. It is interesting to explain these oddities in order to understand the mechanism of interpretation.

The name Abdeel (Jr 36:26) existed at about at the same time as Abdiel (1Ch 5:15). As the name Abdeel means 'servant [of] God', the name Abdiel could be understood to mean 'my servant [is] God' which is surprising. There are two possible explanations, either Abdiel is an archaic Hebrew genitive in *i* meaning 'servant [of] God' or a paragogic vowel *i* has been added to slightly modify the tone without changing the sense of the name that is 'servant-of-me [of] God'. For example, the name Abshalom (2Ch 11:20,21) has also been written Abishalom (1K 15:2,10). It is not easy to decide between the two explanations. However, as the archaic cases (genitive, nominative, accusative) disappeared early enough (before 1100 BCE), it seems more likely to explain these variants in proper nouns by some paragogic vowels[418], so, the name Abihu (Lv 10:1) which is very ancient (time of Moses) must be translated by 'my father [is] He', not by 'father [of] He' that is 'God'!

RESOLUTION OF SOME CASES (EX. SAMUEL)

In most dictionaries[419] the name Samuel is shown to mean in Hebrew 'Name of God' what completely contradicts the biblical etymology which connects this name to 'asked to God'

(1S 1:20). Indeed, even though biblical etymologies look more like wordplays than rigorous definitions there is nevertheless a link between the grammatical sense of the name and its biblical explanation. The definition 'Name of God' for the Hebraic name Shemuel supposes that it is an archaic nominative which, as was seen previously, is very improbable. A reference work recognized that if the Sumerian name Shumu-ilum (God's name) existed, there was not enough chance that there is a link between these two names. To resolve this difficulty the author of this work[420] proposed a conjugate form of a verb 3H as an alternative, that is Shamû-el 'we loft God' or 'Loftiness of God'. However, this explanation has two inconveniences, firstly the proposed root is uncommon in Hebrew and secondly, the sense of the name has nothing to do with the biblical explanation. An alternative improvement consists of supposing an old form Shim-Hu'-'il which means 'name [of] him [is] God' or 'His name [is] God' which contradicts the Bible itself because the name of God is not 'God' but Yah or Yehowah.

A final argument is to check that the definition 'Name of God' can not fit. Indeed, if this name resulted from an archaic form it would have been pronounced Shimu-il, because the word 'name', Shém in Hebrew, results from a more ancient pronunciation Shim[421]. In the Septuagint this name was vocalized Samuel and not Simuel or Semuel. On the other hand the name Shém (Gn 10:22) which means 'name', was vocalized Sèm and not Sam, the name Shemiramoth 'name [in the] heights' (1Ch 15:18) was vocalized Sémiramoth and not Samiramoth, the name Shemida 'Name he knows' (Nb 26:32) was vocalized Sum(aér) and not Sam(aér). So the vocalization Sam- of the name Samuel does not allow an interpretation of the name Samuel into 'Name of -'.

To try to reconcile the grammatical sense of the name and its explanation in the Bible an author[422] suggested translating Shemuel by She-me-el that is 'what is from God'. This explanation is cunning but the presence of the *u* inside the name remains inexplicable. An explanation could nevertheless reconcile all these difficulties. Indeed, Gesenius[423] proposed an explanation of the name Samuel by a contraction of the name Shammu'a'el which means 'being heard of God'. Firstly, the first part Shammu'a (2S 5:14) of the Name is very common and its meaning is 'being heard'. Secondly the explanation 'being heard of God' is close to the biblical definition 'asked to God'. Thirdly, the contraction Shammu'a'el into Shamu'el that is to say: *u-a-* into *u-*, is normal because the drop out of the vowel *a* inside a word is very frequent in Hebrew. Lastly, Shamu'el became Shemu'el around the third century before our era when the first *a* dropped out in the same way that Zakaryah and Natanyah became Zekaryah and Netanyah.

CONTRACTION IN SOME VOWELS (EX. YÔEL)

For example, the name Zerubabel came from an old form Zeru'a-babel which means 'seed of Babel'. This name corresponds to the Akkadian name Zer-babili (seed of Babel), or perhaps to Zarut-babili (begotten of Babel), which has been adopted in Hebrew with the same meaning. Thus, Zeru('a)babel meaning 'seed of Babel' in Hebrew became Zerubabel. The fusion of the group *u-a* into a simple *u* is often seen especially inside a word.

Name	Meaning	Hebrew form	Reference
Ge'û'él	majesty of God	Ga'(a)w(ah)-'él	Nb 13:15
Miṣwot	commandments	Miṣw(ah)-ôt	Nb 15:22
Yiśra'él	He will contend, God	Yiśra(h)'él	Gn 32:28
'Elohim	Gods/ God	'Elo(a)h-im	2K 1:12

Thus, the name Ga'aw(ah)'el became Ga'ow'el that is Ga'û'el then Ge'û'el. More generally there were contractions in the theophoric names. For example, Yehowah-nathan became Yehow(ah)nathan that is Yehônathan, sometimes there was a double contraction like Yehowah-'el which became Y(eh)ow(ah)'el that is Yô'el, in the same way that the name Ga'(a)w(ah)'el became Ga'û'el (then Ge'û'el), or Mitsw(ah)ot became Mitswot.

CONFUSION DUE TO A FOREIGN INFLUENCE (EX. ZERUBABEL)

When a name has a foreign origin, the risks of confusion in the explanation of the etymology are higher. For example the name Zerubabel possesses two senses which are close in Akkadian (seed and begotten) but it is possible to propose some other explanations. For example, in Akkadian *zuru* means 'strength, shoulder', so Zurubabili can be translated by 'strength of Babel'. This choice may be justified by the fact that the Septuagint has vocalized this name Zoro-babel and the Hebrew translation of 'strength of Babel' is Zero'a-Babel which may deformed into Zerubabel. A final argument which helps to decide among various possible senses is to consider the plausible and logical aspects of the choice. As the deportation to Babylon was a humiliation the name 'strength of Babylon' must be eliminated. The name 'seed of Babylon' seems more likely, but the Septuagint kept the vocalization Zoro- which supposes a former Zuru- or Zaru- corresponding to the sense 'begotten' in Akkadian. It is possible that the Akkadian name was Zaru(t)babel 'begotten of Babel' and that this name was translated into Hebrew Zeru('a)babel because the sense 'to sow' was common. For example the name Yizr'e'el came from the verbal form Yizr'a'el which means 'God will sow seed', which is in accordance with its prophetic meaning (Hos 2:22,23). Seeing Zerubabel's role, it seems logical to think that the Jews recognized in him a prophetic role of 'seed'.

CONFUSION DUE TO ETYMOLOGY (EX. BABEL)

The case of Babylon's name is exemplary. Indeed, this name is very old, but what perplexes the grammarians is the incompatibility between the well established biblical etymology, which connects this name with the root 'to mix, to confuse' (Gn 11:9) and the grammatical meaning given by some archaeological evidences, which is 'gate of God'.

The age of the city is confirmed by an inscription[424] of the king of Agade (Akkad) called Shar-kali-sharri (-2217-2193) who mentions his restoring of two temple-towers at Babylon. This precision implying that this city existed prior to his reign, and furthermore this restoration suppose that the city had decayed, is in agreement with the biblical record of a desolation of the city after the Flood (Gn 11:8). The Sumerian stories relate the event of a universal flood and distinguish between the kings before the Flood and after the Flood in their list of kings.

In the most ancient documents, the name of the city is always written in Sumerian in the form KA.DINGIR.RA(K) which means 'Gate of God'. This name was translated into Akkadian as Bab-ilum. Afterwards, once the Sumerian language had disappeared, this name would have been read as Bab-ili (Gate of god), or sometimes as Bab-ilani (Gate of each individual god). In this time the expression 'Gate of God' was understood as 'Gate of Heavens' or 'Heavenly Gate', which is in agreement with the concepts of this epoch, for example, to express his admiration Jacob said: «How fear-inspiring this place is! This is nothing else but the house of God and this is the gate of the heavens» (Gn 28:17). The place-name Bab-Ea (Gate of Ea) is mentioned in the inscriptions[425] of a city dated around 2200 BCE. Ea is one of the main gods of the Akkadians, sometimes written Aya in the most ancient texts.

It seems illogical that the builders of a city would call it 'confusion' especially as the Bible recorded that these builders were presumptuous because they hoped its top would be in the heavens (Gn 11:4). This is probably where the name 'Gate of heavens' came from. Which language was used to name the city? As the Sumerian language is the most ancient known at the moment, one can not suppose a pre-Sumerian pronunciation. However, the Bible clarifies that before the Flood there was only one single language (Gn 11:1) which confirms some Sumerian stories. The following extracts can read[426]: «Formerly it was a time when the lands of Shubur and Hamazi, Sumer where are spoken so many languages to each other (...) honored Enlil in a single language.» or: «The leader of the gods, the Lord of Eridu, endowed with wisdom, changed the words of their mouth, put in it some discord, in the language of the man which had been unique.» According to the Bible this unique language could be Hebrew, it is possible that in archaic Hebrew this city was called 'gate of heavens' that is 'Bab-ilum'.

In conclusion, the Bible kept an almost exact transcription of this antique city, however the etymology of the name was modified. Moreover, it should be noted that the Hebraic transcription is Babel (בָּבֶל) and not Bab'el (בָּבְאֵל) which would have kept the exact etymology of the name of this city. As previously seen, the biblical definition is based more on a play on words (like Gilgal 'wheel' instead of Galîl (?) 'rolling away' according to Joshua 5:9) than on a rigorous definition and the Babylonians themselves proceeded in the same way, believing that the same sound is connected to the same sense. In Hebrew to express 'confusion' or 'discomfiture' the word *mehumah* is used (Dt 28:20). Thus, according to the Bible, the word Babel, the 'gate of heavens', came to be owing to a wordplay *babelulah* (בְּבְלוּלָה) that is 'in the mix-up', or Babîl (בָּבִיל) 'in the confusion', which remains close to the name Babel. The change BLL into B-BL is identical with the name Bezalel (Ex 31:3) written B-ṢL-'L (בְּצַלְאֵל), which means 'in [the] shadow of God'. The word ṢĕL 'shadow' comes from the verb ṢaLaL (to be shaded) in the same way that the Aramaic passive participle BîL comes from the verb BaLaL (to mix).

CONFUSION DUE TO ETYMOLOGY (EX. YEHOWAH)

The vocalization of the divine name involves a unique process because this name which was accepted for almost five centuries is now being revocalized due to former witnesses or according to its presumed etymology. This method is unprecedented, for example, the legendary hero of Mesopotamia Gilgamesh, is now much better known due to numerous archaeological discoveries from very ancient witnesses (before 2000 BCE), however the spelling of this name is far from being uniform. For example the following variants can be seen[427]:

Sumerian	giš-bil-ga-meš
	giš-bil-maš/mez
	giš
Hittite	giš-gim-maš
Neo-Babylonian	giš-gim-maš
Hurrite	gal-ga-mi-šun
Akkadian	giš-bil-meš
	kal-ka-meš
	kal-ga-imin

As Gilgamesh is a Sumerian hero it seems logical to give superiority to Sumerian testimonies, but even in that case there are several variants:

Oldest witness	giš-bil-ga-meš	Gishbilgamesh
	(giš.bil-pap-ga-meš)	
Syllabic witness	gi-il-ga-meš	Gilgamesh
Etymology	bil-ga-meš	Bilgamesh

At the moment, specialists read (or rather interpret) this name as 'the ancestor who is a young man' that is Bilgamesh. However, even though this etymology is likely to be correct (?), the change of the name Gilgamesh into Bilgamesh (or into Gishbilgamesh) was never envisaged. The modification of the Iehouah's respectable name into Yahve was accepted on some bases, which are nevertheless much more questionable.

Very early etymology intervened, not to vocalize the divine name again (which was little used) but 'to explain the real sense' of this name. Indeed, the Hebraic Bible gives an etymological definition of this name in Exodus 3:14 which is "I shall be which (who) I shall be". Generally the Talmud and Targums commented on this sentence by clarifying[428] that God strengthened his servants by saying to them 'I shall be [with you]'. One finds this same notion in the Christian Greek Scriptures «If God is for us, who will be against us» (Rm 8:31). However, the translators of the Septuagint (towards -280), under the influence of Greek philosophy, modified this etymology by translating this sentence into "I am the being" that is 'I am He who is', God becoming 'the one who is'. Then at the beginning of the third century there was a slight development of this definition. In the Christian environment, Clement of Alexandria explained that God's name Iaoue means 'the one who is and who will be.' In the Jewish environment the Targum of Jonathan[429] explained that in, Deuteronomy 32:29, that God's name means "I am the one who is and who was and I am the one who has to be". At the end of the twelfth century Maimonides explained the name as meaning: 'The necessary being'. But in no way did these etymologies serve to find the original vocalization of the Tetragram.

When the understanding of the Hebraic language rose again in Europe during the thirteenth century, some scholars tried to vocalize this name YHWH from an existing verbal form. The choice was only between two possibilities: YeHaWèH (piel form 3rd person of masculine singular), which means 'He will make to be' or 'He will constitute' a Hebraic reconstituted form and YiHWèH a West Aramaic form (peal imperfect, 3rd person of masculine singular) which means, 'He will be'. The vocalization *yehaweh* had the favor of a few cabalists and the vocalization *yihweh* had the favor of some Hebrew Christian scholars. The vocalization YiHWèH rather than YèHèWéH[430] derives from the word YeHU'a (Qo 11:3) meaning 'He will be'.

However no verbal form[431] corresponded exactly to the biblical definition. Additionally, the form *yehaweh* would come from an Aramaic root HWH (see the *piel* form YeḤaWèH of the verb ḤWH in Psalm 19:3), not from a Hebrew root HYH (see the *piel* form YeḤaYèH of the verb ḤYH in Job 36:6). The normal *piel* form of the verb HYH would be, according to Hebrew, the form *yehayeh*, not *yehaweh*.

3rd person	Meaning	1st person	Meaning
YeHaWèH	He will constitute	'ahawèh	I shall constitute
YiHWèH	He will be (Aram.)	'èhwèh	I shall be (Aram.)
YiHYèH	He will be	**'èhyèh**	**I shall be**
YaHaYèH	He will cause to be	'ahayèh	I shall cause to be

Even the modern hypothetical form 'I shall cause to become' or 'I shall cause to be' *Yahayèh* (hiphil form 3rd person of masculine singular) does not agree with the biblical form 'I shall [prove to] be' that is: *'èhyèh* in Hebrew. Two explanations have been put forward to try to resolve the differences between the biblical sense and the grammatical meaning. These were to suppose that either the Masoretes had incorrectly vocalized the form 'I shall be' or that the theophoric names which all begin by Yeho- have lost their link with the Tetragram. For example, Johannes Wessel Gansfort who proposed Iohauah for the name of the Father in his comment on the prayer called 'Our Father' (around 1480), supposed that the sentence "I shall be who I shall be" *eheieh azer eheieh* in his Latin manuscript could be vocalized *aheieh azer aheieh*. The Masoretic vocalization had shown itself to be very reliable; some scholars preferred to reconstruct an archaic vocalization of the Tetragram based on its etymology 'He will be' or 'He is'. The first to start this process was probably Gilbert Genebrard in 1568, who proposed the verbal form Iehue or Iihue for the divine name corresponding to the Aramaic *yihweh*, rather than Iehoua, the usual Hebrew name. This method of identifying a proper noun with its verbal shape is nevertheless contradicted by several cases in the Bible. It can be seen that the Masoretic spelling is in agreement with the vocalization of the Septuagint, but is not in agreement with its own grammatical vocalization implied from its etymology. For example:

Name	M.T.	Etymology	Meaning	LXX
Joseph	YÔSéPh	YÔSÎPh	He will add	Ioseph
Judah	YeHÛDaH	YeHÔDèH	He will laud	Iouda
Seth	ŠéTh	ŠaTh	He has set	Sèth
Jehovah	YeHoWaH	YiHWeH	He will be	(Kurios)

Therefore, those who want to revocalize Jehovah into Yihweh or Yahweh should also change the names of Joseph into Yosiph, Judah into Yehodeh, Seth into Shath, etc., which was never done even by the translators of the Septuagint.

CONFUSION DUE TO A LACK OF DATA (EX. EUATEOSE)

Unfortunately this case is very frequent. For example, several Cypriot coins[432] have been found at Salamis dated 450 BCE, bearing the Greek inscription: E-u-wa te-o-se written in the Cypriot syllabary. However, this inscription is too short to be correctly interpreted. Is it about an unknown king named Evanthes (Ευανθης) or is the inscription Ieoua Theos (Ιεουα θεος) that is Iehoua God, as seen on a German coin[433] of 1635?

Salamis was a city where the Jews lived for a long time (Ac 13:5). Furthermore, this coin is engraved on each side with a ram. According to Herodotus around 450 BCE there was a period of freedom owing to a liberation struggle. It should be noted that the Greek word *theos* is correctly written in te-o-se, which would be different if it was question of the name Evanthes, which would have been written E-wa-(ne)-te-se in the Cypriot syllabary (at that time the consonant *n* was frequently omitted before another consonant).

However, the name Evanthes may be written Evantheus (Ευανθευς) according to the Dorian genitive (Evanthes's), that is E-wa-(ne)-te-u-se. On the other hand, it is impossible to know if the Jews had been allowed to mint money for a special event, such as the coronation of a king. It is interesting to note that the oldest Jewish coin (5th century BCE) found near Gaza, used the name YHW (Yahu). The name Iehoua should be written I-e-u-wa in the Cypriot syllabary, but very often at this time (in fact even before 1000 BCE) the sound ye- became e- (or dy- and then z-). For example[434], the word *yepar** (γηπαρ) meaning 'liver' became *e-par* in academic Greek but *ie-cur* in Latin, the word *yenter** meaning 'sisters-in-law' became *ei-nateres* in academic Greek but *ja-nitrices* in Latin, etc. The Greek philosopher Plato (-427 -347) already knew these variants, that is to say an ancient *ie-* which has been changed into a more recent *e-* in certain words, and he pointed out some of them (for example in his work entitled *Kratylos 426c*).

CONFUSION DUE TO VOCALIZATION VARIATIONS (EX. JUPITER)

In time, some names undergo such great changes of vocalization that the "original form" becomes impossible to rediscover. For example the Latin name Jupiter is understood in Latin as Jou-pater that is 'Ioue father'. The beginning Jou- has been kept in the words 'Jov-ial' and 'Jou-rnal'. Due to declensions this name Ioue may be spelt Iouis or Iouei. The name Ioue came from an older form Dyeu because in Sanskrit, an Indo-European language, the word Dyaus means 'Day, luminous sky'. For example on an Etruscan shelf dated 250 BCE the name Iouei is spelt Diuvei (Etruscan language partly generated the Latin tongue). This part has been kept in some words like Diu-rnal, Di-vine, De-vin, Deus, Dio-gene (begotten by Zeus), Dio-trephes (Fed by Zeus), etc. The Greek name Zeus came from an older form Dios, probably because the letter D was pronounced D̲ that is Dj then Z. The name Dios is spelt Diwos in an old Greek inscription[435] dated around 550 BCE.

Era	1500 BCE			500 BCE
	Diwos ⇒	Dios	⇒ D̲ios (Djios)	⇒ Zeus
			⇒ Deus	⇒ Deus
			⇒ Deos (T̲eos ?)	⇒ Theos
	Diwei ⇒	Diuvei	⇒ Iouei	⇒ Jove

According to these complex changes it can supposed that there was a possible "archaic" form Dyew, but the form Deiw is also acceptable because in the linear B an old Mycenaean language (dated around 1500 BCE) the Greek classic Dii is spelt Di-we. The problem also occurs with the spelling of the name of the god Yam ('Sea'), which is sometimes changed into Yaw, that is ia-u, because the pronunciation of *m* and *w* was probably confused in certain Semitic languages. Some examples can be seen at Ugarit[436] (14th century BCE) where the name of the god Yam (ym) was also spelled Yaw (yw), at El-Amarna[437] (14th century BCE) where the Akkadian word *a-wa*-da is also spelled *a-ma*-da in the same letter (EA 38) and the name Bir-*yaw*-aza is also written Bir-*yam*-aza (EA 7), at Kanish[438] (18th century BCE) where the Akkadian word annu-*wa* is also spelled annu-*ma* in the same letter and the name T*awi*-nîya is also written T*am*-nîya, at Taanach[439] (15th century BCE) where the name Aḫi-yawi is also written Aḫi-yami and in Persia (6th century BCE) where the name Dari-*yaw*-ush (Darius) is also read Dari-*yam*-ush.

Lack of *nomina sacra* in the earliest Christian papyrus

The papyrus P52 is dated 125 CE, and contains the verse of John 18:31-33. Owing to the shape of this piece of sheet (dark part) it is possible[440] to reconstruct the whole codex to which it belonged (around 130 pages of 18 lines per page with an average of 33 characters per line, and 29/30 on the verso).

ΟΙ.ΙΟΥΔΑΟΙ.ΗΜΕΙΝ.ΟΥΚ.ΕΞΕΣΤΙΝ.ΑΠΟΚΤΕΙΝΑΙ
ΟΥΔΕΝΑ.ΙΝΑ.Ο.ΛΟΓΟΣ.ΤΟΥ.ΙΗΣΟΥ.ΠΛΗΡΩΘΕ.ΟΝ.ΕΙ
ΠΕΝ.ΣΗΜΑΙΝΩΝ.ΠΟΙΩ.ΘΑΝΑΤΩ.ΗΜΕΛΛΕΝ.ΑΠΟ
ΘΝΗΣΚΕΙΝ.ΙΣΗΛΘΕΝ.ΟΥΝ.ΠΑΛΙΝ.ΕΙΣ.ΤΟ.ΠΡΑΙΤΩ
ΡΙΟΝ.Ο.ΠΙΛΑΤΟΣ.ΚΑΙ.ΕΦΩΝΗΣΕΝ.ΤΟΝ.ΙΗΣΟΥΝ
ΚΑΙ.ΕΙΠΕΝ.ΑΥΤΩ.ΣΥ.ΕΙ.Ο.ΒΑΣΙΛΕΥΣ.ΤΩΝ.ΙΟΥ
ΔΑΙΩΝ.ΑΠΕΚΡΙΘΗ.ΙΗΣΟΥΣ.ΑΠΟ.ΣΕΑΥΤΟΥ.ΣΥ

(John 18:31-33)

In the papyrus P90 dated 150 CE which contains[441] the verses of John 18:36-19:7, the name of Jesus is this time shortened into JS according to the process of *nomina sacra*, like the word *Kurios* (Lord) which is written KS. So, when the *sacred name* was absent the word 'Lord' had to be written without abbreviation. For example, in this codex the verse of John 12:38 have appeared:

ΙΝΑ.Ο.ΛΟΓΟΣ.ΗΣΑΙΟΥ.ΤΟΥ.ΠΡΟΦΗΤΟΥ.ΠΛΗΡΩ
ΘΗ.ΟΝ.ΕΙΠΕΝ.ΚΥΡΙΕ.ΤΙΣ.ΕΠΙΣΤΕΥΣΕΝ.ΤΗ.ΑΚΟΗ
ΗΜΩΝ.ΚΑΙ.Ο.ΒΡΑΧΙΩΝ.ΚΥΡΙΟΥ.ΤΙΝΙ.ΑΠΕΚΑΛΥ
ΦΘΗ   **(John 12:38)**

However this part of the gospel of John quoted a verse from the book of Isaiah and in all the Septuagints of this period (before 150 CE) there are none with the name *Kurios* (Lord) instead of the Tetragram. For example:

ΙΝΑ.Ο.ΛΟΓΟΣ.ΗΣΑΙΟΥ.ΤΟΥ.ΠΡΟΦΗΤΟΥ.ΠΛΗΡΩ
*ΘΗ.ΟΝ.ΕΙΠΕΝ.*𐤉𐤄𐤅𐤄*.ΤΙΣ.ΕΠΙΣΤΕΥΣΕΝ.ΤΗ.ΑΚΟΗ*
*ΗΜΩΝ.ΚΑΙ.Ο.ΒΡΑΧΙΩΝ.*𐤉𐤄𐤅𐤄*.ΤΙΝΙ.ΑΠΕΚΑΛΥ*
ΦΘΗ   **(Isaiah 53:1 [LXX])**

There are only two ways to explain this modification, where the Tetragram was exchanged by the word 'Lord'. Either the Christians changed this name after 150 CE (more exactly between 70 and 135 CE) because they did not understand it anymore, or they changed it before 150 CE (more exactly before the previous period) for theological reasons but *without there being any archaeological witnesses*. The first explanation seems more logical because if the Christians (Judeo-Christians) had changed this name during the first century (before 70 CE) this teaching would have been seen in the NT especially among a Jewish environment, what is never the case. For example, Jesus should have said «I have made you known to them under your new name 'Lord'» but as a Jew he said nothing new on this very important matter (John 17:6, 26). It should be remembered that the book of John (who was a Jew) was written around 98 CE and he kept the short name Yah rather than Lord in his book of Revelation (Rv 19:1-6) when he wrote the Hebrew word Allelu-ia instead of Allelu-adonai. Even in 129 CE, Aquila who was a Christian converted to Judaism kept in his translation of the Septuagint the Tetragram embedded in a Greek text. It is interesting to note that Rabbi Tarphon (*Šabbat 116a*), between 90 and 130 CE, related the problem of the destruction of heretical (Christian) texts that contained the Tetragram.

Thus, between 70 and 135 CE, the Christian copyists (most of them were heathens who had become Christians) simplified the 'strange' writing YHWH [KURIOU] into a 'sacred name' $\overline{\text{KU}}$, consequently the expression KURIOS YHWH [O THEOS] became $\overline{\text{KS}}$ o $\overline{\text{TS}}$, and KURIOU IESOU XRISTOU became in the same way $\overline{\text{KU}}$ $\overline{\text{IU}}$ $\overline{\text{XU}}$. In time, many other sacred names appeared[442].

Finally those who would like to keep the Jewish tradition, which appeared only from the third century BCE, by replacing the divine name with YHWH (not pronounced) should act in the same way with the name of Jesus replacing it with JS as was done during the three first centuries of Christianity!

Pronunciation of the name y-h-w3

How should we pronounce the Egyptian word y-h-w3 (Shneider's transliteration)? Whether this orthography does or does not represent a conscious attempt on the part of Egyptian scribes to record vowels has always been a matter of controversy. Even at the present time, it is hard to know if the Egyptian orthography is syllabic (as the Akkadian), consonantal and sometimes partly vocalic (as the Hebrew) or anything else. Therefore because of this difficulty, there is a general agreement to accept the conventional vocalization: 3 = a, ÿ = i, w = u, (lack of vowel) Ø = e. This system seems to be consistent because of two main reasons. Firstly, these sounds a, i, u, e are common to other tongues of this epoch (Akkadian, Hittite, Sumerian) and secondly, there are three 'mothers of reading' in the Egyptian tongue[443] (at least since 2000 BCE) which are justly 3, ÿ and w. For example:

Signs:	🕊	🕊	🕊	🕊	🕊	🕊	🕊	🕊
Transcr.	h-3	h-ÿ	h-w	hØ	y-3	y-ÿ	y-w	yØ
Reading	ha	hi	hu	he	ya	yi	yu	ye

According to this conventional system, the word y-h-w3 would be read yehua, but several scholars prefer the syllabic reading, yahwa. Is this reading really better?

The hypothesis of the syllabic reading was proposed by W.F. Albright (but he thought that until 1300 BCE the system was consonantal and after this date some groups remained alphabetic!)[444], who dealt with the representation of vowels in the Egyptian script. He collected words written in the syllabic style of Egyptian writing and sought to define the rules governing such writing. He made extensive use of comparison with Northwest Semitic languages. Later on, E. Edel made comparisons between Hittite names in Egyptian spellings and the spelling in cuneiform texts. He concluded that the vocalic values given by Albright (and by Helck in 1971) are not precise. In his opinion, the cuneiform Hittite demonstrates that in Northwest Semitic words written in Egyptian script, any vowel may have stood in the syllable! However, at the present time, many scholars think that in the Execration texts, the scribes had almost achieved a pure system of *matres lectionis*, writing consonants plus a distinct vowel sign, but from the time of the 18th Dynasty, the scribes incorporated more syllabic signs, perhaps under the influence of the cuneiform script which they had adopted at that time for use in international diplomatic correspondence[445]. Furthermore, to confirm some Egyptian vowels, Greek and Coptic are used. However, all these assertions are open to criticism.

OWING TO COPTIC AND GREEK WITNESSES

Firstly, most of the usual Greek witnesses are not reliable, even from an Egyptian source! Thus, the Greek historian Herodotus (-495 -425) gave in his books the name of several Pharaohs, the Egyptian priest Manetho who is principally famed for having written a history of Egypt (before 250 BCE) named many kings, but these names are unusable to find the genuine vowels (and even the consonants) as one can see with the following sample of different Pharaohs[446].

EGYPTIAN NAME	GREEK1 HERODOTUS	GREEK2 MANETHO	GREEK3 SEPTUAGINT
Snefru	-	Sôris	
Ḥufu	Ḵéopa	**Souphis**	
Djedef-Râ	Didoufri	Ratoisès	
Ḥâfrâ	**Képhrèna**	Souphis	
Menkaurâ	Mukérinos	**Menḵérès**	
Šepseskarâ	-	**Séberḵérès**	
Menkarâ	Nitocris	Nitocris	
Uaḥabrâ	Apriès	**Oua**phris	Ouaphrè Ḥæphra' [MT]

Manetho's list seems to fit a little better (very often one syllable at least is correct), furthermore, it is interesting to note that in his full list, the Greek vowel *e* (é, è, e) is used very often (for example: Menchérès, Séberchérès and so forth).

Secondly, 'usual' Coptic appeared too late (third century of our Common Era) to give any reliable information concerning the Late-Egyptian vowels[447], furthermore many Coptic cognates do not follow the rule of usual Egyptian vocalizations[448]. It is interesting to note that Coptic, in spite of it being alphabetic, has one syllabic sign (ti). Furthermore, in Bohaïric and in Saïdic the two main dialects, there is a specific sign to note a vowel very close to the Hebrew *shewa*, that is to say, a kind of weak *e*. Meroitic is more interesting because it appeared sooner (third century BCE) than Coptic. It is interesting to note that Meroitic, in spite of it being alphabetic, has four syllabic signs (ne, se, te, to). Furthermore, in this language, which came partly from the Egyptian, there are only four vowels (a, i, o, e) and two semi-consonants (y, w). The vowel *e* may also represent a lack of vowel. A final remark on this matter, Walaf is a language which kept numerous features of the Old Egyptian and it is interesting to note that it has four true vowels (a, i, u, e) corresponding to the Egyptian signs (3, ÿ, w, Ø)[449].

OWING TO AKKADIAN WITNESSES

Thirdly, the numerous witnesses coming from Akkadian, mainly Hittite names written in the syllabic cuneiform system, seem to be impressive because of two reasons. First, this system is very old and contemporary of the Late-Egyptian period and also that in this system there are four identified vowels (a, i, u, e). Unfortunately, the reality is not so easy. For example, an Egyptian scribe of the Ramesses period wrote a treatise in Egyptian and in Akkadian, but he translated the royal name (vocalized in the conventional system):

Usermaatre- Setepenre- Ramessu-   Meryamum (Egyptian)
Washmuria- Shatepnaria- Riamashesha- Maiamana (Akkadian)

It is easy to see the great difficulty to identify, at the present time, the "true" vowels, even in the case of well-known names like Ramessu (Riamashesha) or in other documents[450]:

Amenhotep Nebmaatre Neferkheperure (Egyptian)
Amanhatpi Nibmuaria Naphurria   (Akkadian)

Several discrepancies may be explained. Firstly, discrepancies coming from the Egyptian tongue:

1-   Hypocoristica are exceedingly common. For example, the name S-s-ÿ-sw-w (and also the short form S-s) is a hyporisticon of R'-ms-s-s (Ramesses II) which was read Sésoôsis (or Sesostris) by the Greek writers. Therefore, there is a risk of errors.

2-   Metathesis are very frequent[451]. For esthetical reasons a name may be written in different ways. For example, L-w-ÿ-s3 and L-ÿ-w-s3, Ti-ÿ-y and Ti-y-ÿ, and so forth.

3-   Plene or defective writing are possible with Egyptian words. For example, the Hebrew word *ha yæm* (הַיָּם) meaning 'the sea' is written p3 y-m' and also p3 y-w-m'. This word is pronounced in the present day as: Fai-yum (iom/ éiom in Coptic). The Hebrew word *yad* (יָד) meaning 'hand, monument' is written y-w-d[452]. It seems reasonable to accept the letter *w* as a mater lectionis for *u* (or *o*). This kind of comparison shows similarities of Egyptian with other Semitic languages (alphabetic). Furthermore, the names of several Egyptian primeval hieroglyphs are Semitic![453]

Secondly, discrepancies that come from the Akkadian tongue:

1-   Polyphonous signs. Each Akkadian sign may be polyvalent[454].

2-   Incomplete system of vowels writing. Very often the vowels *e* and *i* are not clearly distinguished. For example, Pa-tu-**re**-si may also be read Pa-tu-**ri**-si and so forth. The worst case is the sign ⟨⟩ which may be read; ya, ye, yi, yu, pe, pi, wa, we, wi, wu (...)![455]

3-   The history in the change of the vocalization is not very well-known. Furthermore in all Semitic languages the vowel is a weak element which may easily change in time. For example, in Hebrew, Balaam, Nabau, Galaad (Nu 22:7 32:3; Gn 31:21) became Bilam, Nebô, Gilad, and so forth. But does this law (Barth-Ginsberg's law), which says that a primitive *a* became an *i*, have exceptions? Some scholars suppose that in the Egyptian tongue an initial *i* became an *a*, the contrary of the previous law.

At the present time, before 500 BCE, our knowledge of Hebrew is open to criticism, and for Egyptian and Akkadian the history of the change in vowels is purely speculative[456].

OWING TO THE ONOMASTIC FROM THE LXX

An interesting new method to find the "true" vowels in the Egyptian names is using all these names used in the Septuagint for three reasons. Firstly, it is older (beginning of the third century BCE) than Coptic. Secondly, it is reliable (several samples dated BCE). Thirdly, it was probably written in Alexandria and therefore in an Egyptian milieu which involves a greater accuracy in the transcription of Egyptian names.

	r'-ms-s-sw-w	Gn 47:11
	š3-š3-n-q	1K 11:40
	t3-h-rw-q	2K 19:9
	n-k3-w	2K 23:29
	w3ḥ-'ib-r'	Jr 44:30 (51:30 LXX)
	'in-ti-rw-y-w3-š3	Dn 9:1
	ḥ-š3-y-3-rw-š3	Dn 9:1

The last two Pharaohs are not Egyptian but these names are two transcriptions from Old Persian names written in cuneiform. These names appeared in a late period (around 500 BCE) but, because of this, they are well-known foreign names[457].

NAME	Darius	(Xerxes)	Ahasuerus
GREEK (LXX)	daréios	xerxou (A)	asouèrou (B)
HEBREW (MT)	daryawèš		'aḥašwérôš
ELAMITE	da-ri-ia-ma-u-iš	ik-si-ir-sa	
AKKADIAN	da-ri-ia-muš	ḫi-si-'-ar-sa	
ELEPHANTINE	daryawahûš	ḫašya'rša	
EGYPTIAN	taruyuaša	ḫašayârušâ	
OLD PERSIAN	dâryavauša	kšayâršâ	
ARAMAIC	daryawahûš	ḫašayârš	

In spite of this large amount of data, one can hardly choose between the alphabetic transcription of Elephantine into Hebrew and the alphabetico-syllabic transcription into Old-Persian.

Egyptian hieroglyph

ḫ3 š3 **y 3** rw š3 3   'in ti rw **y w3** š3
ḫashayârushâ   (an)taruyuasha

Old-Persian cuneiform

k̠- š- **y**- **a** r- š- a   d- a r- **y- v- u** š-
k̠shayârshâ   dâryavausha

Aramaic writing

ח ש י א ר ש   ש ו ה ו י ר ד
ḥ š **ya'** r š   d r **y w h w** š
ḥashayârsha   daryawahûsh

One can see a good link with the three former sequences y-3, y-a, ya' and to a lesser extent, with y-w3, ya-va-u, yawahû. Furthermore, the readings ay-va-u and aywahû are also possible[458].

EGYPTIAN TRANSCR.	LXX	MT	REF.
r'-ms-s-s	Raméssè	Ra'mesés	Gn 47:11
š3-š3-n-q	Sousakim	Šišaq	1K 11:40
t3-h-rw-q	Taraka	Tirhaqah	2K 19:9
n-k3-w	Nékao	Nekoh	2K 23:29
w3h-'ib-r'	Ouaprè	Hæpra'	Jr 44:30
p3-t3w-rsÿ	Patourès	Patros	Ezk 30:14
s-w-nw	Suènès	Swénéh	Ezk 30:6
b3s-t-(t)	(bou)bastou	(pi)bèsèt	Ezk 30:17
p3-di-p3-r'	Pétépré	Pôtipar	Gn 39:1
hwt-nn-nsw(t)	-	Hanés	Is 30.14
d3-'-n	Tanéi	Tso'an	Is 30:4
'i-mn-n	Amôn	Amôn	Na 3:8
gs-s-m-w-mw	Gésém	Gošèn (Gèšèm?)[459]	Gn 45:10
p3-'-n-h	Panèk	Pa'néah	Gn 41:45
'iws-n-nt	Asénnét	Asnat	Gn 41:45
niw-(t)-pth	Népta(liim)	Naptuh(im)	Gn 10:13
hwt-k3-pth	Aigüpto	(Mitsrayim)	Gn 12:10

A good agreement can be seen between the LXX and the Masoretic text. Thus it is interesting to compare this reading with the conventional reading and the syllabic one.

TRANSCR.	CONVENT.	SYLLABIC (IN A)	LXX
r'-ms-s-s	**Râ-mes-se-se**	Râ-mas-sa-sa	Raméssè
š3-š3-n-q	Ša-ša-ne-qe	Ša-ša-na-qa	Sousakim
t3-h-rw-q	Ta-he-rue-qe	**Ta-ha-rwa-qa**	Tharaka
n-k3-w	**Ne-ka-u**	Na-ka-wa	Nékao
w3h-'ib-r'	Uah-ib-râ	Wah-ib-râ	Ouaprè
p3-t3w-rsÿ	**Pa-tau-resi**	Pa-taw-rasya	Patourès
s-w-nw	**Se-ue-nu**	Sa-wa-nwa	Suènès
b3s-t-(t)	**Bas-et**	Bas-at	Bast (ou)
p3-di-p3-r'	Pa-di-pa-râ	Pa-di-pa-râ	Pétépré
d3-'-n	Dja-â-ne	Dja-â-na	Tanéi

'i-mn-n	A-men-ne	A-man-na	Amôn
gs-s-m-w-mw	**Ges-se-mu**	Gas-sa-maw	Gésém
p3-'-n-ḫ	**Pa-'a-neḫ**	Pa-'a-naḫ	Panèḳ
'iws-n-nt	**Aus-en-net**	Awas-an-nat	Asénnét
niw-(t)-ptḥ	Niu-peteḥ	Niw-pataḥ	Népta(lim)
ḥwt-k3-ptḥ	ḥut-ka-peteḥ	ḥawat-ka-pataḥ	Aigüpto

As one can see the conventional reading (except *'i* sign is read *a*)* agrees better with the Septuagint than the syllabic reading. Furthermore, it seems that the vowel *a* very often became *e* [e, é, è] (ex. Padiparâ became Pétépré in the LXX). A second test is possible, which is to compare the reverse transcription from Hebrew to Egyptian. In order to avoid mistakes only clearly identified names have been kept[460].

*(It is interesting to note that the Egyptian word for 'cat' is spelled mi-'i-w with this equivalence, that is mi-a-u, which is a good approximation for the word miaow).

	'i-('i3w)-y-w-rw-n	Jos 21:24
	(2Ch 11:10)	
	'i-s-q-3-rw-n-3	Jg 1:18
	'-s-ti-'i-l-ti-'i	Jos 13:12
	b3-'i-3-rw-t-w	Jg 9:21
	b-3-y-ti-'-n-ti-'i	Jos.19:38
	b-3-y-ti-h-'i-d-3-q-3-n-3	Jos 19:27
	b3-i-ti-ḫ-w3-3-rw-n	Jos 16:3
	ti-'i-ms-s-q	Gn 15:2
	t-w-'i-3-l	Jos 17:11
	q-3-ḏ3-3-l	Jos 21:21
	ṯ-rw-w3-3-n	1Ch 4:20
	ḫ3-3-m3-3-ti-'i	Jos 19:35
	ḥw-()-ḏ3-3-w-l	Jos 19:36
	y-b-l-'-mw	Jg 1:27
	y-w-p y-p-w	Jos 19:46
	y-rw-m-t-w	Jos 15:35
	(y-rw-m-w-t)	
	q-3-n-3	Jos 19:28
	r-b-w-n	Dt 1:1
	l-k-ÿ-š3-3	Jos 12:11

	Transliteration	Reference
	l-b3-3-n-ṯ	Jos 19:26
	l-w-ÿ-s3 l-ÿ-w-s3	Jg 18:29
	mi-š3-'i-l	Jos 19:26
	mw-'i-b-w	Dt 34:1
	n-g-b-w	Jos 11:2
	q-ï-n-3 q-ï-y-n-3	Jos 15:22
	s3-rw-n-3	1Ch 5:16
	š3-n-m-'-'i-3	Jos 19:18
	ḏ3-ÿ-d-w-n-w	Jos 19:28
	ḏ3-3-w-l	Jos 19:29
	'i-w-'i-n-'i-w	1Ch 8:12
	m-k-d-'i-w	Jos 17:11
	y-w-d-h-m-'-rw-k	
	y-[3]-ḫ3-3-m3-3	1Ch 7:2
	y-s-ÿ-r-'i-3-l (y-ÿ-s-r-'i-3-l)	Gn 32:29
	ḏ3-3-ÿ-r-p-w-ti-'i	1K 17:9,10
	s-'-r-ÿ (s-'-ÿ-r)	Gn 14:6
	l-ḫ-b-w	Jos 19:28,30
	s3-w-k3	Jos 15:35

READING: TRANSCR.	CONVENT.	LXX	MT
'i-**y**-**w**-**rw**-n	'A**y**u**ru**n	A**i**alôn	'Ayyælôn
'i-s-q-3-rw-n-3	'Asqaruna	Askalôna	'Ashqelôn
'-s-ti-'i-l-ti-'i	'Astaleta	Astarôṭ	'Ashtarôṭ
b-**3**-**y**-**ti**-'-n-ti-'i	**B**a**yt**aneta	**B**a**iṭ**anaṭ	**B**é**yt**a'naṭ
b-**3**-**y**-**ti**-h-'i-	**B**a**yt**ha	**B**è**ṭ**	**B**é**yṭ**
d-3-q-3-n-3	daqana	dagôn	dagon
b3-i-ti-ḥ-w3-3-rw-n	Baṭḥuarun	Baiṭôrôn	Béyṭḥôron
ti-'i-ms-s-q	Tamesseq	Damaskos	Damèsèq
t-w-'i-3-l	Tu'al	Dôr	Do'r
q-3-ḏ3-3-l	Qadjal	Gazara	Gèzèr
ṭ-rw-w3-3-n	Tjeruan	Ṭilôn	Ṭiwlôn
ḥ3-3-m3-3-ti-'i	Ḥamata	Amaṭ	Ḥammaṭ
ḥw-ḏ3-3-w-l	Ḥudjaul	Asôr	Ḥatsôr
y-b-l-'-mw	**Y**eble'amu	**I**éblaam	**Y**ible'am
y-**w**-**p** / y-p-w	**Y**u**p**	**I**op**p**è	**Y**æ**p**ô
y-**rw**-m-w-t	**Y**e**ru**mut	**I**éri mouṭ	**Y**armûṭ
q-3-n-3	Qana	Kana	Qanah
r-b-w-n	Rebun	Lobon	Laban
l-k-ÿ-š3-3	Lekisha	Laḵis	Laḵish
l-b3-3-n-ṭ	Lebanet	Labanaṭ	Libnaṭ
l-w-ÿ-s3	Luisa	Lais	Layish
mi-š3-'i-l	Mish'al	Masal	Mish'al
mw-'i-b-w	Mu'abu	Môab	Mô'ab
n-g-b-w	Negebu	-	Nègèb
q-ÿ-n-3 / **q**-**ÿ**-**y**-n-3	**Qi**y na	**Ki**na	**Qi**ynah
s3-rw-n-3	Saruna	Sarôn	Sharôn
š3-n-m-'-'i-3	Shaneme'a	Sounam	Shûném
ḏ3-ÿ-d-w-n-w	Djidunu	Sidônos	Tsidôn
ḏ3-3-w-l	Djaul	Türiôn	Tsor
'i-w-'i-n-'i-w	'Auan'au	ônô	'ônô
m-k-d-'i-w	Meked'au	Magéddô	Megidô
y-**w**-**d**-	**Yud**		(**Yad**
h-m-'-rw-k	heme'ruk		ha mèléḵ)

y-[3]-ḥ3-3-m3-3	Yaḥama	Iémou	Yaḥmay
y-ÿ-s-r-'i-3-l	Yisra'al	Israèl	Yisra'él
ḏ3-3-ï-r-p-w-ti-'i	Djairputa	Sarépta	Tsarpaṯ
s-'-ÿ-r	Se'ir	Sèir	Sé'ir
l-ḥ-b-w	Leḥebu	Roôb	Reḥob
s3-w-k3	Sauka	Sôḵô	Sôḵoh

As one can see in this table there is a good correlation between the Hebrew vocalizations and their Egyptian equivalents[461]. It is interesting to note the following link:

	Hebrew names	Egyptian transcriptions
ya	Ḥashaya'rsha, yaḥmay	y-3
ya	'Ayyælôn, Yæm, Yad, Yæpô	y-w
ya	Yarmûṯ	y
ye,yi	Yible'am, Yisraél	y

The name **Yarmûṯ** (but **Yérimouṯ** in the Septuagint) appears as an exception, therefore the name **Yahweh** would have probably been written: first **Y-w**-h-w3 (4/7) then **Y-3**-h-w3 (2/7) then **Y**-h-w3 (1/7).

OWING TO A CHECK WITH A WELL-KNOWN NAME.

Another means to verify the vocalization of the Egyptian language is to compare[462] the well-known old name of the Hittite queen Puduhepa[463] (-1297 -1215) which was written in Egyptian hieroglyphs but also in syllabic cuneiforms and in Hittite hieroglyphs.

p- w- d- w- ḥ-ÿ- p3   Egyptian hieroglyphs

pu-   du-   ḫe- pa   Syllabic cuneiforms
bu-   (ḫi-)

				Syllabic cuneiforms
pu-	du-	i-	pa	
bu-				

				Hittite hieroglyphs
pu-	du-	ḫa-	pa	
bu-	tu-	(ḫe/ḫi-)	pa	

As, this princess was of Hittite origin, the Hittite inscriptions (syllabic cuneiform, Hittite hieroglyph) are more likely to give good transcription. But, surprisingly, the sound *hey* is written *ḫa* in the Hittite hieroglyphs and *i* or *ḫe* in the Hittite syllabary (*ḫi* in the Egyptian hieroglyphs).

Hittite syllabary[464]   Cuneiform syllabary[465]

ḫa	ḫe	ḫi	ḫu		ḫa	ḫe	ḫi	ḫu

There are several plausible explanations. The name Puduhepa is probably Hurrite. The sounds *e* and *i*, are very often confused in the Hittite cuneiforms. Furthermore the sign used for *ḫe* is very former and appears specific to this region. In the Hittite syllabary the sign *ḫa* was also pronounced *ḫe* and *ḫi* during the second millennium before our era. In addition this sign *ḫa* was also an ideogram for 'god'. It seems so that the pronunciation *ḫe* is a good compromise (although *ḫai* or *ḫei* may be acceptable). In the Egyptian hieroglyphs the sequence ḫ-ÿ is the closest choice to the sound *ḫe*, because the form p-w-d-w-ḫ-p3 would have been pronounced puduḫpa and not puduḫepa.

ḫa	ḫi	ḫu	ḫ(e)

Thus the name p-w-d-w-ḫ-ÿ-p3 should be read puduḫipa (or maybe puduḫeipa). In the same way ÿ-h-w3 should be read ihua and y-h-w3 should be read yehua. The reading of *e*, when there is no vowel, is normal such as in the case of the name R'-ms-s-s which is read Ra'messes. The Greek historian Herodotus (around 450 BCE) pronounced the names of two pharaohs (who lived around 700 BCE) Nékô and Sabacô (*History II, 152*) that is: Nekau (n-k3-w) and Shabaka (š3-b3-k3), what is a supplementary confirmation of the equivalence 3 = a, w = u, ÿ = i, nothing = e.

In Indo-European languages[466] (before 1500 BCE) there were six vowels, the three short vowels e, a, o and the three long vowels: ê, â, ô, and also a seventh brief vowel the *shewa* ə. In Old Semitic languages[467] there were six vowels, the three short vowels i, a, u and the three long vowels i:, a:, u:. There was probably a seventh brief vowel the *shewa* ə as proved some variants in Akkadian vocabulary. For example, the word ba'lu(m)*, that is baəlu(m), became be:lu(m) meaning 'master', and also ba:lu(m) meaning 'to implore'. It can be noted that the Egyptian name p-t-ḥ could be pronounced owing to *shewas* pətəḥ that is ptəḥ which can be found in the two modern words as Egypte or Co-pt with the part *pte*.

Pronunciation of YHWH's name in the Mesha stele

The Tetragram appears in the Mesha stele which proves that Moabites knew how to read it. Based on this evidence some scholars[468] suggest reconstituting a vocalization Yahwoh of this name according to a supposed pronunciation of Hebrew at this time. This reconstruction is totally speculative for the following reasons:

1   As reconstruction according to biblical Hebrew is not accepted unanimously (even though it is well attested to) it seems improbable to resolve this problem by using a badly known Hebrew.

2   The Hebrew of this stele is abnormal in two important aspects. Firstly it is very defective which means that the vocalization of words cannot be verified, including those which are very well known.

3   Secondly, the spelling of proper nouns is often abnormal. This means that certain names, which normally could be used, would have had a different pronunciation in this stele.

4   Specialists sometimes put forward such complex explanations in order to read each word of this stele that one wonders that perhaps only scholars of this time have been able to read this inscription, which is against common sense.

IS THE HEBREW OF MESHA STELE CORRECT?

Probably no, because differing conclusions result from the same data provided by the Mesha inscription itself. The variety of interpretation underscores the need for caution and highlights the uncertain nature of the evidence, especially as it involves interpreting ambiguous vowel letters[469]. For example, many discrepancies of vocalization can be noted due to the role played by several elements such as the historical spellings, the contraction of diphthongs, the use of *matres lectionis*, etc.

Name	Reference	M.T.	LXX	Mesha
Kiriathaim	Jr 48:23	Qiryataïm	Kariataim	Qiryatén
Diblathaim	Jr 48:22	Diblataïm	Déblataim	Diblatén
Horonaim	Jr 48:34	Horonaïm	Ôrônaim	Hawronén
Dibon	Jr 48:22	Dîbôn	Daibôn	Daybon
Nebo	Jr 48:22	Nebô	Nabau	Naboh
Bozrah	Jr 48:24	Bæṣræh	Bosor	Beṣer
Jahaz	Jr 48:21	Yahṣah	Iassa	Yahaṣ
Medeba	Jos 13:9	Méydba'	Maidaba	Mehadaba'

The ending of -én instead of -ayim, which is the form of masculine plural, is usual in the Mesha inscription. This raises two problems. Firstly, did this discrepancy[470] come from an archaism or an aramaism? Secondly, Moabite writing is very defective and it is not always possible to find a reliable vocalization. For example the pronoun 'myself' is always written *'anoki* in Hebrew but *'anok* in the Mesha inscription probably for *'anok(i)*. Also, the two pronouns 'he' and 'she' are always written *hû'* and *hî'* in Hebrew but only *h'* in the Mesha inscription probably for *h(u)'* and *h(i)'* according to the context. In addition, the word 'night' is written *lélah* rather than *laylah* etc. Furthermore the use of *matres lectionis* seems chaotic, for example the word 'this' is written *zo't* instead of the usual *zot* but, on the other hand, the word 'head' is written *rosh* instead of the usual *ro'sh*, the word 'house' is written either *bét* or *bayt*, etc. Finally, the very name of Mesha's father is itself miswritten on this stele, that is to say Kemosh instead of Kemoshyat (real name).

At the present time it is hard to choose between a vocalic *bét* or a consonantic *bayt* because the contraction of diphthongs may have occured at this epoch. The chronology of these changes is supported by several studies. For Aramaic, 5 phases are proposed: Old A. (-925 -700), Official A. (-700 -200), Middle A. (-200 200), Late A. (200 700). The chronology of the Hebrew language is roughly parallel[471] and the main consequences were: contraction of diphthongs *ay*, *aw* into *é*, *o* and a mute *h* was dropped out. For example, the suffix *hu* became *o/w* and the suffix *éhu* became[472] *aw* (see numerous *qere/ kethib* in the Bible). The Qumran texts enabled us to prove this chronology[473]. The last change: *w* ⇒ *v* ⇒ *b̲* is well known[474].

	-900	-700	-500	-300	-100	200	
HEBREW	הֻא hu'	הֻ / וּה hû	וּה hû	וּ û	וֹ ô	וֹ ô	וֹ ô
ARAMAIC	הֻא hu'a	הֻ, וַ ahu aw	וַ aw	וַ aw	וַ aw	וַ av	וַ ab̲
HEBREW		יְהֻ îhû	יְהֻ îhû	יִוּ îû	יִוֹ îô	יִוֹ îô	יִוֹ îô
ARAMAIC		הֻ, וַ ihu iw	יִו îw	יִו îw	יִו îw	יִו îv	יִו îb̲
HEBREW	הֻא יָה yâh hu'	יָה הֻ / יָה יְהֻ yâh hû	יְהֻ yahû	יְהֻ yahû	יְ yaô	יְ yaô	יְ yaô
ARAMAIC	הֻ יָה yah hu'a	יְהֻ / יְו yahaw	יְ yaw	יְ yaw	יְ yaw	יְ yav	יְ yab̲
	1	**2**	**3**	**4**	**5**	**6**	**7**

During this period, Aramaic greatly increased its influence on Hebrew. For example: it can be noted that Bhadèrèk̲ (Ne 9:19), Khayom (Gn 39:11), Bhašamayim (Ps 36:6), Lha'am (2Ch 10:7) became respectively Badèrèk̲ (Qo 12:5) Kayom (Gn 25:31) Bašamayim (Ps 11:4), and La'am (2Ch 10:10), without the *h* which is the normal spelling in the Masoretic text. Also mînéhû 'kind [of] him', that is 'his kind' (14 times), became mînô (Gn 1:11,12; Lv 11:15,16,22; Dt 14:14,15) and seéhû 'sheep [of] him' (1S 14:34) became séô (Dt 22:1). The vowel *ô* is the normal spelling thus, 'hand [of] him' that is 'his hand' is always written yadô (yadô <yadaû* <yadahû*). However, there is also a second change: pîhû 'mouth [of] him' (22 times) became pîw (55 times) sometimes, in the same verse (Ex 4:15) and 'aḥîhû 'brother [of] him' (4 times) became 'aḥîw (113 times) sometimes in the same verse (2Ch 31:12,13; Jr 34:9,14). Thus, to sum up it is easy to assume a parallel change: -yhw pronounced first -îhû then, -îû and finally -îô in Hebrew or -îw (Aramaic influence).

Many discrepancies in the Hebrew text may be explained because of aramaism rather than archaism. In the same way the Septuagint has been strongly influenced by the Aramaic tongue because numerous Hebrew names of two or three letters ending in a -W were transcribed by an ending of -aÜ in the Septuagint, and -Ô in the Masoretic text. As this came from an original -U, this sound is found in some 'theophoric' names. For example, the names built from Nabû (or Ra'û), begin with Nabou- (or Ragou) in the Septuagint (instead of Nabaü and Ragaü), and Nebû- (or Re'û-) in the Masoretic text.)

NAME (2 letters)	GREEK (LXX)	HEBREW (M.T.)	ASSYRIAN (B.D.B.)	REF.
Ww	Ouaü	Waw	Ûû	Ps 119:41
Zw	Ziou	Ziw	Ziû	1K 6:37
Tw	Taü	Taw		Ps 119:169
Yw	(Iaü)	(Yaw)	(Iû)	
Ḥzw	Azaü	Ḥazô	Ḥazû	Gn 22:22
Ypw	Ioppè	Yapô	Iapû	Jos 19:46
Nbw	Nabaü	Nebô	Nabû	Nb 33:47
Nkw	Nékaô	Nekô	Nikû	2Ch 35:20
'dw	Addô	'Iddô		2Ch 13:22
'kw	Akkô	Akkô	Akkû	Jg 1:31
'sw	Èsaü	'Ésaw		Gn 32:19
R'w	Ragaü	Re'û		Gn 11:18

However, as Hebrew proper nouns of four letters and more are mostly pronounced as they are spelt the translators of the Septuagint had to read them in this way and certain errors of reading on their part confirm this fact. So, the expression 'towards him' ('lyw in Hebrew) was read as it is spelled, that is Èliou (1K 17:2,8; 18:8,17), 'his brothers' ('hyw) was read Akiou (1Ch 26:7), 'hill of Moreh' (gb't hmwrh) was read Gabaat Amôra (Jg 7:1), etc. It can be seen that an expression containing the Tetragram (1K 17:20), and meaning 'towards yhwh' ('l-yhwh) had been read by mistake as Èl-iou, and that the Tetragram was also read as Iouda twice (Jg 1:22; 2 1:12)!

In the Mesha inscription the reading Ḥawronén rather than Ḥôronén is chosen because many scholars agree with an "archaic" pronunciation *aw* which became *ô* in time. But this theory is highly dependent on a hypothetical change[475] from a primeval consonantic reading towards a later vocalic reading. This theory is also based on the "dogma" of the tri-letters root (probably wrong)[476], which says, for example, the word 'day', *yôm* in Hebrew, came from an old *yawm* written ywm. Unfortunately, this word might also be written ym in the "archaic" past and be pronounced *yam*, because the plural form is *yam-im* and not *yom-im* Therefore the "archaic" pronunciation of the word *yôm* may be *yam, yawm, yawwam, yawwum,* etc., and also *yôm*! In facing so many difficulties how did an ordinary Moabite read this inscription? For example, Nebo is the name of a city which came from the very well-known Nabu, but in the inscription of Mesha this name is written NBH instead of the usual NBW. Many scholars propose to read the H letter as a *mater lectionis* for the sound *ô*, but this solution is unlikely, because this abnormal writing resulted from a historical spelling of the pronoun 'him' -*Hu* which became -*Ho* (see Gn 9:21; 1K 19:23; etc.) and this explanation remains true for some names. (Nekahu means in Hebrew 'Him who afflicted' !, and Nabahu means 'Him who called')

Name	Origin	Phonetic Heb.	Historic Heb.	LXX
writing	N-k3-w	N-K-W	N-K-H	Νεχαω
(Nekô)	Ne-ka-u	NeKaW	NeKaHu	Nékaô
writing	Na-bû	N-B-W	N-B-H	Ναβαυ
(Nebô)	Nabû	NaBaW	NaBaHu	Nabau

Therefore, the way of reading seems very simple. The ending in H for usual words is, most of the time, a consonant and the vocalization depending on the context, -*Hu* when it is a masculine singular suffix and -*Ha* when it is feminine. For some ambiguous readings or with foreign names, *matres lectionis* may be used, in this case H represent the sound A (ends of words) Y the sound I and W the sound U, what is usual in all the Semitic languages at this time[477], but for well-known names a defective reading is frequent. For example, the names written YHṢ and BṢR could be pronounced YiHaṢa and BæṢRa according to the Masoretic text and the Septuagint. The name QRḤH which means 'baldness' could be pronounced QæRḤæH. However, the best check comes from foreign names because in this case Moabites had to use a "natural reading".

NATURAL READING AND MATRES LECTIONIS SYSTEM.

From a Moabite point of view the three names Israel Omri and Jehovah are of foreign origin. It can be noted that the ending Y of the name Omry is always read I and never aY. The beginning Y of the name Ysrael is always read I or Yi but ever Ya (the name Kamošyat [Kmšyt] was read Kamišiti at Ebla)[478].

Akkadian	-850	Ḫu-um-ri-i	Humri
Moabite	-850	ʿmry	
Greek	-250	Ambri	Amri
Hebrew	500	ʿÆmrî	Omri
Eblaite	-2000	Iš-ra-il	Ishrail
Egyptian	-1200	Y-ÿ-s-r-i-3-l	Yisrial
Moabite	-850	Yśr'l	
Greek	-250	Israèl	Israel
Hebrew	500	Yiśra'él	Yisrael

Therefore among foreign names the "natural reading" of the letter Y is always I, which is its usual value as *mater lectionis*. According to this natural reading the Tetragram Yhwh would be read I-hwh or Yi-hwh. However the meaning of a name could lead to a specific pronunciation. For example the name Yisrael means 'He will contend, God' that is Yisrèh-él in Hebrew, however the ending in -*èh* came from[479] an old -*ah*, thus the verbal form Yisrèh-él could be Yisrah-il, which became Yisraél. Could the name Yi-hwh be understood as a verbal form by Moabites?

The answer is not easy, but probably Moabites could have linked this name with the Aramaic verbal form Yhwh 'He will be', which is found at Sefire[480] in an inscription dated around 750 BCE.

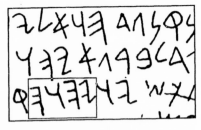

This verbal form is usually vocalized Yihwèh or maybe at this time Yihwah. On the other hand the Hebrew verbal form for 'He will be' is vocalized Yihyèh (or Yihyah) in an inscription found at Kuntillet Ajrud[481] and dated after 800 BCE.

What strengthens the possibility of a vocalization Yihwah is the presence in the same line of Mesha stele, of a H used as *mater lectionis* for the sound A in the verbal form 'He built', that is BNH (Banâ). Last point, the presence of the letter W is rare in names because there are only two in the entire stele (dwdh, hwrnn) but its pronunciation seems to be either û or ô as in Hebrew. The word dwdh may be vocalized *dôdahu* that is 'his beloved' and the name of Horon was well-known and it was been written Huarun in the inscription of Thutmosis III.

Egyptian	-1450	Ḥ-w3-3-rw-n	Ḥuarun
Moabite	-850	Ḥwrn	
Greek	-250	Ôrôn	Oron
Hebrew	500	Ḥôron	Ḥoron

Therefore the pronunciation Yihwah or Yihua in the Mesha inscription is in agreement with all the previous data, furthermore it corresponds to its "natural reading" Ihua. This natural reading is very ancient because the Egyptians used it (20th century BCE) with their system: ÿ = i, w = u, 3 = a, at Ugarit (14th century BCE) three vowels i, u, a, were represented by three different signs, the Hebraic language possessed *matres lectionis* very early even inside names (11th century BCE)[482]. It is as possible as letters y and w served to represent the sounds i, e and u, o respectively because as early as 1500 BCE the Cypriot syllabary had the five sounds: a, e, i, o, u.

The natural reading is the main rule in the Bible.

Reference	Consonants	Vowel letters	MT	LXX
Gn 46:13	PWH	PUA	PUaH	Poua
Nb 26:23	PWH	PUA	PuWaH	Poua
Jg 10:1	PW'H	PU'A	PU'aH	Poua
Gn 26:34	YHWDYT	IHUDIT	YeHUDIT	Ioudéit
Jg 16:4	DLYLH	DaLILA	DeLILaH	Dalila
Gn 25:19	YṢḤQ	IṢaHaQ	YiṢḤaQ	Isaak
Dt 3:21	YHWŠW'	IHUŠUa'	YeHOŠU'a	Ièsoi
Ex 17:9	YHWŠ'	IHUŠa'	YeHOŠu'a	Ièsou
1Ch 24:11	YŠW'	IŠU'a	YéŠU'a	Ièsou
1Ch 11:26	DWDW	DUDU	DODO	Dôdô
Ezk 34:23	DWYD	DUID	DaWID	Daüid
1Ch 27:4	DWDY	DUDI	DODaY	Dôdia
Jos 12:23	GWYM	GUIM	GOYiM	Gôim
Gn 29:35	YHWDH	IHUDA	YeHUDaH	Iouda
Lv 26:42	Y'QWB	I'aQUB	Ya'aQOB	Iakôb
2Ch 27:1	YRWŠH	IRUŠA	YeRUŠaH	Iérousa
Gn 46:17	YŠWH	IŠUA	YiŠWaH	Iésoua
1Ch 2:38	YHW'	IHU'	YéHU'	Ièou
1Ch 3:5	YRW-ŠLYM	IRU-ŠaLIM	YeRU-ŠaLaYiM	Iérou-salèm
Jr 36:14	NTN-YHW	NaTaN-IHU	NeTaN-YaHU	Natan-iou

It can be seen in the table above the pronunciations in the three systems of vocalization are quite close. It should be noted however that the pronunciation according to its letters is generally closer to the Septuagint than to the Masoretic text. Some gaps are more important for the compound names, for example the name Nethanyahu (MT) is read Nathaniou in Septuagint and Nathanihu in the system of reading according to its letters. Which is the right one? In fact the name Nethanyahu comes from the joining of Nathan-yah-hu' 'He has given-Yah-

Himself' which is spelt in Hebrew NTN-YH-HW' and what is vocalized in the system according to its letters in NaTaN-IA-HU' that is Nathaniahu which corresponds to the vocalization of the Masoretic text (with the classic drop of the first a). The reading of the name NTN-YH-HW' is easy but when it was shortened into NTNYHW its reading became ambiguous.

The natural reading of names beginning with Y- is I-, but the "true" vocalization, that is Yi, Ye or I, can not be known as to the present data comes from the Septuagint or from the Masoretic text.

Name	Reference	MT	LXX
Jezebel	1K 16:31	'I-zèbèl	Ié-zabél
Ishbosheth	2S 2:8	'I-šbošèth	Ié-bosthé
Ithamar	Ex 6:23	'I-ṯamar	I-ṯamar
Job	Ezk 14:14	'I-yôb	I-ôb
Jedidiah	2S 12:25	Ye-didyah	I-dédi
Jeshaiah	1Ch 25:3	Ye-šaʿyahu	I-saia
Isaiah	Is 1:1	Ye-šaʿyahu	È-saias
Jehiel	1Ch 15:18	Ye-ḥi'él	I-ièl
Judah	Gn 29:35	Ye-hudah	I-ouda
Jeroham	1Ch 8:27	Ye-roḥam	I-raam
Jerahmeel	1Ch 24:29	Ye-raḥmeél	I-ramaèl
Ezekiel	Ezk 1:3	Ye-ḥèzqé'l	Ié-zékièl
Jehezkel	1Ch 24:16	Ye-ḥèzqé'l	É-zékèl
Ishmael	Gn 25:13	Yi-šmʿa'él	I-smaèl
Israel	Gn 32:29	Yi-sra'él	I-sraèl
Jezreel	Jg 6:33	Yi-zreʿè'l	Ié-zraél
Imna	1Ch 7:35	Yi-mnaʿ	I-mana
Isaac	Gn 17:19	Yi-sḥaq	I-saak
Ibleam	Jg 1:27	Yi-bleʿam	Ié-blaam
Imnah	Gn 46:17	Yi-mnah	Ié-mna
Jeremiah	2Ch 35:25	Yi-rmeyahu	Ié-rémias
Ishbak	Gn 25:2	Yi-šbæq	Ié-sbok
Iscah	Gn 11:29	Yi-skah	Ié-ska

It can be seen that the first syllable of names in the Masoretic vocalization is rather badly linked with the Septuagint. Several phenomena can explain these differences. Iotacism can help a reader to understand the presence of Isaia next to Esaia and Ezekel next to Iezekiel but except for some cases the confusion of sounds ei, ie, i etc., was not very frequent because Hebrew names generally have a good correspondence with Greek names which, in turn, are quite reliable. The influence of Aramaic pronunciation had a role to play, especially in Alexandria. However, this does not explain how names beginning by Ye- became I- in Greek text at the same time as those that are vocalized Yi- become Ié-. Yi-'s transformation into Ye- (Barth-Ginsberg's law) is possible for some names, because this process mainly happened during the third century before our era, for example Yihudah (Iouda) would have become Yehudah. However this explanation contains weaknesses. The former name Yishaq remained Isaak and not Iésaak, on the other hand several names in the old book of Genesis beginning by Yi- became Ié-, but Yihudah did not become Iéouda.

It is finally possible that such confusion results from a hiatus of the Masoretic system itself. It can be noted first that the Masoretes of the West and those of the East had an oral tradition of different reading concerning these names, even with a name as important as Yisrael which is read Israel. In the Masoretic system it is impossible to represent a name beginning with a vowel, except by adding a mute consonant (aleph). For example, the name Israel can be read only Yisrael or Yesrael in this system but it is impossible to read it Israel except by modifying the spelling of this name into 'Israel. So, it is possible that some names beginning with Y- were read I-, but the Masoretic system vocalized them as Yi- or Ye-, which would explain some modifications of pronunciation. For example, 'to Israel' is pronounced in Hebrew 'Le-Yisrael' (but L-Israel in the Ben Naphtali's tradition) 'to Judah' is pronounced L-Ihudah and not Le-Yehudah which would have been possible. So it seems likely that the current name Yehudah pronounced in fact Ihudah (that is Yudah) could be explained by the following. In the first place the Septuagint vocalized the name Iouda, and secondly that the Jews abbreviated the name Ihudah into Iudah, and that the Masoretes not being able to represent the form Ihudah chose an approximation Yehudah.

So most of the names which are read Ye- or Yi- in the Masoretic text and I- in the Septuagint may be effectively read I- originally. Some spelling mistakes in old inscriptions confirm this reading in I-. The name Jezebel is read 'Izèbèl in the Masoretic text which appears to be the right pronunciation of a vocalic Y (I) rather than a consonantal Y (Ye), what confirms Ithamar a frequent and very ancient name. In an inscription dated 700 BCE the name Jezebel is written inaccurately YZBL and not 'YZBL, which supposes a natural reading I-ZaBaL. However, the name 'Izèbèl, which means in Hebrew 'where [is] honor', may also be a voluntary deformation of the name YiZBoL, which means, '[Baal] He will honor' (Gn 30:20). Even in the Masoretic text the name Jesse is written either Yishay (1Ch 2:12) or 'Ishay (1Ch 2:13) and Iessai in the Septuagint!

Name	Jezebel	Yahats	Jabneh	Judah
Reference	1K 16:31	Nb 21:23	2Ch 26:6	Gn 29:35
MT	'Izèbèl	Yahṣ(ah)	Yabnèh	Yehudah
LXX	Iézabél	Ias(sa)	Iabnè	Iouda
Consonants in the Bible	'yzbl	yhṣ	Ybnh	yhwdh
Voc. reading	'I-zabal	I-haṣ	I-bna	I-huda
Con. reading	'i-zabal	Ya-haṣ	Ya-bnah	Ya-hudah
Consonants on old seals	Yzbl	y'hs	yhbnh	yhwdh
Voc. reading	I-zabal	I-'ahas	I-habna	I-huda
Con. reading	Ya-zabal	Ya-'ahas	Ya-habnah	Ya-hudah

An inscription dated 750 BCE contains the name Yahats (normally written YHṢ) but inaccurately written Y'HṢ which proves that the reading Ya- was not natural. In the Bible the name YHṢ could be naturally read according to its letters in IHaṢ as Jahz(eel) (Gn 46:24) that is that YHṢ-'L is read IHaṢ-'éL and not YaHaṢ-'éL. To avoid such an error the writer preferred the less ambiguous writing Y'HṢ which means 'He divided' (Gn 32:7) which can be read naturally as IAHaṢ, also the name Jahaz (Nb 21:23) that is YHṢH is always read naturally in the Bible IHaṢA that is Iassa (LXX) and YaHṢaH (MT), but ever YaHaṢaH.

It can be seen that the vocalic reading (rather than the consonantal reading) of inscriptions on old seals (before 700 BCE) is in good agreement with the Masoretic readings. Furthermore the name Jabneh came from an old, but unusual *hiphil* form which means, 'He will cause to build'. For example, Jabneel (Jos 15:11) means 'God will cause to build'. The usual form in the Bible is the *qal* form Yibnèh 'He will build' like in the name Ibnijah (1Ch 9:8) which means 'He will build, Yah'. This last name is written YBNYH and it is pronounced according to its letters IBNIA which is in good agreement with the Masoretic Yibnyah. Therefore, in Hebrew names beginning with Ya- are less numerous than those beginning with Yi- or Ye-, very often they came from a contraction, like Yeha-bnèh into Ya-bnèh, or Ya'-boq (he got dusty) into Ya-boq (Gn 32:22-24), Yah-hu' into Ya-hu, etc, or from a foreign influence, like Yabin (Jos 11:1), Yarhaʻ (1Ch 2:34), Yaziz (1Ch 27:31), etc.

GREEK ALPHABET CAME FROM A NATURAL READING

As most of the features of the archaic Greek alphabet resemble those of the West Semitic script of around 1100 BCE, serious consideration can be given to the theory of an early adoption by the Greeks[483]. The inscription of Mesha was written at the time of the poet Homer (850 BCE) and the main difference between the Greek and the Phoenician of these writers was the notation of vowels. It is interesting to note which sounds Greeks preferred to pronounce with some Phoenician letters, which is their natural reading. The orthography of the Aramaic portion of the Tell Fekherye Bilingual[484] (dated before 9th century BCE) proves that for a long time three vowels were used, *waw* for û, *yod* for î, and *he* for final â. For example, numerous words were read "according to their natural reading" in this old inscription:

Writing	Reading	Writing	Reading
ṬBH	ṬaBA	BTNWR	BaTaNUR
TYṬB	TIṬaB	YGTZR	YiGTiZaR
DMWT'	DaMUTa'	'DQWR	'aDaQUR
GWGL	GUGaL	YLQḤ	YiLQaḤ
'LYM	'aLIM	NHR	NaHaR
TṢLWTH	TaṢLUTA	LMT	LaMaT
WLKBR	WaLaKaBaR	RḤMN	RaḤMaN

As a general rule the 'natural reading' was mainly used to vocalize proper names.

Fekherye		Reading according to:			
Alphabetic	Syllabic	Akkadian	M.T.	LXX	reference
ḤBWR	Ḥa-bur	ḤaBUR	ḤaBOR	Abôr	2K 18:11
NYRGL	(Nè-iri-gal)	NIRGaL	NèRGaL	Nèrigĕl	2K 17:30
GWZN	Gu-za-ni	GUZaN	GOZaN	Gôzan	2K 18:11
HDDSKN	Adad-si-ka-ni	HaDaDSiKaN	HaDaD-	Adad-	Gn 36:35
SSNWRY	Šamaš-nu-ri	SaSNURI	SiS-	Sos-	1Ch 2:40
(YHWH)	-	(YiHWA)	(YeHoWaH))		

The word YHWH meaning 'He will [prove to] be' is found in the Sefire inscription (dated 750 BCE). The normal vocalization is YiHWèH, but more probably YiHWaH at this time (because the sound -èH comes from an old -aH), which is in agreement with its 'natural reading'.

Before 550 BCE, the Greeks could partly read Phoenician writings because they read from right to left in the same way as Hebrew. Furthermore, the earliest Greek letter forms and names are very similar (called Cadmeian letters by Herodotus), and some even identical, to the equivalent West Semitic letters (around 850 BCE). A Greek of this time could have partially read the names of the stele of Mesha!

Letter Form	MOABITE Name	Reading	GREEK Name	Reading
A	aleph	'	alpha	A
E	he	H	e-psilon	É
H	heth	Ḥ	eta	È
Y	waw	W	u-psilon	Ü
Z	yod	Y	iota	I
O	aïn	'	o-micron	O

It can be seen that the Greek reading appeared as a fixed and simplified natural reading[485] of the Hebrew names.

Before ninth century BCE, to establish the "true" reading of Hebrew names is difficult. Nevertheless, a verification is still possible owing to the name among different places names in alphabetic and syllabic writing at Ugarit[486] (dated 14th century BCE), although the general agreement between the defective reading (alphabetic) and its syllabic equivalent is not great. However there remains a noteworthy link between the "natural reading" of the Masoretic consonantal writing and its syllabic reading despite Ugaritic is a sister tongue of Hebrew. In addition, specific cuneiform signs were used for the Alphabetic writing rather than paleo-Hebrew at Tell Fekherye.

Ugarit Alphabetic	Syllabic	Reading according to: Consonant	M.T.	LXX	reference
'KY	A-ki-ia	'KW	'Akô	Akkô	Jg 1:31
'RWDN	a-ru-a-di-ia	'RWDY	'Arwadi	Aradion	Gn 10:18
ADDD	Aš-da-di	'ŠDWD	'Ašdôd	Asĕdôt	Jos 11:22
-	Aš-qu-lu-nu	'ŠQLWN	'Ašqelôn	Askalôna	Jg 1:18
ATR	Aš-šur	'ŠWR	'Ašur	Assour	Is 31:8
GBL	Gu-ub-li	GBL	Gebal	Bübliôn	Ezk 27:9
ḤT	Ḫa-at-ti	ḤT	Ḥĕt	Ket	Gn 27:46
KRGMŠ	Kar-ga-miš	KRKMYŠ	Karkemiš	Karkamis	Jr 46:2
KN'N	Ki-na-ḫi	KN'N	Kena'an	Kana'an	Gn 9:18
LBNN	La-ab-a-na	LBNWN	Lebanôn	Libanou	Jos 11:17
ṢDN	Ṣi-du-na	ṢYDWN	Ṣidôn	Sidôna	Gn 10:15

Did Yehowah come from a change?
(YAH ⇒ YAHU ⇒ YEHOWAH)

This change looks very feasible but several facts disprove it. Firstly, such an off-glide seems to be unlikely[487], secondly this explanation creates a discrepancy with the Bible which says that Yah and Yehowah are two very old names (Ex 3:15; 15:2) that one can praise alike (Ps 146:1). On the other hand, archaeology gives an opposite evolutionary alternative that is to say Yhwh became Yhw then finally Yh!

To be compatible with these facts, a very ingenious explanation is proposed: When the primeval men spoke of God, they said 'Oh, He' that is to say in Hebrew 'Ya Hua' that gave the two forms Yah and Yahûa' which became by a phonological change Yehowah. Yet the impression remains that the defenders[488] of these theories are carried away by their fantasy into a sphere where scientific control is no longer possible. For example, these authors don't explain why Ya developed into Yahwah and not into another form. The only point open to test is the phonological evolution. Actually, if one examines the variation of different proper names[489], there is apparently a change from the sequence 'a-u-a' toward a sequence 'e-o-a'.

REF.	-1400 -1200	-800 -600	-300 -100	-100 +100
Jg 1:18	Ašqaluna	Asqaluna	Askalôna	Ašqelôn
Is 39:1		Marduk	Marôdak	Merodak
Nb 21:29	Kammus	Kamuš	Kamôs	Kemôš
Nb 32:3	Nabû	Nabû	Nabau	Nebô
2K 25:8		Nabû-zéra-iddina	Nabou zardan	Nebû zar'adan
1Ch 5:41		Nabû-kudurri-uṣur	Nabou kodonosor	Nebû kadrè'ṣar
Jr 39:13		Nabû-šézi-banni	Nabou sazaban	Nebû šazban
2K 19:37		Aššur-aḥ-iddina	Asor dan	'ésar ḥadon

Jg 1:18		Amqarruna	Akkarôn	ʿèqrôn
Gn 19:1	(Saduma)		Sodoma	Sedoma
2K 23:29		Neka'û	Nékaô	Nek̲o
Is 20:1		šarrukîn	Arna	Sargôn
Dn 1:7			Abdénagô	ʿab̲édnegô
Est 1:16			Mouk̲aios	Memûk̲an
Est 1:10			Aman	Mehûman
Jos 15:11			Sak̲karona	Šikerônâ
Jos 18:15			Naptô	Nèptôaḥ
Nb 22:5			Patoura	Pet̲ôra
		a - u - (*)	a - ô - (a)	e - ô - (a)

A change a-u-a towards e-ô-a seems to be convincing, however the greater part of these names came from foreign origins (Philistia, Assyria, Babylonia, etc.) therefore, they have been Hebraized to be written in the Bible. An important problem to solve is first, to make a reliable identification with the biblical names, for example, concerning Saduma the link is open to criticism[490], secondly, to evaluate the evolution of the language itself and thirdly to evaluate the influence of the modifications due to transcription from one tongue to an other. Thus to avoid a modification from a transcription the best choice to test this evolution is to use only some old Hebrew names.

REF.	-1400 -1200	-800 -600	-300 -100	-100 +100
Jos 11:10	Ḥaṣura		Asôr	Ḥaṣôr
Ezr 3:7	Yapu	Yappû	Ioppè	Yap̲ô
Jos 21:24	Ialuna		Ialôn /Ailon	ʾAyalona
Jg 13:2			Manôé	Manôaḥ
Jos 16:6			Ianoka	Yanôḥa
Ezr 2:8			Zat̲oua	Zatû'
Ne 11:30			Zanôé	Zanôaḥ
		a - u - (*)	a - ô - (a)	a - ô - (a)

Unfortunately, with these Hebrew names, there is no significant evolution, the sequence a-u-a became a-ô-a. Therefore, this modification of the sequence a-u-a (foreign language) ⇒ e-o-a (Hebrew) results mainly from a Hebraisization of foreign names, because the Jews are very fond of this sequence. For example:

REF.	HEB. NAME	FRE.	LXX -300 -100	MT -100 +100
1Ch 3:5	יְרוּשָׁלַיִם	667	Iérousalèm	Yerušalém
1S 9:1	בְּכוֹרַת	1	Békôrat	Bekôrat
1Ch 4:17	אֶשְׁתְּמֹעַ	5	Éstémôn	'Èštemoa'
Gn 10:26	אַלְמוֹדָד	2	Élmôdad	'Almôdad
Jos.19:4	אֶלְתּוֹלַד	2	Éltoulad	'Éltolad
Ezk 47:16	בְּרוֹתָה	1	Bérôta	Bérôtâ
Gn 35:8	דְּבוֹרָה	10	Débbôra	Debôrâ
Jos 15:22	דִּימוֹנָה	1	Dimôna	Dîmônâ
Ne 11:9	הַסְּנוּאָה	1	Asana	Hasenû'â
2K 23:36	זְבוּדָה	1	-	Zebûdâ
Nb 34:9	זִפְרֹנָה	1	Zéprôna	Ziprônâ
1Ch 3:19	זְרֻבָּבֶל	22	Zorobabél	Zerubabèl
Nb 33:29	חַשְׁמֹנָה	2	Sélmôna	Hašmônâ
Gn 29:35	יְהוּדָה	806	Iouda	Yehûdâ
Jg 7:1	יְרֻבַּעַל	14	Iérobaal	Yeruba'al
2K 15:33	יְרוּשָׁא	1	Iérousa	Yerûša'
2Ch 27:1	יְרוּשָׁה	1	Iérousa	Yerûšâ
1Ch 9:12	יְרֹחָם	10	Iéroam	Yeroḥam
Jg 21:19	לְבוֹנָה	1	Lébôna	Lebônâ
Jg 7:22	מְחוֹלָה	3	Méoula	Meḥôlâ
2S 21:8	מְחֹלָתִי	2	Mooulatéi	Meḥolati
Ne 11:28	מְכֹנָה	1	Makna	Mekonâ
1Ch 4:34	מְשׁוֹבָב	1	Mosôbab	Mešôbab
Nb 3:6	מְשֻׁלָּם	25	Mésoulam	Mešulam
Gn 4:18	מְתוּשָׁאֵל	2	Matousala	Metûša'él
Ne 7:50	נְקוֹדָא	4	Nékôda	Neqôda'

Ne 7:26	נְטֹפָה	2	Nétopa	Netopâ
1Ch 2:54	נְטוֹפָתִי	11	Nétôpati	Netôpatî
Nb 33:34	עַבְרֹנָה	2	Ébrôna	ʽAbronâ
Ex 4:25	צִפֹּרָה	3	Séppora	Siporâ
1K 11:26	צְרוּעָה	1	Saroua	Serûʽâ
Gn 25:1	קְטוּרָה	4	Kéttoura	Qetûrâ
Gn 22:24	רְאוּמָה	1	Rééma	Re'ûmâ
2K 22:14	תִּקְוָה	7	Tékoué	Teqôʽâ
1Ch 8:5	שְׁפוּפָן	2	Sôparpak	Šepûpan
1Ch 9:7	סְנֻאָה	2	Sanaa	Senû'â
			é - ô - (a)	e - ô - (a)

Thus the sequence e-o-a is very frequent in the Hebrew names and most of the time, this sequence has been preserved correctly in the Septuagint. On the other hand, it is interesting to know the reverse transcription, that is to say e-o-a (Hebrew) ⇒ (foreign language). To avoid some fortuitous coincidence, only a few names have been selected because only a clear context allows the reader to make an accurate identification.

-2300 -2000	-1400 -1200	-800 -600	-300 -100 LXX	-100 +100 MT
Urusalima	Urusalim	Urusalimmu	Iérousalèm	Yerušalém
		Yahudu	Iouda	Yehûdâ
		Yaua	Ièou	Yéhû'
		Yakukînu	Iôakim	Yehôyakin
		Yauhazu	Iôakaz	Yeho'ahaz
		Hazaqiyau	Ézékiou	Hizqiyahû
		a - u - (*)	é - ô - (a)	e - ô - (a)

It is easy to verify there is no trace of this first *a* in the Septuagint nor in the Masoretic text. Once again, the problem of transcription, Hebrew to foreign language, may explain the difference. In actual fact, the yeho form in Assyrian-Babylonian cannot be distinguished from the yahu form[491], for example, Yehû' and Yehûdâ, two Hebrew names very close to Yhwh, can be read[492] on the black obelisk of Shalmaneser III (-850) and in the Babylonian chronicle of Nebuchadnezzar (-600):

Ia - u - a   Ia -a-ḫu-du

Therefore, there is an Akkadianization of these Hebrew names, thus, this e-o-a sequence (Hebrew) is converted to a-u-a (Akkadian) because very often the first vowel in Assyrian transcriptions is *a* in spite of the true vowel. Furthermore, the cuneiform sign[493] for a phonetic *ia* may be read also *ie, ii* or *iu*. Thus, according to some scholars the reading *Ia* is open to question, for example, the name Ia-'a-su (Yô'ash) may be read Iu-'a-su (Ia-na may be read Ie-na and so forth)[494]. Consequently, this modification is quite normal as Yehud is pronounced Yahud in Arabic and Yhwh is vocalized Yahuwa[495]. Last but not least, very often the vocalization of some proper names is inexplicable[496].

<small>CHANGES WHICH ARE PROVED</small>

In this period; *hû'* became *hû*, at the end of some words, for example: 'Èlîhû' is written 'Èlîhû (1Ch 26:7 27:18; Job 32:4 35:1). On the other hand, the pronoun *hû'* itself is very often written hw (see the inscription from Khirbet Beit Lei dated around 700 BCE and the papyri from Elephantine dated around 500 BCE). However, it remained written h' in the Arad ostraca during this period, and hw at the end of words. It is interesting to notice that the word 'TNH-HW is written 'TNHW in the Lakish ostracon n°3 line 12 (idem n°4 line 7).

In Hebrew, *Yâ hû'* 'Yah himself' became Yahû at the end of the theophoric names, on the other hand, these names are written *yaw* in Aramaic, because the pronunciation of the *h* was dropped. For example -why is written[497] -wy.

Another interesting example is about the theophoric names, written -yhw in Judaea (Hebrew) but -yw in Samaria (Aramean)[498]. But the difference of pronunciation was not so important -yahû and -yaw. Sometimes, the two spellings are mentioned[499]:

Sheban-yahû   Azar-yahû
Sheban-yaw   Azar-yaw

In this field, the Masoretes mainly kept the names of Hebrew origin, but there is an exception: 'Aḥyô (2S 6:3,4; 1Ch 8:14,31 9:37 13:7) thus, this Hebrew spelling is unusual compared to 'Aḥiyahû (1K 14:4,5,6,18; 2Ch 10:15) therefore, the name 'Aḥyô reflects an Aramaic origin 'Aḥyaw[500]. Thus, this process produced different abbreviations:

Yah-hû' (יָה הוּא) gave Yahû (יְהוּ) with an Aramaic abbreviation Ya(h)û that is Yaw (יַ)
Yehow(ah) (יְהֹוָה) gave Yehô- (יְהֹ) with a Hebrew abbreviation Y(eh)ô- that is Yô- (יֹ)

Religious trials of the first century

AMONG THE JEWS

While the trial of Jesus is the most famous, certain elements appear contradictory as to the motive for his condemnation and the procedure followed by the authorities.

To understand these difficulties[501] we must remember that the Jewish Supreme Court, the Sanhedrin, was a body officially recognized by the occupying power and endowed with competence in judicial and administrative matters and in legal exegesis, existing as a single institution under the presidency of the High Priest (After the destruction of Jerusalem in 70 CE, the Sanhedrin ceased to exist in its previous form). The Sanhedrin in the time of Jesus was restricted to the eleven toparchies of Judaea proper. It consequently had no judicial authority at all over Jesus whilst he remained in Galilee. He came directly under its jurisdiction only in Judaea (Lk 23:7). In a sense, of course, the Sanhedrin exercised such moral jurisdiction over all the Jewish communities throughout the world (Ac 9:2: 22:5: 26:12), and in that sense over Galilee too. The Sanhedrin judged civil and religious crimes, but it had authority only over Jewish citizens and being under the Roman authority, the execution of its judgments had to be overseen by these authorities (Ac 22:30). For example, the Talmud of Jerusalem (*Sanhedrin 18a*) tells us that 40 years before the destruction of the Temple, that is in 30 CE, the Romans had deprived the Jews of capital punishment. With the trial of Jesus taking place in 33 CE, the Jews could indeed tell Pilate that they could not put Jesus to death (Jn 18:31). However, this limitation concerned only civil crimes, because the Romans did not want to take charge of religious crimes (Ac 18:14-16; 23:29; 25:19). Moreover, Pilate pointed out that he had full authority to judge civil crimes (Jn 19:10) yet, he did not want to judge a religious crime (Jn 18:31) even though this crime was punishable by death (Jn 19:7). With reference to Judaea, Josephus states explicitly that the emperor delegated to Coponius, Judaea's first Roman prefect (from 6 to 9 CE), the power to rule on his behalf, and exercise his authority, including the right to inflict capital punishment (*The Jewish War II:117*). In Jewish law the only religious crimes which were punishable by death, at this time, were profanation of the Temple (Nb 4:15) and blasphemy against God's name (Lv 24:16), which explains why the chief priests tried at first to condemn Jesus on these grounds (Mc 14:55). For example, in a extract from a letter to Agrippa I (-10 to 44), Philo asserted that entry into the Holy of Holies by a Jew, even a priest, or even the High Priest when not expressly ordered, constituted a crime punishable by 'death without appeal'. Literary and epigraphic evidence indicate that a non-Jew, even if a Roman citizen (*The Jewish War VI:126*), was to be put to death if apprehended in the inner Temple court.

BLASPHEMY

This crime is clearly codified in the Law of Moses and the culprit was to be stoned to death outside the camp (Lv 24:14-16). For example, this procedure was unjustly applied to execute Naboth (1K 21:13,14). The chief priests tried to apply this charge against Jesus, but several elements made their plan fail. First of all the false witnesses did not agree among themselves (Mt 26:59,60), and secondly the charge of blasphemous sayings was a matter of interpretation.

In order for that charge to be valid the accused person must have cursed God's name, with two conditions, that is to blaspheme God and to use his name, or more rarely to directly blaspheme God's name. Apostasy being considered as blasphemous sayings, could entail the death penalty (Jn 10:33) if the accused person also used God's name before the final verdict of the court (*Sanhedrin 56a, 7:5*). In this particular case, Jesus did not so use the divine Name and he demonstrated that the charge of blasphemous sayings was untrue (Jn 10:31-39). In the time of Jesus there existed blasphemous sayings and blasphemy against God (Mt 12:31). If blasphemous sayings (generally apostasy) were proved, the accused person was excluded and cursed by the community. It was this threat which hung over the Jews who became Christian (Jn 9:22; 12:42). They did not risk death, but rather exclusion or excommunication (Ac 8:1). However, to satisfy the Jewish religious leaders, the civil authorities did put some Christians of Jewish origin to death (Jn 16:2) on vague charges of sedition (Ac 12:1-3; 19:40; 24:5) or disturbing public order (Ac 16:20; 17:6).

THE TRIAL OF JESUS

The chief priests who wanted to eliminate Jesus (Mt 26:4) tried to put him to death (Mt 26:59) by using the only charge which allowed for capital punishment (Jn 19:7), the charge of blasphemy (Mt 26:65). Since there had obviously been no direct blasphemy against God, in order for that charge to work it was also necessary that Jesus use the divine name before the final verdict, which he did not do, using substitutes such as Power (Mt 26:64), Above (Jn 19:11), God (Mk 15:34). So, the charge remained potential -"He is liable to death" but could not become actual -"he is condemned to death", because, although the high priest ripped his outer garments, he asked «What is your opinion?» (Mt 26:65-66). Furthermore the high priest alone ripped his garments proving that the other members of the Sanhedrin did not fully agree. Having failed, the chief priests then changed the charge of blasphemy (religious crime), into a crime of lese-majesty (civil crime), but for this, the approval of Roman authorities was necessary (Lk 23:1,2). This charge of *crimen laesae majestis* was perfectly understood by Pilate, but he did not retain it (Lk 23:13,14). The law called *lex Julia majestis* promulgated in 48 BCE recognized as a crime any activity against the sovereign power of Rome. Finally, Pilate accepted unwillingly to execute Jesus but simply to restore law and order and to protect his career (Lk 23:22-24).

It was mainly for this last reason that Christians of pagan origin would be put to death. Roman historian Tacitus, wrote that to silence rumors about the fire of Rome in 64 CE, Nero put to death Christians who were already the object of popular hatred (*The Annals XV, XLIV*). Pliny the Younger, the governor of Bithynia around 111 CE, expressed his perplexity over the absence of any legal motive for the execution of Christians (*Letters of Pliny X:96,3-5; 97,1*).

STEPHEN'S TRIAL

The procedure followed is similar to the one that was followed for the trial of Jesus. First of all Stephen was accused of blasphemous sayings and thus was brought before the Sanhedrin (Ac 6:11,12). Stephen was considered to be a blasphemer, because he was accused of apostasy (Ac 6:14), which charge he attempted to refute. His argumentation should have exonerated him, but in his defense he quoted the episode of the burning bush (Ex 3:1-15) with the revelation of the Name (Ac 7:30-33) which led him to use the divine name three times (Ac 7:31,33,49). On the other hand, refusing to name God could have convinced the audience that Stephen implicitly recognized that he spoke blasphemous sayings. The fact of using the divine name was not reprehensible in itself, because prohibition on its use would appear only by the middle of the second century, but to use it when on trial for blasphemy before the final verdict meant execution by stoning (*Sanhedrin 7:5*), which indeed occurred (Ac 7:58). A few Judeo-Christians were executed in this 'legal' way (Ac 26:10). There were not simply vigilante killings because Saul, who was a legal expert, approved of Stephen's execution (Ac 22:20). Some Bible scholars propose the idea that it was the last sentence about Jesus, which condemned Stephen. This is impossible for two reasons. The first is that the proceedings were dealing with blasphemy against the Name and not the charge of apostasy which would have only entailed a prison sentence (Ac 8:3; 22:4) and exclusion from the synagogue (Jn 12:42), not capital punishment. Secondly, the prohibition on the use of the name of Jesus did exist (Ac 4:18; 5:28), but the penalty in that case was flogging (Ac 5:40) not death. This penalty was often applied (Mt 10:17; Ac 22:19) on Christians of Jewish origin but not on Christians of heathen origin.

PAUL'S TRIAL

The procedure followed was still the same. The Jews, around 58 CE, wanted to eliminate Paul (Ac 22:22) who was then brought before the Sanhedrin (Ac 22:30). However, knowing perfectly well what had happened to Stephen (Ac 22:20) and knowing that in any case the crowd would molest him (Ac 21:31,35) after his judgment, Paul skillfully transformed a likely charge of sedition, profanation of the Temple (Ac 21:28) and apostasy (Ac 21:21) into a charge concerning different faiths (Ac 23:6), which definitively held up his trial. (A few years before, around 50 CE, a Roman soldier who heedlessly tore up a Torah scroll was put to death for profanation of the Temple by Procurator Cumanus (*The Jewish War II:231*)). It would seem that Paul in a previous trial had not acted as skillfully, since he was indeed stoned and left for dead outside the city (Ac 14:19).

JAMES' TRIAL

There is no record in the Scriptures of James' death. The secular historian Josephus, however, says that during the interval between the death of Governor Festus, about 62 CE, and the arrival of his successor Albinus, the high priest Ananus (Ananias), «conveyed the judges of the Sanhedrin and brought before them a man named James, the brother of Jesus (Ga 1:19) who was called the Christ, and certain others. He accused them of having transgressed the law and delivered them up to be stoned» (*Jewish Antiquities XX: 200*). The stoning of James, a Christian of Jewish origin, appears to be the last to be recorded.

AMONG THE ROMANS

The Romans easily accepted new religions with the express condition (at the risk of death) that they be licit i.e. authorized by the State according to the ancient law called *lex superstitio illicita*. At the beginning of our era, since Christians were mainly of Jewish origin, the Romans did not easily distinguish between the two groups. The Jewish religion being a licit religion, the Judeo-Christian should have been able to use the divine name without risk of being pursued for blasphemy by the Roman authorities. Whereas it was legal for a Roman to become Jewish, the law on superstitions was nevertheless invoked to condemn Judeo-Christians (Ac 16:21).

This charge seems paradoxical, because it was possible only if a new god had been introduced, but certain philosophers believed this was the case in hearing talk about Jesus (Ac 17:18). A second possibility is that, as in the first century, since the Romans knew that the Jews worshiped a god who was not named, the use of a name unknown to them, would have led to belief in the introduction of a new religion (Ac 18:13). For that reason, Paul carefully avoided using the Tetragram, in his defense, but preferred substitutes such as God, Lord of the heaven and earth, the Divine Being (Ac 17:21-31). The proconsul Gallio considered that a quarrel on names (Ac 18:15) did not come from the law on superstitions, but from the Jewish law alone. Theoretically, the law on superstitions could apply to the Jews or to the Judeo-Christians only if they mentioned the divine name, a god unknown to the Romans. However even in that case, the penalty was not necessarily death but expulsion. For example, historian Valerius Maximus relates that around 139 BCE Praetor Cornelius Hispalus sent back Jews who had tried to convert Romans to the worship of Jova Sabaoth (Sabazi Jovi). However, under pressure from the crowd which hated Christians, historian Suetonius wrote «that punishments were inflicted on the Christians, a class of men given to a new and mischievous superstition» (*The Lives of Caesars -Nero, XVI, 2*).

The charge of sedition was ambiguous, because any disorder could have been perceived as a revolt (Ac 19:40). If a citizen was at the same time Jewish and Roman, Roman authority prevailed. For example in Paul's case, the first charge was apostasy (Ac 21:21; case n°8 see hereafter) then profanation of the Temple and sedition [against Jewish authorities] (Ac 21:28; case n°6 and 7) understood as sedition [against Roman authorities] (Ac 21:38; case n°5) but modified into apostasy (Ac 22:22-25; case n°8). When they had stretched him out for the whipping, Paul said to the army officer standing there: "Is it lawful for You men to scourge a man that is a Roman and uncondemned?" (Ac 22:26-29) Therefore the legal authority could not have been the Sanhedrin but only that of the Governor (Ac 23:28-30; case n°3). To clear up the question of judgement authority, Paul appealed to Caesar (Ac 25:11) but in this case as the real charge remained religious, from a Roman point of view it was not valid (Ac 25:27).

Crime	Incurred penalty	Proper authorities	
Murder of a Roman	Capital punishment	Governor	1
Crime* of a Jew by a Jew	Capital punishment	Sanhedrin (judgment) but Governor for the execution after 30 CE	2
Murder of a Jew by a Roman	Capital punishment	Governor	3
Illicit religion of a Roman	Eviction or capital punishment	Governor	4
Sedition against Roman authorities	Capital punishment	Governor	5
Sedition against Jewish authorities	Flogging and excommunication	Sanhedrin	6
Profanation of the Temple	Capital punishment	Sanhedrin	7
blasphemous (apostate) sayings	Flogging and excommunication	Sanhedrin	8
Blasphemy	Capital punishment	Sanhedrin	9

* homosexuality, bestiality, idolatry, sorcery, etc. (Sanhedrin 7:4)

Numbering system changes

The Jews used the biblical numbering system in their letters, but very early (before the seventh century BCE) they borrowed from Egypt its simpler numbering system especially for trade (contracts and weights)[502]. For example, they used Hieratic signs for the following numbers: 5, 10, 20, 30, 50, 300.

In about the fourth century BCE, due to Greek influence they began to use the Greek numbering system instead of the previous Egyptian system. It seems that the number YW (י) had been used as a liquid measure[503].

Then, from the third century BCE, the Greek numbering system began to spread in the Jewish world. From this time, most dated Jewish coins used a Greek numbering. The oldest dated coin (265 BCE), issued in Phoenicia, bears Greek alphabetic numerals in a decimal system[504]. This system was used as a rule for dated Jewish coins[505] from the second century BCE to the second century CE.

Coin Inscriptions: Date

		Date
ΒΑΣΙΛΕΩΣ ΑΝΤΙΟΧΟΥ ΕΥΕΡΓΕΤΟΥ ΑΠΡ		
(ΑΠΡ = 1 + 80 + 100 = 181 SE =		131 BCE)
מלכא אלכסנדרוס שנת כ	(שנת כ = year 20 =	83 BCE)
מלכא אלכסנדרוס שנת כה	(שנת כה = year 25 =	78 BCE)
ΗΡΩΔΟΥ ΒΑΣΙΛΕΩΣ LΓ	(LΓ = year 3 =	37 BCE)
ΦΙΛΙΠΠΟΥ ΤΕΤΡΑΡΧΟΥ LΙΣ	(LΙΣ = year 16 =	30 CE)
שקל ישראל א	(א = 1 =	66 CE)
שקל ישראל שב	(שב = year 2 =	67 CE)
שקל ישראל שג	(שג = year 3 =	68 CE)
שקל ישראל שד	(שד = year 4 =	69 CE)
שקל ישראל שה	(שה = year 5 =	70 CE)
LΙΕ ΒΑΣ ΑΓΡΙΠΠΑ	(LΙΕ = year 15 =	76 CE)
שנה אחת לגאלת ישראל	(שנה אחת = year 1 =	132 CE)
שב לחר ישראל	(שב = year 2 =	133 CE)

Numbering:		Jewish coins in:	
	Greek	Greek	Hebrew
1	A	-	א
2	B	B	ב
3	Γ	Γ	ג
4	Δ	-	ד
5	E	E	ה
6	Σ	Σ	-
7	Z	Z	-
8	H	H	-
9	Θ	-	-
10	I	I	-
11	IA	AI	-
12	IB	IB	-
13	IΓ	-	-
14	IΔ	IΔ	-
15	IE	IE	-
16	IΣ	IΣ	-
17	IZ	-	-
18	IH	IH	-
19	IΘ	IΘ	-
20	K	K	כ
21	KA	KA	-
22	KB	-	-
23	KΓ	KΓ	-
24	KΔ	KΔ	-
25	KE	KE	כה

An anomaly can be found in the above table. The Greek number 11 was written IA on the Roman coin dated 25 CE bearing the inscription IOYΛIA LIA, meaning 'Julia (Livia, mother of Tiberius) year 11', but was written AI on the Jewish coin dated 71 CE bearing the inscription ΒΑCΙΛΕΩC ΜΑΡΚΟΥ ΑΓΡΙΠΠΟΥ ΕΤΟΥC AI ΤΟΥ, meaning 'Of the King Marcus Agrippa of year 11'. It was probably in order to avoid confusion with the divine name IA that the Greek number 11 (IA) was written with the letters inverted. For the same reason the Hebrew numbers 15 and 16 could not have been written YH (יה) and yw (יו), but rather TW (טו) and TZ (טז), because as the Talmud points out, before our common era the two divine names YH (יה) and

YHW (יהו) which were stamped on jars, had begun to be removed in order to protect their holiness (*'Arakin 6a; Šabbat 61b*). Thus, the two Hebrew numbers 15 and 16 became 'sacred numbers'. Probably, this Jewish custom of 'sacred numbers' paved the way for the Christian custom of *nomina sacra* (sacred names) which appeared during the period 70-135 CE.

The papyrus P52, dated 125 CE, contains no *nomina sacra*, but the author of a work written between 115 and 135 CE (*Epistle of Barnabe 9:8*)[506] made a link between the number 318 of Genesis 14:14 written TIH in Greek and the T (standard) of IH (Jesus). This last remark proves that, at this time, the acronym IH was a normal abbreviation of the Greek name IHCOUC, which was always written $\overline{\text{IC}}$ after 135 CE as in the papyrus P90 dated 150 CE. Irenaeus explained in his book (*Against Heresies I:3,2*) that some Gnostics thought of deriving mystic information from these Greek abbreviations, because IH (iota, eta) represented the Greek number 18. The method of writing a line over a number was commonly used during the first century CE in order to distinguish it (for example in the writing of dates)[507].

Part 5

Index and notes

Bibliographical notes

1.1 THE POWER OF THE NAME

[1] Le Robert - Dictionnaire Universel des noms propres (préface) pp. 12,13
[2] Encyclopedia Universalis Art. Nom pp. 384-7
[3] **F. Vigouroux** - Dictionnaire de la Bible Art. Nom
Ed.Letouzey et Ané 1908 pp. 1670-8

A. Westphal - Dictionnaire Encyclopédique de la Bible 3e édition Art. Nom pp. 224-6,294-6
O. Odelain R. Séguineau - Dictionnaire des noms propres de la Bible
Paris 1988 Ed. Cerf
L. Pirot A. Robert H. Cazelles - Dictionnaire de la Bible Supplément Art. Onomastique
Ed. Letouzey et Ané 1960 pp. 732-44.
M. Viller F. Cavallera - Dictionnaire de la Spiritualité Art. Nom
Ed. Beauchesne 1982 pp. 398-410
A. Chouraqui - La vie quotidienne des hommes de la Bible
Ed.Hachette 1978 pp. 146,308-10
R. de Vaux - Les Institutions de l'Ancien Testament
Ed. Cerf 1989 pp. 74-8,165
Watchtower - Insight on the Scriptures Vol. 2
New York 1988 Ed. Watch Tower Bible and Tract Society pp. 464-468
[4] **J.M Durand** - Documents épistolaires du palais de Mari. tome III
in: LIPO Paris 2000 Éd. Cerf p. 23

1.2 TO KNOW GOD'S NAME

[5] **L. Pirot A. Clamer** - La Sainte Bible Tome I,2 Exode
Paris 1956 Ed. Letouzey et Ané p. 84
[6] **Osty** - Bible note sur Gen.3:1
1973 Seuil p. 40
[7] Code de droit canonique annoté (Can.1172)
Université pontificale de Salamanque. Ed.Cerf/Tardy 1989 p. 646

1.3 JESUS, SATAN, THEIR CONTROVERSY OVER THE NAME

[8] Encyclopédie de l'Islam
Leyde 1960 Ed. E.J. Brill Tom.I p.418; Tom IV p. 85

1.4 THE NAME READ DISTINCTLY

[9] **J. Bonsirven** - Textes rabbiniques des deux premiers siècles
Roma 1955 Ed. Pontificio Istituto Biblico pp. 50,51
[10] **D.N. Freedman** - The Massoretic Text and the Qumran Scrolls: A Study in Orthography.
1962 in Textus 2 p. 91
[11] **Herbert Marks** -Biblical Naming and Poetic Etymology
in: Journal of Biblical Literature 114/1 1995 Ed. The Society of Biblical Literature pp. 21-42
J. Barr - Etymology and the Old Testament
in: Oudtestamentische Studiën XIX. Leiden 1974 Éd. E.J. Brill pp. 1-28
[12] **A. Strus** - Nomen Omen
in: Analecta Biblica 80. Rome 1978 Éd. Biblical Institute Press pp. 82-89
[13] **Herbert Marks** - Biblical Naming and Poetic Etymology
in: Journal of Biblical Literature 114/1. 1995 Ed. The Society of Biblical Literature pp. 21-42

J. Barr - Etymology and the Old Testament
in: Oudtestamentische Studiën XIX. Leiden 1974 Éd. E.J. Brill pp. 1-28
[14] **J.B. Pritchard** - Ancient Near Eastern Texts
Princeton 1969 Ed. Princeton University Press p. 69 note 112
F.M.Th. Böhl in: Archiv für Orientforschung n°XI (1936) pp. 191-218
[15] **G.J. Thierry** - The Pronunciation of the Tetragrammaton
Leiden 1948 O.T.S. vol.. V Ed. E.J. Brill pp. 30-42
B. Alfrink - La prononciation 'Jehova' du tétragramme
Leiden 1948 O.T.S. vol.. V Ed. E.J. Brill pp. 43-62
A. Lukyn Williams - The Tetragrammaton -Jahweh, Name or Surrogate?
Z.A.W. vol.54 1936 pp. 262-9
F. Vigouroux - Dictionnaire de la Bible
Paris 1912 Ed. Letouzey et Ané pp. 1220-42
F. Dunand - La transcription du tétragramme dans les traductions grecques de la Bible.
in: Papyrus grecs bibliques Volumina de la Genèse et du Deut.
Le Caire 1966 Ed. IFAO p.39-64
B.D. Eerdmans - The name Jahu
Leiden 1948 O.T.S. vol.. V Ed. E.J. Brill pp. 1-29
[16] **J. Margain** - Les particules dans le Targum Samaritain
in: Hautes études orientales n°29 Paris 1993 Ed. Librairie Droz, Genève pp. 177,256
K. Beyer - Die Aramäischen Texte vom Toten Meer
Göttingen 1984 Ed. Vandenhoeck & Ruprecht pp. 126-128
[17] **A. Saenz-Badillos** - A History of the Hebrew Language
Cambridge 1996 Ed. Cambridge University Press pp. 152-154
[18] **Theodoreti episcopi Cyrensis** - Quæst. In I paral. Cap IX
1864 Paris Éd. Migne Patrologia Græcæ LXXX p. 806
[19] **A. Vincent** - La religion des Judéo-araméens d'Éléphantine
Paris 1937 Éd. Librairie orientaliste Paul Geuthner pp. 33-35
[20] **J.C. de Moor** - An Anthology of Religious Texts from Ugarit
Leiden 1987 Ed. E.J. Brill pp. 24,25
[21] **L. Pirot A. Clamer** - La Sainte Bible
Paris 1956 Éd. Letouzey et Ané p. 152
[22] **J. du Verdier** - Nova methodus hebraica punctis masoreticis expurgata
in Linguæ hebraicæ Paris 1847 Éd. J.P. Migne pp. 883-890
[23] **D. Barthélemy** - Critique textuelle de l'Ancien Testament
in Orbis Biblicus et Orientalis 50/3 Göttingen 1992 Éd. Universitaires Fribourg p. 667
[24] **W. Randall Garr** Dialect Geography of Syria-Palestine 1000-586 B.C.E.
Philadelphia 1985 Ed. U. of Pennsylvania Press pp. 12,35-41,54-58,106-109
[25] **A. Saenz-Badillos** - A History of the Hebrew Language
Cambridge 1996 Ed. Cambridge University Press pp. 50-55
D.N. Freedman - The Massoretic Text and the Qumran Scrolls.: A Study in Orthography.
Ed. Textus 2, 1962 pp. 88-102
D.N. Freedman K.A. Mathews - The Paleo-Hebrew Leviticus Scroll
Ed. A.S.O.R. 1985 pp. 52-54,58,68,79,82
E. Qimron - The Hebrew of the Dead Sea Scrolls
in: Harvard Semitic Studies n°29 Atlanta 1986 Ed. Scholars Press p. 59
[26] **G. Bergsträsser** - Introduction to the Semitic Languages
Indiana 1995 Ed. Eisenbrauns p. 8
[27] **E. Tov** - Textual Criticism of the Hebrew Bible
Minneapolis 1992 Ed. Van Gorcum p. 115
[28] **D.N. Freedman K.A. Mathews** - The Paleo-Hebrew Leviticus Scroll
1985 Ed. A.S.O.R. pp. 55,56
[29] **M. Harl G. Dorival O. Munnich** - La Bible grecque des Septante
C.N.R.S. 1988 Ed. Cerf pp. 159,160

[30] **M. Burrows** - The Dead Sea Scrolls of St. Mark's Monastry
New Haven 1950 Ed. A.S.O.R.
[31] **E.L. Sukenik** - The Dead Sea Scrolls of the Hebrew University
Jerusalem 1955 Ed. The Magnes Press
[32] **G. Gertoux** - In Fame Only? A Historical of the Divine Name
Paris 1998 B.O.S.E.B. T594GER pp. 31-33
[33] **V.A. Tcherikover A. Fuks** - Corpus Papyrorum Judaicarum
1957 Harvard University Press pp. 132,133
[34] **E.J. Revell** - The Development of Segol in an Open Syllable as a Reflex of *a*
in: Linguistics and Biblical Hebrew. Winona Lake 1992 Ed. W.R. Bodine pp. 17-28

2.1 FROM ADAM TO MOSES

[35] **R. Labat A. Caquot M. Sznycer** - Les religions du Proche-Orient
Paris 1970 Ed. Fayard-Denoël
- Prières de l'Ancien Orient
in: Documents autour de la Bible. Paris 1989 Ed. Cerf
[36] **G. Contenau** -De la valeur du nom chez les Babyloniens
in: Revue de l'histoire des religions LXXXI n° 3 1920 pp. 316-324 G.
G. Contenau -La civilisation d'Assur et de Babylone
In: Grandes civilisations disparues.
Genève 1975 Ed. Famot pp. 125,138,150,185
[37] **P. Barguet** - Les textes des sarcophages égyptiens du moyen empire
in: Littératures anciennes du Proche-Orient n°12
Paris 1986 Ed. Cerf pp. 107,211,269,287,303-09,359-63,461,664
[38] **R.J. Thibaud** - Dictionnaire de mythologie et de symbolique Égyptienne
1996 Ed. Dervy pp. 21,221,222
[39] Encyclopædia Universalis. Art. Égypte Religion p. 1014
[40] **G. Pettinato** - The Archives of Ebla. An Empire Inscribed in Clay
New York 1981 pp. 248,249,260,261,276-283
É. Lipinski - Dictionnaire encyclopédique de la Bible
Turnhout 1987 Ed. Brepols pp. 1348-9
[41] **D. Faivre -** L'idée de Dieu chez les Hébreux nomades
Paris 1996 Ed. L'Harmattan p. 197
[42] **A. Finet** - Yahvé au Royaume de Mari
in Res Orientales vol. V Bures-sur-Yvettes 1993 p. 20
[43] **G. Pettinato** - BAR Interviews
in: Biblical Archaeology Review Sept./Oct. 1980 Vol.VI n°5 pp. 49-52
[44] **H. Barwell Huffmon** -Amorite Personal Names in the Mari Texts
Baltimore 1965 Ed. The Johns Hpkins Press pp. 13-161
[45] **R. de Vaux** -Histoire ancienne d'Israël
Paris 1986 Éd. J. Gabalda pp. 324,325
[46] **É. Lipinski** - Étymologie et signification
in: Dictionnaire encyclopédique de la Bible Turnhout 1987 ÉdBrepols p. 1349
[47] **J.B. Pritchard** - Ancient Near Eastern Texts
Princeton 1969 Ed. Princeton University Press p. 69 note 112
F.M.Th. Böhl in: Archiv für Orientforschung n°XI (1936) pp. 191-218
[48] **J.A. Fitzmyer** - The Aramaic Inscriptions of Sefire
in: Biblica et orientalia -19/A
Roma 1995 Ed. Pontifico Istituto Biblico pp. 18-20, 126 pl. IX
[49] **J.B. Pritchard** - Ancient Near Eastern Texts
Princeton 1969 Ed. Princeton University Press pp. 553-555
[50] **A. Zivie** - Les tombes imprévues de Bubasteion
in: Historia thématique n°69 janvier-février 2001 pp. 9,34-37

[51] **P. Barguet** - Les textes des sarcophages égyptiens du moyen empire
in: Littératures anciennes du Proche-Orient n°12.
Paris 1986 Ed. Cerf pp. 176,189,196,267,
[52] **C. Nims R. Steiner -** A Polemical Poem from the Aramaic text in Demotic script.
in: Journal of Near Eastern Studies vol.43. 1984 pp. 89-113
[53] **W.L. Moran** - Les lettres d'El Amarna
in: Littérature du Proche-Orient n°13 Éd. Cerf p. 581
[54] **J.B. Pritchard** - Ancient Near Eastern Texts
Princeton 1969 Ed. Princeton University Press p. 416
[55] **I.J. Gelb** - Pour une théorie de l'écriture
Paris 1973 Flammarion pp. 163-166
[56] **J. Briend M.J. Seux** -Textes du Proche-Orient ancien et histoire d'Israël
Paris 1977 Ed. Cerf p. 89
[57] **F.M. Cross** - Newly Discovered Inscribed Arrowheads of the 11th Century BCE.
in: Biblical Archaeology Today 1990.
1993 Jerusalem Ed. Israel Exploration Society pp. 533-542
[58] **P. Joüon T. Muraoka** -A Grammar of Biblical Hebrew Part One
in: Subsidia biblica -14/I
Roma 1993 Ed. Pontifico Istituto Biblico p. 128 §41e
[59] **E. Lipinski** - Formes verbales dans les noms propres d'Ébla et système verbal sémitique.
in: La lingua di Ebla. Seminario di Studi Asiatici XIV
Napoli 1981 Ed. Istituto Universitario Orientale pp. 191-210
[60] **P. Fronzaroli** – La langue d'Ébla
in: Les dossiers histoire et archéologie n°83 mai 1984 p. 42
[61] **H. Bardwell Huffmon** - Amorite Personal Names in the Mari Texts:
A structural and Lexical Study. Baltimore 1965 Ed. The Johns Hopkins Press pp. 64,76,82
[62] **J.M. Durand** - Documents épistolaires du palais de Mari
in: LAPO n°16 Paris 1997 Éd. Cerf pp. 292-299
[63] **S. Moscati** - An Introduction to the Comparative Grammar of the Semitic Languages.
Wiesbaden 1980 Ed. O. Harrassowitz pp. 141-143
[64] **J. Barr** - Sémantique du langage biblique
Paris 1988 Éd. Cerf pp. 1-22

2.2 FROM MOSES TO DAVID

[65] **G. Dossin** – Une mention des Cananéens dans une lettre de Mari
in: Syria n°50 1973, pp. 277-282
[66] **M. Hadas-Lebel** - Histoire de la langue hébraïque
Paris 1986 Ed. Publications Orientalistes de France pp. 62-64
[67] **John F. Healey** - Les débuts de l'alphabet
in: La naissance des écritures. Paris 1994 Éd. Seuil pp. 257-279
Joseph Cohen - L'écriture hébraïque
Lyon 1997 Éd. du Cosmogone pp. 18-61
[68] **P. Grimal** - Dictionnaire de la mythologie grecque et romaine
Paris 1999 Éd. Presses Universitaires de France pp. 71-73
[69] **Menahem Stern** - Greek and Latin Authors on Jews and Judaism
Jerusalem 1976 Ed. Israel Academy of Sciences and Humanities pp. 26-34
[70] **B.Z. Wacholder** - Eupolemus. A Study of Judeo-Greek Literature
Cincinnati 1974 Ed. Hebrew Union College-Jewish Institute of Religion pp. 71-96
[71] **B. Albrektson** -On the Syntax of אהיה אשר אהיה in Exodus 3:14
in: Words and Meanings
Cambridge 1968 Ed. Cambridge University Press pp. 15-28
[72] **James Barr** -Sémantique du langage biblique
Paris 1988 Ed. Cerf pp. 78,79,132;133

[73] **J. Orr** -The International Standard Bible Encyclopaedia Vol. II
Grand Rapids 1984 Ed. WM. B. Eerdmans Publishing CO. p. 1266
[74] **T. Reinach** - Textes d'auteurs grecs et romains relatifs au Judaïsme
Hidesheim 1983 Ed. Georg Olms Verlag p. 60
[75] **A. Strus** -Nomen Omen
in: Analecta Biblica 80. Rome 1978 Éd. Biblical Institute Press pp. 82-89
[76] **M. Reisel** - The Mysterious Name of Y.H.W.H
in: Studia Semitica Neerlandica. Assen 1957 Ed. Van Gorcum pp. 41,52
[77] **J.B. Pritchard** - Ancient Near Eastern Texts
Princeton 1969 Ed. Princeton University Press pp. 230-232,554,555
R. de Vaux -Histoire ancienne d'Israël
Paris 1986 Éd. J. Gabalda pp. 78-84
[78] **J. Tyldesley** - Hatshepsout la femme pharaon
Monaco 1997 Éd. Rocher pp. 34-42,184
[79] **J. Leclant** - Les fouilles de Soleb
in: Annuaire du Collège de France 1980-1981 pp. 474-475
J. Leclant - Les fouilles de Soleb
in: Nachrichten der Akademie der Wissenscaften in Göttingen I 1965 pp. 205-216
[80] **J. Leclant** - Le "Tétragramme" à l'époque d'Aménophis III
in: Near Eastern Studies. Wiesbaden 1991 Ed. Otto Harrassowitz pp. 215-219
M.C. Astour - Yahweh in Egyptian Topographic Lists
Bamberg 1979 in: Festschrift Elmar Edel pp. 17-32
[81] **W.L. Moran** - Les lettres d'El Amarna
in: LIPO n° 13 Paris 1987 Éd. Cerf pp. 604,605
V. Nikiprowetzky - Dictionnaire de l'Égypte ancienne
In: Encyclopædia Universalis Paris 1998 Éd. Albin Michel pp. 169,170
[82] **J.M. Durand** - Documents épistolaires du palais de Mari
in: LIPO n° 18 Paris 2000 Éd. Cerf p. 205
R. de Vaux - Histoire ancienne d'Israel
Paris 1986 Éd. Gabalda pp. 106-112,202-208
[83] **J.B. Pritchard** - Ancient Near Eastern Texts
Princeton 1969 Ed. Princeton University Press p. 242
[84] **W.A. Ward** - A New Look at Semitic Personal Names and Loanwords in Egyptian.
in: Chronique d'Égypte LXXI(1996) N° 141
Ed. Fondation Égyptologique Reine Élisabeth Bruxelles pp. 17-47
[85] **J.D. Fowler** - Theophoric Personal Names in Ancient Hebrew
in: J.S.O.T. Sup. n° 49 Sheffield 1988 Ed. Academic Press pp. 122-125

2.3 FROM DAVID TO ZEDEKIAH

[86] **J.M. Durand** - Documents épistolaires du palais de Mari
in: LAPO n° 16 Paris 1997 Éd. Cerf pp. 292-299
[87] **J. Huehnergard** - Ugaritic Vocabulary in Syllabic Transcription
in: Harvard Semitic Studies n° 32 Atlanta 1987 Ed Scholars Press pp. 236-239
René Labat - Manuel d'épigraphie Akkadienne
Paris Ed. Librairie Orientaliste Paul Geuthner S.A. p. 101
Gary A. Rendsburg - Eblaitica: Essays on the Ebla Archives and Eblaite Language.
Indiana 1990 Ed. Eisenbrauns pp. 96,97,111,116,118
[88] **Z. Meshel** - Kuntillet 'Ajrud a Religious Centre From the Time of the Judaean Monarchy on
the Border of Sinai. Jerusalem 1978 The Israel Museum Cat. n° 175 pp. 10-24
Z. Meshel C. Meyers - The Name of God in the Wilderness of Zin
in. Biblical Archeologist March 1976 pp. 6-10
[89] **J.M. Hadley** - Some Drawings and Inscriptions on Two Pithoi From Kuntillet 'Ajrud.
in: VT XXXVII Leiden 1987 pp. 180-211

Amihai Mazar - Archaeology of the Land of the Bible
New York 1990 A.B.R.L. pp. 446-451
[90] **F.M. Cross** - The Seal of Miqnêyaw, Servant of Yahweh
in: Ancient seals and the Bible pp. 55-63, Pl. IX-X
Malibu 1983 Congress International institute for Mesopotamian Studies , Undena publications
[91] **W.G. Sever** -Iron Epigraphic material From the Area of Khirbet El-Kom
in: H.U.C.A. XL-XLI Cincinnati 1969-70 pp. 139-201
J.M. Hadley -The Khirbet El-Qom Inscription
in: V.T. XXXVII Leiden 1987 pp. 50-62
[92] **P. Bar-adon** -An Early Hebrew Inscription in a Judean Desert Cave
I.E.J Vol. 25 Jerusalem 1975 pp. 226-232
[93] **J. Naveh** -Old Hebrew Inscriptions in a Burial Cave
in: I.E.J. Vol.13 Jérusalem 1963 pp. 74-92
J.A. Sanders -Near Eastern Archaeology in the Twentieth Century
in: Essays in honor of N. Glueck -New York 1970 pp. 299-306
A. Lemaire -Prières en temps de crise: Les inscriptions de Khirbet Beit Lei
in: RB LXXXIII Paris 1976 pp. 558-568
P.D. Miller - Psalms and Inscriptions
in: SVT XXXII Leiden 1981 pp. 311-332
[94] **G. Barkay** - The Priestly Benediction on Silver Plaques From Ketef Hinnom in Jerusalem.
in: Tel Aviv Vol.19 n°2 1992
R. Martin-Achard - Remarques sur la bénédiction sacerdotale
in: Études Théologiques & Religieuses Tome 70 1995/1 pp. 75-84
[95] **J. Bonsirven** - Textes Rabbiniques des deux premiers siècles
Roma 1955 Ed. Pontificio Istituto Biblico pp. 50-51
[96] **Y. Aharoni** -I.E.J. Vol.16 n°1
Jérusalem 1966 pp. 1-7
[97] **Y. Aharoni** -Arad Inscriptions
Jerusalem 1981 Ed. The Israel Exploration Society pp. 1-35
[98] **J.G. Février** -Histoire de l'écriture
1984 Ed. Payot p. 213
[99] **E.M. Blaiklock R.K. Harrison** -The New International Dictionary of Biblical Archaeology
Michigan 1983 Ed. Regency p. 284
A. Lemaire -Inscriptions hébraïques Tome I, Les Ostraca
In: LAPO n°9 Paris 1977 Ed. Cerf pp. 93-143
[100] **G.I. Davies** - Ancient Hebrew Inscriptions, Corpus and Concordance
Cambridge 1991 Ed. Cambridge University Press pp. 366-367
[101] **K.A.D. Smelik** -Writings from Ancient Israel
Westminster pp. 150-186
[102] **L.H. Vincent** -Les épigraphes Judéo-araméennes postexiliques
in: Revue Biblique LVI
Paris 1949 Ed. J. Gabalda pp. 274-294
[103] **J.A. Fitzmyer** -A Wandering Aramean
California 1979 Ed. Scholars Press pp. 82 §95,181 §69
[104] **H.G. May** -An Inscribed Jar from Megiddo
1933 In: American Journal of Semitic Languages L, pp. 10-14
[105] **P. Benoit J.T. Milik R. de Vaux** -Les grottes de Murabbaât
Oxford 1961 Ed. Clarendon Press p. 100
[106] **A. Van den Branden** -Grammaire Phénicienne
1969 Beyrouth Éd. Librairie du Liban pp. 5,6
[107] **D.N. Freedman** -The Massoretic Text and the Qumran Scrolls.
A Study in Orthography. Ed. Textus 2, 1962 pp. 88-102
D.N. Freedman K.A. Mathews -The Paleo-Hebrew Leviticus Scroll
Ed.A.S.O.R. 1985 pp. 52-54,58,68,79,82

[108] **A. Lemaire** -Inscriptions hébraïques Tome I, Les Ostraca
in: Littérature anciennes du Proche-Orient n°9
Paris 1977 Ed. Cerf pp. 47,48,253
[109] **L.H. Vincent** -Les épigraphes Judéo-araméennes postexiliques
in: Revue Biblique LVI Paris 1949 Ed. J. Gabalda p. 277 note 4

2.4 FROM ZEDEKIAH TO SIMON THE JUST

[110] **M. Hadas-Lebel** - Histoire de la langue hébraïque
1986 Ed. Publications Orientalistes de France pp. 95-105
[111] **P. Grelot** -Documents Araméens d'Égypte
in: Littératures anciennes du Proche Orient n°5. Paris 1972 Ed. Cerf
J.A. Fitzmyer -A wandering Aramean
California 1979 Ed. Scholars Press pp. 219-230
[112] **B. Porten A. Yardeni** - Textbook of Aramaic Documents from Ancient Egypt, 2 Contracts
1989 Ed. Israel Academy of Sciences and Humanities pp. XLIV,64,74,75
[113] **A. Dupont-Sommer** - Yaho et Yaho-Sebaoth sur les ostraca araméens inédits d'Éléphantine.
in: C.R.A.I..L. 1947 pp. 175-191
[114] **F.I. Andersen A. Dean Forbes** -Spelling in the Hebrew Bible
Rome 1986 Ed. Biblical Institut p. 324
[115] **K. Beyer** -Die aramäischen Text,vom Toten Meer
Göttingen 1983 Ed. Vandenhoek Ruprecht p. 451
E. Qimron -The Hebrew of the Dead Sea Scrolls
in: Harvard Semitic studies n°29 Atlanta 1986 Ed. Scholars Press aut. p. 23 §100.7 p. 58 §322
[116] **J.D. Fowler** -Theophoric Personal Names in Ancient Hebrew
in: J.S.O.T. Supplement n°49. Sheffield 1988 Ed. Academic Press pp. 325-364
M.H. Silverman - Religious Values in the Jewish Proper Names at Elephantine
in: Alter Orient und Altes Testament.
Vluyn 1985 Ed. Verlag Butzon & Bercker Kevelaer pp. 215 221
B. Porten A. Yardeni - Textbook of Aramaic Documents from Ancient Egypt, 2 Contracts
1989 Ed. Israel Academy of Sciences and Humanities pp. XLVII,XLVIII
B. Porten A. Yardeni - Textbook of Aramaic Documents from Ancient Egypt, 3 Literature
1993 Ed. Israel Academy of Sciences and Humanities pp. LVII,LVIII
[117] Codex Vaticanus gr.244 folio 2r; Codex Urbinatus gr.84 folio 215r
[118] **Y. Aharoni** - Excavations at Ramath Rahel 1954
in: I.E.J. vol.6 n°3 1956 pp. 144-151
Y. Aharoni - Excavations at Ramath Rahel 1961-62
Roma 1964 Ed. Centro di studi semitici pp. 20-46 pl.19,20
[119] **C.E. Carter** - TheEmergence of Yehud in the Persian Period
in: JSOT n°294 Sheffield 1999 Ed. Sheffield Academic Press pp. 22-29
[120] **G.I. Davies** - Ancient Hebrew Inscriptions, Corpus and Concordance
Cambridge 1991 Ed. Cambridge University Press pp. 25,364,365
[121] **J. Naveh** - The Development of the Aramaic Script
in: Proceedings of the Israel academy of sciences and humanities vol.5 Jerusalem 1976 pp. 1-59
[122] **U. Rappaport** - The First Judean Coinage
1981 in: Journal of Jewish Studies 32 pp. 1-17
J. Naveh - Early History of the Alphabet
Jerusalem 1982 Ed. The Magnes Press pp. 112-119
[123] **E. Stern** - The Material Culture of the Land of the Bible in the Persian Period
Jerusalem 1973 Ed. I.E.S. pp. 200-205
M. Kochman -"Yehud Medinta" in the Light of the Seal Impression
in: Cathedra 24 Jerusalem 1982 Ed. Yad Izhak Ben-Zvi Publications pp. 4-29
[124] **F. Moore Cross** - Judean Stamps
in: Eretz-Israel vol.9. Jerusalem 1969 Ed. I.E.S. pp. 20-27

Y. Meshorer S. Qedar -The Coinage of Samaria in the Fourth Century BCE
in: Numismatic Fine Arts International. Jerusalem p. 43
[125] **L. Mildenberg** - Yehud: A Preliminary Study of the Provincial Coinage of Judaea.
in: Essays in honour of M. Thompson, Wetteren 1979 pp. 183-196
A. Kindler - Silver Coins Bearing the Name of Judea from the Early Hellenistic Period.
in: I.E.J. vol.24 n°2 1974 pp. 73-145
[126] **S.A. Cook** - The Yahu Coin
in: Z.A.W. vol.56 1938 pp. 268-271
[127] **N. Avigad** - A New Class of Yehud Stamps
in: I.E.J. vol.7 n°3 1957 pp. 146-153
[128] **C.C. McCown** - Tell En-Nasbeh, Archaeological and Historical Results
New Haven 1947 Ed A.S.O.R. pp. 156-174 pl. 57
[129] **J. Maltiel-Gerstenfeld** - 260 years of Ancient Jewish Coinage
Tel Aviv 1982 Ed. Kol printing service pp. 41,42,103-109
Y. Meshorer -A Treasury of Jewish Coins from the Persian Period to Bar-Kochba. Jerusalem
1997 Ed. Yad Izhak Ben-Zvi Publications pp. 171-256
[130] **S. Moscati** -L'epigrafia Ebraica antica,1935-1950
Roma 1951 Ed. Pontificio Istituto Biblico pp. 88-91
[131] **D. Diringer** -Le Iscrizioni antico-ebraiche Palestinesi
1934 Firenze pp. 128-137
L.H. Vincent -Les épigraphes Judéo-araméennes postexiliques
in: Revue Biblique LVI Paris 1949 pp. 274-294
M. Delcor -Des diverses manières d'écrire le tétragramme sacré dans les anciens documents
hébraïques. in: Études bibliques et orientales de religions comparées
Leiden 1979 Ed. E.J. Brill pp. 22-24
[132] **J. Naveh** -Dated Coins of Alexander Janneus
Jerusalem 1968 in: Israel Exploration Journal N°18 pp. 24,25
[133] **Z. Zevit** - A Chapter in the History of Israelite Personal Names
in: B.A.S.O.R. 250 pp. 3-14
[134] **A. Caquot** -Charges et fonctions en Syrie-Palestine
in: Comptes rendus de Janvier-Mars 1986.
Paris. Éd. Académie des Inscriptions & Belles-Lettres pp. 305-307
[135] **B. Porten A. Yardeni** - Textbook of Aramaic Documents from Ancient Egypt, 1 Letters.
1989 Ed. Israel Academy of Sciences and Humanities pp. 67-70
B. Porten A. Yardeni - Textbook of Aramaic Documents from Ancient Egypt, 3 Literature
1993 Ed. Israel Academy of Sciences and Humanities pp. 258,259
[136] **E.M. Laperrousaz** - La Palestine à l'époque Perse
Paris 1994 Ed. Cerf pp. 245-260
[137] **Eusèbe** - Préparation évangélique XIII,12,1
in: Sources Chrétiennes n°307 Paris 1983 p. 311
[138] **A. Pelletier** - Lettre d'Aristée à Philocrate
in: Sources Chrétiennes n°89 Paris 1962 Ed. Cerf pp. 234-237
[139] **Menahem Stern** - Greek and Latin Authors on Jews and Judaism Tom.I
Jerusalem 1976 Ed. The Israel Academy of Sciences and Humanities pp. 20-44
[140] **W. Horbury D. Noy** - Jewish Inscriptions of Graeco-Roman Egypt
1992 Ed. Cambridge University Press, Inscription n°22

2.5 FROM SIMON THE JUST TO JESUS

[141] **M. Harl** - La langue de Japhet
Paris 1992 Ed. Cerf pp. 267-75
M. Carrez -Manuscrits et langues de la Bible
1991 Ed.Société Biblique Française pp. 32-47

[142] **M. Hadas-Lebel** - Histoire de la langue Hébraïque
1986 Ed. Publications Orientalistes de France pp. 148-158
[143] **M. Harl G. Dorival O. Munnich** - La Bible Grecque des Septante
1988 Ed. Cerf CNRS p. 58
[144] **Z. Aly L. Koenen** - Three Rolls of the Early Septugint: Genesis and Deuteronomy.
Bonn 1980 Ed. R.Habelt Verlag
[145] **B.M. Metzger** - Manuscripts of the Greek Bible
New York 1991 Oxford University Press pp. 33-36,59-64
[146] **P. Harlé D. Pralon** - La Bible d'Alexandrie 3 Le Lévitique
Paris 1988 Ed. Cerf pp. 195,196
[147] **A. Pietersma** - Kyrios or Tetragram: A renewed Quest for the Original LXX
in: De Septuaginta: Studies in honour of J.W. Wevers
1984 Ed. Beuben Publications pp. 99-101
[148] **Josephus** - Jewish Antiquities XII, 43
in: Loeb Classical Library Cambridge 1998 Ed. Harvard University Press p.25
[149] Université de Louvain - Recueil Lucien Cerfaux Tome I
1954 Ed. J. Duculot S.A. Gembloux pp. 149-172
[150] **Ralph Marcus** - Jewish Antiquities Books XII-XIII
Cambridge 1998 Ed. Loeb Classical Library pp. 462-466
[151] **S. Haïk Vantoura** - La musique de la Bible révélée
Paris 1978 Ed. Dessain et Tolra
[152] **L. Pirot** - La Sainte Bible tome V
Paris 1937 Ed. Letouzey et Ané p. XXIII
[153] **J.A. Fitzmyer** - A Wandering Aramean
California 1979 Ed. Scholars Press pp. 88,89
[154] **M. Reisel** - The Mysterious Name of Y.H.W.H
in: Studia Semitica Neerlandica. Assen 1957 Ed. Van Gorcum pp. 41,52
[155] Les manuscrits de la Mer morte
in: Les dossiers d'archéologie n°189 janvier 94 p. 46
[156] **E. Tov** - From Nahal Hever 8HevXIIgr
Oxford 1990 Ed. Clarendon Press
[157] **E.G. Turner** -Theological Text
in: The Oxyrhynchus Papyri Vol.L, papyrus n°3522
London 1983 Ed. Egypt Exploration Society pp. 1-3; pl.I
[158] **J. Naveh** - Dated Coins of Alexander Janneus
in: Israel Exploration Journal vol. 18, Jerusalem 1968 pp. 20-26
[159] **B. Porten A. Yardeni** - Textbook of Aramaic documents from ancient Egypt,3 Literature.
1993 Ed. Israel Academy of Sciences and Humanities p. XXXVI
[160] **J.A. Fitzmyer** -A Wandering Aramean
California 1979 Ed. Scholars Press pp. 61,82 §95,181 §69
D.N. Freedman -The Massoretic Text and the Qumran Scrolls: A Study in Orthography.
Ed. Textus 2, 1962 pp. 88-102
D.N. Freedman K.A. Mathews- The Paleo-Hebrew Leviticus Scroll
Ed. A.S.O.R. 1985 pp. 52-54,58,68,79,82
E. Qimron -The Hebrew of the Dead sea Scrolls
in: Harvard Semitic studies n°29 Atlanta 1986 Ed. Scholars Press p. 59
[161] **K. Beyer** -Die aramäischen Texte vom Toten Meer
Göttingen 1984 Ed. Vandenhoeck & Ruprecht pp. 126-128
[162] **B. Cardauns** -M. Terentius Varro Antiquitates rerum divinarum
Wiesbaden 1976 Ed. Akademie der Wissenschaf tom.I p.22 n°17 tom.II p. 146
E. Norden - Varro über den Gott der Juden
Tübingen 1921 p. 298
[163] **P.W. Skehan** -Qumran cave 4 IV
in: Discoveries in the Judaean Desert IX. Oxford 1992 Ed. Clarendon Press p. 174

[164] **Diodore de Sicile** -Naissance des dieux et des hommes I:94,2
Paris 1991 Ed. Les Belles Lettres p. 112
[165] **Irénée de Lyon** -Contre les hérésies I:4,1 I:21,3
Paris 1991 Ed. Cerf
[166] **J.M. Robinson** - The Apocryphon of John II:1,24
in: The Nag Hammadi Library. Leiden 1988 Ed. E.J. Brill p. 119
[167] **A. le Boulluec** -Les Stromates V,VI:34,5
In: Sources chrétiennes n°278,279 Paris 1981 Ed Cerf
[168] **Tertullien** -Contre les valentiniens XIV:3
in: Sources chrétiennes n°280 . Ed. Cerf 1980 p. 115
[169] **S.R. Driver** -Recent Theories on the Origin and Nature of the Tetragrammaton.
in: Studia Biblica vol.1 1885 pp. 1-20
[170] **Biblica** -vol.22 1941 pp. 339-355
R. Devreesse - Introduction à l'étude des manuscrits grecs
Ed. Paris 1954 pp. 108-111
Origène -Commentaires sur St Jean 1:1 (II:7)
in: Sources chrétiennes n°120 . Ed. Cerf 1966 p. 213
Origène -Contre Celse VI:32
in: Sources chrétiennes n°147. Ed. Cerf 1969 p. 259
[171] **Eusebii Pamphili** - Demonstrationis Evangelica IV:17,23 X:8,28
in: Patrologiæ Græcæ XXII Éd. J.P. Migne Paris pp. 334,766
[172] **St Epiphane** -The Panarion of St Epiphanius Bishop of Salamis XXXVI:10,1
Ed. Oxford University Press 1990 pp. 79,114
[173] **St Jerome** -S. Hieronymi presbyteri opera
in: corpus christianorum Series Latina vol. LXXII (Psalm 8:2) Ed. Brepols 1959 p.191
[174] **N.F. Marcos A.S. Badillos** -Theodoreti Cyrensis Quaestiones in Octateuchum. Exodus XV
Madrid 1979 Ed. Cardenal Cisneros p. 112
[175] **M. Simon** - Jupiter-Yahvé Sur un essai de théologie pagano-juive
1976 in: Numen Vol. XXIII,1 p. 49
[176] **M. Nisard** - De la langue latine IX,55
Paris 1875 in: Macrobe Varron Pomponius Méla Ed. Firmin-Didot p. 561
[177] **S. Augustini** - De consensu evangelistarum
Paris 1845 Éd. Migne Patrologiæ Latina XXIV pp. 1055-1058
[178] **Marcel Simon** - Jupiter-Yahvé Sur un essai de théologie pagano-juive
1976 in: Numen Vol. XXIII,1 pp. 41-66
[179] **G. Le Rider** - La naissance de la monnaie
Paris 2001 Éd. Presses Universitaires de France pp. 209,280,281

2.6 FROM JESUS TO JUSTIN

[180] **A. Dupont Sommer** - Les écrits esséniens découverts près de la mer morte
1959 Ed. Payot pp. 176,214
[181] **J.A. Sanders** -The Psalms Scroll of Qumrân Cave 11
in: Discoveries in the Judaean Desert of Jordan IV Oxford 1965 Ed. Clarendon Press pp. 24-38
[182] **M Delcor** -Des diverses manières d'écrire le tétragramme sacré dans les anciens documents
hébraïques in: Etudes bibliques et orientales de religions comparées.
Leiden 1979 Ed. E.J. Brill pp. 1-29
L.H. Schiffman -The Use of Divine Names
in: Sectarian Law in the Dead Sea Scrolls. Ed. Scholars Press pp. 132-154
[183] **J.P. Siegel** -The Employment of Palaeo-Hebrew Characters for the Divine Names at Qumran
in the Light of Tannaitic Sources
in: H.U.C.A. n°42 1971 pp. 159-172
[184] **P.W. Skehan** -The Divine Name at Qumran, in the Masada Scroll, and in the Septuagint
in: B.I.O.S.C.S. n°13 1980 Ed. The Catholic University of America. pp. 14-44

[185] **M. Burrows** -The Dead Sea Scrolls of St. Mark's Monastry
New Haven 1950 Ed. A.S.O.R.
[186] **A. Sperber** -A Grammar of Masoretic Hebrew
Copenhagen 1959 Ed. E. Munksgaard p. 183
E. Qimron -The Hebrew of the Dead Sea Scrolls
in: Harvard Semitic Studies n°29 Atlanta 1986 Ed. Scholars Press p. 21
[187] **A. Lemaire** -Le nom du Dieu d'Israël.
in: Le monde de la Bible N°110. Paris avril 1998 pp. 10,11
[188] **Flavius Josèphe** - La guerre des Juifs (V,438) Tome III
1982 Ed. Les Belles Lettres p. 172
[189] **Flavius Josèphe** -Les Antiquités Juives (II,275) ou (II,12,4)
1992 Ed. Cerf p. 130
[190] **F.I. Andersen A.D. Forbes** - Spelling in the Hebrew Bible
in: Biblica Orientalia 41 Rome 1986 Ed. Biblical Institut Press p. 92
[191] **A. Dupont-Sommer** - La règle de la communauté VI,27-VII,2
in: Les écrits esséniens découverts près de la mer morte. 1959 Ed. Payot p. 164
Flavius Josèphe - La guerre des Juifs II,145
1980 Ed. Les Belles Lettres p. 34
[192] **E. Qimron** -The Hebrew of the Dead Sea Scrolls
in: Harvard Semitic Studies n°29 . Atlanta 1986 Ed. Scholars Press p. 57
[193] **R. Le Déaut** -Targum du pentateuque II
in: Sources chrétiennes n°256. 1979 Ed. Cerf pp. 32 §12,49 §5,220,22,457 §23
[194] **P. Joüon** -Grammaire de l'hébreu biblique
Rome 1987 Ed. Institut Biblique Pontifical p. 108 §48d
[195] **R.A. Nicholson** -Studies in Islamic Mysticism.
1921 Cambridge p. 96
I. Goldziher -Die Richtungen der Islamischen Koranauslegung.
1952 Leiden pp. 260-2
P. Benoit J.T. Milik R. de Vaux -Les grottes de Murabbaât
Oxford 1961 Ed. Clarendon Press pp. 286-290
[196] **Ali-Rhida Arfa** - Quatre textes d'Ibn ʿ Arabî, Abdol-Karîm et Gîlî
1978 Paris in: Dieu et l'être. Ed. Études Augustiniennes C.N.R.S. pp. 191-202
[197] **G. Scholem** - Les grands courants de la mystique juive
1994 Paris Éd. Payot pp. 81-83
[198] **Ryszard Rubinkiewicz** - L'apocalypse d'Abraham en vieux slave
1987 Lublin Éd. Société des Lettres de l'Université Catholique de Lublin
[199] **A. Crampon**- La Sainte Bible
Paris 1905 Ed. Cie de Jésus p. 143 note 58
[200] **A. Hamman** -La vie quotidienne des premiers chrétiens
1971 Ed. Hachette pp. 95-126
[201] **M. Harl G. Dorival O. Munnich** -La Bible grecque des septante
1988 Ed. Cerf/C.N.R.S. pp. 274-288
[202] **G. Howard** -Biblical Archaeology Review Vol IV n°1
march 1978 pp. 12-14
[203] **S.C. Mimouni** - Le judéo-christianisme ancien, essais historiques
Paris 1998 in: collection Patrimoines Éd. Cerf pp. 161-188
[204] **M. Hadas-Lebel** -Histoire de la langue hébraïque
1986 Ed. Publications Orientalistes de France pp. 117-158
[205] **P.E. Kahle** -The Cairo Geniza
Oxford 1959 Ed. B. Blackwell pp. 222-225
C.H. Roberts -Manuscript, Society and Belief in Early Christian Egypt
Oxford 1979 Ed. University Press pp. 28-31
[206] **L. Vaganay C.B. Amphoux** -Initiation à la critique textuelle du Nouveau Testament.
1986 Ed. Cerf pp. 138-147

[207] **M. Harl G. Dorival O. Munnich** - La Bible grecque des Septante
1988 Ed. Cerf CNRS pp. 142-167
[208] **G. Howard** - The Tetragram and the New Testament
1977 J.B.L. vol.96 pp. 63-83
[209] **V. Morabito** - Les Samaritains de Sicile
in: Études sémitiques et samaritaines Lausanne 1998 Éd. Zèbre pp. 195-197
[210] **Origène** - Selecta in Psalmos 2.2
in: Patrologiæ Greca XII pp. 1103-1104. Turnholti (Belgium) Ed. Brepols
[211] **F. Crawford Burkitt** - Fragments of the Books of Kings According to the Translation of
Aquila 1898 Cambridge pp. 3-8
[212] **C.P. Thiede** - Qumrân et les Évangiles
Paris 1994 Ed. F.X. de Guilbert pp. 22,23,112,113
[213] **B.M. Metzger** -A Textual Commentary on the Greek new Testament
Stuttgart 1975 Ed. United Bible Societies
[214] **G.D. Kilpatrick** -The Principles and Practise of New Testament Textual Criticism
in: Bibliotheca ephemeridum theologicarum lovaniensium XCVI;
Leuven pp. 207-222
[215] **J. Daniélou** -Théologie du judéo-christianisme
1974 Ed. Desclée/Cerf pp. 235-262
[216] **D. Bertrand** - Les Pères apostoliques
Paris 1991 in: Foi Vivante Ed. Cerf
[217] **J.P. Audet** - La Didachè, instructions des apôtres
in: Études Bibliques. 1958 Ed. J. Gabalda pp. 188-191
[218] **P. van Imschoot** - Dictionnaire Encyclopédique de la Bible
Paris 1960 Ed. Brepols Turhout pp. 1700-04
N.Lewis Y.Yadin J.Greenfield -The Documents from the Bar-Kokhba Period in the Cave of
Letters Jerusalem 1989 Ed. Israel Exploration Society pp. 17,42,43,52,60,139,
[219] **J. Daniélou** -Théologie du judéo-christianisme
1974 Ed. Desclée/Cerf pp. 235-262
[220] **N.A. Dahl A.F. Segal** -Philo and the Rabbis on the Names of God
in: Journal for the study of judaism . Leiden 1978 Ed. E.J. Brill pp. 1-28
[221] **Philon** - De vita Mosis
in: Les œuvres de Philon d'Alexandrie n°22. Lyon 1967 Ed. Cerf pp. 243,251
[222] **Philon** - De mutationem nominum 11-15
in: Les œuvres de Philon d'Alexandrie n°18. Lyon 1964 Ed. Cerf pp. 37-39
[223] **Philon** - in: Les œuvres de Philon d'Alexandrie. Lyon Ed. Cerf.
1962 n°19 p.119 - De somniis I,230
1963 n°7-8 p.117- De gigantus quod deus sit immutabilis 109
1965 n°5 p.117- Quod deterius potiori insidiari soleat 160
1966 n°15 p.249- Quis rerum divinarum heres sit 170
[224] **Philon** - in: Les œuvres de Philon d'Alexandrie. Lyon Ed. Cerf.
1964 n°18 p.87- De mutatione nominum 121
[225] **A. Wartelle** - Saint Justin Apologies I,10,1 I,61,11 I,63,1 II,12,4
in: Études Augustiniennes. Paris 1987 Ed. I..C.P. pp. 109,183,185,205,215
[226] **D. Barthélemy** - Les devanciers d'Aquila
in: V.T.S. vol. X Leiden 1963 Ed. E.J. Brill pp. 203-212
[227] **J. Naveh** - Early History of the Alphabet
Leiden 1982 Ed. E.J. Brill p. 121 pl. 15
[228] **M. Simon A. Benoit** - Le Judaïsme et le Christianisme antique
1991 Ed. P.U.F. pp. 144-162
[229] **J.M. Robinson** - The Nag Hammadi Library
Leiden 1988 Ed. E.J. Brill pp. 220-224
[230] **S.C. Mimouni** - Le judéo-christianisme ancien, essais historiques
Paris 1998 in: collection Patrimoines Éd. Cerf pp. 475-493

[231] **P. Schaff** - Literary Contest of Christianity with Judaism and Heathenism
in: History of the Churc Vol II Chap III, 1997 Oak Harbor WA Logos Research Systems

2.7 FROM JUSTIN TO JEROME

[232] **J.M. Robinson** - The Nag Hammadi Library
Leiden 1988 Ed. E.J. Brill pp. 38-52
[233] **D. Barthélemy** -Justin martyr. Œuvres complètes
Paris 1994 Ed. J.P. Migne pp. 220,188
[234] **A. Rousseau** - Irénée de Lyon: Contre les hérésies I,14,4 II,32,5 IV,17,6
Paris 1991 Ed. Cerf pp. 81,263,460
[235] **C.H. Roberts** - Manuscript, Society and Belief in Early Christian Egypt
Oxford 1979 Ed. University Press pp. 26-48
[236] **C. Rabin** - University Library Cambridge
in: Textus vol. II 1962 Jerusalem Ed. Magnes Press
[237] **I.osepho Cozza-Luzi** -Prophetarum codex Graecus Vaticanus 2125
Rome 1890, Biblioteca Vaticana pp. 205,509,588
[238] **B.M. Metzger** -Manuscripts of the Greek Bible
New York 1991 Ed; Oxford University Press pp. 35,94,95
[239] **G. Stanton** - Parole d'Évangile?
Paris 1998 Éd. Cerf Novalis pp. 57,106-109, pl. 9
[240] Textus vol I 1960 Ed. Magnes Press Jerusalem p. IV
S. Olofsson -The LXX version
In: Coniectanea Biblica n°30
Stockholm 1990 Ed. Almqvist & Wiksell Internationl p. 49
[241] **G.E. Weil** -Fragment inédit de ms babylonien
in: Textus vol VI . Jerusalem 1968 Ed. Magnes Press pp. 100-103
M.L. Klein -A Palestinian Fragment-Targum
In: Textus vol X. 1982 Jerusalem Ed. Magnes Press pp. 28-31
A. Chester -Divine Revelation and Divine Titles in the Pentateuchal Targumim
Tübingen 1986 Ed. J.C.B. Mohr p. 325
[242] **A.S. Hunt** -The Oxyrhynchus Papyri VII
London 1910 pp. 1,2
[243] **P.E. Kahle** - The Cairo Geniza
Oxford 1959 Ed. B. Blackwell pp. 318-335
[244] **A. Abécassis** - La mystique du Talmud
in: Encyclopédie juive. Paris 1994 Ed. Berg International pp. 152,153
[245] **Montfaucon** - L'antiquité expliquée et représentée en figures vol.II
Paris 1722
K. Preisendanz -Papyri Graecae Magicae I
Leipzig 1928 II Berlin 1931 Stuttgart 1974 XVIIa 1-2
Kopp -Paleographia critica vol.3,4
Mannheim 1817-1829
C.W. King-The Gnostics and their Remains. London 1864
[246] **M. Philonenko** -L'anguipède alectorocéphale et le dieu Iaô
in: C.R.A.I.L. Paris 1979 Ed. Klincksieck pp. 297-304
Campbell Bonner -Studies in Magical Amulets
Oxford 1950 Ed.University Press Pl. I-XXI
Hans Dieter Betz -The Greek Magical Papyri in Translation
1992 Ed. The University of Chicago press p. XLVII
A. Delatte Ph. Derchain - Les intailles magiques gréco-égyptiennes Paris 1964
[247] **J. Naveh** - A Recently Discovered Palestinian Jewish Aramaic Amulet
in: Arameans, Aramaic and the Aramaic literary tradition.
Tel-Aviv 1983 Ed. Bar-Ilan University Press pp. 81-88

J. Naveh S. Shaked - Amulets and magic bowls
Jerusalem 1985 Ed. Magnes Press pp. 40-61
J.A. Montgomery -Aramaic Incantation Texts from Nippur
Philadelphia 1913 Ed. University Museum pp. 145,146,165,209,210
[248] **B. Alfrink** -La prononciation 'Jehova' du tétragramme
in: O.T.S. vol V 1948 pp. 43-62 Pap. gr. CXXI 1.528-540 (3rd century) British Museum Library
[249] **J.M. Robinson** - The Nag Hammadi Library
Leiden 1988 Ed. E.J. Brill pp.210,217
[250] **Eusèbe de Césarée** - Préparation Évangélique XI,6,36-37
in: Sources chrétiennes n°292. Paris 1982 ed. Cerf p.87
[251] **J. Margain** -Essais de sémantique sur l'hébreu ancien
Paris 1976 Ed. Geuthner p. 173
M. Simon A. Benoit -Le judaïsme et le christianisme antique
Paris 1991 Ed. Presses Universitaires de France pp. 50-201
[252] **St Jerome** - S. Hieronymi presbyteri opera
in: corpus christianorum Series Latina vol. LXXII (Psaume 8:2) Ed. Brepols 1959 p. 191
[253] **C. Wessely** - Studien zur Palaeographie und Papyruskunde vol.XI
Leipzig 1911 p. 171
[254] **J. Naveh** - Early History of the Alphabet
Leiden 1982 Ed. E.J. Brill p. 124
[255] **Origène** -Origenis Hexaplorum tomus II (Psalm 26:1; 27:4,7; 28:1;Jes. 1,2)
1964 Ed. Georg olms verlagsbuchhandlung Hildesheim pp. 124,-127, 431
[256] **G. Mercati** Psalterii Hexapli Reliquiae.Pars prima.
Codex Rescriptus Bybliothecae Ambrosiane O39. Rome 1958 pp. 11,97,101
B.M. Metzger -Manuscripts of the Greek Bible
New York 1991 Oxford University Press pp. 108,109
[257] **B.M. Metzger** - Manuscripts of the Greek Bible
New York 1991 Ed. Oxford University Press p. 35
[258] **P. de Lagarde** - Onomastica Sacra
Hildesheim 1966 Ed. Georg Olms Verlagsbuchhandlung pp. 205,206,230
[259]- Ad tomum III operum S. Hieronymi appendix
in: Patrologiæ Latina XXIII Éd. J.P. Migne Paris 1845 pp. 1275-1280
[260] **Eusèbe de Césarée** - La préparation évangélique I,9,21
in: Sources chrétiennes n°206 Éd. Cerf Paris 1974 pp. 179,303-305
[261] **S.A. Kaufman** - The History of Aramaic vowel reduction.
in: Arameans, Aramaic and the Aramaic literary Tradition.
Ramat-Gan 1983 Ed. Bar-Ilan University Press pp. 47-55
A. Dupont-Sommer - La tablette cunéiforme araméenne de Warka
in: Revue d'Assyriologie XXXIX (1944) pp. 60-61

2.8 FROM JEROME TO THE MASORETES

[262] **A. Deissmann -** Die Septuaginta-Papyri
1905 Heidelberg Ed. Carl Winter's Universitätsbuchhandlung pp. 86-93
[263] **F. Bovon P. Geoltrain** - Écrits apocryphes chrétiens
in: Bibliothèque de la Péiade. Paris 1997 Éd. Gallimard pp. 317,1562-3
[264] **Balthafar Corderius** - Catena Petrvm Græcorvm in Sanctvm Ioannem
Parisii 1630 Bibliothèque des Sources Chrétiennes Lyon p.244
Roma Biblioteca Vallicelliana **ms. E40** (10th CE) fol. 153v line 33
[265] **Codex Coislinanus**
Paris Bibliothèque Nationale Coislin Gr. 1 fol. 1-4 (6th CE)
[266] **Eberhard Nestle** - Jacob von Edessa über den Schem hammephorasch und andere
Gottesnamen. in: Zeitschrift der Deutschen morganländischen Gesellschaft
Leipzig 1878 tom.XXXII pp. 465-508,735

[267] **Photii** - Epistvlæ et Amphilocia n°162 vol. 2
1984 Ed. BSB BG Teubner Verglagsgesellschaft pp. 121,122
[268] **S. Isidori Hispalnesis episcopi.** - Etymolgiarum lib. VII
in: Patrologiæ Latina LXXXII Éd. J.P. Migne Paris 1859 pp. 259-262
[269] **Albini seu Alcuini.** - Lib. De Divinis officiis caput XXXVIII-XXXIX
in: Patrologiæ Latina CI Éd. J.P. Migne Paris 1851 pp. 1239-1244
[270] **John F. Healey** - Les débuts de l'alphabet. Vers l'alphabet arabe
in: La naissance des écritures Paris 1994 Éd. Seuil p. 312
[271] **G.E. Weil P.Rivière M. Serfaty** -Concordance de la cantilation
1978 Ed. C.N.R.S. C.A.T.A.B. pp. I-XVI
[272] **P.E. Kahle** - The Cairo Geniza
Oxford 1959 Ed. B. Blackwell pp. 339-344
I. Yeivin - Geniza Bible Fragments
Jerusalem 1973 Ed. Makor Publishing Ltd
H. L. Stack - Codex Babylonian of Petrograd
New York 1971 Ed. Ktav Publishing House
[273] **P.E. Kahle** - The Cairo Geniza
Oxford 1959 Ed. B. Blackwell pp. 51-75
[274] **D. Barthélemy** - Critique textuelle de l'Ancien Testament
in: Orbis Biblicus et Orientalis Éd. Université de Fribourg 50/1 1982 p. *108; 50/2 1986 p.*5§2
[275] **P. Cassuto** - Isomorphie consonantique et hétéromorphie vocalique
in: Bible et Informatique: méthodes, outils, résultats, Jérusalem 9-13 Juin 1988.
Lyon 1988 Ed. C.A.T.A.B. pp. 177-207
[276] **P.E. Kahle** - The Cairo Geniza
Oxford 1959 Ed. Basil Blackwell p. 65
[277] **Angel Sàenz-Badillos** - A History of the Hebrew language
Cambridge 1996 Ed. Cambridge University Press pp. 94-102
P. Joüon T. Muraoka - A Grammar of Biblical Hebrew
in: Subsidia Biblica 14/I. Roma 1993 Ed. Pontificio Istituto Biblico p. 94 §26e
[278] **P. Kahle** - Masoreten des Ostens
Hildesheim 1966 Ed. Georg Olms Verlagbuchhandlung pp. 36,37
C. Sirat - Codices litteris exarati () 1020 Tome I
Turnout 1997 Éd. Brepols pp. 80-85
[279] **J.J.L. Bargès** - Libri psalmorum David Regis et prophetae. Versio à R. Yaphet ben Heli
Paris 1861 Ed. Instituti Imperialis Gallicani Bibliopolam p. 184
[280] **P. Benoit, J.T. Milik, R. de Vaux** - Les grottes de Murabbaât
Oxford 1961 Ed. Clarendon Press pp. 286-290
[281] **P.L.B. Drach** De l'harmonie entre l'Église et la synagogue
Gent (Belgium) 1978 Ed. Socii Sancti Michaelis pp. 480,481
[282] **Paul E. Kahle** -The Cairo Geniza
Londres 1947 pp. 172,173 note 4
[283] **P. Joüon T. Muraoka** - A Grammar of Biblical Hebrew
in: Subsidia Biblica 14/I. Roma 1993 Ed. Pontificio Istituto Biblico p. 73 §6
[284] **P.E. Kahle** - The Cairo Geniza
Oxford 1959 Ed. Basil Blackwell pp. 318-32
[285] **E. Levine** - The Targum to the Five Megillot
Jerusalem 1977 in: Codex Vatican Urbinati I Ed. Makor Publishing Ltd

2.9 FROM THE MASORETES TO MAIMONIDES

[286] **P.E. Kahle** - The Masoretic Text of the Bible and the Pronunciation of Hebrew.
in: J.J.S. n°7 1956 pp. 133-153
[287] **D.N. Freedman A. D. Forbes F.I. Andersen** - Studies in Hebrew and Aramaic Orthography
in: Biblical and Judaic Studies San Diego 1992 pp. 21,256-258

[288] Jerusalem 1971 **D.S. Loewinger** Ed. Makor Publishing
[289] Jerusalem 1976 **M.H. Goshen Gottstein** Ed. Magnes Press
[290] Copenhagen 1959 **Alexander Sperber** Ed Ejnar Munksgaard
[291] Jerusalem 1973 **Israël Yeivin** Ed. Makor Publishing Ltd.
[292] Copenhagen 1956 **Alexander Sperber** Ed Ejnar Munksgaard
[293] New York 1971 **Hermann L. Stack** Ed. Ktav Publishing House
[294] Jerusalem 1980 **E. Levine** Ed. Makor Publishing Ltd.
[295] Jerusalem 1972 **Israël Yeivin** Ed. Makor Publishing Ltd.
[296] **P. Guillemette M. Brisebois** - Introduction aux méthodes historico-critiques .
In: Héritage et projet n°35. Québec 1987 Ed.Fides pp.59-63
[297] Gn 3:14 9:26 18:17; Ex 3:2 13:3,9,12,15 14:1,8; Lv 23:34 25:17; Dt 31:27 32:9 33:12,13; 1S
1:11; 1K 3:5; Jr 2:37 3:1,21,22,23,25 4:1,3,4,8; 5:2,3,9,18,19,22,29; 6:9; 8:13 30:10 36:8; Ezk
33:23 44:5 46:13; Os 10:3; Na 1:3; Ml 3:23; Ps 15:1 40:5 47:6 100:5 116:5,6; Pr 1:29
[298] 1K 2:26; Is 50:4; Jr 1:6 7:20; Ezk 2:4 3:11,27 5:5 8:1 12:10 13:16 14:21,23 16:36 17:9 20:39
21:33 22:31 23:32 24:6,14; 26:21 28:2 30:22 33:25 35:11 36:2 39:17 43:27 46:16; Za 9:14; Ps
73:28
[299] **P. Kahle** - Masoreten des Westens
Stuttgart 1927 Ed. V.V.W. Kohlhammer p. 17/1 sheet 930 p.19/3 sheet 946 p.24/8 sheet 1017
[300] **Meira Polliak** -The Karaite Tradition of Arabic Bible Translation. A linguistic & Exegetical
Study of Karaite Translations of the Pentateuch from the Tenth & Eleventh Centuries C.E.
Leiden E.J. BRill 1997
Geoffrey Khan - Karaite Bible Manuscripts from the Cairo Geniza.
Cambridge 1990 p. 72
[301] **G. Khan** - The Medieval Karaite Transcriptions of Hebrew into Arabic Script
in: Israel Oriental Studies 12 (1992) pp. 159-176
G. Khan - The Orthography of Karaite Hebrew Bible Manuscripts in Arabic Transcription
in: Journal of Semitic Studies 38 (1993) pp. 49-70
[302] **Ibn 'Ata' Allâh** - Traité sur le nom ALLÂH translated by Maurice Glotton
Paris, Les Deux Océans 1981 pp. 146,147
[303] **Fares Chidiaq & William Watts** -The Holy Bible
London, 1857 (Yahuwah in Ex 6:3, 6, 8, etc.)
The Dominican Fathers -The Dominican Bible
Iraq, 1875 (Yahuwah footnote of Ex 3:14 and Yahwah in footnote of Ex 6:3)
Van Dyke & Boustany -The Holy Bible
Beirut, 1865 (Yahwah in Ex 3:15; 6:3)
The Jesuit Fathers -The Holy Bible
Beirut, 1880 (Yahwah in Ex 6:3)
[304] **D. Barthélemy** - Les traditions anciennes de division du texte biblique
in: Selon les Septante. Paris 1995 Éd. Cerf pp.33-38
[305] **G. Dahan** - Les intellectuels chrétiens et les Juifs au Moyen Age
in: Patrimoines Judaïfme. Paris 1990 Ed. Cerf
[306] **Petrus Alfunsus** - Dialogi Petri Alphonsi ex judæo christiani
in: Patrologiæ Latina CLVII Éd. J.P. Migne Paris 1854 pp. 607-612
[307] **Petri Blesensis** - Contra perfidiam Judæorum
in: Patrologiæ Latina CCVII Éd. J.P. Migne Paris 1855 p. 833
[308] **M. Maïmonide** - Le guide des égarés
in: collection "Les Dix Paroles" Paris 1979 Ed. Verdier
[309] **J. Hallévi** - Le Kuzari, apologie de la religion méprisée
in: collection "Les Dix Paroles" Paris 1993 Ed. Verdier
[310] **Gioacchino da Fiore** - Expofitio (...) in Apocalipfim
Venise 1527 Bibliothèque de la Part-Dieu Lyon SJ TH37/3 fol. 35-37
[311] **L. Tondelli** - Il Libro delle figure dell'abate Gioachino da Fiore
Torino 1953 Ed Societa Editrice Internazionale tom.I pp. 225,226 tom.II tav.XIa,XIb

[312] **Innocentii III papæ** - Sermones de sanctis. Sermo IV, in circumcisione domini.
in: Patrologiæ Latina CCXVII Éd. J.P. Migne Paris 1855 pp. 465-47
Innocentii III - Sermon de circumcisione domini
1229? Roma Biblioteca Vaticana CodexVaticanus Latinus n°700 f.13r
[313] **S.A. Hirsch E. Nolan** - The Greek Grammar of Roger Bacon
Cambridge 1902 Ed. E. Nolan pp. 200-208
[314] **A. Fabre d'Olivet** - Grammaire Hébraïque p.19
1985 Paris in: La langue hébraïque restituée Ed. L'âge d'homme p. 19
[315] **A. Landgraf** - Écrits théologiques de l'école d'Abélard
Louvain 1934 in: Spicilegium Sacrum Lovaniense n°14. pp. 128-285

2.10 FROM MAIMONIDES TO TYNDALE

[316] **E. Longpré** - Dictionnaire de Théologie Catholique
Paris 1924 Tome 8 pp. 2467-2470
[317] **Guillelmi de Mara** - De hebræis et græcis vocabulis glossarum Bibliæ
1279 Bibliothèque Municipale de Toulouse ms.402 part 3 fol. 230-280
[318] **Gerardus de Hoyo** - De Liber Triglossos
1260? Bibliothèque de l'Arsenal ms.904 fol. 28
[319] **Raymvndvs Martini** - Pvgio Christianorvm
Paris 1300? Bibliothèque Sainte Geneviève ms.1405 fol. 162b
[320] **M. Quereuil** - La Bible française du XIIIe siècle
in: Publications romanes et françaises n°183 Paris 1988 Éd. Droz pp. 65-67
[321] **Raymvndi Martini** - Pvgio Fidei
Lyon 1651 Bibliothèque La Part Dieu. 21296 pp. 448,514-546
[322] **J. Carreras Artau** - La Allocutio super Tetragrammaton de Arnoldo de Vilanova.
Madrid-Barcelona 1949 in: Sefarad 9 pp. 75-105
[323] **Porcheto de Salvaignis** - Victoria Porcheti adversus impios Hebraeos
1380 Bibliothèque municipale de Dijon ms.231 fol. 169
[324] **M. Idel** - Maïmonide et la mystique juive
in: Patrimoines judaïfme 1991 Paris Cerf pp. 11-89
[325] **A. Abulafia** - Otsar Eden Ganouz, ms. Oxford, 1580, fol. 16b-17a
[326] **A. Abulafia** - Maftéah ha-Raayon, ms. Vatican, 291, fol. 21a
[327] **A. Abulafia** - Séfer ha-Edout, ms. Rome, Angelica 38, fol. 14v-15r, ms. Munich 285, fol. 39b
[328] **N. Séd** - Celui qui est
in: Patrimoines 1986 Ed. Cerf pp. 25-27
[329] **G. Scholem** -Le Nom et les symboles de Dieu dans la mystique juive
in: Patrimoines judaïsme 1988 Ed. Cerf pp. 78-83
[330] **D. Lortsch** - Histoire de la Bible française
1989 Montreux Ed. P.E.R.L.E. pp. 12-16
[331] **Alfonso de Valladolid (Abner de Burgos)** - Mostrador de Justicia
1350? Bibliothèque Nationale ms. Espagnol 43 fol. 1-11
[332] **Paulus de Sancta Maria** - Additiones ad Postillam Nicolai de Lyra. Vol.I
1429 Bruxelles Bibliothèque Royale Albert Ier, ms.240 fol. 36-38
[333] **Nicolai de Cusa** - Opera omnia. Sermo I In principio erat verbum
Hamburg 1970 Ed. Felix Meiner. Ed. Heidelbergensis Tom.XVI,1 pp. 1-19
Nikolaus de Cusa - Codex Cusanus 220 fol. 56,57
Berkastel-Kues (Germany) 1430 Bibliothek des Cusanus Stites
[334] **Nicolai de Cusa** - Opera omnia. Sermo XX Nomen eius Jesus
Hamburg 1977 Ed. Felix Meiner. Academia Litterarum Heidelbergensis Tom.XVI,3 pp. 301-317
[335] **Nicolai de Cusa** - Opera omnia. Sermo XXIII, XXIV Domine, in lumine vultus tui.
Hamburg 1984 Ed. Felix Meiner. Academia Litterarum Heidelbergensis Tom.XVI,4 pp. 358-433
[336] **Nicolai de Cusa** - Opera omnia. Sermo XLVIII Dies sanctificatus
Hamburg 1991 Ed. Felix Meiner. Academia Litterarum Heidelbergensis Tom.XVII,2 pp.200-212

[337] **Nicolai de Cusa** - Opera omnia. Sermo LXXI
Hamburg 200* Ed. Felix Meiner. Academia Litterarum Heidelbergensis Tom.XVII,4 pp.
[338] **Dionysii Carthvsiani** -Enarrationes piæ ac eruditæ, in quinque Mofaique legis libros. Cap VI.
1534 British Museum Library 3837.g.7. fol. CLVI
[339] **Marsilii Ficini Florentini** - Liber de Chriftiana Religione. Capitum XXX
Florence 1471? British Museum Library C.**9**.b.**4**. fol. 83b
[340] **L. Gorny** - La Kabbale
Paris 1977 Éd. Belfond pp. 113-147
[341] **Paulus de Heredia** - Epistola Neumia filii Haccanae de Secretia
Roma 1488 Bibliothèque Nationale Française Res D-67975 fol. 1-5
[342] **Johann Reuchlin** - De Verbo Mirifico. liber III Cap. XII-XIX
Basle 1494 British Museum Library IB.37366
[343] **Jacques Lefèvre d'Étaples** - Qvincvplex Pfalterium Cap. LXXII,CL
Lyon 1509 Bibliothèque La Part Dieu. Res.105024 pp. 109, 127b, 143b, 148b, 231, 231b
[344] **Jacques Lefèvre d'Étaples** - Nicolas de Cvsa Excitionvm
1514 Bibliothèque de l'Arsenal Fol.B.1298(2) fol. XII,XIV,LII,LIV
[345] **Ioannis Pici Mirandvlæ** - Dispvtianvm adversvs astrologos liber V,VI
1496 Lyon. Bibliothèque La Part Dieu. inc.645 Liber V,VI
[346] **Sebastiani Castellionis** - Biblia Sacra
1697 Francfurti Bibliothèque minicipale de Grenoble R276
[347] **Adrian Reland/ J. Drusii** - Decas exercitationum philologicarum de vera pronunciatione
Jehova. 1707 British Museum Library 1568/3014 pp. 148-150
[348] **Avg. Ivstiniani** - Psalterium (Psalm L)
1516 Bibliothèque Lyon La Part Dieu Rés 100035
[349] **Sebastianvs Castalio** - Dialogorvm sacrorvm
1549 Lvgdvni Bibliothèque La Part Dieu 800472 pp. 1-60
[350] **Sebastian Chateillon** - La Bible novvelement translatée
1555 Bale Ed. Iehan Heruage Bibliothèque mun. de Toulouse Rés.A.XVI.68

2.11 FROM TYNDALE TO THE AMERICAN VERSION

[351] **Petrus Galatinus** - Opus toti chriftiane reipublice maxime utile, de arcanis catholice ueritatis
Lyon 1518 Bibliothèque La Part Dieu. 100766 Liber II pp. XLI-LVIII
[352] **Olivetanus Pierre Robert** - La Bible
1535 Lyon Bibliothèque de la Part Dieu Rés.23748
[353] **Joannes Wessel Gansfortius** - Tractatus () Wesseli. De Oriatione. Pars III
Zwolle 1521 British Library 477.a.41(3) lib III, cap XI-XII fol XXXIX
[354] **M. Luther** - Ain Epiftel aufz dem Prophete Jeremia
Wittemberg 1527 Bayerische Staatsbibliothek München Exeg.659
[355] **Sebastianum Munsterum** - Chaldaica grammatica
Basileae 1527 Bibliothèque Lyon La Part Dieu Res 341641 p.16
[356] **Johann Georg Walch** - Sämtliche Schriften. Zwanzigster Theil, welcher die Schriften [ ]
Magdeburg 1747 column 2528,2564,2565
[357] **G.F. Moore** - Old Testament & Semitic Studies Vol.I
in: Notes on the Name -1. The pronunciation Jehovah
[358] **Sebastiani Munsteri** - En tibi lector Hebraica Latina
Basileae 1534 Bibliothèque Nationale Française A37(1) pp. 56v,57
[359] **J. Calvin** - Sermons de M. Iean Caluin fur le V. liure de Moyfe nommé Deuteronome
Geneue 1567 Bibliothèque Lyon La Part Dieu 100830 pp.184-190
[360] **J. Calvin** - Commentarii Ioannis Calvini in qvinqve libros Mosis 21321
1573 Genevæ Éd. Gaspard de Hus Bibliothèque Lyon La Part Dieu pp. 44,45
[361] **Olivetanus Pierre Robert** - Bible
1535 Bibliothèque de la Part Dieu Rés.23748

[362] **Roberti Stephani** - Liber Psalmorvm Davidis
1556 Bibliothèque de la Part Dieu 327510
[363] **Sancte Pagnino** - Biblia
1528 Lyon Bibliothèque La Part Dieu. Rés.317377
[364] **Sancte Pagnino** - Thefaurus Linguæ fanctæ
1548 Lyon Bibliothèque La Part Dieu. 341631 pp. 223,418
[365] **Adrian Reland/ J. Drusii** - Decas exercitationum philologicarum de vera pronunciatione
Jehova. 1707 British Museum Library 1568/3014
[366] **Ioannis Merceri** - In Genesim primum Mosis librum .. commentarius
1598 Paris Bibliothèque Nationale Française A-1736 p. 41
[367] **M. Serueto** - De trinitatis erroribvs
1531 Bibliothèque d'Aix en Provence Res.s.23 fol. 98-101
[368] **Angelo Caninio Anglarenfi** - De nomine Iesv et Iova
in: Institutiones lingua Syriacæ 1554 Lyon Bibliothèque La Part Dieu. 349745(3)
[369] **G. Genebrardo** - S. Trinitate
1569 Lyon Bibliothèque La Part Dieu. 329938 pp. 56-62
[370] **B. Aria Montano** - Davidis Regis (..) Psalmi
1574 Parisiis Lyon Bibliothèque La Part Dieu 327652 pp. 8,9
[371] **Roberto Bellarmino** - Institvtiones Lingvae Hebraicae
1596 Lyon Bibliothèque La Part Dieu. 811323 pp. 183-188
[372] **Immanuel Tremellius** - Biblia
1579 Francfort. Bibliothèque de la Part-Dieu Lyon. SJ E134/101
[373] **Hieronymi Prodi** - In Ezechielem explanationes
1596 Bibliothèque de la Part-Dieu Lyon. 27001 pp. 47,48
[374] **Lvdovici Alcasar** - Vestigatio arcani sensvs in apocalypsi
1616 Bibliothèque de la Part-Dieu Lyon. 20333 pp. 106-114
[375] **A. Strus** -Nomen Omen
in: Analecta Biblica 80. Rome 1978 Éd. Biblical Institute Press pp. 17,82-89
[376] **A. Caquot** - Les énigmes d'un hémistiche biblique
in: Dieu et l'être
1978 Paris Ed. Études Augustiniennes C.N.R.S. p. 24 note 23
[377] **B. Spinoza** -Traité Théologico-politique
Paris 1965 Ed. GF Flammarion pp. 59,231
B. Spinoza - Abrégé de grammaire hébraïque
Paris 1987 Ed. Librairie J. Vrin pp. 25-27
P. Cassuto - La place de l'hébreu (Thèse n°8716404 C)
1991 Lyon Université J. Moulin Lyon III pp. 97-99,333-6
[378] **A. Fabre d'Olivet** - Grammaire Hébraïque p.19 / Cosmogonie de Moïse pp. 28,67-71.
in: La langue hébraïque restituée. 1985 Ed. L'âge d'homme
[379] **P.L.B. Drach** - De l'harmonie entre l'église et la synagogue
1978 Belgium Ed. Socii Sancti Michaelis pp. 370,473-498
[380] **J.H. Levy** - The Tetra(?)grammaton
in: The Jewish Quarterly Review Vol.XV (1903)
1966 Ed. Ktav Publishing House pp. 97-99
[381] **P. Joüon** - Grammaire de l'Hébreu biblique
Rome 1923 Ed. Institut Biblique Pontifical p. 49 §16f note 1
[382] **A. Westphal** - Dictionnaire Encyclopédique de la Bible
Valence 1973 Éd. Imprimeries Réunies pp. 294,295,839
[383] **J.D. Eisenstein** - Ozar Wikuhim
Israel 1969 pp. 310-315
[384] **G. Howard** - Hebrew Gospel of Matthew
Georgia 1995 Ed. Mercer University Press pp. 160,229-32
[385] **Elias Hutter** - Novum Testamentum Domini Nostri Iesu Christi
Nuremburg 1599

[386] **John Eliot** - The New Testament of Our Lord and Saviour Jesus Christ
Cambridge Massachuset 1661
[387] **E. Ledrain** - Histoire d'Israël
Paris 1879 Éd. A. Lemerre p. 130
[388] **M. Taillé** - Dieu et dieux: noms et Nom
1982 Ed. Université catholique de l'ouest p. 220
[389] **A.J. Kolatch** -Le livre juif du pourquoi
Genève 1990 Éd. MJR pp. IX,347

2.12 THE NAME OF JESUS, ITS LINKS WITH THE NAME

[390] **W.E. Vine** - An Expository Dictionary of New Testament Words
Nashville 1985 Ed. Thomas Nelson Publishers p. 333
[391] **P. Joüon T. Muraoka** - A Grammar of Biblical Hebrew
in: Subsidia biblica 14/I
Roma 1993 Ed. Pontificio Istituto Biblico §29h p. 101
[392] **G.I. Davies** - Ancient Hebrew Inscriptions. Corpus and Concordance
Cambridge 1991 Ed. Cambridge University Press p. 369
[393] **B. Davidson** - The Analytical Hebrew and Chaldee Lexicon
Massashussetts 1990 Ed. Hendrickson Publishers p. 354
[394] **G. Scholem** - Les grands courants de la mystique juive
Paris 1994 Éd. Payot pp. 81-83
[395] **Eusebii Cæsarienisis** - Commentaria in Psalmos
in: Patrologiæ Græcæ XXIII
Paris 1857 Éd. J.P. Migne pp. 99-100,685-8, 702-4
[396] Ad tomum III operum S. Hieronymi appendix
in: Patrologiæ Latina XXIII
Paris 1845 Éd. J.P. Migne pp. 1275-1280
[397] **P.W. Skehan J.E. Sanderson** Qumran Cave 4.IV Paleo-Hebrew and Greek Biblical Ms.
in: Discoveries in the Judaean Desert IX
Oxford 1992 Ed. Clarendon Press p. 63
[398] **E. Ulrich F.M. Cross** Qumran Cave 4.VII Genesis to Numbers
in: Discoveries in the Judaean Desert XII
Oxford 19924 Ed. Clarendon Press pp. 101,212,213
[399] **W. Weidmüller** - Der rätselhafte Gottesname YHWH
in: Archiv für Gesschichte des Buchwesens VI 3/4
Frankfurt 1965 pp. 1407-1426
J. Servier - Noms divins
In: Dictionnaire critique de l'ésotérisme Paris 1998 Éd. Presses Universitaires de France p. 936
[400] **Y. Yadin J.C. Greenfield** - The Documents from the Bar Kokhba Period in the Cave of
Letters. Jerusalem 1989 Ed. Israel Exploration Society pp. 19,162
[401] **S.C. Mimouni** - Le judéo-christianisme ancien, essais historiques
Paris 1998 in: collection Patrimoines Éd. Cerf p. 237 note 4, 239

3.1 THE CONTROVERSY COMES TO AN END

[402] **Avgvstini Evgvbini** - Cosmopoeia in Cap II Genesis
Lvgdvni 1535 Bibliothèque de la Part-Dieu Res 100089 p. 150
[403] **Johann Babor** - Die Bibel
Vienna 1805 Ed. Johann Babor
[404] **A. Crampon** - Supplementum ad commentaria in scripturam sacram R.P. Cornelii a Lapide
Paris 1856 Ed. Ludovicus Vives Bibliopola

[405] **Lippomanus Aloysius** - Catena in Exodum
Paris 1550 Bibliothèque de la Part-Dieu
[406] **J. Drusii** - Tetragrammaton sive de nomine dei proprio
1696 in: Critici Sacri Tom. VI,IX
Bibliothèque I.C.L. de Lyon H-31-B-I-1/6 pp.2141-2189, H-31-B-I-1/9 p. 451
[407] **Ioannis Cappelli** - Critica Sacra
Paris 1650 Bibliothèque I.C.L. de Lyon A2631 pp. 666-739

3.2 CONCLUSION CONCERNING THE NAME

[408] **B. Couroyer** - La Bible de Jérusalem
Paris 1986 Éd. Cerf p. 87 note k
[409] **D.N. Freedman** - The Anchor Bible Dictionary vol. 6
New York 1992 Ed. Doubleday p. 1011
[410] **W.F. Albright** - From the Stone Age to Christianity
Baltimore 1940 Ed. The Johns Hopkins Press pp. 196-199
[411] **L. Pirot, A. Clamer** - Bible (Exode)
Paris 1956 Ed. Letouzey et Ané p. 83
[412] **J. du Verdier** - Nova methodus hebraica punctis masoreticis expurgata
Paris 1847 Éd. J.P. Migne pp. 883-890
[413] **W. Weidmüller** - Der rätselhafte Gottesname YHWH
in: Archiv für Gesschichte des Buchwesens VI 3/4 Frankfurt 1965 pp. 1407-1426
J. Servier - Noms divins
In: Dictionnaire critique de l'ésotérisme Paris 1998 Éd. Presses Universitaires de France p. 936
[414] **J. Astruc** -Conjectures sur les mémoires originaux dont il paroit que Moyse s'est servi.
1753 Bruxelles
[415] **C. Mopsik** -Le livre hébreu d'Hénoch
Dijon 1989 in: Collections «Les Dix Parole» Éd. Verdier pp. 39,40
Yehuda Liebes -The angels of the call of Chofar and Yochoua the Prince of the Face (in Hebrew) Jerusalem 1987 in: Jerusalem Studies in Jewish Thougnt Vol.6 (1-2) pp. 176-196
[416] **A. Caquot** - Léviathan et Behémoth
in: Semitica XXV (1975) pp. 111-122
I.B.S.A. - The New World
Brooklyn 1942 Ed. Watchtower Bible and Tract Society, Inc. pp. 314-320
[417] **V. Malka** - Proverbes de la sagesse juive
Paris 1994 Éd. Cerf p. 97

APPENDIX
INTERPRETATION OF THE HEBREW NAMES

[418] **P. Joüon T. Muraoka** - A Grammar of Biblical Hebrew Part One
in: Subsidia biblica -14/I Roma 1993 Ed. Pontifico Istituto Biblico pp. 278-285 §93
[419] **F. Brown S.R. Driver C.A. Briggs** - Hebrew and English Lexicon
Oxford 1951 Ed Clarendon Press p. 1028
[420] **J.D. Fowler** - Theophoric Personal Names in Ancient Hebrew
in: J.S.O.T. Sup. n°49 Sheffield 1988 Ed. Academic Press p. 124
[421] **C.F. Jean** - Grammaire hébraïque élémentaire
Paris 1950 Éd. Letouzey et Ané p. 63
[422] **J. Auneau** - Dictionnaire encyclopédique de la Bible
Turnhout 1987 Ed. Brepols p. 1165
[423] **H.W.F. Gesenius** - Hebrew-Chaldee Lexicon to the Old Testament
Michigan 1979 Ed. Baker Book House p. 833
[424] **G. Rachet** - Civilisations de l'Orient ancien
Paris 1999 Éd. Larousse p. 80

[425] **A.M. Mahdi** -Important centre Agadéen (La Babylonie)
in: Dossiers histoire et archéologie n°103 mars 1986 p. 67
[426] **S.N. Kramer** - L'histoire commence à Sumer
Paris 1994 Éd. Flammarion pp. 152,269
[427] **R.J. Tournay** - L'épopée de Gilgamesh
in: L.A.P.O. n°15 Paris 1994 Éd. Cerf pp. 7-10
[428] **N. Séd** - Celui qui est
in: Patrimoines 1986 Ed. Cerf pp. 45,46
[429] **R. le Déaut** - Targum du Pentateuque
in: Sources chrétiennes n°271 Éd. Cerf p. 277
[430] **B. Davidson** - The Analytical Hebrew and Chaldee Lexicon
Massachussetts 1990 Ed. Hendrickson p. 51
[431] **A.S. Halkin** - 201 Hebrew Verbs
New York 1970 Ed. Barron's Educational Series pp. 66,67,90,91
[432] **M. Amandry** - Le monnayage des royaumes Chypriotes
in: Dossiers d'archéologie n°205 Dijon 1995 Ed. Faton p. 104
M. Iacovou - Monnaies de Chypre
1994 Nicosie Éd. Banque de Chypre Fondation Culturelle, pp. 11-21
[433] Deutsche Taler
1967 Ed. Germany's Federal Bank
[434] **M. Lejeune** - Phonétique historique du mycénien et du grec ancien
Paris 1987 Éd. Klincksieck pp. 161-173
[435] **J. Chadwick** - Le linéaire B, p.212
B.F. Cook - Les inscriptions grecques, p. 401
L. Bonfante - L'étrusque, p. 477
In: La naissance des écritures Paris 1994 Éd. Seuil
[436] **J.C. de Moor** - An Anthology of Religious Texts from Ugarit
Leiden 1987 Ed. E.J. Brill pp. 24,25
[437] **W.L. Morand** – Les lettres d'El-Amarna
in: Littératures Ancienne du Proche-Orient n°13, Paris 1987, Ed Cerf, p. 23 n. 38 p. 578, 589
[438] **C. Michel** - Correspondance des marchands de Kanish
in: Littératures Ancienne du Proche-Orient n°19, Paris 2001, Ed Cerf, pp.106,157
[439] **A. Murtonen** – A Philological and Literary Treatise on the Old Testament Divine Names
in: Studia Orientalia XVIII:1, Helsinki 1952, pp. 90-92

LACK OF NOMINA SACRA IN THE CHRISTIAN PAPYRUS

[440] **C.H. Roberts** - An Unpublished Fragment of the Fouth Gospel in the John Rylands Library
in: Bulletin of the John Rylands Library 20 (1936) pp. 45-55
[441] **E.G. Turner** -Theological Text
in: The Oxyrhynchus Papyri Vol.L, papyrus n°3522
London 1983 Ed. Egypt Exploration Society pp. 3-8; pl. II
[442] **L.W. Hurtado** - The origin of the nomina sacra: A proposal
in: Journal of Biblical Literature n°117(4) 1998 pp. 655-673

PRONUNCIATION OF THE NAME Y-H-W3

[443] **I.J. Gelb** - Pour une théorie de l'écriture
1973 Éd. Flammarion pp. 187-190
[444] **W.F. Albright** - The Vocalization of the Egyptian Syllabic Orthography
New York 1966 Ed. Kraus Reprint Corporation 1934 American Oriental Society) pp. 11-25
[445] **D. Sivan Z. Cochavi-Rainey** - West-Semitic Vocabulary in Egyptian Script of the 14th to the
10th cent. BCE 1992 Ed. Ben-Gurion University of the Negev Press pp. 1-5

[446] **J. Yoyotte P. Vernus** - Dictionnaire des Pharaons
Paris 1996 Éd. Noesis
[447] **P. Vernus** - Le Néo-Égyptien
in: Les langues dans le monde ancien et moderne.
Langues Chamito-Sémitique. 1988 Paris pp. 183,190
[448] **W.A. Ward** - A New Look at Semitic Personal Names and Loanwords in Egyptian
in: Chronique d'Égypte LXXI (1996) Fasc.141
Bruxelles Éd. Fondation Égyptologique Reine Élisabeth pp. 41-47
[449] **Cheikh Anta Diop** - Nouvelle recherche sur l'Égyptien ancien et les langues Négro-
Africaines modernes Paris 1988 Éd. Présence Africaine p. 18
[450] **D.M. Rohl** - A Test of Time
London 1995 Ed. Century pp. 18,156-162
[451] **W.V. Davies** - Les hiéroglyphes Égyptiens
in: La naissance des écritures. 1994 Paris Éd. Seuil p. 113
[452] **J.E. Hoch** - Semitic Words in Egyptian Texts of the New Kingdom and Third Intermediate
Period Princeton 1994 pp. 52-57
[453] **P. Vernus** - L'Égypto-Copte. I La langue Égyptienne
in: Les langues dans le monde ancien et moderne.
Langues Chamito-Sémitique. 1988 Paris p.163
[454] **R. Caplice D. Snell** - Introduction to Akkadian
in: Studia Pohl: Series Maior 9 Rome 1988 Ed. Biblical Institute Press pp. 6-8
[455] **Gotthelf Bergsträsser** - Introduction to the Semitic Languages
Indiana 1995 Ed. Eisenbrauns pp. 253-259
[456] **S. Moscati** - An Introduction to the Comparative Grammar of the Semitic Languages
Wiesbaden 1980 Éd. Otto Harrassowitz pp. 22,56
[457] **F. Vigouroux** - Dictionnaire de la Bible Art. Assuérus
Paris 1893 Éd. Letouzey et Ané pp. 1139,1140
[458] **P. Lecoq** - L'écriture cunéiforme vieux-perse
in: Les inscriptions de la Perse achéménide. 1997 Éd. Gallimard pp. 59-72
[459] **J.E. Hoch** - Semitic Words in Egyptian Texts of the New Kingdom and Third Intermediate
Period (n°522 Anastasi Papyri An.IV 1b,2 D15) Princeton 1994 p. 354
[460] **S. Ahituv** - Canaanite Toponyms in Ancient Egyptian Documents
Jerusalem 1984 Ed. The Magnes Press pp. 45-205
[461] **J. Simons** -Handbook for the Study of Egyptian Topographical Lists relating to Western Asia
Leiden 1937 Ed. E.J. Brill pp. 16-21
[462] **Keith C. Seele** - Beurteilung der Syllabischen Orthographie des Ägyptischen
in: JNES vol.VIII Chicago 1949 Ed. The University of Chicago Press pp. 44-47
[463] **Jesús-Luis Cunchillos** -Lettre de Pudugiba(t) grande reine du Hatti à Niqmadu roi d'Ougarit
in: Textes Ougaritiques Tome II, LAPO 14, Éd. Cerf 1989 pp. 363-421
C.F.A Scaeffer - Matériaux pour l'étude des relations entre Ugarit et le Hatti
In: Ugaritica III tom. VIII Paris 1956 Éd. Librairie orientaliste P. Geuthner pp. 12-20
Elmar Edel - Zur Schwurgötterliste des Hethitervertrags
In: Zeitschrift für Ägyptische Sprache Berlin 1963 p. 34
[464] **I.J. Gelb** -Pour une théorie de l'écriture
Paris 1973 Éd. Flammarion p. 95
[465] **R. Labat** - Manuel d'épigraphie Akkadienne
Paris 1999 Éd. Librairie orientaliste P. Geuthner pp. 11-22,101
[466] **M. Lejeune** - Phonétique historique du mycénien et du grec ancien
Paris 1987 Éd. Klincksieck pp. 190-204
[467] **D. Cohen** - Le chamito-sémitique
in: Les langues dans le monde ancien et moderne.
Langues Chamito-Sémitique. 1988 Paris pp. 10,11

PRONUNCIATION OF YHWH'S NAME IN THE MESHA STELE

[468] **W. Vischer** - Yahwo plutôt que Yahwé
in: Études Théologiques et Religieuses Tom. 50 Montpellier 1975 pp. 195-202
[469] **K.P. Jackson J.A. Dearman** - Studies in the Mesha Inscription and Moab
Atlanta 1989 Ed. Scholars Press pp. 93-130
[470] **Joshua Blau** - Short Philological Notes on the Inscription of Mesha
in: Maarav vol.2 n° 2 Santa Monica 1980 pp. 143-157
[471] **A. Saenz-Badillos**- A History of the Hebrew Language
Cambridge 1996 Ed. Cambridge University Press pp. 50-55
[472] **D.N. Freedman** -The Massoretic Text and the Qumran Scrolls.: A Study in Orthography
Ed. Textus 2, 1962 pp. 88-102
D.N. Freedman K.A. Mathews- The Paleo-Hebrew Leviticus Scroll
Ed. A.S.O.R. 1985 pp. 52-54,58,68,79,82
E. Qimron -The Hebrew of the Dead Sea Scrolls
in: Harvard Semitic Studies n°29 Atlanta 1986 Ed. Scholars Press p. 59
[473] **D.N. Freedman K.A. Mathews** -The Paleo-Hebrew Leviticus Scroll
1985 Ed. A.S.O.R. pp. 52-58,68,79,82
[474] **J. Margain** - Les particules dans le Targum Samaritain
in: Hautes études orientales n°29
Paris 1993 Ed. Librairie Droz, Genève pp. 177,256
K. Beyer -Die Aramäischen Texte vom Toten Meer
Göttingen 1984 Ed. Vandenhoeck & Ruprecht pp. 126-128
[475] **Joshua Blau** - Some difficulties in the Reconstruction of "Proto-Hebrew"
in: BZAW n° 103
Berlin 1968 Ed. M. Black G. Fohrer pp. 29-43
[476] **G. Bohas** - Matrices et étymons. Développements de la théorie
Lausanne 2000 Éd. Zèbre pp. 57,155-157
[477] **D.N. Freedman A.D. Forbes F.I. Andersen** - Studies in Hebrew and Aramaic Orthography
in: Biblical and Judaic Studies vol.2
Indiana 1992 Ed. University of California p. 167
[478] **E. Lipinski** – Formes verbales dans les noms propres d'Ebla
in: La lingua di Ebla
Napoli 1981, Ed Istituto Universitario Orientale XIV p. 195
[479] **E.J. Revell** - The Development of Segol in an Open Syllable as a Reflex of *a*
in: Linguistics and Biblical Hebrew
Winona Lake 1992 Ed. W.R. Bodine pp. 17-28
[480] **J.A. Fitzmyer -** The Aramaic Inscriptions of Sefire:
in: Biblica et orientalia -19/A
Roma 1995 Ed. Pontificio Istituto Biblico pp. 18-20, 126 pl. IX
[481] **G.I. Davies** - Ancient Hebrew Inscriptions. Corpus and Concordance
Cambridge 1991 Ed Cambridge University Press p. 81
[482] **J. Naveh** - Early History of the Alphabet
Jerusalem 1982 Ed. The Magnes Press p. 89 note 52
[483] **J. Naveh** - Early History of the Alphabet
Jerusalem 1982 Ed. The Magnes Press pp. 175-186
[484] **D.N. Freedman A.D. Forbes F.I. Andersen** - Studies in Hebrew and Aramaic Orthography
in: Biblical and Judaic Studies vol.2
Indiana 1992 Ed. University of California pp. 137-170
[485] **C. Higounet** - L'écriture
in: Que sais-je? n°653 Éd. Presses Universitaires de France pp. 59-63
[486] **M.C. Astour, D.E. Smith** – Ras Smamra Parallels, Vol. II. Places Names
in : Analecta Orientalia 50
Roma 1975 Ed. Pontificium Institutum Biblicum pp. 251-369

DID YEHOWAH COME FROM A CHANGE?

[487] **F.I. Andersen A.D. Forbes** - Spelling in the Hebrew Bible
in: Biblica Orientalia 41
Rome 1986 Ed. Biblical Institut Pres p. 92
[488] **S. Mowinckel** - The Name of the God of Moses
in: H.U.C.A. vol.XXXII
Cincinnati 1961 pp. 131-133
[489] **J. Briend M.J. Seux** - Textes du Proche-Orient ancien et histoire d'Israël
Paris 1977 Ed. Cerf
J.B. Pritchard - Ancient Near Eastern Texts Relating to the Old Testament
Princeton 1950, 1969
[490] **G. Pettinato** -Bar Interviews
in: Biblical Archaeology Review Sept./Oct. 1980 Vol.VI n°5 pp. 46-47
[491] **M. Reisel** - The Mysterious Name of Y.H.W.H.
in: Studia Semitica Neerlandica
Assen 1957 Ed. Van Gorcum pp. 42-43
[492] **T.C. Mitchell** - The Bible in the British Museum
London 1992 Ed. British museum pp. 47,82
[493] **J. Huehnergard** - Ugaritic Vocabulary in Syllabic Transcription
in: Harvard Semitic Studies n°32
Atlanta 1987 Ed. Scholars Press pp. 236-239
René Labat - Manuel d'épigraphie Akkadienne
Paris Ed. Librairie Orientaliste Paul Geuthner S.A. p. 101
[494] **Gary A. Rendsburg -** Eblaitica: Essays on the Ebla Archives and Eblaite Language
Indiana 1990 Ed. Eisenbrauns pp. 96,97,111,116,118
[495] **I. Goldziher** Die Richtungen der Islamischen Koranauslegung
Leiden 1952 pp. 260-262
[496] **I.J. Gelb -** Pour une théorie de l'écriture
1973 Ed. Flammarion p. 167
[497] **J.A. Fitzmyer** -A wandering Aramean
California 1979 Ed. Scholars Press pp. 82 §95,181 §69
[498] **A. Lemaire** -Inscriptions hébraïques Tome I, Les Ostraca
in: Littérature anciennes du Proche-Orient n°9
Paris 1977 Ed. Cerf pp. 23-81
[499] **L.H. Vincent** -Les épigraphes Judéo-araméennes postexiliques
in: Revue Biblique LVI
Paris 1949 Ed. J. Gabalda p. 277 note 4
[500] **S. Mowinckel** -The Name of the God of Moses
in: H.U.C.A. vol XXXII
Cincinnati 1961 p. 130

RELIGIOUS TRIALS OF THE FIRST CENTURY

[501] **E. Schürer** - The Great Sanhedrin in Jerusalem
in: The history of the Jewish people in the age of Jesus Christ Vol. II
1986 Edinburgh Ed. Matthew Black F.B.A. pp. 199-226
E. Schürer - Judaea under Roman Governors
In: The history of the Jewish people in the age of Jesus Christ Vol. I
1987 Edinburgh Ed. Matthew Black F.B.A. pp. 357-398
J. Massonnet - Sanhédrin
In: Dictionnaire de la Bible, Supplément Paris 1991 Ed. Letouzey & Ané pp. 1357-1413

NUMBERING SYSTEM CHANGES

[502] **A. Lemaire** - Inscriptions hébraïques Tome 1
1977 Paris, Ed. Cerf, pp. 277-281
[503] **B. Porten A. Yardeni** - Textbook of Aramaic documents from ancient Egypt, 3 Literature
1993 Ed. Israel Academy of Sciences and Humanities p. XXXVI
[504] **J. Naveh** - Dated Coins of Alexander Janneus
in: Israel Exploration Journal volume 18, Jerusalem 1968, pp. 24,25
[505] **J. Maltiel-Gerstenfeld** - 260 Years of Ancient Jewish Coins
1982 Tel Aviv Ed. Kol Printing Service Ltd.
[506] **S.C. Mimouni** - Le judéo-christianisme ancien, essais historiques
in: collection Patrimoines, Paris 1998, Éd. Cerf p. 237 note 4, 239
[507] **G.H.R. Horsley** - New Documents Illustrating Early Christianity
Sydney 1981, Ed. Macquarie University pp. 52,56

General Index